Lecture Notes in Computer Science 3965

Commenced Publication in 1973
Founding and Former Series Editors:
Gerhard Goos, Juris Hartmanis, and Jan van Leeuwen

Marco Bernardo   Alessandro Cimatti (Eds.)

Formal Methods for Hardware Verification

6th International School on Formal Methods for the Design
of Computer, Communication, and Software Systems, SFM 2006
Bertinoro, Italy, May 22-27, 2006
Advanced Lectures

 Springer

Volume Editors

Marco Bernardo
Università degli Studi di Urbino "Carlo Bo"
Istituto di Scienze e Tecnologie dell'Informazione
Piazza della Repubblica 13, 61029 Urbino, Italy
E-mail: bernardo@sti.uniurb.it

Alessandro Cimatti
Istituto Trentino di Cultura (ITC)
Istituto per la Ricerca Scientifica e Tecnologica (IRST)
Loc. Panté, Povo, 38050 Trento, Italy
E-mail: cimatti@irst.itc.it

Library of Congress Control Number: Applied for

CR Subject Classification (1998): D.2, D.3, F.3, C.3, C.2.4

LNCS Sublibrary: SL 2 – Programming and Software Engineering

ISSN   0302-9743
ISBN-10   3-540-34304-0 Springer Berlin Heidelberg New York
ISBN-13   978-3-540-34304-2 Springer Berlin Heidelberg New York

Springer is a part of Springer Science+Business Media

springer.com

© Springer-Verlag Berlin Heidelberg 2006
Printed in Germany

Typesetting: Camera-ready by author, data conversion by Scientific Publishing Services, Chennai, India
Printed on acid-free paper   SPIN: 11757283   06/3142   5 4 3 2 1 0

Preface

This volume presents a set of papers accompanying the lectures of the sixth edition of the International School on Formal Methods for the Design of Computer, Communication and Software Systems (SFM).

This series of schools addresses the use of formal methods in computer science as a prominent approach to the rigorous design of computer, communication and software systems. The main aim of the SFM series is to offer a good spectrum of current research in foundations as well as applications of formal methods, which can be of help for graduate students and young researchers who intend to approach the field.

SFM 2006 was devoted to formal techniques for hardware verification and covered several aspects of the hardware design process, including hardware design languages and simulation, property specification formalisms, automatic test pattern generation, symbolic trajectory evaluation, BDD-based and SAT-based model checking, decision procedures, refinement, theorem proving, and the verification of floating point units.

The opening paper by Bombieri, Fummi, and Pravadelli provides a general view on simulation-based modeling and verification strategies for developing embedded systems. In particular, the paper is focussed on describing state-of-the art co-simulation approaches and verification strategies based on fault simulation and assertion checking.

The paper by Drechsler and Fey reviews the basic concepts and algorithms for the postproduction test of integrated circuits. The then authors present an advanced SAT-based tool for automatic test pattern generation.

The paper by Claessen and Roorda concentrates on simulation-based model-checking techniques, which do not need to represent the states of the design, but only the values that flow through each signal. In particular, the authors introduce a high-performance simulation-based model-checking technique called symbolic trajectory evaluation.

The paper by Cabodi and Murciano overviews binary decision diagrams (BDD) and their application in formal hardware verification. The paper by Gupta, Ganai, and Wang illustrates instead a promising alternative to BDD-based symbolic model-checking methods that relies on Boolean satisfiability (SAT).

The paper by Cimatti and Sebastiani deals with decision procedures for verification problems that can be represented as satisfiability problems in some decidable fragments of first-order logic. The authors focus on integration techniques for combining technology for propositional satisfiability and solvers able to deal with the theory component.

The paper by Manolios addresses theorem-proving systems and shows how they can be employed to model and verify hardware using refinement. Theorem proving is considered also in the closing paper by Harrison, where it is used for the verification of floating-point algorithms.

We believe that this book offers a comprehensive view of what has been done and what is going on worldwide in the field of formal methods for hardware verification. We wish to thank all the lecturers and all the participants for a lively and fruitful school. We also wish to thank the entire staff of the University Residential Center of Bertinoro (Italy) for the organizational and administrative support.

May 2006   Marco Bernardo and Alessandro Cimatti
                                                       SFM 2006 Directors

Table of Contents

Hardware Design and Simulation for Verification

Nicola Bombieri, Franco Fummi, and Graziano Pravadelli

Università di Verona, Strada le Grazie 15, 37134 Verona, Italy
{bombieri, fummi, pravadelli}@sci.univr.it

Abstract. The development of more and more complex embedded systems constitutes a very challenging task for EDA experts, due to their HW/SW-mixed nature joint to the high demand for quality and reliability. Recently, both industrial engineers and academic researchers have developed a very large number of techniques for dynamic verification in terms of co-simulation, which, in particular, address the different nature of hardware and software components of an embedded system. However, a widely accepted methodology does not exist. Thus, this paper is intended to provide a general view on simulation-based modeling and verification strategies for developing embedded systems. In particular, the paper is focussed on describing state-of-the art co-simulation approaches and verification strategies based on fault simulation and assertion checking.

1 Introduction

An embedded system can be defined as a computer that is a component in a large system and that relies on its own microprocessor [1, 2]. Thus, it can be viewed as a mix of cooperating hardware and software parts, which are able to provide a wider and more adaptable set of complex functionality with respect to ASIC and ASIP, without requiring the large amount of resources needed by general purpose systems. Examples of embedded systems include controllers for industrial processes, automotive appliances, medical devices, multimedia portable systems, data acquisition systems, etc. The main characteristic of embedded systems is the reactivity: they must continuously react to asynchronous input events. Furthermore, since such systems are particularly suited in real-time contexts, where tasks must be performed within a given deadline, predictability (determinism) can become a key issue. In such application domains, the adaptability is required too. In fact, when determinism is required, it must be preserved also when the system is operating in a highly non-deterministic environment.

Even if embedded systems historically operate with bounded resources, as memory and computational power, nowadays they are increasing their resources, leveraging on the improvements of silicon technology. In fact, technology scaling always offers new opportunities and new challenges to system designers. Moore's law predicts a doubling on systems complexity (expressed as the number of transistors per integrated circuits) every couple of years. Chips composed of tens of million of gates, and therefore of more than a hundred million transistors, are

M. Bernardo and A. Cimatti (Eds.): SFM 2006, LNCS 3965, pp. 1–29, 2006.
© Springer-Verlag Berlin Heidelberg 2006

today feasible in commercial production lines with a 90 nm technology. Thus, a system that yesterday was developed as a set of several chips connected on a printed board, nowadays can be developed in a single chip, composed of several complex subsystems integrated on the same silicon die. Such a system is known as *System-on-a-Chip* (SoC) and it represents a strong paradigm for embedded systems [3]. Several advantages make this way to develop a system very attractive for system developers. When the system complexity increases, the number of pins also tends to increase, so it becomes simpler and cheaper to connect many subsystems on a single chip than several chips on a printed board. Furthermore, the on-chip wire capacitances are smaller than their on-board counterparts, and this implies higher performance and lower energy requirements.

On the other side, developing a single, very complex, SoC poses many challenges for the developers. First, when the technology scales, designers have to face new issues, like the short channel effects [4] and the crosstalking problem [5]. Even if such problems are usually faced by foundries, the system developers must be aware of them, because high-level design choices can have a strong impact on lower levels of abstraction.

Another issue is represented by the power quest [6]. The energy budget for embedded systems is usually strictly limited. Those systems are often battery-based, and the improvements on the battery capacitance cannot keep pace with the increase on the system complexity. Thus, to obtain a usable system (in terms of activity time), the designer must take into account the optimization of the energy consumption. Such an optimization is pressing also for the higher power density involved in modern integrated circuits. As the gate size reduces and the power consumption increases, the power density to dissipate strongly increases. Current high-performance systems, as the state of the art microprocessors, have already reached very high power densities, and, in the near future, power density is expected to increase even more. Those levels of power density imply a high quantity of heat to dissipate and this fact causes an increasing cost of the package to use. Moreover, the higher temperature of functioning has a direct impact on the reliability and on the life time of the systems. Therefore, the energy consumption minimization of a system is nowadays a key issue for the developer, which has to keep it under control at every stage of the design process.

Also the development time spent is a key factor that must be accurately considered when an embedded system is designed. The growing complexity of the development of such systems pushes towards component reuse [2]. Designers are bound to use use pre-designed subsystems, called *Intellectual Property* (IP) components, as far as possible. Such components can be of several kinds, ranging from cell libraries over blocks which perform a standard task (e.g., MPEG decoder, USB controller, etc.), to very complex components, like processor cores (ARM, MIPS and other families of microprocessors are commercially available as pre-designed IP cores). IP components are specified at several levels of abstraction, so that they can be used during all steps of the system design flow. Moreover, they are often customizable and configurable, thus designers can use them in their own systems, tuning them according to their needs.

The modern approach of design reuse introduces the concept of *platform* [7]. A platform is a fully defined interconnection structure and a collection of customizable IP blocks. A developer can start from an available platform and configure it choosing the parameters for the given IP blocks, adding new hardware devices, and removing useless IP blocks. A platform is then conceived as a highly reusable system that a designer can adapt to his own needs and purposes.

The need of taking into account all the previous challenges, and the intrinsic heterogeneous nature of embedded systems (HW and SW) makes the development of such systems a harder task compared with more traditional digital systems. In particular, the high demands for quality and reliability for embedded systems have led to complementary quality assurance efforts: hardware engineers have developed techniques for verification in terms of co-simulation, which, in particular, addresses the different nature of hardware and software components. Thus, these techniques are tailored for design and verification flows which comprises dedicated models for the hardware and the software parts.

In this context, the paper is intended to provide a review of design and verification techniques based on simulation for developing embedded systems. The paper is organized as follows. Section 2 describes a typical embedded system design flow. Section 3 is devoted to present techniques for simulation and co-simulation. Section 4 focuses on verification approaches which exploit testbenches and assertions, and the related issues. Section 5 reports some experimental results for the verification techniques presented in Section 4. Finally, concluding remarks are summarized in Section 6.

2 Design Modeling

The design of an embedded system is a very challenging task which involves the cooperation of different experts: system architects, SW developers, HW designers, verification engineers, etc. Each of them operates on different views of the system starting from a very abstract informal specification and refining the model through the abstraction layers reported. At every level of abstraction, a model of an embedded system can be viewed as a black box that processes the information received at its inputs to produce corresponding outputs. This I/O mapping defines the behavior of the system.

Figure 1 represents the classical design modeling flow where system level is refined by applying the new *transactional level modeling* (TLM) style [8]. A TLM-based design flow starts from an abstract system description and it evolves toward more detailed implementations till it gets to RTL. In particular, verification activity involves three main phases: first, the design implemented at the higher abstraction level is validated considering the system functionality; then, once the design is optimized following architecture exploration and performance analysis, it is validated taking into account the temporal behavior. Finally, whenever a step of the refinement flow implies a change in the system design, a further verification check is required in order to preserve the *golden model* functionality ascertained at the preceding step.

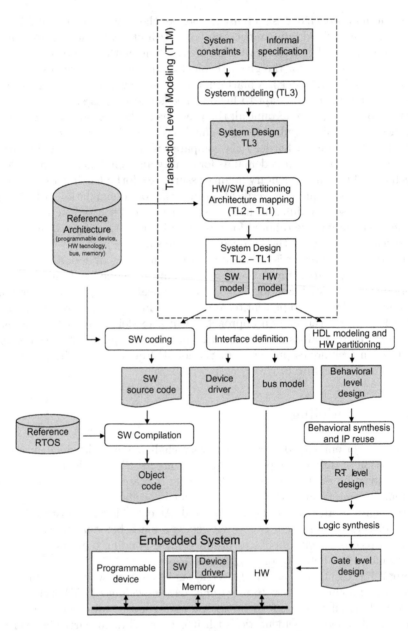

Fig. 1. Embedded system design flow

In spite of its name, *transaction-level* does not denote a *single* level of description; rather, it refers to a group of abstraction levels, each varying in the degree of functional or temporal details used and expressed.

A common agreement on terminology for TLM levels is still missing so far. Different interpretations (and terminology for the same concepts) have been

Level	Use	Features
TL3	Executable specifications and first level of functional partitioning of data and control. System proof of concepts.	➢ Implementation architecture-abstract. ➢ Untimed functionalities modeling. ➢ Event-driven simulation semantics. ➢ Point-to-point Initiator-Target connection. ➢ Abstract data types.
TL2	Hardware architectural performance and detailed behavior analysis. HW/SW partitioning and co-development. Cycle performance estimation.	➢ Mapping ideal architecture into resource-constrained world. ➢ Memory/Register map accurate. ➢ Event driven simulation with time estimation. ➢ Bit-width and transfer-size constrained data types to allow mapping to bus bursts or fragments of bursts. ➢ Split, pipelined with time delays.
TL1	Detailed analysis and low level SW development. Modeling CA interfaces for abstract simulation models of IP blocks such as embedded processors. CA performance simulation.	➢ Clock-accurate protocols mapped to the chosen HW interfaces and bus structure. ➢ Interface pin are hidden. ➢ Byte-accurate data Transactions have internal structure (protocols, data, clock). ➢ Transactions map directly to bus cycles. ➢ Parametizable to model different bus protocol and signal interfaces.

Fig. 2. TLM levels use and features

proposed by both industry and academia [8, 9, 10, 11]. However, factoring out common elements, key concepts are:

1. To implement a system at higher level means to implement the system in a more abstract way, that is to leave implementation details in order (mainly) to speed-up simulation for functional verification purposes.
2. To implement a system at lower level means to add implementation details to the system in order to simulate it in a more accurate way (for performance analysis purpose).

Hence, taking OCP-IP definition as reference, main use and features of every TLM level (e.g., TL3, TL2, and TL1) are summarized in Figure 2.

SystemC, as a broad-range level of abstraction modeling language, well addresses TLM. However, lack of established standards and methodologies means that each organization adopting TLM has to invent its own usage methodologies and API's. In addition to this redundant cost, these methodologies easily differ, making IP exchange and reuse more difficult. In this context, OSCI TLM library [12] based on SystemC represents a valuable set of templates and implementation rules aiming at establishing a reference for TLM API's implementation.

A typical TLM-based SoC design flow consists of the following steps.

– **System modeling (TL3).** Informal specification and system constraints are analyzed to provide a *system level model* of the design. At this level, there is no distinction between the HW components and the embedded SW. Indeed, the embedded system is considered as an interconnection of independent functional blocks which communicate by using blocks of words (messages) or shared memory. Implementation details like communication protocols, delay analysis, computation algorithms, etc. are not taken into consideration. The most important issues of system modeling are represented by *efficiency* (i.e., the model must be quickly developable), *flexibility* (i.e., the model must be easily adaptable to explore different design implementations), and *functionality* (i.e., the behavior of the system must reflect the informal specification and it must satisfy the system constraints). Finite state machines (FSMs) [13], Labeled Transition Systems [14], Kripke structures [15], Petri nets [16, 17], process networks [18], etc. are valuable alternatives to formally model the functionality of embedded systems at such a level. The adoption of such semantic models makes the system level a good target for formal verification issues. However, to evaluate different architectural alternatives and to carry out performance analysis, semantic models are typically translated into simulatable descriptions. In this context, SystemC [19] is a very suitable language for system level modeling[1]: it joins the flexibility of C++ and the standard features of the traditional hardware description languages (HDLs), like VHDL [20], Verilog [21], etc.

- **HW/SW partitioning and architecture mapping (TL2, TL1).** The system level description is then mapped onto an architecture to obtain a transactional level model. This requires to decide which tasks will be implemented by SW and which ones by HW. The partitioning is actually a critical design choice, since there is no unique way to decide which task must be mapped into HW and which ones into SW. Moreover, some decisions about the configuration of the final system must be taken. In particular, the designers must select the following components:
  - the programmable device where the SW will run;
  - the memory model;
  - the HW/SW communication architecture and the bus typology;
  - the HW technology (ASIC, FPGA, etc.) where HW tasks will be mapped.

  HW/SW partitioning and architecture mapping provides a *transactional level model* where the communication is completely separated from computation. The focus is on the data rather than on the way transfer is executed. At this level, simulation is used intensively for evaluating different architectures. Thus, the transactional model aims at minimizing the amount of events and the information processed during simulation in order to reduce the verification time. SystemC represents an attractive alternative also at the transactional level, since it allows one to describe very accurately both SW and HW components. In this way, HW/SW partitioning is simplified, because functional tasks can be moved from SW to HW and viceversa without the need of code translations, which are required when two different languages are used to model SW and HW components.

---

[1] SystemC is a C++ class library which can be used to define methodologies to effectively model software algorithms, hardware architectures, and HW/SW interfaces. The class library includes a simulation engine (the *SystemC kernel*) that can be linked with the user descriptions. This allows us to obtain a single executable which exhibits the behavior of the modeled system.

- **SW coding.** After partitioning, SW and HW parts follow a different design
flow. In particular, SW tasks are implemented by using a programming language (C/C++ represents an immediate solution when SystemC is adopted
at system and transactional levels), and typical SW engineering techniques
are used to optimize the resulting code. At this level, SW developers consider
the HW part as a black box which communicates with SW via device drivers.
Thus, SW coding must take into account constraints depending on the programmable device selected during the architecture mapping, and constraints
depending on the communication interface.
- **SW compilation.** After the coding, the SW is compiled to object code. The
compilation process generally depends on a Real Time Operating System
(RTOS) which is selected to take care of load distribution, task scheduling,
and communication with the HW interface. However, in some cases, RTOS
may be absent, and the SW directly interacts with the device driver.
- **Interface definition.** Splitting the design tasks in HW components and
pieces of SW introduces the need for an interface between the two parts
that, often, is not specified in the initial requirements. This interface has to
translate the timing information from the SW to the HW, and viceversa,
because HW and SW rely on very different timing models. The HW model
is typically event driven, while the SW model is cycle based, assuming it
is executed by a programmable device. For this reason, the design of the
interface between SW and HW parts is one of the most challenging task in the
embedded system design flow. It requires to implement the device drivers for
the programmable devices where the SW runs, and the communication bus
to connect HW components, memory and programmable devices. The device
drivers represent the interface between the RTOS and the HW components.
Its purpose consists of hiding the HW to the SW layers by providing a set of
functions to control the operation of the peripheral devices. Complementary,
the purpose of the bus consists of defining the communication protocol taking
into account many parameters like cost, bandwidth, reliability, etc..
- **HDL modeling and HW partitioning.** The HW model generated at the
transactional level must be refined and optimized by executing different synthesis steps to obtain a gate-level description. Historically, the highest level
of abstraction for HW components is represented by the *behavioral level*. The
HW model is implemented by using an HDL focussing on the logic function
of the HW components and ignoring implementation details. Moreover, the
HW model is possibly partitioned into various interacting modules that better characterize the different HW units. Some books dealing with Electronic
Design Automation (EDA) [22] make a more accurate classification and refer to this level as the *functional level*, while a behavioral level model is
intended as a functional representation of the design coupled with a description of the associated timing relations. Any of these two abstraction levels
keeps the complexity of digital system models quite low, allowing their rapid
simulation.
- **Behavioral synthesis and IP reuse.** The functional/behavioral model of
each HW component is further refined into a *Register Transfer Level (RTL)*

model by means of behavioral synthesis. The functionality of the design is decomposed and represented by a structural connection of combinational and sequential components (generally described as finite state machines with datapath (FSMD) [23]). At this level, IP reuse is performed too. Thus, already existing components are connected with new ones to provide the final RTL model. IP reuse sensibly decreases the time-to-market and it allows designers to concentrate the effort in implementing the very critical functionality of the system.

- **Logic Synthesis.** Finally, logic synthesis is used to translate the RTL model to a *gate-level* model, where the design is mapped into a structural view of primitive components (AND, OR, flip-flop, etc.) from which the physical mask can be easily generated to physically produce the circuit.

A verification/testing phase is mandatory after each step of the embedded system design flow to avoid the propagation of errors between the different abstraction levels. Indeed, synthesis is a dangerous process since it may introduce further bugs. This can be due to different causes: incorrect use of synthesis tools, incorrect code writing style that may prevent the synthesis tool to adequately infer the required logic, bugs of the synthesis tool, etc..

Thus, most of the publications focusing on the field of EDA start claiming the importance of verification [24] and testing [22] for shipping successful embedded systems. While the purpose of testing is to verify that the design was manufactured correctly, verification aims at ensuring that the design meets its functional intent before manufacturing. In particular, functional verification of embedded systems is the process of ensuring that the logical design of the system satisfies the architectural specification by detecting and removing every possible design error. As digital systems become more complex with each generation, verifying that the behavior is correct has become a very challenging task. Between 60% and 80% of the design group effort is now dedicated to verification [24]. The trend is particularly crucial for embedded systems, which are composed of a heterogeneous mix of hardware and software modules, and where the presence of design errors in the early phases of the design flow may lead to a complete failure of time-to-market fulfillment. In this context, both formal verification and simulation-based verification represent effective solutions to remove design errors.

There exist formal verification approaches to deal with the analysis and check of each of the grey products in Fig. 1. On the contrary, since one needs executable specifications to do simulation, simulation-based verification plays a predominant role in the later stages of the design process, i.e. once a design is already available, while formal verification must do most of the work at the border with the higher levels of abstraction. Typical abstraction-bridging verification tasks include checking a system level design vs. constraints or abstract specifications, checking the behavioral level design vs. partial models, checking component design vs. behavioral properties. Of course, the different approaches cover different aspects, thus they belong to different communities of scientists (like requirement engineering at the specification level, code analysis around a compilation task, etc.). Indeed, advanced design process methodologies always foresee verification loops when working on a single artefact (e.g., to get the system constraints or the system level design right), and verification approaches for the transformations from one or more intermediate products to another one (e.g. given a system level design and a reference architecture, get the architecture-specific incarnation of that model right).

As we see, a large area of the design flow is common ground between simulation-based verification and formal verification, indicating a large potential for synergies between the two techniques which are still insufficiently exploited.

3   Design Simulation

Dynamic verification faces the correctness of a design by means of simulation-based techniques. In dynamic verification the model functionality is essentially verified by generating a high number of input stimuli (test set) that are simulated to observe the behavior of the design under verification at primary outputs. The test set generated at a specific abstraction level can be re-used (and possibly incremented) at the lower levels after each synthesis step up to manufacturing test.

Traditional simulation-based approaches can be adopted to verify the whole embedded system before HW/SW partitioning, as well as, HW and SW components separately after HW/SW partitioning. However, the most challenging task is to perform *co-verification* between HW and SW components. The integration and the synchronization of HW and SW modules requires a permanent control of consistency and correctness that can be efficiently achieved only by exploiting a co-simulation environment.

3.1   Co-simulation Approaches

Co-simulation becomes a mandatory step after HW/SW partitioning. For this reason, several co-simulation platforms [25, 26, 27, 28, 29, 30, 31, 32] have been developed in the past years. In spite of the variety of architectural targets, performance efficiency, and description languages, we can classify these different solutions in three main categories: *homogeneous, heterogeneous,* and *semi-homogeneous* co-simulation environments.

Homogeneous Environments. Homogeneous environments use a single engine for the simulation of both HW and SW components (see Fig. 3). The Ptolemy [25] and Polis [26] environments are pioneering works in that direction. In these approaches, homogeneity is achieved by abstracting away the distinction between hardware and software parts that are described as functional blocks. Homogeneous environments simplify the design modeling and they provide good simulation performance. However, they are suitable only in a very initial phase of the design, prior to HW/SW partitioning, since the HW and SW sides needs different techniques and different tools when the abstraction level decreases toward a real implementation.

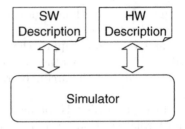

Fig. 3. A homogeneous co-simulation environment

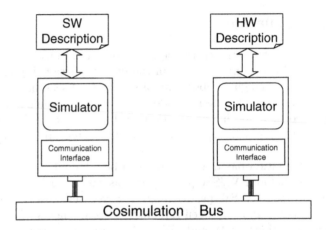

Fig. 4. A heterogeneous co-simulation environment

Heterogeneous Environments. Heterogeneous environments ensure a more accurate tuning between HW and SW components in comparison to homogeneous ones. This allows us to use a level of abstraction lower than the behavioral for HW and to evaluate the SW in its compiled (binary code) form. Such a binary code is obtained, from the high level SW description, using standard tools as a compiler, an assembler and a linker (see Fig. 1).

Most of the heterogeneous frameworks essentially address the same problem: how to efficiently link an event-driven hardware simulator and a cycle-based Instruction Set Simulator (*ISS*)[2] (see Fig. 4). In order to model the connection between HW components and the microprocessor, where the SW will be executed, a communication channel (a bus) is needed. However, such a bus causes the reduction of the simulation speed, because it requires to model the signals involved in the communication. Thus, the resulting simulation is very slow.

Earlier HW/SW co-simulation frameworks [29, 30, 31] were mainly focused on HW described in several hardware description languages, like Verilog, VHDL or SystemC, and on software developed in various programming languages, like C, C++, Java, etc.

---

[2] An ISS provides an accurate simulation of a programmable device allowing to verify SW before hardware is available.

All these heterogeneous approaches are quite similar in that their main effort aims at solving the issue of controlling and synchronizing two (or more) simulation engines. This heterogeneous style is sub-optimal in terms of simulation performance and ease of integration, since there is the burden of the communication between two very different engines. However it was the only possible choice when VHDL or Verilog was the highest possible description level for modeling HW. Some commercial tools, such as Mentor Graphics Seamless [28] and Synopsys Eaglei [27], also provide heterogeneous co-simulation capabilities. However, they only allow HW/SW co-simulation at bus level, where each bus transaction involves all signals necessary to accomplish the bus function, thus degrading the co-simulation performance.

Semi-Homogeneous Environments. The advent of design flows based on SystemC allowed the definition of efficient *semi-homogeneous* approaches [33, 34, 35, 36, 37], where the bus is not modeled at signal level. Rather, the bus is usually modeled with a small number of simple functions which provide information on the time required by the communication, without the need to evaluate each signal. By using such bus abstractions, the model results less accurate compared with a heterogeneous description where the bus is completely modeled, but the simulation speed is considerably faster. Moreover, in a semi-homogeneous approach, the accuracy is higher than the one obtained with an unpartitioned (homogeneous) description. Thus, the semi-homogeneous environments lie between the heterogeneous and the homogeneous ones, exploiting both their benefits, and allowing us to reach an optimal tradeoff between accuracy and simulation speed.

Semi-homogeneous approaches are homogeneous from the language point of view, since both HW and SW are described using C++ constructs (note that SystemC is simply a C++ library). This definitely simplifies the implementation of the initial model, as well as the subsequent HW/SW partitioning. However, these approaches are heterogeneous from the simulation point of view, since HW and SW can be executed using different simulators: the SystemC simulation kernel for the HW components and an ISS for the SW programs.

In this way, a more accurate performance estimation can be achieved, since the heterogeneous model reflects closely the final embedded system. All these environments are based on two basic issues (see Fig. 5):

- *Interprocess communication (IPC).* IPC is a software mechanism to allow different processes to communicate, even on different computers. It is used to realize the communication between the ISS, where the SW part runs in its binary form, and the SystemC simulator, that models the HW part. The simulators run as distinct processes on a host system.
- *Bus wrapper.* A wrapper is a SW layer which allows an existing piece of software to interact with an environment that is different from its originally intended one. The bus wrapper allows the use of a high level model of the bus within an environment where the SW model is cycle-accurate and the HW is modeled at a signal-accurate level of abstraction. Such a bus wrapper

ensures synchronization between the system simulation and the ISS, and it translates the information coming from the ISS into cycle-accurate bus transactions.

Most of these approaches [33, 34, 35] define a *custom interface* between the bus wrappers and the ISS. This makes the integration of new processor cores within the co-simulation framework harder, because the ISS needs to be modified to support the IPC primitives defined by the co-simulation system. This issue is addressed in [32], where a standardized interface between the bus wrapper and the ISS is proposed. It is based on the remote debugging primitives of GDB [38], which is both an instruction-level debugger and an ISS. In this way, any ISS that can communicate with GDB (that is, basically any, since GDB is a SW application) can also become part of a system-level co-simulation environment. The approach of [32] still suffers from some performance bottlenecks, since the ISS and the SystemC simulators evolve in lock-step, because the synchronization is driven by the host operating system via IPC.

In [36] the authors solve some limitations of previous approaches by proposing two alternatives co-simulation methodologies that allow a SystemC description of hardware and an ISS to efficiently co-execute. The two proposed solutions differ with respect to the simulation kernel (SystemC or ISS) that drives the co-simulation. The aim is to reduce the overhead of the IPC calls, which are very expensive in terms of time. When the master is the HDL simulator, the reduction of the IPC calls can be achieved by using and optimizing the bus wrapper, in order to minimize the amount of data exchanged between the two engines. On the other side, when the master is the ISS, it is possible to exploit the system calls of the RTOS. In fact, a device driver can be added to the RTOS, and the communication between SW and HW is handled by the software, invoking the device driver routines.

The timing synchronization is also an important issue in a co-simulation environment. Both simulators, the ISS and the HW simulator, have their own timing

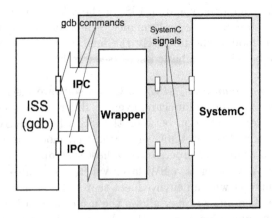

Fig. 5. A semi-homogeneous co-simulation environment based on SystemC and ISS

information. Forcing the two sides to remain strictly synchronized can be too burdening for the performance. However, relaxing too much the synchronization, can impact the simulation accuracy. Several tradeoffs between accuracy and performance are addressed in the literature [39, 40, 41]. It is possible to annotate the SW execution delay into the application (and RTOS) code [39, 40], or to add a channel between the simulators in order to exchange timing information [41]. The latter approach allows better portability, since it is independent of the used RTOS. Furthermore, it allows a fine tuning of the performance/accuracy trade-off, because the granularity of the exchanged timing information can be varied.

4 Simulation for Verification

Simulation represents the main verification technique when the functionality of large heterogeneous embedded systems has to be verified. In particular, simulation techniques for embedded systems verification are classified in two main categories:

- Simulation by testbenches.
- Assertion-based verification.

Next sections present the key concepts that distinguish the two techniques. Moreover, some approaches are described to evaluate the quality of verification carried out by using testbenches and assertions. Finally, a transaction-based verification (TBV) approach is presented to show how testbenches and assertions defined at higher levels of abstraction (e.g., at transaction level) can be reused at lower levels (e.g., at RTL).

4.1 Simulation by Testbenches

Simulation techniques based on testbenches essentially validate the model functionality by dynamically generating a high number on input stimuli (test set) that are simulated to observe the behavior of the design under verification (DUV) at primary outputs. What we need to perform such a dynamic verification is: a simulatable model of the design, a simulator, a testbench to apply stimuli to the primary input of the design, and a "method to establish the correctness" of the design with respect to the results of the simulation. Generally, the stimuli generator and the simulation engine are integrated in a single SW application, called automatic test pattern generator (ATPG).

While the first three ingredients of dynamic verification are almost straightforward, the last one is the crucial aspect. If state explosion is the big problem of formal verification, the big problem of simulation is represented by the lack of exhaustiveness of the verification process. Thus, like for formal verification, dynamic verification is very good in finding bugs, but it cannot ensure their absence. Simulation can hypothetically provide an exhaustive answer to the problem of design correctness only if the set of all possible input stimuli, applied to the design, results, after design simulation, in a set of values for the primary outputs consistent with the set of expected values. Unfortunately, this is almost impossible for two reasons: the set of expected values is typically not available, and the set of input stimuli for sequential circuits is exponentially large in time and space. Thus, the quality of dynamic verification, and in particular the quality of the generated set of stimuli, is measured by means of *code coverage* or *fault coverage*. Depending on which of these two strategies is used, we can distinguish between two kinds of dynamic verification: *logic simulation* and *fault simulation*.

Logic simulation. In logic simulation, the quality of the set of stimuli is measured by using code coverage. This is a class of metrics that has been used in software engineering [42] for quite some time to analyze whether test suites cover the required functionality. The most popular metrics adopted in logic simulation are: *statement coverage*, *condition coverage* and *path coverage*.

- *Statement Coverage.* It measures how much of the total lines of code are executed by the test set. To bring the statement coverage metric up to 100%, a desirable goal, it is necessary to understand what conditions are required to cause the execution of the uncovered statements. Then, it is necessary to understand why they never occurred. It is because the test set does not contain a stimulus able to activate the condition or it is because the condition can never occur? In the first case, a larger number of (or higher quality) test cases must be generated. On the contrary, if the condition can never occur, the code in question is effectively unreachable. Thus, either the code (and the condition) could be removed, or the design requires some most general refinement to allow the activation of the condition.
- *Condition Coverage.* It measures the various ways paths through the code are executed. Consider for example an `if` statement whose condition is `((a < 10) or (a > 20))`. The `then` part of such a statement can be executed in two ways: when the value of `a` is less than 10 (first term of the condition) and when the value of `a` is greater than 20 (second term of the condition). Thus, it is evident that the statement coverage of a code can be 100%, while the condition coverage is lower. To increase condition coverage, it is necessary to identify the possible terms of conditions that are not executed, and if these terms can never be excited or they cannot be activated by the current test set.
- *Path Coverage.* It measures all possible ways you can execute a sequence of statements. Again it is important to determine the possible conditions that cause the uncovered path to be executed, and if these conditions can never occur or they cannot be activated by the current test set. Full 100% path coverage is very difficult to achieve, since the number of paths in a sequence of statements grows exponentially with the number of control-flow statements.

What does 100% code coverage means? Not much, it indicates how thoroughly the generated test set exercises the source code, but it does not provide precise indications about the correctness of the DUV. Nevertheless, code coverage can help to identify possible corner cases that are not exercise by the testbench, and that can be symptoms of design errors.

Fault simulation. Traditional code coverage metrics derived from SW testing represent a low cost popular solution. However, they are based on controllability information, i.e., the activation of statements, branches or sequences of statements, and they do not address observability requirements, i.e., to see whether effects of possible errors activated by tests can be observed at the DUV outputs. The fact that a statement with a bug has been activated by input stimuli does not mean that the observed outputs will be incorrect. An alternative approach is represented by the use of high-level fault models [43], which include the characteristics of both coverage metrics and logic-level fault models [44]. Thus, fault simulation consists of simulating a design in presence of logical faults, which emulate the effect of physical faults on the behavior of a system description. Faults can be modeled by means of different fault models, targeting various kind of errors that may affect a design, depending on the considered abstraction level. Independently from its typical implementation (perturbed assignment, operator substitution, mutants, saboteurs, etc.), an high-level fault provides an abstraction of a possible design error, since it produces perturbed DUV behaviors. Thus, the analysis of its nature allows an effective verification of the expected and unexpected behavior of the DUV, particularly when faults are directly injected into TL or RTL code, which is very familiar to the designer.

Comparing the fault simulation results with those of the fault-free simulation of the same design, simulated by using the same test set, we can determine the *fault coverage* as the ratio between the number of faults detected by the test set and the number of simulated faults. In such a way, the fault coverage is used as a metrics to evaluate the quality of testbenches as well as to reveal design errors. Achieving 100% fault coverage is generally harder than 100% statement or condition coverage. Then, stimuli generators targeted to fault coverage allow a wider exploration of the DUV state space. Thus, they provide better test cases with respect to ones obtained by using traditional coverage metrics. For this reason, fault simulation is generally preferred to logic simulation. Indeed, as for code coverage, we cannot completely ensure the correctness of the design by relying on the fault coverage. In fact, even a test set which achieves 100% fault coverage may still fail to detect faults modeled by a different fault model.

4.2   Assertion-Based Verification

Functional verification based on assertions represents a valuable alternative to fault simulation [45]. Assertion-based verification (ABV) joins formal verification and simulation based verification to provide a more powerful and easy way to verify complex digital systems. To test these complex systems, too much time is spent constructing tests as design deficiencies are discovered, requiring testbenches to be rewritten or modified, as the previous testbench code did not address the newly discovered complexity. This process of working through the bugs causes defects in the testbenches themselves. ABV dramatically improves the efficiency of verifying correct behavior, detecting bugs and fixing bugs throughout the design process. Thus, more and more it is proposed into SoC verification methodologies.

In ABV, *assertions* are the central focus of the verification process; they detect bugs and guide testbenches in the stimuli production. An assertion, sometimes called a checker or monitor, is a precise description of what behavior is expected when a given input is presented to the design. It raises the level of verification from RTL to TL where users can develop tests and debug their designs closer to design specifications. Consequently, design functions are exercised efficiently (with minimum required time) and monitored effectively by detecting hard-to-find bugs. This methodology is called assertion based verification, since the assertions are the primary basis for ensuring that the DUV meets the criteria of design quality. ABV supports two methods: dynamic verification using simulation, and formal or semi-formal verification using model checking. In this second case, for historical reasons, the term *property* is usually adopted instead of assertion. However, the terms assertion and property are interchangeable, thus, in the following we use the more traditional term property.

Similarly to simulation by testbenches, ABV can prove the presence of bugs, but not their absence. Indeed, a design which satisfies all the defined properties is not guaranteed to be correct. In fact, the verification engineers can forget to written some properties, missing a complete verification. Thus, a design implementation that satisfies an incomplete set of properties cannot be considered bug-free. For this reason, a mechanism is needed to evaluate the quality of the defined properties, as well as a metric is used to evaluate the quality of testbenches for simulation. In this case, we use the term property coverage to indicate the percentage of the DUV behaviors checked by the defined properties.

Different papers [46, 47, 48, 49, 50] have been proposed to address the problem of property coverage. The majority of them [46, 47, 48, 49] propose formal method-based methodologies which statically analyze the effectiveness of properties in covering all states of the DUV. The main limitation of such techniques is represented by the state explosion problem that may arise in case of medium-large DUVs.

A different approach based on dynamic verification is presented in [50], where the property coverage is computed by analyzing, via simulation, the property capability of detecting DUV perturbations. In this case, the proposed property coverage methodology is applied on a set of properties which hold on the DUV, and an high-level fault model is used to generate different perturbations that modify the original functionality of the DUV implementation. The presence of a detectable fault implies that the behavior of the perturbed implementation differs from the behavior of the unperturbed one. Thus, while the set of properties is satisfied by the original unperturbed implementation, at least one of them should be refuted if checked on the perturbed implementation. On the contrary, the set of defined properties is unable to completely explore the DUV state space, thus it is incomplete. Summarizing, the property coverage methodology proposed in [50] can be described as follows:

1. a checker is generate for each defined property, by using for example FoCs [51];
2. the DUV is perturbed by using an high-level fault model to obtain a set of faulty implementations whose behavior differs from the fault-free one;

3. faulty implementations are simulated and their behavior is monitored by the checkers. Fault f is *covered* by property p if its checker fails during the simulation of the faulty implementation corresponding to f.

If a checker fails in presence of a fault f, the corresponding property p is able to distinguish between the faulty and the fault-free DUVs. This means that p covers the logic cone of the DUV that may be affected by f. Thus, according to the selected fault model, the property coverage C_P of a set of properties P is defined as:

$$C_P = \frac{\text{\# of faults covered by at least one property } p \in P}{\text{\# of generated perturbations}}. \tag{1}$$

All faulty implementation, whose behavior differs from the faulty-free one, must be covered by the property set, i.e. property coverage must achieve 100%. A lower property coverage is symptom that the property set is incomplete, and new properties must be added to addresses the uncovered perturbations.

4.3   Reuse by Transactor-Based Verification

Fault simulation and ABV are generally faster than formal verification techniques, and they allow to effectively verify large systems reducing the risk of incurring in the state explosion problem. This motivates the recent trend of proposing design and verification methodologies based on TLM, simulation and ABV (see Figure 6). However, such a tendency should not leave out of consideration the concept of *reuse* to further save time. Reuse has to be intended in two directions: from TL to RTL and viceversa. In the first case, verification engineers are interested in reusing testbenches and properties, once the TL components are refined into RTL descriptions. On the contrary, the second case is motivated by the fact that many vendors provide standard IPcores together with corresponding verification kits including testbenches and properties. In this way, already

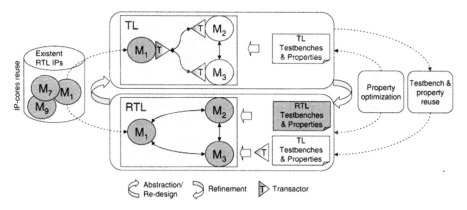

Fig. 6. Reuse of IP-cores, testbenches and properties in a mixed TL-RTL design and verification flow

existing IP-cores can be composed and integrated with new ones to create different and more complex systems. However, already existent IP-cores are generally available at RTL, while new components are modeled at transaction level. Thus, TL-RTL mixed descriptions are becoming very common in practice to quickly obtain high-level design implementations.

The benefits deriving from the reuse of testbenches and properties for ABV moving through all transactional levels till to RTL and the reuse of RTL IP-cores in a TLM context are evident. However, this arouses new challenges for both designers and verification engineers. In fact, it is evident the lack of methodologies and tools to automatically derive the RTL implementation, once the TL design has been carried out. The refinement process from TL to RTL is much more difficult than logic synthesis from RTL to gate level. A synthesizable RTL design contains all information required by the synthesis tool to generate the corresponding gate-level netlist. On the contrary, a TL description is very far from including the implementation details which must be added at RTL. Then, a fully automatized process to convert TL designs into RTL implementations is still an utopia. For this reason, it is mandatory that new design and verification methodologies are proposed in order to efficiently check the correctness of the TL-to-RTL manual conversion.

In this context, some approaches based on Transactor-based Verification (TBV) have been recently proposed from both EDA companies and academic researchers [52, 53, 54, 55]. Despite of technical details, all of them exploit the concept of *transactor* to allow a mixed TL-RTL co-verification (Triangle shape in Figure 6). A transactor works as a translator from a TL function call to an RTL sequence of statements, i.e., it provides the mapping between transaction-level requests, made by TL components, and detailed signal-level protocols on the interface of RTL IPs. Thus, testbenches and properties, defined to check the TL design, can be directly reused, through the transactor, to verify the RTL implementation. This avoids time-consuming and error-prone manual conversion of testbenches and properties moving from TL to RTL.

Figure 7 shows how the transactor is exploited to reuse TL testbenches and assertions on the RTL design [52, 53]. The testbench carries out one transaction at time, composed by two TL function calls (write() and read()). First, data are provided to the RTL design by means of write(addr, data). The transactor converts the write() call to the RTL protocol-dependent sequence of signals required to drive control and data inputs of the design under verification. Moreover, the write status is reported to the testbench to notify about successes or errors. Then, the testbench asks for the DUV result by calling read(addr, &res). The transactor waits until the DUV result is ready by monitoring the output control ports, and, finally, it gets the output data. Then, testbench can carry on with the next transaction. If property checking is desired, the parameter of the function calls (addr, data, write_status, &res, read_status), which represent inputs and outputs of the RTL computation, are provided to the checkers. The testbench is modeled at transaction level, thus, properties are checked when write() and/or read() return according to the aim of properties.

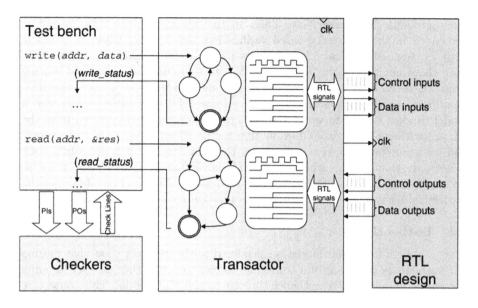

Fig. 7. The role of the transactor in TBV

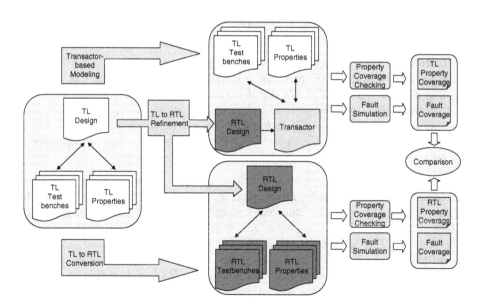

Fig. 8. Evaluation methodology flow

The effectiveness of the TBV with respect to a fully RTL verification, which requires to manually convert TL testbenches and properties into RTL ones, has been proved in [56]. The comparison methodology is summarized in Figure 8. The TL design is refined in an equivalent RTL description by following a standard semi-automatic TL design flow. Then, in the upper side, the RTL module is embedded in the transactor-based verification architecture, where it interacts with TL testbenches and TL properties through the transactors. In this way, both the simulation engine and the ABV infrastructure are unchanged moving from TL to RTL. On the contrary, in the lower side of the Figure, the RTL description communicates directly with ad-hoc RTL testbenches. Moreover, a model checker is used to verify the RTL properties manually derived from the TL properties. Such a twofold evaluation methodology, based on fault coverage and assertion/property coverage, shows that the transactor-based verification is not only valuable for time savings and conversion error avoidance, but also because it is at least as effective as RTL verification. Next sections describes the theoretical basis upon which the TBV evaluation methodology relies.

4.4 Testbench Reuse

A general high-level fault model is considered to theoretically show that reusing TL testbenches by means of a transactor allows to detect the same set of faults detectable by applying a testbench directly to the RTL model. This conjecture relies on the following definitions and theorem.

Definition 1. *Given the implementation, $\mathcal{I}$, of the DUV, a set of faults, $\mathcal{F} = \{f_1, \ldots, f_n\}$, a set of perturbed implementations, $\mathcal{I}_\mathcal{F} = \{\mathcal{I}_f | f \in \mathcal{F}\}$, the environment, $\mathcal{E}$, where $\mathcal{I}$ is embedded, and the set of FSM retroactive networks originated by $\mathcal{E}$, $\mathcal{N}_{\mathcal{I}\mathcal{E}} \cup \mathcal{N}_{\mathcal{I}_\mathcal{F}\mathcal{E}}$ [3], where $\mathcal{N}_{\mathcal{I}_\mathcal{F}\mathcal{E}} = \{\mathcal{N}_{\mathcal{I}_f\mathcal{E}} | f \in \mathcal{I}_\mathcal{F}\}$, a fault $f \in \mathcal{F}$ is:*

Detectable *if there is at least an input sequence, $\iota = (i_1, \ldots, i_n)$, such that at least one output of $\mathcal{I}$ differs from the respective output of $\mathcal{I}_f$ when ι is simultaneously applied to $\mathcal{I}$ and $\mathcal{I}_f$. We say that ι is a test sequence for f on $\mathcal{I}$.*

 $\mathcal{E}$-**detectable** *if there is at least an input sequence $\iota = (i_1, \ldots, i_n)$, such that at least one output of $\mathcal{N}_{\mathcal{I}\mathcal{E}}$ differs from the respective output of $\mathcal{N}_{\mathcal{I}_f\mathcal{E}}$ when ι is simultaneously applied to $\mathcal{N}_{\mathcal{I}\mathcal{E}}$ and $\mathcal{N}_{\mathcal{I}_f\mathcal{E}}$. We say that ι is a test sequence for f on $\mathcal{N}_{\mathcal{I}\mathcal{E}}$ [4]. We call $\mathcal{E}$-det the set of $\mathcal{E}$-detectable faults.*

Definition 2. *Under the same conditions of Def. 1 and assuming that the implementation $\mathcal{I}$ is modeled at transaction level, a fault is **TLM-detectable** if there is a test vector such that the outputs of the unperturbed and perturbed DUVs differ when the test vector is simultaneously applied to both the designs. The fault is **TLM-undetectable** if such a test vector does not exist.*

Definition 3. *Under the same conditions of Def. 1 and assuming that the implementation $\mathcal{I}$ is modeled at RTL, a fault is **RTL-detectable** if there is a test sequence such that the outputs of the unperturbed and perturbed DUVs differ when the test sequence is simultaneously applied to both the designs. The fault is **RTL-undetectable** if such a test sequence does not exist.*

---

[3] An FSM retroactive network $\mathcal{N}_{\mathcal{I}\mathcal{E}}$ is composed of two FSMs: $\mathcal{I}$, which describes the DUV, and $\mathcal{E}$, which models the environment where $\mathcal{I}$ is embedded. Some output lines of $\mathcal{I}$ are connected to the input lines of $\mathcal{E}$, and some output lines of $\mathcal{E}$ are connected to input lines of $\mathcal{I}$.

[4] Note that ι is also a test sequence for f on $\mathcal{I}$.

It is worth to note that, at TL, testbenches are composed of test vectors, while, at RTL, we need test sequences generally composed of more than one test vector. This is due to the fact that TLM is untimed (eventually a clock can be introduced at level 1), thus the result of a transaction is instantaneously available once a single test vector is applied. On the contrary, at RTL the design is generally modeled as an FSMD where the result is available after a number of clock cycles and it may depends on values provided to the primary inputs at different times. When a TL testbench is applied to an RTL design, the transactor converts test vectors in the corresponding test sequences modeling the communication protocol needed by the RTL design. From this observation the following definition derives.

Definition 4. *Under the same conditions of Def. 1 and assuming that the implementation $\mathcal{I}$ is modeled at RTL and wrapped by a TL-to-RTL transactor as defined in Section 4.3, a fault is[5]:*

- *Functionally T-detectable, if there is a test vector such that the outputs of the transactor connected to the unperturbed and perturbed DUVs are available at the same time and they differ, once the transactor has simultaneously applied the test sequence derived from the test vector to both the designs.*
- *Timing T-detectable, if there is a test vector such that the outputs of the transactor connected to the unperturbed and perturbed DUVs are available at different times, but they are equal, once the transactor has simultaneously applied the test sequence derived from the test vector to both the designs.*
- *Functionally and timing T-detectable, if there is a test vector such that the outputs of the transactor connected to the unperturbed and perturbed DUVs are available at different times, and they differ, once the transactor has simultaneously applied the test sequence derived from the test vector to both the designs.*
- *T-detectable, if it is functionally T-detectable and/or timing T-detectable.*
- *T-undetectable, if for each test vector the outputs of the transactor connected to the unperturbed and perturbed designs are available at the same time and they are equal, once the transactor has simultaneously applied the test sequence derived from the test vector to both the designs.*

Theorem 1. *An RTL-detectable fault is also T-detectable.*

Proof: If a fault is RTL-detectable there exist a test sequence such that it propagates the effect of the fault to at least one output of the perturbed RTL DUV (Def. 3). Note that, such a test sequence respects the protocol imposed by the environment constraints that must be connected to the RTL DUV as required by Def. 1.

Let us consider that the fault is propagated to a data output. Accordingly to the transactor implementation described in Section 4.3 and Def. 4, such a fault

---

[5] Please, note that in this case the environment constraints are directly modeled by the transactor.

becomes functionally T-detectable (then, T-detectable) when the RTL design is connected to a TL testbench through the transactor. In fact, the same test sequence generated by the RTL testbench can be obtained by applying an opportune test vector to the transactor (which acts like the environment constraints).

On the contrary, let us consider that the fault is propagated to a control output. In this case, the communication protocol between the transactor and the perturbed RTL DUV is necessarily changed. This causes that: the result of the perturbed DUV is provided to the transactor with a timing discrepancy with respect to the unperturbed DUV. Thus, according to Def. 4, the fault is timing T-detectable (then, T-detectable).   □

Theorem 1 shows that the TBV is at least as effective as the RTL verification from the fault coverage point of view. The Theorem assumes that the TL testbenches are able to produce a set of test vectors that can be converted from the transactor into a set of test sequences which includes the test sequences directly generated by the RTL testbenches. However, such an assumption is reasonable, since it is much more difficult to create efficient RTL testbenches than TL ones [52].

4.5 Property Reuse

Let us compare now TL property coverage and RTL property coverage to show the effectiveness of reusing TL properties at RTL through TBV, instead of converting them into properties specifically tailored to the RTL design. The desired goal is to show that TL properties cover the same set of behaviors covered by the corresponding RTL properties.

As already described, the property coverage measures the quality of properties to detect design errors in all parts of the DUV description. It is computed by analyzing the capability of properties to highlight differences between the unperturbed and the perturbed implementations of the same design. If a property, which holds on the unperturbed design, fails in presence of a fault, then the behavior perturbed by the fault is covered by the property.

Definition 5. *Under the same assumption of Definition 1, the RTL property coverage, C_P^{RTL}, and the TL property coverage, C_P^{TL}, are defined as:*

$$C_P^{RTL} = \frac{\text{\# of faults that causes an RTL property failure}}{\text{\# of RTL-detectable faults}} \tag{2}$$

$$C_P^{TL} = \frac{\text{\# of faults that causes a TL property failure}}{\text{\# of T-detectable faults}} \tag{3}$$

Given the previous Definition and Theorem 1, TL property coverage and RTL property coverage can be compared. In fact, the methodology presented in [50] for RTL property coverage can be reused for TL property coverage, provided that, the definition of RTL-detectable faults is substituted with the definition of T-detectable faults.

For sake of completeness, it is worth to note that a set of assertions, achieving 100% property coverage on the TL design, may not achieve 100% on the RTL design. This is due to the fact that at TL no properties can be defined related to communication protocols and timing between events, since such details are not modeled at transaction level. However, this observation does not affect the effectiveness of reusing TL properties at RTL, since they allows to check the functionality of the RTL design. Then, new RTL properties must be added only to verify timing and communication protocols.

5 Experimental Results

This section reports some experimental results showing the effectiveness of the simulation-based techniques, described in Section 4, to verify a complex embedded system. Moreover, an experimental confirmation is reported to show the effectiveness of reusing test benches and properties by TBV.

The case study is represented by the STMicroelectronics *Face Recognition System* shown in Figure 9. In particular, the *ROOT, DIV* and *DISTANCE* modules are considered, since they were selected to become HW components. Their characteristics are showed in Table 1 whose columns report the number of gates and flip-flops, and the number of TL and RTL faulty implementations generated to perform functional verification by using test benches and ABV.

Table 1. Characteristic of the case study

Module	Gates	FFs	TL faults	RTL faults
ROOT	7802	155	196	1627
DIV	11637	269	1017	2333
DISTANCE	40663	100	2327	3061

5.1 Functional Verification by Test Benches and ABV

The TL descriptions of *ROOT, DIV* and *DISTANCE* have been verified by using both fault simulation by test benches and ABV. In particular, a set of test sequences have been generated by using Laerte++ [57], a functional ATPG equipped with different pseudo-deterministic engines, and the corresponding fault coverage has been computed. Then, a set of properties have been defined and their effectiveness have been evaluated by computing the related property coverage. Table 2 reports the achieved results, where *FC%, #TV, PC%* and *#Prop.* refer, respectively, to the fault coverage, the number of generated test vectors, the property coverage and the number of defined properties.

5.2 TBV Evaluation

The effectiveness of TBV has been experimentally confirmed by comparing the fault coverage and the property coverage achieved by reusing TL test benches and properties through TBV, and the fault coverage and property coverage achieved by generating ad-hoc RTL test benches and by manually converting TL properties into corresponding RTL ones.

Table 2. Fault coverage and property coverage at TL

Module	ATPG		ABV	
	FC%	#TV	PC%	#Prop.
ROOT	99.0	23	99.0	11
DIV	99.0	20	99.0	5
DISTANCE	99.0	8	99.0	3

Fault Coverage Comparison. Table 3 reports the results related to the fault coverage comparison. Columns *FC%*, *#TV* and *Time* show, respectively, the achieved fault coverage, the number of test vectors generated by Laerte++, and the time required to generate/simulate such vectors, for TBV and the RTL verification flow. In particular, *TBV (reuse)* is related to the reuse of TL test benches at RTL via transactor, while *TBV (reuse+ATPG)* is related to the integration of the TL test benches by adding new test vectors generated by applying an Laerte++ to the RTL module via transactor. As expected from theoretical results reported in Section 4, the TBV fault coverage is greater than or equal to the RTL one for all the modules. Moreover, it is interesting to note that the number of test vectors and the time required by TBV is lower than the corresponding RTL quantities. In particular, the time spent by TBV is extremely lower than the one needed at RTL. This derives from the fact that, at RTL, test vectors must be completely generated ex-novo. On the contrary, TBV can reuse the ones generated during the verification of the TL descriptions. Thus, fault simulation is required instead of ex-novo test generation when TBV is applied. Indeed, the reuse of high-quality TL test vectors could be insufficient

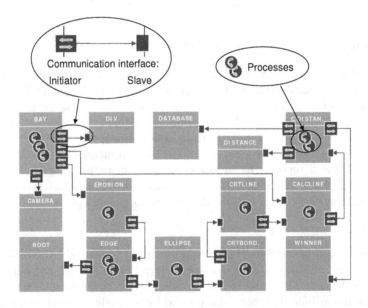

Fig. 9. The Face Recognition System

Table 3. Fault coverage comparison by reusing test benches through TBV

Design	TBV (reuse)			TBV (reuse+ATPG)			RTL		
	FC%	#TV	Time(s.)	FC%	#TV	Time(s.)	FC%	#TV	Time(s.)
ROOT	94.5	23	23	98.5	25	145	97.8	741	2050
DIV	84.3	20	31	97.0	191	112	86.6	1073	1774
DISTANCE	90.7	8	57	98.9	15	316	94.2	254	11540

to achieve an high-fault coverage also on the RTL design (*TBV (reuse)*). For this reason, the TL test benches have been integrated by generating new test vectors achieving the fault coverage reported in *TBV (reuse+ATPG)*. Thus, the TBV time is composed by summing the time required for fault simulation and the time required for test bench integration.

Property Coverage Comparison. Table 4 shows the property coverage percentage (*PC%*) achieved by applying the ABV methodology. As already reported in Table 2 the TL description of the considered modules has been verified by defining a total number of 19 properties which achieve 99% property coverage. After TL-to-RTL refinement the RTL implementation was verified by:

1. reusing TL properties through TBV (*TL Prop. Reuse*);
2. converting the TL properties into RTL ones (*Manual Conv.*);
3. adding new properties to check implementation details and the communication protocol added at RTL (*New ad-hoc Prop.*).

After RTL refinement, the TL properties have been checked on the RTL implementation by using TBV. Then, they have been manually converted into RTL properties and verified by using the SMV model checker. Finally, the corresponding property coverage have been computed and compared on the RTL implementation. The results reported in Table 4 confirms the effectiveness of TBV, since property coverages achieved by TL property reuse and manual conversion are equal for all modules. However, as observed in Section 4.5, TL properties are not enough to completely verify the RTL implementations, even if they do it at TL. This emphasizes the fact that TL properties, but also the corresponding RTL properties, are not able to identify perturbations that affect behaviors depending on timing synchronization or communication protocols typical of the RTL implementation. This has been confirmed by analyzing the

Table 4. Experimental results

		ROOT		DIV		DISTANCE		TOTAL	
		#Prop	PC%	#Prop	PC%	#Prop	PC%	#Prop	PC%
TLM	TL Prop.	11	99%	5	99%	3	99%	19	99%
RTL	TL Prop. Reuse	11	95%	5	86%	3	87%	19	89%
	Manual Conv.	11	95%	5	86%	3	87%	19	89%
	New ad-hoc Prop.	1	99%	3	96%	4	96%	8	97%

nature of high-level faults not covered by the TL properties. Thus, column *New ad-hoc Prop.* reports the final property coverage achieved after new properties have been added to check the timing synchronization and the communication protocol.

6   Concluding Remarks

In this work, the key concepts of actual embedded system design flows have been presented. Transaction level modeling has been showed as the emerging system level modeling style that, starting from an abstract system description, evolves toward more detailed descriptions till an RTL implementation. Software coding, interface definition and HW modeling have been introduced to complete the design process till the logic level. Then, the work have dealt with the use of co-simulation techniques for dynamic verification. In particular, homogeneous and heterogeneous co-simulation environments based on SystemC and ISS have been presented. Finally, the application of simulation to dynamic verification techniques, based on fault simulation and ABV, has been described. In this context, fault coverage and property coverage have been introduced to provide metrics able to evaluate the quality of such a dynamic verification. Moreover, the transaction-based verification has been presented as an efficient strategy to reuse IP-cores, test benches and properties, throughout the TL-to-RTL design flow.

References

1. Wolf, W.: What is embedded computing? IEEE Computer **35**(1) (2002) 136–137
2. Ernst, R.: Codesign of embedded systems: Status and trends. IEEE Design and Test of Computers **15**(2) (1998) 45–54
3. Bergamaschi, R.A., Cohn, J.: The a to z of socs. In: IEEE. (2002) 791–798
4. Sze, S.M.: Physics of Semiconductor Devices. John Wiley and Sons (1981)
5. S.Hall, Hall, G., McCall, J.: High-Speed Digital System Design: A Handbook of Interconnect Theory and Design Practices. John Wiley and Sons (2000)
6. Benini, L., Poncino, M.: Ambient intelligence: a computational platform perspective. In: Ambient intelligence: impact on embedded system design, Kluwer Academic Publishers (2003) 31–50
7. Sangiovanni-Vincentelli, A., Martin, G.: Platform-based design and software design methodology for embedded systems. IEEE Design and Test of Computers **18** (2001) 23–33
8. Cai, L., Gajski, D.: Transaction level modeling: An overview. In: IEEE CODES + ISSS. (2003) 19–24
9. Ghenassia, F., et al.: Using Transactional Level Models in a SoC Design Flow. Kluwer Academic Publishers (2003)
10. Donlin, A.: Transaction level modeling: Flows and use models. In: IEEE CODES + ISSS. (2004) 75–80
11. Kogel, T., Haverinen, A., Aldis, J.: Ocp tlm for architectural modeling. OCP methodology guideline, http://www.ocpip.org (2005)
12. Rose, A., Swan, S., Pierce, J., Fernandez, J.M.: Transaction level modeling in systemc. White paper. http://www.systemc.org (2004)

13. Lee, D., Yannakakis, M.: Principles and methods of testing finite state machines - a aurvey. Proc. of the IEEE **84**(8) (1996) 1090–1123
14. Valenzano, A., Sisto, R., Ciminiera, L.: An abstract execution model for basic lotos. IEEE Software Engeneering Journal **5**(6) (1990) 311–318
15. Clarke, E., Grumberg, O., Peled, D.: Model Checking. MIT Press (2000)
16. Cortes, L., Eles, P., Peng, Z.: Hierarchical modeling and verification of embedded systems. In: Proc. of IEEE Euromicro Symposium on Digital System Design. (2001) 63–70
17. Gomes, L., Barros, J.P.: On structuring mechanisms for petri nets based systems design. In: IEEE. (2003) 431–438
18. Ernst, R., Jerraya, A.A.: Embedded system design with multiple languages. In: Proc. of IEEE Conference on Asia and South Pacific Design Automation. (2000) 391–396
19. Inc.: (SystemC User's Guide) http://www.systemc.org.
20. Armstrong, J., Gray, F.: VHDL Design Representation and Synthesis. Prentice Hall (2000)
21. Sagdeo, V.: The Complete Verilog Book. Kluwer Academic Publisher (1998)
22. Breuer, M., Abramovici, M., Friedman, A.: Digital Systems Testing and Testable Design. IEEE Press (1990)
23. Gajski, D., Dutt, N., Allen, S., Wu, C., Lin, Y.: High-Level Synthesis: Introduction to Chip and System Design. First edn. Kluwer Academic Publishers (1992)
24. Bergeron, J.: Writing Testbenches: Functional Verification of HDL Models. Kluwer Academic Publishers, Norwell Massachusetts (2000)
25. Buck, J., Ha, S., Lee, E., Messerschmitt, D.: Ptolemy: A framework for simulating and prototyping heterogeneous systems. International Journal in Computer Simulation **4**(2) (1994) 155–182
26. Balarin, F., Chiodo, M., P.Giusto, H.Hsieh, A.Jurecska, L.Lavagno, C.Passerone, A.Sangiovanni-Vincentelli, E.Sentovich, K.Suzuki, B.Tabbara: Hardware-Software Co-Design of Embedded Systems: The Polis Approach. Kluwer Academic Press (1997)
27. Synopsys Inc.: (Eaglei) http://www.synopsys.com/products.
28. Mentor Graphics Inc.: (Seamless CVE) http://www.mentor.com/seamless.
29. Liem, C., Nacabal, F., Valderrama, C., Paulin, P., Jerraya, A.: System-on-chip co-simulation and compilation. IEEE Design and Test of Computers **14**(2) (1997) 16–25
30. Valderrama, C., Nacabal, F., Paulin, P., Jerraya, A.: Automatic vhdl-c interface generation for distributed co-simulation: Application to large design examples. Design Automation for Embedded Systems **3**(2/3) (1998) 199–217
31. Coste, P., Hessel, F., Marrec, P.L., Sugar, Z., Romdhani, M., Suescun, R., Zergainoh, N., Jerraya, A.: Multilanguage design of heterogeneous systems. In: Proc. of IEEE International Workshop on Hardware-Software Codesign. (1999) 54–58
32. Benini, L., Bertozzi, D., Bruni, D., Drago, N., Fummi, F., Poncino, M.: Systemc co-simulation and emulation of multi-processor soc designs. IEEE Computer **36**(4) (2003) 53–59
33. Liu, J., Lajolo, M., Sangiovanni-Vincentelli, A.: Software timing analysis using hw/sw co-simulation and instruction set simulator. In: Proc. of IEEE International Workshop on Hardware/Software Co-design. (1998) 65–69
34. Semeria, L., Ghosh, A.: Methodology for hardware/software co-verification in c/c++. In: Proc. of IEEE Asian and South Pacific Design Automation Conference (ASP-DAC). (2000) 405–408

35. Lahiri, K., Raghunathan, A., Lakshminarayana, G., Dey, S.: Communication architecture tuners: a methodology for the design of high-performance communication architectures for system-on-chips. In: Proc. of ACM/IEEE Design Automation Conference (DAC). (2000) 513–518

36. Fummi, F., Martini, S., Perbellini, G., Poncino, M.: Native iss-systemc integration for the co-simulation of multi-processors soc. In: Proc. of IEEE Design Automation and Test in Europe. (2004) 564–569

37. Moussa, I., Grellier, T., Nguyen, G.: Exploring sw performance using soc transaction-level modelling. In: Proc. of IEEE Design Automation and Test in Europe. (2003) 120–125

38. : (Gnu project web server) http://www.gnu.org/software/.

39. Yoo, S., Bacivarov, I., Bouchhima, A., Paviot, Y., Jerraya, A.: Building fast and accurate sw simulation models based on hardware abstraction layer and simulation environment abstraction layer. In: Proc. of IEEE Design Automation and Test in Europe. (2003) 550–555

40. Bacivarov, I., Yoo, S., Jerraya, A.: Timed hw-sw cosimulation using native execution of os and application sw. In: Proc. of IEEE International High Level Design Validation and Test Workshop. (2002) 51–56

41. Formaggio, L., Fummi, F., Pravadelli, G.: A timing-accurate hw/sw co-simulation of an iss with systemc. In: Proc. of IEEE International Conference on Hardware/Software Codesign and System Synthesis. (2004) 152–157

42. Myers, G.: The Art of Software Testing. Wiley - Interscience, New York (1979)

43. Ghosh, S., Chakraborty, T.: On behavior fault modeling for digital designs. International Journal of Electronic Testing: Theory and Applications 2(2) (1991) 135–151

44. Breuer, M., Abramovici, M., Friedman., A.: Digital Systems Testing and Testable Design. IEEE Press (1990)

45. Synopsys Inc.: Assertion-based verification. White paper. www.synopsys.com (2003)

46. Hoskote, Y., Kam, T., Ho, P.H., Zao, X.: Coverage estimation for symbolic model checking. In: Proc. of ACM/IEEE DAC. (1999) 300–305

47. Katz, S., Grumberg, O., Geist, D.: Have i written enough properties? - a method of comparison between specification and implementation. In: Proc. of IFIP CHARME. (1999) 280–297

48. Chockler, H., Kupferman, O., Kurshan, R.P., Vardi, M.Y.: A practical approach to coverage in model checking. In: Proc. of CAV. (2001) 66–78

49. Jayakumar, N., Purandare, M., Somenzi, F.: Dos and don'ts of ctl state coverage estimation. In: Proc. of ACM/IEEE DAC. (2003) 292–295

50. Fummi, F., Pravadelli, G., Toto, F.: Coverage of formal properties based on a high-level fault model and functional ATPG. In: IEEE ETS. (2005) 162–167

51. Abarbanel, Y., Beer, I., Gluhovsky, L., Keidar, S., Wolfsthal, Y.: Focs - automatic generation of simulation checkers from formal specifications. In: CAV). Volume 1855 of Lecture Notes in Computer Science., Springer-Verlag (2000) 538–542

52. Brahme, D., Cox, S., Gallo, J., Glasser, M., Grundmann, W., Ip, C.N., Paulsen, W., Pierce, J., Rose, J., Shea, D., Whiting, K.: The transaction-based verification methodology. Technical Report CDNL-TR-2000-0825, Cadence Berkeley Labs (2000)

53. Norris Ip, C., Swan, S.: A tutorial introduction on the new systemc verification standard. White paper. www.systemc.org (2003)

54. Bombieri, N., Fedeli, A., Fummi, F.: On psl properties re-use in soc design flow based on transactional level modeling. In: IEEE MTV. (2005)

55. Jindal, R., Jain, K.: Verification of transaction-level systemc models using rtl testbenches. In: ACM/IEEE MEMOCODE. (2003) 199–203
56. Bombieri, N., Fummi, F., Pravadelli, G.: On the evaluation of transactor-based verification for reusing tlm assertions and testbenches at rtl. In: IEEE DATE. (2006)
57. Fin, A., Fummi, F. In: LAERTE++: An Object Oriented High-Level TPG for SystemC Designs. Kluwer Academic Publishers (2004)

Automatic Test Pattern Generation*

Rolf Drechsler and Görschwin Fey

Institute of Computer Science, University of Bremen, 28359 Bremen, Germany
{drechsle, fey}@informatik.uni-bremen.de

Abstract. The postproduction test of integrated circuits is crucial to ensure a high quality of the final product. This test is carried out by checking the correct response of the chip under predefined input stimuli – or test patterns. These patterns are calculated by algorithms for *Automatic Test Pattern Generation* (ATPG).

The basic concepts and algorithms for ATPG are reviewed in this chapter. Then, an advanced SAT-based ATPG tool is introduced and emprically evaluated.

1 Introduction

After producing a chip the functional correctness of the integrated circuit has to be checked. Otherwise products with malfunctions would be delivered to customers which is not acceptable for any company. During this postproduction test input stimuli are applied and the correctness of the output response is controlled. These input stimuli are called test patterns. Many algorithms for *Automatic Test Pattern Generation* (ATPG) have been proposed in the last 30 years. But due to the ever increasing design complexity new techniques have to be developed that can cope with todays circuits.

While classical approaches are based on backtracking on the circuit structure, since the early 80s several approaches based on *Boolean Satisfiability* (SAT) have been proposed (see e.g. [41, 30, 44, 43]). In [41] comparisons to more than 40 other "classical" approaches based on FAN, PODEM and the D-algorithm are provided showing the robustness and effectiveness of SAT-based techniques. In contrast to the early work in the 80s, where ATPG was often reduced to PROLOG or logic programming, the ATPG techniques developed by Larrabee [27] and Stephan et al. [41] used many simplification and learning approaches, like global implications [44]. By this, these algorithms combined the power of SAT with algorithms from the testing domain.

Recently, there is a renewed interest in SAT, and many improvements for proof engines have been proposed. SAT solvers make use of learning and implication procedures (see e.g. [31, 32]). These new proof techniques led to breakthroughs in several applications, like formal hardware verification [9].

In this chapter we give an introduction to ATPG. The basic concept and classical ATPG algorithms are reviewed. Then, the formulation as a SAT problem is considered. Therefore modern SAT solvers are explained and the transformation

---

* This work was supported in part by DFG grant DR 287/15-1.

M. Bernardo and A. Cimatti (Eds.): SFM 2006, LNCS 3965, pp. 30–55, 2006.

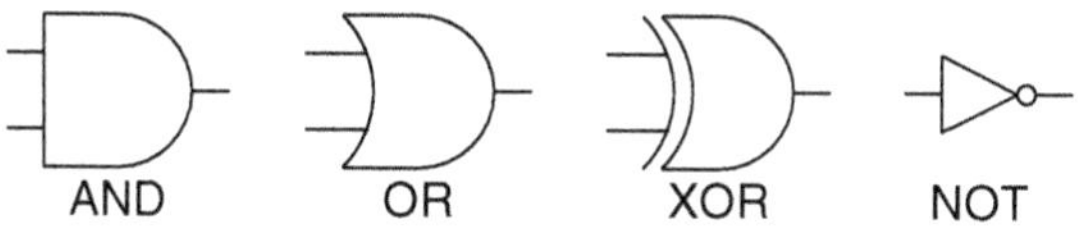

Fig. 1. Basic gates

of ATPG onto SAT is discussed. Advanced techniques for SAT-based ATPG are explained for the ATPG tool *PASSAT* (PAttern Search using SAT). This tool uses techniques recently developed for SAT solvers that are today commonly applied in the verification domain. In contrast to previous SAT approaches, that only considered Boolean values, we study the problem for a multi-valued logic encoding, i.e. PASSAT can also consider unknown values and tri-states. The influence of different branching heuristics is studied to tune the SAT solver towards test generation, i.e. variable selection strategies known from SAT and strategies applied in classical ATPG [18, 17]. Experimental results on the ISCAS benchmarks and large industrial circuits are given to demonstrate the efficiency of the approach.

The chapter is structured as follows: In the next section the basic concepts to keep the presentation self-contained are introduced. Also classical ATPG algorithms based on the circuit structure are briefly reviewed. In Section 3 important concepts from SAT and SAT solvers are reviewed. The reduction of the ATPG problem to a SAT problem and improvements to exploit the circuit structure and handle practical multi-valued circuits are presented in Section 4. Dedicated variable selection strategies for SAT solvers applied to ATPG are investigated in Section 5. Experimental results are reported in Section 6. Finally, we conclude in Section 7.

2 Preliminaries

This section provides the necessary notions to introduce the ATPG problem. First, circuits and fault models are presented. Then, the reduction of a sequential ATPG problem to a combinational problem is explained. Finally, classical ATPG algorithms working on the circuit structure are briefly reviewed. The presentation is kept brief, for further reading we refer to [21].

2.1 Circuits

In this work a circuit is assumed to be composed of the set of basic gates shown in Figure 1. These are the well-known gates that correspond to Boolean operators: AND, OR, XOR and NOT. Extending this library to other Boolean gates if necessary is straightforward. The connections between gates are defined by an underlying graph structure. Additionally, for gates that represent non-symmetric functions (e.g. multiplexors or tri-state elements) a unique order for the inputs is given by ordering the predecessors of a gate.

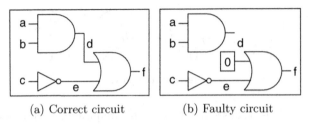

(a) Correct circuit   (b) Faulty circuit

Fig. 2. Example for the SAFM

2.2   Stuck-at Fault Model

After producing a chip the functional correctness of this chip with respect to the Boolean gate-level specification has to be checked. Without this check an erroneous chip would be delivered to customers that may result in a malfunction of the final product. This, of course, is not acceptable. On the other hand a large range of malfunctions is possible due to defects in the material, process variations during production etc. But directly checking for all possible physical defects is not feasible. Therefore an abstraction in terms of a *fault model* is introduced.

The *Stuck-At Fault Model* (SAFM) [5] is well-known and widely used in practice. In this fault model a single line is assumed to be stuck at a fixed value instead of depending on the input values. When a line is stuck at the value 0, this is called a *stuck-at-0* (SA0) fault. Analogously, if the line is stuck at the value 1, this is a *stuck-at-1* (SA1) fault.

Example 1. Consider the circuit shown in Figure 2(a). When a SA0 fault is introduced on line d the faulty circuit in Figure 2(b) is resulting. The output of the AND-gate is disconnected and the input of the OR-gate constantly assumes the value 0.

Besides the SAFM a number of other fault models have been proposed, e.g. the cellular fault model [16], where the function of a single gate is changed, or the bridging fault model [23], where two lines are assumed to settle to a single value. These fault models mainly cover static physical defects like opens or shorts. Dynamic effects are covered by delay fault models. In the path delay fault model [40] a single fault means that a value change along a path from the inputs to the outputs in the circuit does not arrive within the clock-cycle time. Instead of paths the gate delay fault model [20, 42] considers the delay at gates.

In the remainder of this chapter only the SAFM is considered further due to the high relevance in practical applications. This relevance can be attributed to two observations: the number of faults is in the order of the size of the circuit and fault modeling in the SAFM is relatively easy, i.e. for the static fault model the computational complexity of test pattern generation is lower compared to dynamic fault models.

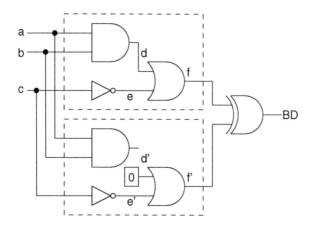

Fig. 3. Boolean difference of faulty circuit and fault free circuit

2.3   Combinational ATPG

Automatic Test Pattern Generation (ATPG) is the task of calculating a set of test patterns for a given circuit with respect to a fault model. A test pattern for a particular fault is an assignment to the primary inputs of the circuit that leads to different output values depending on the presence of the fault. Calculating the Boolean difference of the faulty and fault free circuit yields all test patterns for a particular fault. This construction is similar to a Miter circuit [4] as it can be used for combinational equivalence checking.

Example 2. Again, consider the SA0 fault in the circuit in Figure 2. The input assignment $a = 1$, $b = 1$, $c = 1$ leads to the output value $f = 1$ for the correct circuit and to the output value $f = 0$ if the fault is present. Therefore this input assignment is a test pattern for the fault d SA0. The construction to calculate the Boolean difference of the fault free circuit and faulty circuit is shown in Figure 3.

When a test pattern exists for a particular fault, this fault is classified as being *testable*. When no test pattern exists, the fault is called *redundant*. The decision problem to classify a fault as redundant or testable is NP-complete. The aim is to classify all faults and to create a set of test patterns that contains at least one test pattern for each testable fault.

  Generating test patterns for circuits that contain state elements like flip-flops is computationally more difficult, because the state elements can not directly be set to a particular value. Instead the behavior of the circuit over time has to be considered during ATPG. A number of tools have been proposed that directly address this sequential problem, e.g. HITEC [33]. But in practice, the resulting model often is too complex to be handled by ATPG tools. Therefore the *full scan mode* is often considered to overcome this problem by connecting all state elements in a scan chain [45, 13]. In the test mode the scan chain combines all state elements into a shift register, in normal operation mode the state elements

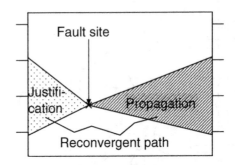

Fig. 4. Justification and propagation

are driven by the ordinary logic in the circuit. As a result the state elements can be considered as primary inputs and outputs for testing purposes and a combinational problem results.

2.4 Classical ATPG Algorithms

Classical algorithms for ATPG usually work directly on the circuit structure to solve the ATPG problem for a particular fault. Some of these algorithms are briefly reviewed in the following. For an in-depth discussion we refer the reader to text books on ATPG, e.g. [21].

One of the first complete algorithms dedicated to ATPG was the *D-algorithm* proposed by Roth [34]. The basic ideas of the algorithm can be summarized as follows:

- An error is observed due to differing values at a line in the circuit with or without failure. Such a divergence is denoted by values D or $\overline{D}$ to mark differences 1/0 or 0/1, respectively.
- Instead of Boolean values, the set $\{0, 1, D, \overline{D}\}$ is used to evaluate gates and carry out implications.
- A gate that is not on a path between the error and any output does never have a D-value.
- A necessary condition for testability is the existence of a path from the error to an output, where all intermediate gates either have a D-value or are not assigned yet. Such a path is called a potential D-chain.
- A gate is on a D-chain, if it is on a path from the error location to an output and all intermediate gates have a D-value.

On this basis an ATPG algorithm can focus on justifying a D-value at the fault site and propagating this D-value to an output as shown in Figure 4. The algorithm starts with injecting the D-value at the fault site. Then, this value has to be propagated towards the outputs. For example to propagate the value D at one input across a 2-input AND-gate the other input must have the non-controlling value 1. After reaching an output the search proceeds towards the inputs in the same manner to justify the D-value at the fault site. At some stages in the search decisions are possible. For example to produce a 0 at the output of an AND-gate either one or both inputs can have the value 0. Such a decision may be wrong and may lead to a conflict later on. For example due to a reconvergence as shown in Figure 4 justification may not be possible due to conditions from propagation. In this case, a backtrack search has to be applied. In summary the D-algorithm is confronted with a search space of $O(2^s)$ for a circuit with s signals including inputs, outputs and internal signals.

A number of improvements have been proposed for this basic procedure. PO-DEM [18] branches only on the values for primary inputs. This reduces the search space for test pattern generation to $O(2^n)$ for a circuit with n primary inputs. But as a disadvantage time is wasted, if all internal values are implied from a given input pattern that finally does not detect the fault. FAN [17] improves upon this problem by branching on stems of fanout points as well. This allows to calculate conditions for a test pattern due to the internal structure of the circuit as well. The branching order and value assignments are determined by heuristics that rely on observability measures to predict a "good" variable assignment for justification or propagation, respectively. Moreover the algorithm keeps track of a justification frontier moving towards the inputs and a propagation frontier moving towards the outputs. Therefore FAN can make the "most important decision" first – based on a heuristic – while the D-algorithm applied a more static order doing only propagation at first and justification afterwards. SOCRATES [35] includes the use of global static implications by considering the circuit structure. Based on particular structures in the circuit indirect implications are possible, i.e. implications that are not directly obvious due to assignments at a single gate, but implications that result from functional arguments across several gates. These indirect implications are directly applied during the search process to imply values earlier from partial assignments and, by this, prevent wrong decisions. HANNIBAL [25] further improves this idea. While SOCRATES only uses a predefined set of indirect implications, HANNIBAL learns from the circuit structure in a preprocessing step. For this task recursive learning [26] is applied. In principle, recursive learning is complete itself, but too time consuming to be used as a stand alone procedure. Therefore learning is done in a preprocessing step. During this step the effect of value assignments is calculated and the resulting implications are learned. These implications are stored for the following run of the search procedure. In HANNIBAL the FAN algorithm was used to realize this search step.

These algorithms only address the problem of generating a test pattern for a single fault. In the professional application such basic ATPG procedures are complemented by a preprocessing step and a postprocessing step. In the preprocessing phase easy-to-detect faults are classified in order to save run time afterwards. Postprocessing concentrates on test pattern compaction, i.e. reducing the number of test patterns in the test set.

3   Boolean Satisfiability

Before introducing an ATPG engine based on *Boolean Satisfiability* (SAT) the main concepts of SAT and modern SAT solvers are reviewed. Also the standard conversion of a given circuit into constraints for a SAT solver is introduced.

3.1   SAT Solver

SAT solvers usually work on a database that represents the Boolean formula in *Conjunctive Normal Form* (CNF) or product of sums. A CNF is a conjunction (product) of clauses, where each clause is a disjunction (sum) of literals. Finally, a literal is a variable or its complement.

Example 3. The following Boolean formula is given in CNF:

$$f(a,b,c,d) = \underbrace{(a + \bar{c} + d)}_{w_1} \cdot \underbrace{(a + \bar{c} + \bar{d})}_{w_2} \cdot \underbrace{(a + c + d)}_{w_3} \cdot \underbrace{(a + c + \bar{d})}_{w_4} \cdot \underbrace{(\bar{a} + \bar{b} + c)}_{w_5}$$

The objective during SAT solving is to find a satisfying assignment for the given Boolean formula or to proof that no such assignment exists. A CNF is satisfied if all clauses are satisfied. A clause is satisfied if at least one literal in the clause is satisfied. The literal a is satisfied if the value 1 is assigned to variable a. The literal $\bar{a}$ is satisfied if the value 0 is assigned to variable a.

Modern SAT solvers are based on the DLL procedure that was first introduced in [7] as an improvement upon [8]. Often the DLL procedure is also referred to as DPLL. In principle this algorithm explores the search space of all assignments by a backtrack search as shown in Figure 5. Iteratively, a decision is done by choosing a variable and a value for this variable according to a *variable selection strategy* (Step 1). Then, implications due to this assignment are carried out (Step 2). When all clauses are satisfied the problem is solved (Step 3). Otherwise the current assignment may only be partial and therefore no conclusion is possible yet. In this case further assignments are necessary (Step 4). If at least one clause is not satisfied under the current (partial) assignment *conflict analysis* is carried out as will be explained in more detail in Section 3.2. Then, a new branch in the search tree is explored by switching the variable value (Step 6). When there is no decision to undo the search space has been completely explored and therefore the instance is unsatisfiable (Step 7).

3.2   Advances in SAT

Only after some substantial improvements over the basic DLL procedure in the recent past SAT solvers became a powerful engine to solve real world problems. In particular these improvements were efficient *Boolean Constraint Propagation* (BCP), *conflict analysis* together with *non-chronological backtracking*, and sophisticated *variable selection strategies*.

BCP carries out implications due to previous decisions. In order to satisfy a CNF all clauses must be satisfied. Now assume, that under the current partial

1. *Decision*:
   Choose an unassigned variable and assign a new value to the variable.
2. *Boolean Constraint Propagation*:
   Carry out implications resulting from the previous assignment.
3. *Solution*:
   If all clauses are satisfied, output the current variable assignment and return "satisfiable".
4. If there is no unsatisfied clause due to the current assignment proceed with Step 1.
5. *Conflict analysis*:
   If the current assignment leads to at least one unsatisfied clause, carry out conflict analysis and add conflict clauses.
6. *(Non-chronological) Backtracking*:
   Undo the most recent decision, where switching the variable could lead to a solution, undo all implications due to this assignment and switch the variable value. Goto Step 2.
7. *Unsatisfiable*:
   Return "unsatisfiable".

Fig. 5. DLL procedure

assignments all but one literals in a clause evaluate to 0 and the variable of the last literal is unassigned. Then, the value of this last variable can be implied in order to evaluate the clause to 1.

Example 4. Again, consider the CNF from Example 3. Assume the partial assignment $a = 1$ and $b = 1$. Then, due to clause w_5 the assignment $c = 1$ can be implied.

After each decision BCP has to be carried out and therefore the efficiency of this procedure is crucial for the overall performance. In [32] an efficient architecture for BCP was presented for the SAT solver CHAFF (the source code of the implementation ZCHAFF can be downloaded from [3]). The basic idea is to use the *two literal watching scheme* to efficiently detect, where an implication may be possible. Two literals of each clause are watched. Only if one of these literals evaluates to 0 upon a previous decision and the other literal is unassigned an implication may occur for the clause. If no implication occurs, because there is a second unassigned literal this second literal is watched. For each literal a watching list is stored to efficiently access those clauses where the a particular literal is watched. Therefore instead of always touching all clauses in the database only those that may cause an implication are considered.

Conflict analysis was first proposed in [31] for the SAT solver GRASP. In the traditional DLL procedure only the most recent decision was undone, when a conflict, i.e. a clause that is unsatisfied under the current assignment, was detected. In contrast a modern SAT solver analyzes such a conflict. During BCP a conflict occurs, if opposite values are implied for a single variable due to different clauses. Then, the reasons (i.e. the decisions) that were responsible for this conflict are detected. From this reasons a *conflict clause* is created to prevent the solver to reenter the same search space. Finally, the SAT solver backtracks to

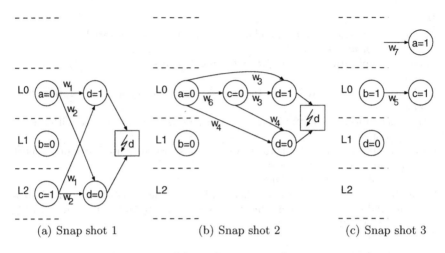

(a) Snap shot 1   (b) Snap shot 2   (c) Snap shot 3

Fig. 6. Decision stack

the decision before the last decision that participated in the conflict. Switching the value of the last decision that lead to the conflict is done by BCP due to the inserted conflict clause. Therfore this value assignment becomes an implication instead of a decision.

Example 5. Again, consider the CNF from Example 3. Each time the SAT solver makes a decision, this decision is pushed onto the decision stack. Now, assume that the first decision at decision level $L0$ is the assignment $a = 0$. No implications follow from this decision. Then at $L1$ the solver decides $b = 0$. Again, no implications follow. At $L3$ the solver decides $c = 1$. Now according to clause w_1 the assignment $d = 1$ is implied, but also due to w_2 the assignment $d = 0$ is implied. Therefore a conflict with respect to variable d occurs. This situation is shown in Figure 6(a). The decision stack is shown on the left hand side. The solver tracks reasons for assignments using an *implication graph* (shown on the right hand side). Each node represents an assignment. Decisions are represented by nodes without predecessors. Each implied assignment has as its predecessors the reason, that caused the assignment. The edges are labeled by the clauses that cause an assignment. In the example the assignments $a = 0$ and $c = 1$ caused the assignment $d = 1$ due to clause w_1. Additionally, this caused the assignment $d = 0$ due to w_2 and a conflict is resulting. By traversing the graph backwards the reason for the conflict, i.e. $a = 0$ and $c = 1$, can be determined.

Now it is known that this assignment must be avoided in order to satisfy the CNF. This information is stored by adding the *conflict clause* $w_6 = (a + \bar{c})$ to the CNF. Thus, the same non-solution space is never re-entered during further search – this is also called *conflict based learning*. The decision $c = 1$ is undone. Due to $a = 0$ and the conflict clause w_6 the assignment $c = 0$ is implied which is called a *failure driven assertion*.

The implication $c = 0$ triggers a next conflict with respect to d as shown in Figure 6(b). The single reason for this conflict is the decision $a = 0$. Therefore the conflict clause $w_7 = (a)$ is added. Now, the solver backtracks above decision level $L0$. This happens because the decision $b = 0$ was not a reason for the conflict. Instead *non-chronological backtracking* occurs – the solver undoes any decision up to the most recent decision that was involved in the conflict. Therefore in the example the decisions $b = 0$ and $a = 0$ are undone.

Due to the conflict clause w_7 the assignment $a = 1$ is implied independent of any decision as shown in Figure 6(c). Then, the decision $b = 1$ is done at $L0$. For efficiency reasons the SAT solver does not check whether all clauses are satisfied under this partial assignment, but only detects conflicts. Therefore a satisfying assignment is found by deciding $d = 0$ at $L1$.

In summary, this example on an informal basis showed how a modern SAT solver carries out conflict analysis and uses conflict clauses to remember non-solution-spaces. A large number of added conflict clauses may result in memory problems. This is resolved by removing conflict clauses from time to time which does not change the initial problem instance. A formal and more detailed presentation of the technique can be found in [31]. The algorithms to derive conflict clauses have been further improved, e.g. in [46, 12]. A result of this learning is a drastic speed-up of the solving process – in particular also for unsatisfiable formulas.

The last major improvement of SAT solvers results from sophisticated variable selection strategies. Basically the SAT solver dynamically collects statistics about the occurrence of literals in clauses. A dynamic procedure is used to keep track of conflict clauses added during the search. An important observation is that locality is acchieved by exploiting recently learned information. This helps to speed up the search. An example is the *Variable State Independent Decaying Sum* (VSIDS) strategy employed in [32]. A counter exists for each literal to count the number of occurrences in clauses. Each time a conflict clause is added the counters are incremented accordingly. The value of these counters is regularly divided by two which helps to emphasize the influence of more recently learned clauses. But a large number of other heuristics has also been investigated, e.g. in [29, 19, 22].

Another ingredient to modern SAT solvers is a powerful preprocessing step as proposed in [10, 11, 22]. The original CNF is usually a direct mapping of the problem onto a CNF representation. No optimizations are carried out, e.g. unit clauses are frequently contained in this original CNF, but these can be eliminated without changing the solution space. When preprocessing the CNF formula optimizations are applied to make the representation more compact and to improve the performance of BCP.

Due to these advances SAT solvers have become the state of the art for solving a large range of problems in CAD, e.g. formal verification [24, 2], debugging or diagnosis [39, 1, 14], and test pattern generation.

3.3   Circuit to CNF Conversion

A SAT solver can be applied as a powerful black-box engine to solve a problem. In this case transforming the problem instance into a SAT instance and the

Table 1. Transformation of an AND-gate into CNF

(a) Truth-table	(b) Clauses	(c) Minimized

$a\, b\, c$	$c \leftrightarrow a \cdot b$		
0 0 0	1		
0 0 1	0	$a + b + \bar{c}$	
0 1 0	1		$a + \bar{c}$
0 1 1	0	$\cdot\, a + \bar{b} + \bar{c}$	$\cdot\quad b + \bar{c}$
1 0 0	1		$\cdot\, \bar{a} + \bar{b} + c$
1 0 1	0	$\cdot\, \bar{a} + b + \bar{c}$	
1 1 0	0	$\cdot\, \bar{a} + \bar{b} + c$	
1 1 1	1		

SAT solution into a solution for the original problem is crucial. In particular for SAT-based ATPG one step is the transformation of the circuit into a CNF. For example in [27] the basic procedure has been presented.

The transformation of a single AND-gate into a set of clauses is shown in Table 1. The goal is to create a CNF that models an AND-gate, i.e. a CNF that is only satisfied for assignments that may occur for an AND-gate. For an AND-gate with two inputs a and b, the output c must always be equal to $a \cdot b$. The truth-table for this CNF formula is shown in Figure 1(a). From the truth-table a CNF formula is generated by extracting one clause for each assignment were the formula evaluates to 0. These clauses are shown in Table 1(b). This CNF representation is not minimal and can therefore be reduced by two-level logic minimization, e.g. using SIS [36]. The clauses in Table 1(c) are the final result.

Now, the generation of the CNF for a complete circuit is straightforward. For each gate clauses are generated according to the type of the gate. The output variables and input variables of a gate and its successors are identical and therefore establish the overall circuit structure within the CNF.

Example 6. Consider the circuit shown in Figure 2(a). This circuit is translated into the following CNF formula:

$$\underbrace{(a + \bar{d}) \cdot (b + \bar{d}) \cdot (\bar{a} + \bar{b} + d)}_{d \leftrightarrow a \cdot b}$$

$$\cdot\, \underbrace{(c + e) \cdot (\bar{c} + \bar{e})}_{e \leftrightarrow \bar{c}}$$

$$\cdot\, \underbrace{(\bar{d} + f) \cdot (\bar{e} + f) \cdot (d + e + \bar{f})}_{f \leftrightarrow d + e}$$

An advantage of this transformation is the linear size complexity. Given a circuit where n is the sum of the numbers of inputs, outputs and gates, the number of variables in the SAT instance is also n and the number of clauses is in $O(n)$.

A disadvantage is the loss of structural information. Only a set of clauses is presented to the SAT solver. Information about predecessors and successors of a node is lost and is not used during the SAT search. But as will be shown later this information can be partially recovered by introducing additional constraints into the SAT instance.

4   SAT-Based ATPG

In this section SAT-based ATPG is explained in detail. The basic problem transformation is presented at first. Then, an improvement of this basic transformation by exploiting structural information is shown. This is enhanced for the practical application to multi-valued circuits.

4.1   Basic Problem Transformation

The transformation is formulated for a single fault. Then, the process iterates over all faults to generate a complete test set. Alternatively, the SAT-based engine can be integrated within an ATPG tool that uses other engines as well.

First, the fault site is located in the circuit. Then, the parts of the circuit that are influenced by the fault site are calculated as shown in Figure 7. From the fault site towards the outputs all gates in the transitive fanout are influenced, this is also called *fault shadow*. Then, the cone of influence of the outputs in the fault shadow is calculated. These gates have to be considered when creating the ATPG instance. Analogously to the construction of the Boolean difference shown in Figure 3 a fault free model and a faulty model of the circuit are joined into a single SAT instance to calculate the Boolean difference between both versions. All gates not contained in the transitive fanout of the fault site have the same behavior in both versions. Therefore only the fault shadow is duplicated as shown in Figure 8. Then, the Boolean difference of corresponding outputs is calculated. At least one of these Boolean differences must assume the value 1 to obtain a test pattern for the fault. In Figure 8 this corresponds to constraining the output of the OR-gate to the value 1. Now, the complete ATPG instance is formulated in terms of a circuit and can be transformed into a CNF. If the SAT solver returns a satisfying assignment this directly determines the values for the primary inputs to test the fault. If the SAT solver returns unsatisfiable, the considered fault is redundant.

4.2   Structural Information

As explained earlier most of the structural information is lost during the transformation of the original problem into CNF. But this can be recovered by additional constraints. This has been suggested for the SAT-based test pattern generator TEGUS [41]. Improvements on the justification and propagation have been proposed in [44, 43].

In particular the observations from the D-algorithm as explained in Section 2.4 are made explicit in the CNF. Now, three variables are used for each gate g:

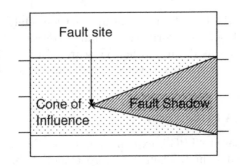

Fig. 7. Influenced circuit parts

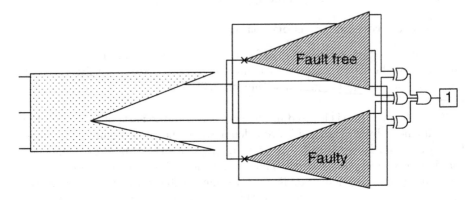

Fig. 8. Influenced circuit parts

- g_f denotes the value in the faulty circuit.
- g_c denotes the value in the correct circuit.
- $g_d = 1$, iff g is on a D-chain.

This notation allows to introduce additional implications into the CNF:

- If g is on a D-chain, the values in the faulty and the correct circuit are different: $g_d \rightarrow (g_f \neq g_c)$.
- If g is on a D-chain, at least one successor of g must be on the D-chain as well: Let $h^i, 1 \leq i \leq q$ be the successors of g, then $g_d \rightarrow \bigvee_{i=1}^{q} h_d^i$.
- If a gate g is not on a D-chain, the values in the faulty and the correct circuit are identical: $\overline{g}_d \rightarrow (g_f = g_c)$.

Without these implications the fault shadow in the fault free version and the faulty version of the circuit are only connected via the variables on the cut to the shared portions of the circuit. In contrast the g_d variables establish direct links between these structures. Therefore implications are possible even when the cut variables are not assigned yet. Moreover the information about successors of a gate and the notion of D-chains are directly encoded in the SAT instance.

4.3   Encoding

In this section the techniques to handle non-Boolean values are discussed. These techniques have been proposed for the tool PASSAT [37]. First, the use of multi-valued logic during ATPG is motivated and the four-valued logic is introduced. Then, different possibilities to encode the multi-valued problem in a Boolean SAT instance are discussed.

Four-Valued Logic. For practical purposes it is not sufficient to consider only the Boolean values 0 and 1 during test pattern generation as it has been done in earlier approaches (e.g. [41]). This has mainly two reasons.

At first circuits usually have tri-state elements. Therefore, besides the basic gates already shown in Figure 1 also tri-state elements may occur in a circuit. These are used if a single signal is driven by multiple sources. These gates behave as follows:

- **BUSDRIVER**, Inputs: a, b, Output: c
  Function: $c = \begin{cases} Z, \text{ if } a = 0 \\ b, \text{ if } a = 1 \end{cases}$

- **BUS0**, Inputs: $a_1, \ldots, a_n$, Output c
  Function: $c = \begin{cases} 0, \text{ if } a_1 = Z, \ldots, a_n = Z \text{ or } \exists i \in \{1, \ldots, n\} \, a_i = 0 \\ 1, \exists i \in \{1, \ldots, n\} \, a_i = 1 \end{cases}$
  Note, that the output value is not defined, if there are two inputs with the opposite values 0 and 1.

- **BUS1** behaves as BUS0, but assumes the value 1 if not being driven.

From a modeling point of view the tri-state elements could be transformed into a Boolean structure with the same functionality, e.g. by inserting multiplexers. But during test pattern generation additional constraints apply to signals driven by tri-state elements. For example, no two drivers must drive the signal with opposite values or if all drivers are in the high impedance state the driven signal has an unknown value. The value Z is used to properly model these constraints and the transition function of tri-state elements.

Environment constraints that apply to a circuit are another problem. Usually the circuit is embedded in a larger environment. As a result some inputs of the circuit may not be controllable. Thus, the value of such a non-controllable input is assumed to be unknown during ATPG. The logic value U is used to model this situation. This has to be encoded explicitly in the SAT instance, because otherwise the SAT solver would also assign Boolean values to non-controllable inputs.

Therefore a four-valued logic over $\{0, 1, Z, U\}$ is considered in PASSAT.

Boolean Encoding. The multi-valued ATPG problem has to be transformed into a Boolean problem to use a modern Boolean SAT solver on the four-valued logic. Therefore each signal of the circuit is encoded by two Boolean variables. One encoding out of the $4! = 24$ mappings of four values onto two Boolean values has to be chosen. The chosen encoding determines which clauses are needed to

Table 2. Boolean encodings

(a) Set 1

s	x	$\overline{x}$
0	a	b
1	a	$\overline{b}$
U	$\overline{a}$	b
Z	$\overline{a}$	$\overline{b}$

(b) Set 2

s	x	$\overline{x}$
0	a	b
1	a	$\overline{b}$
U	$\overline{a}$	$\overline{b}$
Z	$\overline{a}$	b

(c) Set 3

s	x	$\overline{x}$
0	a	b
1	$\overline{a}$	$\overline{b}$
U	$\overline{a}$	b
Z	a	$\overline{b}$

(d) Example: Set 1, $a = 0$, $b = 0$, $x = c_s$

s	c_s	c_s^*
0	0	0
1	0	1
U	1	0
Z	1	1

model particular gates. This, in turn, influences the size of the resulting SAT instance and the efficiency of the SAT search.

All possible encodings are summarized in Tables 2(a)-2(c). The two Boolean variables are denoted by x and $\overline{x}$, the letters a and b are placeholders for Boolean values. The following notations define the interpretation of the tables more formally:

- A signal s is encoded by the two Boolean variables c_s and c_s^*.
- $x \in \{c_s, c_s^*\}, \overline{x} \in \{c_s, c_s^*\} \setminus \{x\}$
- $a \in \{0, 1\}, \overline{a} \in \{0, 1\} \setminus \{a\}$
- $b \in \{0, 1\}, \overline{b} \in \{0, 1\} \setminus \{b\}$

Example 7. Consider Set 1 as defined in Table 2(a) and the following assignment: $a = 0$, $b = 0$, $x = c_s$. Then, the encoding in Table 2(d) results.

Thus, a particular encoding is determined by choosing values for a, b and x. Each table defines a set of eight encodings.

Note, that for encodings in Set 1 or Set 2 one Boolean variable is sufficient to decide, if the value of s is in the Boolean domain, i.e. in $\{0, 1\}$, or in the non-Boolean domain, i.e. in $\{U, Z\}$. In contrast encodings in Set 3 do not have this property. This observation will be important when the efficiency of a particular encoding for SAT solving is determined.

Transformation to SAT Instance. The clauses to model a particular gate type can be determined if a particular encoding and the truth-table of the gate are given. This is done analogously to the procedure in Section 3.3. The set of clauses can be reduced by two-level logic-optimization. Again, the tool ESPRESSO contained in SIS [36] was used for this purpose. For the small number of clauses for the basic gate types ESPRESSO is capable of calculating a minimal representation. The following example illustrates this flow.

Example 8. Table 3(a) shows the truth-table of an AND-gate $s = t \cdot u$ over $\{0, 1, Z, U\}$. The truth-table is mapped onto the Boolean domain using the encoding from Example 7. The encoded truth-table is shown in Table 3(b) (for compactness the notation "$\neq 0\ 0$" is used to denote that at least one of two variables must be different from 0; "$-$" denotes "don't care"). A CNF is extracted from this truth-table and optimized by ESPRESSO.

Table 3. AND-gate over $\{0, 1, Z, U\}$

(a) 4-valued

t	u	s
0	$-$	0
$-$	0	0
1	1	1
U	$\neq 0$	U
Z	$\neq 0$	U
$\neq 0$	U	U
$\neq 0$	Z	U

(b) Encoded

c_t	c_t^*	c_u	c_u^*	c_s	c_s^*
0	0	$-$	$-$	0	0
$-$	$-$	0	0	0	0
0	1	0	1	0	1
1	0	$\neq 0$	0	1	0
1	1	$\neq 0$	0	1	0
$\neq 0$	0	1	0	1	0
$\neq 0$	0	1	1	1	0

Table 4. Number of clauses for each encoding

Set	NAND	NOR	AND	BUS	BUS0	BUS1	BUSDR.	XOR	NOT	OR	All
1	8	9	9	10	11	10	9	5	5	8	100
2	9	8	8	10	10	11	9	5	5	9	100
3	11	11	11	8	9	9	11	5	6	11	108

Table 5. Number of gates for each type

circ.	IN	OUT	FANO.	NOT	AND	NAND	OR	NOR	BUS	BUSDR.
p44k	2356	2232	6845	16869	12365	528	5484	1128	0	0
p88k	4712	4565	14560	20913	27643	2838	16941	5883	144	268
p177k	11273	11031	33605	48582	49911	5707	30933	5962	0	560

Results for all possible encodings are presented in Table 4. For each gate type the number of clauses needed to model the gate are given. Besides the well-known Boolean gates (AND, OR, ...) also the non-Boolean gates $BUSDRIVER$, $BUS0$ and $BUS1$ are considered. The last column All in the table gives the sum of the numbers of clauses for all gate types.

All encodings of a given set lead to clauses that are isomorphic to each other. By mapping the polarity of literals and the choice of variables the other encodings of the set are retrieved. Particularly, Boolean gates are modeled efficiently by encodings from Set 1 and Set 2. The sum of clauses needed for all gates is equal for both sets. The difference is that for example the encodings of one set are more efficient for $NAND$-gates, while the encodings of the other set are more efficient for NOR-gates. Both gate types occur with a similar frequency in our industrial benchmarks as shown in Table 5. The same observation is true for the other gates where the efficiency of the encodings differs. Therefore no significant trade-off for the encodings occurs on the benchmarks.

In contrast more clauses are needed to model Boolean gates if an encoding of Set 3 is used. At the same time this encoding is more efficient for non-Boolean gates. In most circuits the number of non-Boolean gates is usually much smaller than the number of Boolean gates. Therefore more compact SAT instances will result if an encoding from Set 1 or Set 2 is used. The behavior of the SAT

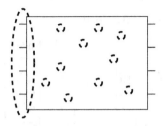

Fig. 9. Decision variables in dedicated variable selection strategies

solver does not necessarily depend on the size of the SAT instance, but if the same problem is encoded in a much smaller instance also a better performance of the SAT solver can be expected. These hypotheses are strengthened by the experimental results reported in Section 6.

5   Variable Selection

A SAT solver traverses the search space by a back-tracking scheme. While BCP and conflict analysis have greatly improved the speed of SAT solvers, the variable selection strategy is crucial for an efficient traversal of the search space. But no general way to choose the best variable is known, as the decision about satisfiability of a given CNF formula is NP-complete [6]. Therefore SAT solvers have sophisticated heuristics to select variables as explained in Section 3. Usually the heuristic accumulates some statistics about the CNF formula during run time of the SAT solver to use this data as the basis for decisions. This leads to a trade-off between the quality of a decision and the overhead needed to update the statistics. Also, the quality of a given heuristic often depends on the problem domain. The default variable selection strategy applied by ZCHAFF is the quite robust VSIDS strategy that has been explained earlier.

Decisions based on variable selection also occur in classical test pattern generation. Here, usually structural methods are employed to determine a good choice for the next selection. Besides the default variable selection strategy from ZCHAFF our tool PASSAT provides two strategies similar to strategies known from classical ATPG: selecting primary inputs only or selecting fanout points only.

Making decisions on primary inputs only was the improvement of PODEM [18] upon the D-algorithm. Any other internal value can be implied from the primary inputs. This yields a reduction of the search space and motivates to apply the same strategy for SAT-based test pattern generation as well. For SAT solving this is done by restricting the variable selection of the SAT solver to those variables corresponding to primary inputs or state bits of the circuit. Within these variables the VSIDS strategy is applied to benefit from the feedback of conflict analysis and current position in the search space. Figure 9 visualizes this strategy. Only the variables in the dotted oval are allowed for selection.

Restricting the variable selection to fan-out gates only has been proposed in FAN [17] for the first time. Again, the idea is to restrict the search space while getting a large number of implications from a single decision. Conflicts resulting from a decision are often due to a small region within the circuit. These conflicts are detected with less effort, if fan-out gates and primary inputs are selected instead of only primary inputs. PASSAT applies the VSIDS strategy to select fan-out gates or primary inputs. In Figure 9 this corresponds to the areas in the dotted oval and in the circles within the circuit. Including primary inputs in this selection strategy is crucial for the SAT procedure because this ensures that all other variable assignments can be implied from decision variables. This is necessary because otherwise conflicts may remain undetected.

The experiments in Section 6.4 show that some heuristics are quite robust, i.e. can classify all faults, while others are fast for some faults but abort on other faults. Therefore an iterative approach turned out to be most effective:

1. One strategy is run with a given time out.
2. If the first strategy does not yield a test pattern a second, more robust, strategy is applied.

Experimental results show that this approach ensures fast test pattern generation where possible, while a more sophisticated search is done for the remaining faults. For our experiments selecting only inputs was used as the first strategy, and selecting any variable as the second.

6   Experimental Results

In this section we report experimental results to validate the efficiency of particular techniques of PASSAT. This tool is based on the SAT solver ZCHAFF [32, 3] that provides the advanced SAT techniques discussed earlier. First, PASSAT is compared to previous FAN-based and SAT-based approaches for ATPG. Then, the influence of the multi-valued encoding is studied. The variable selection strategies are evaluated in another experiment. Finally, results for industrial benchmarks are presented.

6.1   Redundancy Identification

In a first experiment we studied redundancy identification. As a hard example a 40 bit multiplier has been considered. The results for TEGUS in comparison to PASSAT are shown in Figure 10. Reported are run times of an ATPG run for different redundant faults. As can easily be seen, with an increasing number of conflict clauses the run time of TEGUS grows significantly, while our approach shows only a slight increase in run time. The redundancy is detected due to unsatisfiability of the CNF formula. Therefore TEGUS has to exhaust the whole search space by checking all possible assignments before recognizing a fault as redundant. In contrast PASSAT prunes large parts of the search space due to conflict analysis and non-chronological backtracking. Simplified, more conflict clauses mean pruning a larger part of the search space.

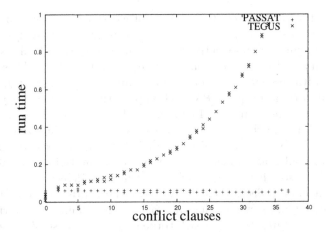

Fig. 10. Redundancies: conflict clauses vs. run time

6.2 ISCAS Benchmarks

In a next series of experiments we study the run time behavior of the two SAT-based approaches for the benchmarks from ISCAS85 and ISCAS89. To demonstrate the quality of SAT-based approaches a comparison to an improved version of Atalanta [28], that is based on the FAN algorithm [17], is given[1]. Atalanta was used to also generate test patterns for each fault. The back-track limit was set to 10. The results are shown in Table 6. The first column gives the name of the benchmark. Then the run time is given in CPU seconds for each approach. Run times for Atalanta with fault simulation and without fault simulation are given in Columns *fs* and *no fs*, respectively. On circuits "s35932" and "s38584.1" Atalanta gave no results, when fault simulation was disabled. For TEGUS and PASSAT the run time to generate the SAT instance and the time for SAT-solving are separately given in Columns *Eqn* and *SAT*, respectively.

Both SAT approaches are significantly faster than the classical FAN-based algorithm and solve all benchmarks in nearly no time. No fault simulation has been applied in the SAT approaches, therefore the run times should be compared to Atalanta without fault simulation. Especially for large circuits the SAT approaches show a run time improvement of several orders of magnitude. But even when fault simulation is enabled in Atalanta the SAT approaches are faster by up to more than two orders of magnitude (see e.g. "s35932" and "s38584.1").

Considering only the SAT approaches, TEGUS is faster for these simple cases. Here test patterns for all faults are generated. In this scenario the speed-up gained by PASSAT for difficult faults as seen in Section 6.1 is overruled by the overhead for sophisticated variable selection and conflict analysis. Furthermore the simple two-valued encoding is used in these experiments. The situation changes, if more complex circuits or tri-states are considered (see below).

---

[1] Atalanta is available as public domain software from *http://www.ee.vt.edu/~ha/cadtools/cadtools.html*.

Table 6. Results for the Boolean circuit model

Circ.	Atalanta fs	no fs	TEGUS Eqn	SAT	PASSAT Eqn	SAT
c432	0.02	0.05	0.02	0.02	0.18	0.08
c880	0.03	0.13	0.00	0.02	0.16	0.02
c1355	0.02	0.90	0.05	0.02	0.29	0.21
c1908	0.12	1.00	0.06	0.00	0.54	0.10
c2670	0.58	3.12	0.04	0.08	0.79	0.12
c3540	0.85	5.73	0.23	0.16	3.17	0.66
c5315	1.12	17.70	0.08	0.04	1.17	0.27
c6288	0.75	49.43	0.21	0.10	4.78	1.79
c7552	5.72	65.93	0.20	0.42	2.61	0.70
s1494	0.08	0.37	0.01	0.00	0.06	0.01
s5378	1.70	18.37	0.03	0.02	0.37	0.06
s9234.1	18.63	83.90	0.14	0.39	3.06	0.47
s13207.1	18.63	127.40	0.29	0.16	3.03	0.61
s15850.1	27.13	204.27	0.68	0.76	7.66	1.52
s35932	87.40	-	0.47	0.09	2.68	0.28
s38417	131.77	1624.78	0.52	0.24	3.56	0.65
s38584.1	86.30	-	0.63	0.14	4.09	0.75

6.3   Encoding

Again, we study the benchmarks from ISCAS85 and ISCAS89 and consider single stuck-at faults. But this time we use the 4-valued encoding allowing tri-states and unknown values as discussed in Section 4.3. The results are shown in Table 7. Additionally, the numbers of testable, redundant and aborted faults are shown in columns *Ct*, *Red* and *Ab*, respectively[2]. As can be seen, TEGUS now has a large number of aborted faults, only for "c6288" all faults can be classified. Often test pattern generation fails even for non-redundant faults, e.g. consider "c432", where 160 detectable faults were aborted. At the same time PASSAT still can fully classify all faults. The increase in run time compared to the Boolean encoding in Table 6 is due to the increased size of the SAT instance as explained in Section 4.3 and due to more decisions that are necessary in this case.

While these results evaluate the performance of different tools under the same encoding, the results in Table 8 help to evaluate the influence of different encodings. As explained in Section 4.3 there are 24 possibilities to choose a particular encoding. As discussed in Section 4.3 a significant trade-off in run time or memory needs can not be expected for the encodings of Set 1 and Set 2. Therefore we chose one encoding from Set 2 and one encoding from the remaining Set 3. The industrial benchmarks already shown in Table 5 were considered. Table 8 reports results for three faults on each circuit. Reported are the name of the circuit, the fault number, and the type of encoding used. The

---

[2] Notice that the numbers might vary slightly to numbers reported in the literature due to the underlying AND/INVERTER graph structure.

Table 7. Results for the 4-valued circuit model

Circ.	TEGUS					PASSAT				
	Ct	Red	Ab	Eqn	SAT	Ct	Red	Ab	Eqn	SAT
c432	241	37	164	0.05	3.28	402	41	0	1.45	0.99
c880	621	0	121	0.11	1.51	742	0	0	1.34	0.97
c1355	1202	0	8	0.47	3.06	1202	8	0	8.60	39.5
c1908	1097	5	81	0.57	5.28	1175	8	0	8.41	12.8
c2670	1724	48	56	0.39	2.47	1730	99	0	6.31	3.79
c3540	1044	89	1266	3.04	76.2	2280	119	0	37.2	34.7
c5315	3653	51	167	2.02	12.3	3811	60	0	23.8	33.8
c6288	5728	2	0	17.8	61.1	5728	2	0	226	638
c7552	4018	61	1045	3.90	36.1	4995	129	0	48.2	143
s1494	1230	12	7	0.05	0.89	1237	12	0	1.23	0.55
s5378	2807	20	46	0.37	2.69	2848	25	0	3.97	3.34
s9234.1	2500	75	132	0.66	6.57	2610	97	0	7.99	2.43
s13207.1	5750	181	685	2.56	107	6362	269	0	45.4	41.4
s15850.1	7666	245	539	5.33	55.4	8116	338	0	63.4	21.7
s35932	26453	3968	4	6.61	8.48	26457	3968	0	31.2	32.7
s38417	20212	149	712	9.22	35.8	20884	189	0	79.7	65.2
s38584.1	24680	1079	857	7.37	27.3	25210	1834	0	40.9	15.1

Table 8. Memory and run time for different encodings

Circ.	No.	Set	Clauses	Cls. %	Variables	Memory	Mem. %	Eqn	Eqn %	SAT	SAT %
p44k	1	1	173,987		56,520	13,713		41		14	
		3	220,375	127	56,520	14,087	103	49	120	78	557
p44k	2	1	174,083		56,542	13,713		43		16	
		3	220,493	127	56,542	14,088	103	51	119	79	494
p44k	3	1	174,083		56,542	13,713		43		15	
		3	220,493	127	56,542	14,088	103	52	121	79	527
p88k	1	1	33,406		10,307	2,824		8		4	
		3	41,079	123	10,307	3,410	121	10	125	7	175
p88k	2	1	33,501		10,328	2,824		9		4	
		3	41,188	123	10,328	3,411	121	9	100	8	200
p88k	3	1	33,517		10,289	2,825		8		8	
		3	41,321	123	10,289	3,412	121	9	113	8	100
p177k	1	1	96,550		34,428	8,900		23		23	
		3	119,162	123	34,428	9,082	102	25	107	247	1074
p177k	2	1	96,536		34,425	8,900		25		28	
		3	119,145	123	34,425	9,082	102	29	116	234	836
p177k	3	1	96,550		34,428	8,899		25		20	
		3	119,162	123	34,428	9,082	102	29	116	237	1185

memory needs were measured in the number of clauses ("Clauses"), the number of variables ("Variables") and memory consumption in kB ("Memory"). Again, run times are measured for generation of the CNF formula ("Eqn") and solving the formula ("SAT"). In all cases the overhead of the encoding from Set 3 over the encoding from Set 2 is shown in percent. On all the test cases the encoding from Set 2 performs significantly better than the encoding from Set 3. As can be expected from the number of clauses needed per gate as shown in Table 4 the memory needs are larger for the encoding from Set 3. The number of variables does not depend on the encoding, but on the number of gates in the circuit and remains the same. The influence of the encoding on the run time is even more remarkable than the influence on the memory needs. The run time for the third fault in p177k is almost 12 times faster if the encoding from Set 2 is applied. Therefore this encoding was chosen as the standard encoding in PASSAT.

6.4   Variable Selection

Next, we study the influence of the different variable selection strategies introduced in Section 5. The 4-valued circuit model is considered. Table 9 shows the results for the default strategy known from ZCHAFF, using fanout-gates only, using inputs only, and the iterative strategy. For the iterative strategy a time out of 1 sec while selecting only inputs was allowed per fault, then the default strategy was applied. In case of the default strategy no time out was used, for the remaining strategies 2 seconds were used to guarantee that a single fault does not block the test generation for remaining faults. The table shows that the default strategy is the most robust strategy among the non-iterative strategies. No abortions occur for this heuristic for the ISCAS benchmarks considered. The selection of fanouts only yields improvements in some cases (e.g. "s35932"), but can not classify all faults in several cases. The reason here is that the reduction of the search space does not compensate for the weak influence of conflict analysis on further decisions. The search space is more drastically pruned, when only inputs are allowed for selection. This yields a large speed up of up to 6 times in case of "s35932". On the other hand difficult faults are often aborted, because internal conflicts during SAT-solving are detected too late. This is the case for "c6288". Therefore the iterative strategy was applied to retrieve a fast solution where possible, while using the more sophisticated VSIDS strategy on all variables, where a fast solution was not possible. As a result the iterative strategy does not lead to any aborted faults. In most cases even a remarkable speed-up compared to the default strategy is gained. The last column of Table 9 shows the percentage of run time needed by SAT-solving using the iterative strategy compared to the default strategy. Only for a few cases a penalty occurs. But the improvement often is significant, e.g. less than 20% are needed in case of "c7552" and "s35932". Especially for the larger benchmarks significant run time improvements were achieved.

6.5   Industrial Circuits

Finally, two industrial circuits from Philips are considered, i.e. large circuits that also contain buses. We gave a 20 second CPU time limit to the SAT solver. The results are given in Table 10. As can be seen for these circuits only very few faults

Table 9. PASSAT with different variable selection strategies

Circ.	Default Ab	Default Eqn	Default SAT	Fanout Ab	Fanout Eqn	Fanout SAT	Inputs Ab	Inputs Eqn	Inputs SAT	Input, Default Ab	Input, Default Eqn	Input, Default SAT	Imp
c432	0	1.41	1.01	0	1.64	0.79	0	1.49	1.53	0	1.47	1.53	0.7
c880	0	1.43	0.86	0	1.44	0.94	0	1.25	0.43	0	1.42	0.28	3.1
c1355	0	8.79	38.80	0	8.70	33.30	1	8.72	8.60	0	8.92	8.72	4.4
c1908	0	8.59	12.60	2	8.83	17.80	13	8.63	16.00	0	9.90	15.80	0.8
c2670	0	5.96	4.09	0	6.30	4.09	5	6.01	6.83	0	6.61	7.70	0.5
c3540	0	38.20	33.80	2	38.40	37.30	2	39.10	15.60	0	39.80	15.30	2.2
c5315	0	24.60	33.30	0	25.20	42.50	0	24.50	8.51	0	24.60	8.31	4.0
c6288	0	229.00	634.00	169	238.00	485.00	517	234.00	635.00	0	715.00	636.00	1.0
c7552	0	49.20	141.00	12	51.00	153.00	2	49.60	24.00	0	50.10	23.50	6.0
s1494	0	1.30	0.51	0	1.30	0.59	0	1.28	0.54	0	1.29	0.55	0.9
s5378	0	4.10	3.26	0	4.65	2.94	0	4.47	1.24	0	4.17	1.48	2.2
s9234.1	0	7.73	5.43	0	8.06	5.60	0	7.90	2.25	0	8.19	2.01	2.7
s13207.1	0	31.60	92.90	30	33.80	100.00	19	32.00	40.00	0	55.40	39.90	2.3
s15850.1	0	62.90	79.70	0	67.40	72.20	0	63.50	20.50	0	63.90	20.70	3.9
s35932	0	31.90	32.60	0	66.00	11.60	0	31.40	5.32	0	32.00	5.34	6.1
s38417	0	80.70	64.60	0	100.00	66.30	0	82.20	31.80	0	82.60	32.50	2.0
s38584.1	0	40.80	26.30	0	68.10	27.50	0	40.50	14.10	0	40.80	14.30	1.8

Table 10. PASSAT for industrial benchmarks

Circ.	Ct	Red	Ab	Eqn	SAT
p88k	127,084	2,354	14	12,186	9,584
p565k	1,203,690	26,426	204	5,291	8,155

remain unclassified, i.e. only 204 for circuit "p565k" that consists of more than 565k gates. For the same benchmark TEGUS gives up on more than 340,000 faults (!) demonstrating how hard the circuit is to test.

7   Conclusions

The problem of generating test patterns for the postproduction test was introduced in this chapter. Basic concepts and classical algorithms have been reviewed. An efficient approach for SAT-based test pattern generation aiming at circuits that include tri-state elements has been shown. Due to recent advances in SAT-solving the approach is more robust than previous ones. Complete test sets for the circuits from ISCAS89 have been calculated. The influence of the variable selection strategy on the efficiency of test pattern generation is crucial. But applying an iterative approach to combine a fast and a robust strategy yields significant improvements. Large industrial circuits that include buses have been studied. Also an industrial circuit with more than 500k gates test pattern have been generated for almost all faults in a very short run time.

Acknowledgment

The authors would like to thank Junhao Shi from the University of Bremen, Germany for his help with the implementation. The authors would also like to thank Andreas Glowatz, Friedrich Hapke and Jürgen Schlöffel from Philips Semiconductors GmbH, Hamburg, Germany for helpful discussions and their support in this work.

Parts of this chapter have been published in [37, 38, 15].

References

1. M.F. Ali, S. Safarpour, A. Veneris, M.S. Abadir, and R. Drechsler. Post-verification debugging of hierarchical designs. In *Int'l Conf. on CAD*, pages 871–876, 2005.
2. A. Biere, A. Cimatti, E. Clarke, and Y. Zhu. Symbolic model checking without BDDs. In *Tools and Algorithms for the Construction and Analysis of Systems*, volume 1579 of *LNCS*, pages 193–207. Springer Verlag, 1999.
3. Boolean Satisfiability Research Group at Princeton University. ZCHAFF, 2004. http://www.princeton.edu/˜chaff/zchaff.html.
4. D. Brand. Redundancy and don't cares in logic synthesis. *IEEE Trans. on Comp.*, 32(10):947–952, 1983.
5. M.A. Breuer and A.D. Friedman. *Diagnosis & reliable design of digital systems*. Computer Science Press, 1976.
6. S.A. Cook. The complexity of theorem proving procedures. In *3. ACM Symposium on Theory of Computing*, pages 151–158, 1971.
7. M. Davis, G. Logeman, and D. Loveland. A machine program for theorem proving. *Comm. of the ACM*, 5:394–397, 1962.
8. M. Davis and H. Putnam. A computing procedure for quantification theory. *Journal of the ACM*, 7:506–521, 1960.
9. R. Drechsler. *Advanced Formal Verification*. Kluwer Academic Publishers, 2004.
10. R. Drechsler. Using synthesis techniques in SAT solvers. In *ITG/GI/GMM-Workshop "Methoden und Beschreibungssprachen zur Modellierung und Verifikation von Schaltungen und Systemen"*, pages 165–173, 2004.
11. N. Eén and A. Biere. Effective preprocessing in SAT through variable and clause elimination. In *SAT 2005*, volume 3569 of *LNCS*. Springer, 2005.
12. N. Eén and N. Sörensson. An extensible SAT solver. In *SAT 2003*, volume 2919 of *LNCS*, pages 502–518, 2004.
13. E.B. Eichelberger and T.W. Williams. A logic design structure for LSI testability. In *Design Automation Conf.*, pages 462–468, 1977.
14. G. Fey, S. Safarpour, A. Veneris, and R. Drechsler. On the relation between simulation-based and SAT-based diagnosis. In *Design, Automation and Test in Europe*, 2006.
15. G. Fey, J. Shi, and R. Drechsler. Efficiency of multiple-valued encoding in SAT-based ATPG. In *Int'l Symp. on Multi-Valued Logic*, 2006.
16. A.D. Friedman. Easily testable iterative systems. In *IEEE Trans. on Comp.*, volume 22, pages 1061–1064, 1973.
17. H. Fujiwara and T. Shimono. On the acceleration of test generation algorithms. *IEEE Trans. on Comp.*, 32:1137–1144, 1983.
18. P. Goel. An implicit enumeration algorithm to generate tests for combinational logic. *IEEE Trans. on Comp.*, 30:215–222, 1981.

19. E. Goldberg and Y. Novikov. BerkMin: a fast and robust SAT-solver. In *Design, Automation and Test in Europe*, pages 142–149, 2002.
20. E. R. Hsieh, R. A. Rasmussen, L. J. Vidunas, and W. T. Davis. Delay test generation. In *Design Automation Conf.*, pages 486–491, 1977.
21. N. Jha and S. Gupta. *Testing of Digital Systems*. Cambridge University Press, 2003.
22. H. Jin and F. Somenzi. CirCUs: A hybrid satisfiability solver. In *SAT 2004*, volume 3542 of *LNCS*, pages 211–223. Springer Verlag, 2005.
23. K. L. Kodandapani and D. K. Pradhan. Undetectability of bridging faults and validity of stuck-at fault test sets. *IEEE Trans. on Comp.*, C-29(1):55–59, 1980.
24. A. Kuehlmann, V. Paruthi, F. Krohm, and M.K. Ganai. Robust Boolean reasoning for equivalence checking and functional property verification. *IEEE Trans. on CAD*, 21(12):1377–1394, 2002.
25. W. Kunz. HANNIBAL: An efficient tool for logic verification based on recursive learning. In *Int'l Conf. on CAD*, pages 538–543, 1993.
26. W. Kunz and D.K. Pradhan. Recursive learning: A new implication technique for efficient solutions of CAD problems: Test, verification and optimization. *IEEE Trans. on CAD*, 13(9):1143–1158, 1994.
27. T. Larrabee. Test pattern generation using Boolean satisfiability. *IEEE Trans. on CAD*, 11:4–15, 1992.
28. H.K. Lee and D.S. Ha. Atalanta: An efficient ATPG for combinational circuits. Technical Report 12, Dep. of Electrical Engineering, Virginia Polytechnic Institute and State University, 1993.
29. J.P. Marques-Silva. The impact of branching heuristics in propositional satisfiability algorithms. In *9th Portuguese Conference on Artificial Intelligence (EPIA)*, 1999.
30. J.P. Marques-Silva and K.A. Sakallah. Robust search algorithms for test pattern generation. Technical Report RT/02/97, Dept. of Informatics, Technical University of Lisbon, Lisbon, Protugal, January 1997.
31. J.P. Marques-Silva and K.A. Sakallah. GRASP: A search algorithm for propositional satisfiability. *IEEE Trans. on Comp.*, 48(5):506–521, 1999.
32. M.W. Moskewicz, C.F. Madigan, Y. Zhao, L. Zhang, and S. Malik. Chaff: Engineering an efficient SAT solver. In *Design Automation Conf.*, pages 530–535, 2001.
33. T.M. Niermann and J.H. Patel. HITEC: A test generation package for sequential circuits. In *European Conf. on Design Automation*, pages 214–218, 1991.
34. J.P. Roth. Diagnosis of automata failures: A calculus and a method. *IBM J. Res. Dev.*, 10:278–281, 1966.
35. M. Schulz, E. Trischler, and T. Sarfert. SOCRATES: A highly efficient automatic test pattern generation system. In *Int'l Test Conf.*, pages 1016–1026, 1987.
36. E. Sentovich, K. Singh, L. Lavagno, Ch. Moon, R. Murgai, A. Saldanha, H. Savoj, P. Stephan, R. Brayton, and A. Sangiovanni-Vincentelli. SIS: A system for sequential circuit synthesis. Technical report, University of Berkeley, 1992.
37. J. Shi, G. Fey, R. Drechsler, A. Glowatz, F. Hapke, and J. Schlöffel. PASSAT: Effcient SAT-based test pattern generation for industrial circuits. In *IEEE Annual Symposium on VLSI*, pages 212–217, 2005.
38. J. Shi, G. Fey, R. Drechsler, A. Glowatz, J. Schlöffel, and F. Hapke. Experimental studies on SAT-based test pattern generation for industrial circuits. In *Int'l Conf. on ASIC*, pages 967–970, 2005.
39. A. Smith, A. Veneris, and A. Viglas. Design diagnosis using Boolean satisfiability. In *ASP Design Automation Conf.*, pages 218–223, 2004.

40. G.L. Smith. Model for delay faults based upon paths. In *Int'l Test Conf.*, pages 342–349, 1985.

41. P. Stephan, R.K. Brayton, and A.L. Sangiovanni-Vincentelli. Combinational test generation using satisfiability. *IEEE Trans. on CAD*, 15:1167–1176, 1996.

42. T. M. Storey and J. W. Barry. Delay test simulation. In *Design Automation Conf.*, pages 492–494, 1977.

43. P. Tafertshofer and A. Ganz. SAT based ATPG using fast justification and propagation in the implication graph. In *Int'l Conf. on CAD*, pages 139–146, 1999.

44. P. Tafertshofer, A. Ganz, and M. Henftling. A SAT-based implication engine for efficient ATPG, equivalence checking, and optimization of netlists. In *Int'l Conf. on CAD*, pages 648 – 655, 1997.

45. M. J. Y. Williams and J. B. Angell. Enhancing testability of large-scale integrated circuits via test points and additional logic. *IEEE Trans. on Comp.*, C-22(1):46–60, 1973.

46. L. Zhang, C. F. Madigan, M. H. Moskewicz, and S. Malik. Efficient conflict driven learning in a Boolean satisfiability solver. In *Int'l Conf. on CAD*, pages 279–285, 2001.

An Introduction to Symbolic Trajectory Evaluation

Koen Claessen and Jan-Willem Roorda

Chalmers University of Technology

1 Introduction

The rapid growth in hardware complexity has lead to a need for formal verification of hardware designs to prevent bugs from entering the final silicon. Model-checking [3] is by far the most popular technique for automatically verifying properties of designs. In model-checking, a model of a design is exhaustively checked against a property, often specified in some temporal logic. Today, all major hardware companies use model-checkers in order to reduce the number of bugs in their designs.

Most model-checking techniques are *state-based*. This means that some kind of representation of all reachable states of the design is used when checking that the temporal properties are fulfilled. One popular way of representing the set of reachable states of a design is by using Binary Decision Diagrams (BDDs) [2]. A BDD is a canonical way of representing a boolean formula over a fixed set of variables. When the set of reachable states of a design can be calculated using BDDs, state-based model-checking techniques work very well. However, for some types of designs, it is very hard to represent all reachable states by BDDs; they grow exponentially in size and lead to a *BDD blow-up*.

A different kind of model-checking technique is *simulation-based* model checking. In simulation-based model-checking, some representation of the values that drive certain signals in the design is used, in order to calculate the resulting values of other signals in the design. In this way, we do not need to represent the states of the design, but only the values that flow through each signal.

Symbolic Trajectory Evaluation. Symbolic Trajectory Evaluation (STE) is a high-performance simulation-based model checking technique, originally invented by Seger and Bryant [13]. STE uses a combination of *three-valued simulation* and *symbolic simulation*. Let us look at a very simple example to understand what this means. The example is inspired by Harrison [5].

Take a look at the circuit in Fig. 1, where a designer has built a 7-input AND-gate out of primitive gates. Inverters are represented in the figure by a block dot ($\bullet$). Suppose it is our job to verify that this circuit actually behaves like a 7-input AND-gate.

One way to do this is to use standard boolean simulation. This means that we simulate the circuit for every possible combination of input values. Since we have 7 inputs, we have to perform $2^7 = 128$ simulation runs. An example of one of these can be described as follows:

$$(\text{in0 is } 0) \ \textbf{and} \ (\text{in1 is } 0) \ \textbf{and} \ (\text{in2 is } 1) \ \textbf{and} \ (\text{in3 is } 0)$$
$$\textbf{and} \ (\text{in4 is } 1) \ \textbf{and} \ (\text{in5 is } 1) \ \textbf{and} \ (\text{in6 is } 0) \implies (\text{out is } 0)$$

The above formula is actually an STE *assertion*, and specifies that with the given input values, the expected output value is 0. Later on, we will define more formally what

M. Bernardo and A. Cimatti (Eds.): SFM 2006, LNCS 3965, pp. 56–77, 2006.

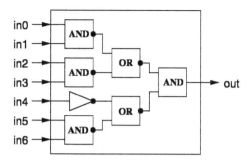

Fig. 1. A 7-input AND-gate

x	$\bullet x$
0	1
1	0
X	X

x y	$x\,\mathrm{AND}\,y$
0 0	0
0 1	0
1 0	0
1 1	1
X 0	0
0 X	0
X 1	X
1 X	X
X X	X

x y	$x\,\mathrm{OR}\,y$
0 0	0
0 1	1
1 0	1
1 1	1
X 0	X
0 X	X
X 1	1
1 X	1
X X	X

Fig. 2. Three-valued extensions of the gates

an STE assertion looks like, but for now, it is enough to know that an STE assertion is of the form $A \implies C$, where A is called the *antecedent*, which specifies with what values we should drive the simulation, and C is called the *consequent*, which specifies the expected results of the simulation.

For a small circuit such as our example circuit, 128 simulation runs might be doable. But for a design of a realistic size, an exponential amount of simulation runs might be too much, and a more efficient alternative should be sought after.

Three-valued simulation. One observation one can make is that, as soon as one input has the value 0, the values of all the other inputs do not matter anymore, since the output must be 0 anyhow. A simulator could actually calculate this; for example, as soon as we know that one of the inputs to an AND-gate is 0, a simulator could calculate that the output is 0, regardless of the value of the other input. It seems that it would somehow be beneficial to introduce a third value in our simulator, a *don't care* or *unknown* value. In STE, the don't care value is written X, and represents the value of a signal that can be either 0 or 1.

When performing simulation with the extra value X, we need to know how the standard gates behave with respect to this new value. In Fig. 2, we can see the *three-valued extensions* of the basic gates. We can see for example that if one of the inputs of an AND-gate is 0, the output is 0, even if the other input is X. However, when one of the inputs is 1, and the other is X, we do not know what the output is, so the output becomes X.

The idea is now that if the value of a certain input does not matter during simulation, instead of performing two simulation runs, one where the input is 0, and one where the input is 1, we perform only one simulation run, namely where the input is X.

In our example, this means that we can reduce the number of simulations to 8 runs. For example, we have one simulation run that checks that if input in0 is 0, the output out is 0:

$$(\text{in0 is } 0) \implies (\text{out is } 0)$$

Here, we use the convention that if inputs are not mentioned in the antecedent, then their value in the simulation run will be X. We can see that setting the input in0 to 0, and all other inputs to X actually leads to the output out getting the value 0.

There are 6 more simulation runs just like the one above:

$$(\text{in1 is } 0) \implies (\text{out is } 0)$$
$$(\text{in2 is } 0) \implies (\text{out is } 0)$$
$$(\text{in3 is } 0) \implies (\text{out is } 0)$$
$$(\text{in4 is } 0) \implies (\text{out is } 0)$$
$$(\text{in5 is } 0) \implies (\text{out is } 0)$$
$$(\text{in6 is } 0) \implies (\text{out is } 0)$$

And finally, we also need to check that the output gets the value 1 when it is supposed to. There is only one simulation run where this is the case:

$$(\text{in0 is } 1) \text{ and } (\text{in1 is } 1) \text{ and } (\text{in2 is } 1) \text{ and } (\text{in3 is } 1)$$
$$\text{and } (\text{in4 is } 1) \text{ and } (\text{in5 is } 1) \text{ and } (\text{in6 is } 1) \implies (\text{out is } 1)$$

So, by using three-valued simulation, we have reduced the number of needed simulation runs for a complete verification from 128 to only 8.

Symbolic simulation. Another way of reducing the number of simulation runs is to use *symbolic simulation*. In symbolic simulation, the values used in simulation are lifted to boolean expressions over *symbolic variables*. In STE, the symbolic expressions are usually represented by BDDs, but other representations are possible [1, 9].

For example, we could pick one symbolic variable for each of the inputs of our AND-gate, and perform one simulation run thusly:

$$(\text{in0 is } a) \text{ and } (\text{in1 is } b) \text{ and } (\text{in2 is } c) \text{ and } (\text{in3 is } d) \text{ and } (\text{in4 is } e)$$
$$\text{and } (\text{in5 is } f) \text{ and } (\text{in6 is } g) \implies (\text{out is } (a \,\&\, b \,\&\, c \,\&\, d \,\&\, e \,\&\, f \,\&\, g))$$

As we said earlier, a BDD is a canonical datastructure for representing boolean expressions over a fixed set of variables. The simulator starts by consluting the antecedent, and computes BDDs for the one-variable expressions that drive the inputs. For each gate, a BDD is calculated for the output, given the BDDs for the inputs. Finally, a BDD is calculated that represents the output of the whole circuit. This BDD is then compared for equality with the BDD specified in the consequent of the STE assertion.

For this symbolic simulation, we needed to compute BDDs containing at most 7 symbolic variables. The worst-case size complexity for BDDs is exponential in the number of symbolic variables. It is therefore often a good idea to reduce the number of variables used. Again, for our simple example, BDDs with 8 variables are not a practical problem, but for realistically sized circuits the number of inputs can be very large, and using BDDs in the way described here is not feasible.

Three-valued symbolic simulation. In STE, we can combine the efficiency of three-valued simulation with the preciseness of symbolic simulation. One way in which we can make use of this combination in our example is by expressing the eight three-valued simulation runs we saw earlier as only one three-valued symbolic simulation run. This can be done by using only three symbolic variables (which we call p, q, and r).

The idea here is that each assignment of 0 and 1 to the three variables represents one three-valued simulation run. Since there are 8 possible assignments, and 8 three-valued simulation runs, this seems to be a good match. Let us make the following (rather arbitrary) choice: When at least one of the variables p, q, r is 0, we want exactly one of the inputs to be 0, and we let $\langle p, q, r \rangle$ be the binary number picking which input is supposed to be 0. When all variables p, q, r are 1, then all inputs are 1. The expected value of the output can then be expressed as $p\&q\&r$.

All this can be expressed by the following STE assertion:

$$((\neg p\&\neg q\&\neg r) \rightarrow \text{in0 is } 0) \textbf{ and } ((\neg p\&\neg q\&r) \rightarrow \text{in1 is } 0) \textbf{ and}$$
$$((\neg p\&q\&\neg r) \rightarrow \text{in2 is } 0) \textbf{ and } ((\neg p\&q\&r) \rightarrow \text{in3 is } 0) \textbf{ and}$$
$$((p\&\neg q\&\neg r) \rightarrow \text{in4 is } 0) \textbf{ and } ((p\&\neg q\&r) \rightarrow \text{in5 is } 0) \textbf{ and}$$
$$((p\&q\&\neg r) \rightarrow \text{in6 is } 0) \textbf{ and}$$
$$((p\&q\&r) \rightarrow (\text{in0 is } 1 \textbf{ and } \text{in1 is } 1 \textbf{ and } \text{in2 is } 1 \textbf{ and}$$
$$\text{in3 is } 1 \textbf{ and } \text{in4 is } 1 \textbf{ and } \text{in5 is } 1 \textbf{ and } \text{in6 is } 1))$$
$$\Longrightarrow (\text{out is } (p\&q\&r))$$

We have used some new notation in the antecedent, namely $P \rightarrow A$, where P is a boolean expression and A is part of the antecedent. Logically, this can be understood as an implication; simulation-wise, this should be read as a conditional statement under which to use the part of the antecedent A.

The above assertion can be checked by performing only one simulation run. This works as follows. The values used by the simulator are now representations of three-valued expressions over a fixed set of (two-valued) symbolic variables (in this case p, q, and r).

The three-valued expressions that are used can be represented in many ways, but most STE tools use BDDs to this. The simplest way is to use a *dual-rail encoding*; a three-valued expression E is represented by a pair of BDDs (E_0, E_1), where E_0 is true exactly when E has the value 0, and E_1 is true exactly when E has the value 1. When both E_0 and E_1 are false, E has the value X. The advantage of using BDDs is that the representations are canonical, so they are easy to compare for equality.

Again, the antecedent is used in order to decide what three-valued expressions to use to drive the inputs. For example, the three-valued expression that drives the input in0 is:

$$\text{if } \neg p\&\neg q\&\neg r \text{ then } 0 \text{ else (if } p\&q\&r \text{ then } 1 \text{ else X)}$$

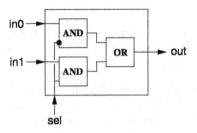

Fig. 3. A multiplexer

The above expression is constructed by gathering all assertions made about in0 in the antecedent. Simplified, this becomes:

$$\neg(\neg p \& \neg q \& \neg r) \& ((p \& q \& r) + \mathsf{X})$$

The other inputs have similar three-valued expressions that drive them.

The simulator can now calculate three-valued symbolic expressions for each of the signals in the circuit, arriving at an expression for the output of the circuit. The expression that is calculated for out is $p \& q \& r$, which verifies the assertion.

Information loss. The power of STE comes from its use of *abstraction*. Abstraction is a technique that allows one to disregard certain specific information during verification, hopefully leading to a cheaper verification process. The cost of using abstraction is the risk of abstracting away too much, resulting in a verification where the outcome is ambiguous, and no conclusions can be drawn.

In STE, two forms of abstraction are used: (1) the value X can be used to abstract from a specific boolean value of a circuit node, and (2) in the simulation, information is only propagated forwards through the circuit (i.e. from inputs to outputs of gates) and, as we will later see, through time (i.e. from time t to time $t+1$).

The three-valued abstraction is induced by the antecedent of the assertion; when the antecedent does not specify a value for a certain node, the value of the node is abstracted away by using the unknown value X. The drawback of this abstraction is the *information loss* inherent to the use of three-valued logic. Let us illustrate this information loss by an example.

Consider the circuit displayed in Fig. 3, consisting of two AND-gates and an OR-gate. The circuit implements a *multiplexer*: if sel is 0, input in0 is routed to the output out, and if sel is 1, input in1 is routed to the output.

A possible STE-assertion for this circuit is:

$$(\text{in0 is } a) \ \text{and} \ (\text{in1 is } a) \Longrightarrow (\text{out is } a)$$

The assertion states that when inputs in0 and in1 both have value a, then the output out has value a as well. It is easy to see that this assertion is true when no abstraction is used. However, when we perform three-valued symbolic simulation, with the expression a for inputs in0 and in1, and the expression X for input sel, we calculate the expression $(a \& \neg \mathsf{X}) + (a \& \mathsf{X})$ for out, which can be simplified to $a \& \mathsf{X}$. This expression is not equivalent to the required value a: when $a = 1$ the simulated expression has value X. Therefore, the property is not proved by STE.

Such an information loss can be repaired by introducing extra symbolic variables. In this case, we can drive the input node sel by a symbolic variable b, yielding the following assertion.

$$(\text{in0 is } a) \ \textbf{and} \ (\text{in1 is } a) \ \textbf{and} \ (\text{sel is } b) \Longrightarrow (\text{out is } a)$$

For this assertion, three-valued symbolic simulation calculates the expression $(a \ \& \ \neg b) + (a \ \& \ b)$ for node out, which can be simplified to a, and the verification succeeds.

A different information loss can happen due to the fact that the STE-simulator only performs *forwards simulation*. This means that information is only propagated forwards through the circuit (i.e. from inputs to outputs of gates) and through time (i.e. from time t to time $t + 1$).

As an example, consider the following assertion for the 7-input AND-gate:

$$(\text{out is } 1) \Longrightarrow (\text{in0 is } 1) \ \textbf{and} \ (\text{in1 is } 1) \ \textbf{and} \ (\text{in2 is } 1) \ \textbf{and}$$
$$(\text{in3 is } 1) \ \textbf{and} \ (\text{in4 is } 1) \ \textbf{and} \ (\text{in5 is } 1) \ \textbf{and} \ (\text{in6 is } 1)$$

Again, without abstraction, this assertion is true. However, this assertion can not be proved with STE. Simulation proceeds as follows: the antecedent does not specify anything for the inputs, so the value X is used for all inputs. Finally, the value X is calculated for the output out, which at the last moment is adjusted to 1, because the antecedent specifies this. Now, the consequent is checked, and it is reported that none of the parts of the consequent hold!

One way to fix this is, again, to introduce extra symbolic variables for all the inputs:

$$(\text{in0 is } a) \ \textbf{and} \ (\text{in1 is } b) \ \textbf{and} \ (\text{in2 is } c) \ \textbf{and} \ (\text{in3 is } d) \ \textbf{and}$$
$$(\text{in4 is } e) \ \textbf{and} \ (\text{in5 is } f) \ \textbf{and} \ (\text{in6 is } g) \ \textbf{and} \ (\text{out is } 1) \Longrightarrow$$
$$(\text{in0 is } 1) \ \textbf{and} \ (\text{in1 is } 1) \ \textbf{and} \ (\text{in2 is } 1) \ \textbf{and}$$
$$(\text{in3 is } 1) \ \textbf{and} \ (\text{in4 is } 1) \ \textbf{and} \ (\text{in5 is } 1) \ \textbf{and} \ (\text{in6 is } 1)$$

Now, simulation proceeds as follows: symbolic variables are used for all inputs, and the expression $a \ \& \ b \ \& \ c \ \& \ d \ \& \ e \ \& \ f \ \& \ g$ is computed for the output out. However, out is assumed to have the value 1 in the antecedent, which in turn means that all symbolic variables a, b, c, d, e, f, and g should be 1; any of these symbolic variables being 0 would contradict the antecedent. Now, the consequent is checked, and the verification succeeds.

So, constructing an STE assertion seems to be a delicate balance between using X's, which is cheap but leads to possible information loss, and using symbolic variables, which is precise, but possibly more expensive.

In the next section, we will look at a larger example, namely the verification of a memory using STE.

2   Verifying a Memory

Let us now take a look at a larger example. Consider a memory circuit, schematically depicted in Fig. 4. It has write and read inputs wr and rd, and an address input vector

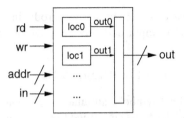

Fig. 4. A simple memory

addr and data input vector in. The output vector is called out. Internally, a number of memory locations are present that can store data.

The circuit has two modes. When rd is 1, the circuit fetches the data stored at the memory location with address addr, and delivers it on the output. When wr is 1, the circuit stores the data from the input vector in in the memory location with address addr. Writing and reading can happen simultaneously; however, a written value can only be read in the next clock cycle.

For simplicity, let us assume that the input and output data vectors have a width of 1 bit, and the address vector has a width of 2 bits. This means there are 4 internal memory locations of 1 bit each.

Now, let us try to verify the following property: If we write a data value *data* on the address *addr*, and in the next clock cycle we read the value from address *addr*, the result should be *data*. As an STE assertion, this property looks as follows:

$$(\text{wr is } 1) \text{ and } (\text{addr}[0] \text{ is } addr_0) \text{ and } (\text{addr}[1] \text{ is } addr_1) \text{ and } (\text{in is } data)$$
$$\text{and } \mathbf{N} \left((\text{rd is } 1) \text{ and } (\text{addr}[0] \text{ is } addr_0) \text{ and } (\text{addr}[1] \text{ is } addr_1) \right)$$
$$\implies \mathbf{N} \left(\text{out is } data \right)$$

We use a new notation here: $\mathbf{N}$ is a next-time operator; $(\mathbf{N}\ A)$ means that A refers to the next point in time. We are using three symbolic variables: *data*, representing the one-bit data we store in the memory, and $addr_0$ and $addr_1$ which together form the two-bit address.

STE simulation of the above assertion involves two points in time. In the first point in time, the input wr is driven with 1, rd is driven with X, addr is driven with $\langle addr_0, addr_1 \rangle$, and in is driven with *data*. In the second point in time, wr is driven with X, rd is driven with 1, addr is again driven with $\langle addr_0, addr_1 \rangle$, and in is driven with X. Lastly, in the second point in time, the STE model-checker checks if out contains the expression *data*.

What happens internally in the simulator?

Before simulation starts, the values of the memory locations need to be decided. Because the antecedent does not specify them, they start off with X:

$$\text{loc0} : \text{X}$$
$$\text{loc1} : \text{X}$$
$$\text{loc2} : \text{X}$$
$$\text{loc3} : \text{X}$$

After one clock cycle has been simulated, at least one memory location should have changed value. But which one? We cannot easily answer this, since it depends on the value of $addr$, which is symbolic and therefore not specific. The answer is that *all* locations have changed value, but the new value depends on both the input data $data$ and on the address $addr$ being written to:

$$\text{loc0}: \text{ if } \neg addr_0 \& \neg addr_1 \text{ then } data \text{ else X}$$
$$\text{loc1}: \text{ if } addr_0 \& \neg addr_1 \text{ then } data \text{ else X}$$
$$\text{loc2}: \text{ if } \neg addr_0 \& addr_1 \text{ then } data \text{ else X}$$
$$\text{loc3}: \text{ if } addr_0 \& addr_1 \text{ then } data \text{ else X}$$

So, each memory location now contains an expression that says: "if the address being written to was my own addres, I have now changed value to $data$, otherwise, I am still X".

What happens in the second simulation cycle? Each memory location loc_i has a local output out_i that is activated with the location's contents as soon as someone reads from the memory at the address belonging to the location. If a read is performed at an other address, the location's local output is 0. The global output out then simply gathers all locations' local outputs with a big OR-bus. Which location's output gets activated, and with which value? The answer is, again, all of them possibly get activated, depending on the address being read.

For example, the local output of loc0, after simulating the second clock cycle is:

$$\text{if } \neg addr_0 \& \neg addr_1 \text{ then } (\text{if } \neg addr_0 \& \neg addr_1 \text{ then } data \text{ else X}) \text{ else } 0$$

In other words, "if the address being read from is my address, then I output my contents, otherwise, I output 0". This can be simplified to:

$$\text{if } \neg addr_0 \& \neg addr_1 \text{ then } data \text{ else } 0$$

So, all locations' local outputs look as follows after the second simulation cycle:

$$\text{out0}: \text{ if } \neg addr_0 \& \neg addr_1 \text{ then } data \text{ else } 0$$
$$\text{out1}: \text{ if } addr_0 \& \neg addr_1 \text{ then } data \text{ else } 0$$
$$\text{out2}: \text{ if } \neg addr_0 \& addr_1 \text{ then } data \text{ else } 0$$
$$\text{out3}: \text{ if } addr_0 \& addr_1 \text{ then } data \text{ else } 0$$

The output out consists of a big OR of the above local outputs, which gets simplified to just $data$, which is what the consequent actually specified. So, the verification of the assertion succeeds.

Larger sizes.   What happens when we want to verify the memory for larger sizes? If the data width is n and the address width is k (which means we have 2^k memory locations with width n), we only need $n + k$ symbolic variables. The structure of the BDDs involved is well-behaved enough so that this does not lead to a BDD blow-up.

Compare this to a standard state-based model-checker, which would have to use one BDD variable for each state holding element in order to represent the states. This would lead to $n \times 2^k$ BDD variables, which quickly becomes infeasible even for small values of k.

Fig. 5. The information lattice

3   STE Theory

In this section, we describe the semantics of STE assertions. The presentation here differs from the usual presentation in the STE literature [13, 6]. However, the semantics we present here is more precise than the semantics usually presented. For a discussion on this topic, see [8, 10].

For an STE semantics, it is important to be faithful to the used abstractions in STE. In the introduction, we have already seen a number of examples that would hold in a standard semantics without abstraction, but which do not hold in STE, showing that the concept of truth in STE is a non-trivial matter. A semantics can be used for reasoning about STE assertions (in order to for example understand why a certain property could not be proven) without having to understand the innards of the used STE model-checker. Here, we present a semantics that defines precisely when an STE model-checker deems a property to be valid.

Preliminaries.   For technical reasons, next to the three values $0, 1$ and X we have already discussed, a fourth value T, called the *over-constrained value*, is used in simulation. This value represents a clash between values; it is the resulting value of a signal that is required to have both the value 0 and 1 during simulation. This happens for example when the antecedent specifies conflicting values for a particular input. The three-valued gate-definitions in Figure 2 are extended to deal with this fourth value in such a way that whenever at least one of their inputs is T their output is also T. We call the set of four simulation values we use $\mathbb{V} = \{0, 1, X, T\}$.

It is handy to define an ordering on $\mathbb{V}$, called the *information order*. The unknown value X contains the least information, so $X \leq 0$, $X \leq 1$, $X \leq T$, while 0 and 1 are incomparable. The over-constrained value T contains most least information, so $0 \leq T$ and $1 \leq T$. If $v \leq w$ it is said that v is *weaker* than w.

We can see that $\mathbb{V}$ with the ordering $\leq$ forms a lattice, see Fig. 5. Thus, we can introduce the *least upper bound* operator, written $\sqcup$ as the least upper bound w.r.t. the ordering $\leq$. We have for instance $0 \sqcup X = 0$, $X \sqcup 1 = 1$, and $T \sqcup 0 = T$ and $T \sqcup X = T$, and in particular $0 \sqcup 1 = T$.

All points in the circuit, that is, inputs, outputs, internal points, and inputs and outputs of registers, are collected in the set $\mathcal{N}$, called the *nodes* of the circuit. A *circuit state*, written $s :$ **State**, is a function from the set of nodes of circuit to the values $\mathbb{V}$. A *sequence*, written $\sigma : \mathbb{N} \to$ **State** is a function from a point in time to a circuit state, describing the behaviour of a circuit over time. The set of all sequences is written **Seq**. A *three-valued sequence* is a sequence that does not assign the value T to any node in any point in time. The set of all three-valued sequences is written $\mathbf{Seq_3}$.

The information order $\leq$ can be naturally extended to states and sequences. State s_1 is weaker than state s_2, written $s_1 \leq s_2$, iff. for every node n, $s_1(n) \leq s_2(n)$.

Sequence σ_1 is weaker than sequence σ_2, written $\sigma_1 \leq \sigma_2$, iff. for every time point t, $\sigma_1(t) \leq \sigma_2(t)$.

Trajectory Evaluation Logic. We have already seen that STE assertions have the form $A \implies C$. Here, A and C are formulas in a language called *Trajectory Evaluation Logic* (TEL). The only variables in the logic are time-independent boolean variables taken from the set V of *symbolic variables*. The language is given by the following grammar:

$$A, B, C ::= n \text{ is } 0$$
$$| \quad n \text{ is } 1$$
$$| \quad A_1 \text{ and } A_2$$
$$| \quad P \to f$$
$$| \quad \mathbf{N} A$$

Here, n is a circuit node, and P is a boolean propositional formula over the set of symbolic variables V.

The operators **is** 0 and **is** 1 are used to make a statement about the boolean value of a particular node in the circuit, **and** is conjunction, $\to$ is used to make conditional statements, and $\mathbf{N}$ is the next time operator. Note that symbolic variables only occur in the Boolean propositional expressions on the left-hand side of an implication. However, given a node n and a boolean formula P, we can write n **is** P as a shorthand for $(P \to n \text{ is } 1)$ **and** $(\neg P \to n \text{ is } 0)$.

The meaning of a TEL formula is defined by a satisfaction relation. In order to decide if a TEL formula is satisfied, we need to have a sequence $\sigma \in \mathbf{Seq}$ as well as a boolean valuation $\phi : V \to \{0, 1\}$. Satisfaction of a TEL formula A, by a sequence σ and a valuation ϕ, written $\phi, \sigma \models A$ is defined as follows:

$$\phi, \sigma \models n \text{ is } b \qquad \equiv \quad b \leq \sigma(0)(n) \ , \ b \in \{0, 1\}$$
$$\phi, \sigma \models A_1 \text{ and } A_2 \quad \equiv \quad \phi, \sigma \models A_1 \text{ and } \phi, \sigma \models A_2$$
$$\phi, \sigma \models P \to A \qquad \equiv \quad \phi \models_{\mathrm{Prop}} P \text{ implies } \phi, \sigma \models A$$
$$\phi, \sigma \models \mathbf{N} A \qquad \equiv \quad \phi, \sigma^1 \models A$$

Here, the following notation is used: The time shifting operator σ^1 is defined by $\sigma^1 (t)(n) = \sigma(t+1)(n)$. Standard propositional satisfiability is denoted by $\models_{\mathrm{Prop}}$.

An interesting property is that, given a valuation ϕ, if a sequence σ makes a TEL formula A true, i.e. $\phi, \sigma \models A$, then any other sequence σ' that is more specific than σ, i.e. $\sigma \leq \sigma'$ makes A true as well.

Circuit models. In order to define when an STE assertion holds for a given circuit, we need to have a model of the circuit. Normally, circuits are represented by their *netlist*, a list of what gates are used and how they are connected. We are going to use a slightly more abstract way of representing circuits, namely by so-called *closure functions*. A closure function can be computed from a given netlist in a standard way (which we will describe), but we want to leave open other possibilities as well.

A closure function $F : \mathbf{State} \to \mathbf{State}$ represents the behaviour of the simulator on the nodes of the circuit. Given current information about the nodes in the circuit as a

Fig. 6. An AND-gate

n	$F(s)(n)$
in0	$s(\text{in0})$
in1	$s(\text{in1})$
out	$(s(\text{in0}) \,\&\, s(\text{in1})) \sqcup s(\text{out})$

Fig. 7. Closure function F for the AND-gate

state $s :$ **State**, the closure function computes the state $F(s) : S$, where all information in s has been propagated forwards through the circuit, leading to a new state.

Let us take a look at an example. Look at the AND-gate displayed in Fig. 6. Its closure function is displayed in Fig. 7. Here, The least upper bound operator in the expression for $F(s)(\text{out})$ combines the value of out in the given state s, and the value for out that can be derived from the values of in0 and in1, being $s(\text{in0}) \,\&\, s(\text{in1})$.

A state $s : \{\text{in0}, \text{in1}, \text{out}\} \to \mathbb{V}$ can be written as a vector $s(\text{in0}), s(\text{in1}), s(\text{out})$. For example, the state that assigns the value 1 to in0 and in1 and the value X to node out is written as 11X. Applying the closure function to the state 11X yields 111. The reason is that when both inputs to the AND-gate have value 1, then by forwards propagation of information, also the output has value 1. Applying the closure function to the vector 1XX yields 1XX. The reason is that the output of the AND-gate is unknown when one input has value 1 and the other value X. The *forwards* nature of simulation becomes clear when the closure function is applied to the vector XX1, resulting in the vector XX1. Although the inputs to the AND-gate must have value 1 when the output of the gate has value 1, this cannot be derived by forwards propagation.

A final example shows how the over-constrained value T can arise. When applying the closure function to the vector 0X1, the result is 0XT. The reason is that in the input state node out has value 1, and node in0 has value 0. From in0 having value 0 it can be derived by forwards propagation that node out should have value 0, therefore node out receives the over-constrained value T.

Circuits with state. To deal with circuits with state, we use the following convention. For each state-holding element in the circuit whit output node n, we always use the name n' (primed) as the input. For example, in Fig. 8, we display a simple memory cell. The current value of the node out$'$ is the same as the value of the node out at the next point in time.

A closure function for the memory cell in Fig. 8 is given in Fig. 9. Consider the state s_1 given in Fig. 10. Applying the closure function to this state yields the state $F(s_1)$. Node p receives value 1 as it is the output of an AND-gate with inputs in and set which both have value 1 in the input state. In the same way, node q receives value 0. Node out$'$ receives value 1, because it is the output of an OR-gate with input nodes p and q. Finally, node out receives value X as its value depends on the *previous* value of node out$'$, its value cannot be determined from the current values of the other nodes.

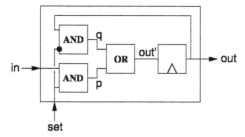

Fig. 8. A memory cell

n	$F(s)(n)$
in	$s(\text{in})$
set	$s(\text{set})$
p	$(s(\text{in}) \ \& \ s(\text{set})) \sqcup s(\text{p})$
q	$(\neg s(\text{set}) \ \& \ s(\text{out})) \sqcup s(\text{q})$
out'	$(F(s)(\text{p}) + F(s)(\text{q})) \sqcup s(\text{out}')$
out	$s(\text{out})$

Fig. 9. Closure function F for the memory cell

When an internal node is given a value in the given state, the least upper bound of this value and the value derived by forwards propagation is used. For instance, driving only node p with value 1 yields state s_2 given in Fig. 10. Applying the closure function F to this state yields state $F(s_2)$. Note that there is no backwards information flow; the closure function does not demand that nodes in and set have value 1, though they are the input nodes to an AND-gate whose output node has received value 1.

Induced closure functions. Given the netlist of a circuit c, a standard closure function for the circuit, called the *induced closure function*, written F_c, can be constructed as follows. Given a state s, for every circuit input n, the value of $F_c(s)(n)$ is $s(n)$. Also, for every output n of a delay element, the value of $F_c(s)(n)$ is given by $s(n)$. Otherwise, if n is the output of for example an AND-gate with input nodes n_1 and n_2, the value of $F_c(s)(n)$ is the least upper bound of $s(n)$ and $F_c(s)(n_1) \ \& \ F_c(s)(n_2)$. In a similar way, values for the outputs of OR-gates and inverters are defined. This definition is well-defined because netlists are acyclic.

The closure functions given in the examples above are actually all examples of induced closure functions.

Properties of closure functions. A closure function F should meet several requirements:

- Closure functions are required to be *monotonic*, that is, for all states s_1, s_2: $s_1 \leq s_2$ implies $F(s_1) \leq F(s_2)$. This means that a more specified input state cannot lead to a less specified result. The reason is that given a more specified input state, more information about the state of the circuit can be derived.
- Closure functions are required to be *idempotent*, that is, for every state s: $F(F(s)) = F(s)$. This means that repeated application of the closure function has the same

n	$s_1(n)$
set	1
in	1
other	X

n	$F(s_1)(n)$
set	1
in	1
p	1
q	0
out'	1
out	X

n	$s_2(n)$
p	1
other	X

n	$F(s_2)(n)$
p	1
out'	1
other	X

Fig. 10. Example states

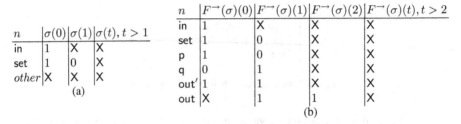

n	$\sigma(0)$	$\sigma(1)$	$\sigma(t), t > 1$
in	1	X	X
set	1	0	X
other	X	X	X

(a)

n	$F^{\rightarrow}(\sigma)(0)$	$F^{\rightarrow}(\sigma)(1)$	$F^{\rightarrow}(\sigma)(2)$	$F^{\rightarrow}(\sigma)(t), t > 2$
in	1	X	X	X
set	1	0	X	X
p	1	0	X	X
q	0	1	X	X
out'	1	1	X	X
out	X	1	1	X

(b)

Fig. 11. Sequences σ and $F^{\rightarrow}(\sigma)$

result as applying the function once. The reason is that the closure function should derive all information about the circuit state in one go.

- Finally, we require that closure functions are *extensive*, that is, for every state s: $s \leq F(s)$. This means that the application of a closure function to a circuit state should yield a state as least as specified as the input state. The reason is that the closure function is required not to loose any information.

The induced closure function F_c, for a circuit c, is by construction monotonic, idempotent and extensive.

Closure over time. In STE, a circuit is simulated over multiple time steps. During simulation, information is propagated forwards through the circuit and through time, from each time step t to time step $t + 1$.

To model this forwards propagation of information through time, a *closure function over time*, notation $F^{\rightarrow} :$ **Seq** $\rightarrow$ **Seq**, is used. Given a sequence, the closure function over time calculates all information that be can derived from that sequence by forwards propagation. Recall that for every state holding element with output n the input to the state holding element is node n'. Therefore, the value of node n' at time t is propagated to node n at time $t + 1$ in the forwards closure function over time.

Let us take a look at an example. For the memory cell, consider the closure function given in Fig. 9, and the sequence σ, given in Figure 11(a). The sequence $F^{\rightarrow}(\sigma)$ at time 0 depends only on the sequence σ at time 0, and is computed by applying the closure function F to $\sigma(0)$. See Figure 11(b).

The sequence $F^{\rightarrow}(\sigma)$ gives node out' value 1 at time 0. Node out' is the input to the delay element with output node out. The value 1 should be propagated from out' at time 0, to out at time 1. Therefore, when calculating the state $F^{\rightarrow}(\sigma)(1)$, the node values given by the state $\sigma(1)$ and the value of node out propagated from the value of node out' at time 0 are combined. Let us call the state that combines these node values $\sigma'(1)$:

$$\sigma'(1)(\text{out}) = \sigma(1)(\text{out}) \sqcup F^{\rightarrow}(\sigma)(0)(\text{out}')$$
$$\sigma'(1)(n) \ = \sigma(1)(n) \qquad\qquad\qquad ,n \neq \text{out}$$

In this case $\sigma'(1)$ is given by: $\sigma'(1)(\text{set}) = 0$, $\sigma'(1)(\text{out}) = 1$, and $\sigma'(1)(n) = X$ for every other node n. Applying the forwards closure F to $\sigma'(1)$ yields state $F^{\rightarrow}(\sigma)(1)$ given in Figure 11(b).

The value of $F^{\rightarrow}(\sigma)(2)$ is given by applying F to $\sigma'(2)$, where $\sigma'(2)$ is calculated in a similar fashion as $\sigma'(1)$, and is given by: $\sigma'(2)(\text{out}) = 1$, and $\sigma'(2)(n) = X$ for all other nodes n. Repeating this procedure gives the complete sequence $F^{\rightarrow}(\sigma)$ given in Figure 11(b).

Now, given a closure function F for a circuit with has a set of outputs of delay-elements S, we inductively define the *closure function over time*, written $F^{\rightarrow} : \mathbf{Seq} \rightarrow \mathbf{Seq}$, as follows:

$$F^{\rightarrow}(\sigma)(0) \ = F(\sigma(0))$$
$$F^{\rightarrow}(\sigma)(t+1) = F(\sigma'(t+1))$$

Here, σ' is defined as:

$$\sigma'(t+1)(n) = \begin{cases} \sigma(t+1)(n) \sqcup F^{\rightarrow}(\sigma)(t)(n'), & n \in S \\ \sigma(t+1)(n), & \text{otherwise} \end{cases}$$

The function $F^{\rightarrow}$ inherits the properties of being monotonic, idempotent and extensive from F.

Trajectories. The last thing we need to do before we can define when circuits satisfy an STE assertion is to define what sequences can be the result of simulating the circuit. We define a *trajectory* to be such a sequence; a sequence in which no more information can be derived by forwards propagation of the closure function. That is, a sequence τ is a trajectory of a closure function when it is a fixed-point of the closure function over time:

$$\tau = F^{\rightarrow}(\tau)$$

Because closure functions are idempotent, applying a forwards closure function $F^{\rightarrow}$ to any sequence always leads to a trajectory. This is the case since:

$$F^{\rightarrow}(\sigma) = F^{\rightarrow}(F^{\rightarrow}(\sigma)), \qquad \text{for all } \sigma \in \mathbf{Seq}$$

We have an immediate link to the simulation-nature of STE; if we create a sequence σ containing all information specified in the antecedent A, applying $F^{\rightarrow}(\sigma)$ corresponds to the result of running the simulator with the antecedent A. $F^{\rightarrow}(\sigma)$ is the *weakest* trajectory τ that still has all information that σ has, and thus the weakest trajectory satisfying A.

Semantics of STE. Using the definition of trajectories of a circuit, we can finally define when an assertion is true. A circuit c with closure function F *satisfies* a trajectory assertion $A \implies C$ iff. for every valuation $\phi : V \to \{0, 1\}$ of the symbolic variables, and for every three-valued trajectory τ of F, it holds that:

$$\phi, \tau \models A \;\Rightarrow\; \phi, \tau \models C$$

The reader can verify that this definition corresponds to the observations made for the examples in the introduction.

Why does the above definition correspond to what an STE simulator actually calculates? The simulator only performs one simulation run, so it definitely does not check the consequent for all trajectories τ that satisfy the antecedent. The secret lies in the properties of the *weakest* trajectory that the simulator calculates; if the consequent C holds for the weakest trajectory τ satisfying A, then the consequent C holds for all trajectories that satisfy A. This is often called the *Fundamental Theorem of STE* [13], and it implies that it is enough to check the consequent C only for the weakest trajectory satisfying A, instead of all trajectories.

4   Abstraction Refinement

A common initial result in an STE verification attempt is that the model-checker cannot prove the assertion because the simulation using the antecedent yields X's at nodes that are required to have a particular boolean value by the consequent. This indicates that the used abstraction was too coarse, leading to a so-called *spurious counter-model*. In contrast, a *real counter-model* is a simulation run that satisfies the antecedent but yields a 0 for a node for which the consequent requires a 1, or vice-versa. A *model* of an assertion is a simulation run that satisfies both the antecedent and the consequent.

When an STE model-checking run produces spurious counter-models but no real counter-models, we say that the result of the verification is *unknown*. In this case, the assertion must be refined (usually by introducing more symbolic variables in the antecedent) until the property is proved, or until a real counter-model is found. Often, a great deal of time is spent on such manual *abstraction refinement* [14, 1]. This is one of the greatest hurdles in using STE.

In this section, we present a new tool called STAR (SAT-based Tool for Abstraction Refinement in STE) that can assist in STE assertion refinement [11]. The tool is based on the concept of a *strengthening*, which is a particular piece of useful information that can help STE-users with manual abstraction refinement; given an STE assertion and a circuit, a strengthening indicates which extra inputs of the circuit need to be given a boolean (non-X) value in order for relevant outputs to also get a boolean value. The tool STAR has two modes; the first mode calculates strengthenings that satisfy the assertion (corresponding to models), and the second mode calculates strengthenings that contradict the assertion (corresponding to real counter-models).

By inspecting a weakest satisfying strengthening, the user can gain intuition about how to refine the assertion by introducing a *minimal* number of extra symbolic variables. On the other hand, a weakest contradicting strengthening gives a *minimal* set of reasons for the failure of the assertion, which can be used to gain intuition about why the circuit

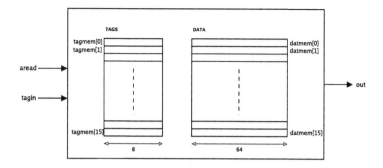

Fig. 12. A Content-Addressable Memory Circuit

does not satisfy the assertion. We give an introduction to the tool STAR by means of a small case-study.

Verifying a CAM. Content-Addressable Memories (CAMs) are hardware implementations of lookup tables. A CAM stores a number of *tags*, each of which is linked to a specific *data-entry*. The basis of a CAM circuit consists usually of two memory blocks, one containing tag entries, and the other the same number of corresponding data entries, see Fig. 12. Given an input tag, the associative-read operation consists of searching all tags in the CAM to determine if there is a match to the input tag, and if so sending the associated data-entry to the output. Verifying this operation is non-trivial [7].

Let us look at a case-study of how a verification engineer might use our tool STAR to derive an STE assertion for verifying the associative-read operation of a CAM. In the case-study, we assume that the verification engineer uses the BDD-based STE model-checker in Intel's in-house verification toolkit Forte [4].

An obvious way of verifying the associative-read operation using STE is to introduce symbolic variables for each tag- and data-entry. When doing so, the antecedent of the assertion specifies that each tag-entry tagmem$[i]$ has symbolic value $tagmem_i$, and each data-entry datmem$[i]$ has symbolic value $datmem_i$. The consequent checks that, for each i, when the input-tag is equal to $tagmem_i$ the output is equal to $datmem_i$.

$$\begin{aligned}
&(\text{aread is } 1) \;\textbf{and}\; (\text{tagin is } tagin) \\
\textbf{and}\;\; &(\text{tagmem}[0] \text{ is } tagmem_0) \;\textbf{and}\; \dots \;\textbf{and}\; (\text{tagmem}[15] \text{ is } tagmem_{15}) \\
\textbf{and}\;\; &(\text{datmem}[0] \text{ is } datmem_0) \;\textbf{and}\; \dots \;\textbf{and}\; (\text{datmem}[15] \text{ is } datmem_{15}) \\
&\qquad\qquad\qquad\Longrightarrow \\
&\qquad ((tagin = tagmem_0) \;\rightarrow\; (\text{out is } tagmem_0)) \\
&\qquad\qquad\qquad\vdots \\
\textbf{and}\;\; &((tagin = tagmem_{15}) \;\rightarrow\; (\text{out is } tagmem_{15}))
\end{aligned} \tag{1}$$

This assertion, however, cannot be handled by BDD-based STE model-checkers. The large number of symbolic variables leads to an immediate BDD-blow up.

Suppose that, instead, the user tries to verify the operation using symbolic indexing [6]. When doing so, a vector of symbolic variables, $index$, is created to index over the potentially matching tag-entries. The antecedent states that the indexed tag-entry has symbolic value $tagin$ and the indexed data-entry has value $data$. So, only variables for

```
Warning: Consequent failure at time 0 on node out[63]
Current value:data[63] + X(!data[63])
Expected value:data[63]
Weak disagreement when:!data[63]
----WARNING: Some consequent errors not reported

data[16]&data[21]&data[61]&data[34]&data[2]&data[7]&data[47]&data[52]&data[20]&
data[60]&data[33]&data[38]&data[6]&data[46]&data[51]&data[19]&data[59]&data[56]&
data[24]&data[32]&data[29]&data[37]&data[5]&data[45]&data[13]&data[42]&data[53]&
data[10]&data[50]&data[18]&data[58]&data[15]&data[26]&data[55]&data[23]&data[63]&
data[31]&data[28]&data[39]&data[36]&data[43]&data[44]&data[40]&data[12]&data[41]&
data[27]&data[49]&data[17]&data[57]&data[14]&data[25]&data[54]&data[22]&data[62]&
data[30]&data[9]&data[35]&data[3]&data[4]&data[0]&data[11]&data[1]&data[8]&data[48]
```

Fig. 13. Forte Output for Assertion 2

Symbolic Variables	
$index$	= 1100
$tagin$	= 00000000
$data$	= 11111111111111111111111111111111111111111111111111111111111111100
Inputs at time 0	
aread	= 1
tagin	= 00000000
Initial Values	
tagmem$_1$	= 00000000
tagmem$_{12}$	= 00000000
datmem$_1$	= --1-
datmem$_{12}$	= 11111111111111111111111111111111111111111111111111111111111111100
Outputs	
out	= 111111111111111111111111111111111111111111111111111111111111111-

Fig. 14. A Weakest Contradicting Strengthening of Assertion (2)

the content of the indexed data-entry and tag-entry are created, instead of variables for all tag- and data-entries. This greatly reduces the number of required symbolic variables.

Using symbolic indexing, the user could arrive at the following assertion.

$$
\begin{aligned}
&(\text{aread is } 1) \ \textbf{and} \ (\text{tagin is } tagin) \\
\textbf{and} \ \ &((index = 0000) \rightarrow ((\text{tagmem}[0] \text{ is } tagin) \ \textbf{and} \ (\text{datmem}[0] \text{ is } data))) \\
\textbf{and} \ \ &((index = 0001) \rightarrow ((\text{tagmem}[1] \text{ is } tagin) \ \textbf{and} \ (\text{datmem}[1] \text{ is } data))) \\
\vdots \quad &\qquad \vdots \qquad\qquad\qquad\qquad\qquad \vdots \\
\textbf{and} \ \ &((index = 1111) \rightarrow ((\text{tagmem}[15] \text{ is } tagin) \ \textbf{and} \ (\text{datmem}[15] \text{ is } data))) \\
&\qquad\qquad\qquad\qquad \Longrightarrow \\
&\qquad\qquad\qquad \text{out is } data
\end{aligned}
\tag{2}
$$

When the user tries to verify this assertion with the model-checker, the result is "unknown". The output of the model-checker is given in Fig. 13: the simulated value for node out[63] is $(data[63] + (X \ \& \ \neg data[63]))$, while the required value is $data[63]$. When the symbolic variable $data[63]$ has value 0, the simulated value of out[63] evaluates to X, indicating a spurious counter-model. The expression $data[16] \& .... \& data[48]$ indicates that only when the data-entry consists of only high bits no spurious counter-model exists.

So, the STE model-checker does not give much help with refining the assertion.

The tool STAR can be used to calculate a weakest contradicting strengthening of Assertion 2, see Fig. 14. The table presents an assignment of the symbolic variables, and a weakest strengthening of the antecedent that together contradict the consequent. Here, only bold-faced values (**0** or **1**) in the table represent strengthened nodes. A normal-faced 0 or 1 represents a node that has received the value 0 or 1 because it was required by the (original) antecedent. For instance, $tagmem_{12}$ is required to have value 00000000 by the antecedent, but $tagmem_1$ is required to have the same value by the strengthening. To increase readability, X's are represented by a dash –; entries for which all values are X have been left out of the table completely.

The table states that

– the value of *index* vector is 1100, so, tag- and data-entry 12 are indexed,
– not only the indexed tag 12 is equal to the input tag *tagin* but also tag 1,
– data-entry 1 differs from the indexed data-entry 12, at the second-last position; data-entry 1 has value 1 at this position, while the indexed data-entry has value 0,
– the value of the output of the CAM at the second-last position is 1 instead of 0 as required by the consequent.

From this, the user can deduce that the assertion in fact does not hold for the circuit because the assertion does not consider the case in which two tag-entries are equal to the input tag. Also, the user can conclude that, apparently, the CAM contains a *bus* that, when given both a 0 and 1 value, chooses the 1 value over the 0 value.

An obvious way of circumventing this problem is to introduce symbolic variables for all tag-entries, and to add the constraint that there is at most one tag-entry equal to the input tag. To do so, many extra symbolic variables are needed; one for each bit of each tag-entry. Therefore, it is not surprising that the resulting assertion yields, again, a BDD blow-up.

To obtain an intuition on how to, instead, refine the assertion by introducing a very small number of extra symbolic variables, the user can calculate a weakest satisfying strengthening of the assertion. The user knows from the output of the model-checker that when all of the data-entries have value 1 no spurious counter-model exists. Therefore, the constraint that at least one of the data-entries has value 0 is given to STAR.

In Fig. 15, a weakest satisfying strengthening calculated by STAR is given. In this strengthening, for each non-indexed tag-entry *either* (1) the tag-entry differs at one position from the input tag, *or* (2) the tag-entry consist only of X's (tag-entries 5 and 11), and the corresponding data-entry contains a zero at the position where the indexed data-entry has a zero, and X's at each of the positions where the indexed data-entry contains a 1.

This can be explained as follows. There are two ways of making sure that a non-indexed data-entry does not corrupt the output: (1) making the tag-entry differ at at-least one position from the input tag, or (2) as the bus in the CAM favors a 1 over a 0, for each tag that potentially matches, having a 0 in the data-entry at each position where the indexed data-entry contains a 0.

As for the verification of the associative read property, no assumptions on the content of the data-entries in the CAM are wanted, the user can ask STAR to generate a weakest satisfying strengthening of assertion (2) that does not strengthen the requirements on the values of data-entries. This strengthening, given in Fig. 16, makes each non-indexed tag-entry differ at one position from the input tag.

Symbolic Variables	
$index$	= 0000
$tagin$	= 00000010
$data$	= 0100000000000000000000000000000000000000000000000000000000000000
Inputs at time 0	
aread	= 1
tagin	= 00000010
Initial Values	
$tagmem_0$	= 00000010
$tagmem_1$	= 1-------
$tagmem_2$	= 1-------
$tagmem_3$	= --1-----
$tagmem_4$	= ------0-
$tagmem_5$	= --------
$tagmem_6$	= -1------
$tagmem_7$	= --1-----
$tagmem_8$	= -1------
$tagmem_9$	= 1-------
$tagmem_{10}$	= 1-------
$tagmem_{11}$	= --------
$tagmem_{12}$	= ---1----
$tagmem_{13}$	= ----1---
$tagmem_{14}$	= ------0-
$tagmem_{15}$	= -1------
$datmem_0$	= 0100000000000000000000000000000000000000000000000000000000000000
$datmem_5$	= 0-000000000000000000000000000000000000000000000000000000000000000
$datmem_{11}$	= 0-000000000000000000000000000000000000000000000000000000000000000

Fig. 15. A Weakest Satisfying Strengthening of Assertion (2)

Inspired by this strengthening, the user can modify the assertion by introducing, for each tag-entry i, a vector of symbolic variables p_i that specifies at which position the tag-entry differs from the input tag when the tag-entry is not indexed. The formula expressing that tag i differs from the input tag $tagin$ at the position encoded by p_i is:

$$
\begin{aligned}
\text{mismatch}(i) = \quad & ((p_i = 000) \rightarrow (\text{tagmem}[i][0] \text{ is } \neg tagin[0])) \\
\textbf{and} \quad & ((p_i = 001) \rightarrow (\text{tagmem}[i][1] \text{ is } \neg tagin[1])) \\
& \vdots \qquad \vdots \qquad\qquad \vdots \\
\textbf{and} \quad & ((p_i = 111) \rightarrow (\text{tagmem}[i][7] \text{ is } \neg tagin[7]))
\end{aligned}
$$

The formula expressing that each of the non-indexed tag-entries differs at at-least one place from $tagin$ is:

$$
\begin{aligned}
A' = \quad & ((index \neq 0000) \rightarrow \text{mismatch}(0)) \\
\textbf{and} \quad & ((index \neq 0001) \rightarrow \text{mismatch}(1)) \\
& \vdots \qquad\qquad \vdots \qquad\qquad \vdots \\
\textbf{and} \quad & ((index \neq 1111) \rightarrow \text{mismatch}(15)))
\end{aligned}
$$

The assertion obtained by adding A' to the antecedent of assertion (2) is exactly the assertion described in [7] and is easily proved by an STE model-checker.

Symbolic Variables	
$index$	$= 1111$
$tagin$	$= 11111110$
$data$	$= 0100000000000000000000000000000000000000000000000000000000000000$
Inputs at time 0	
aread	$= 1$
tagin	$= 11111110$
Initial Values	
$tagmem_0$	$= -------1$
$tagmem_1$	$= ------0-$
$tagmem_2$	$= ---0----$
$tagmem_3$	$= ---0----$
$tagmem_4$	$= ------0-$
$tagmem_5$	$= -------1$
$tagmem_6$	$= -------1$
$tagmem_7$	$= 0-------$
$tagmem_8$	$= ------0-$
$tagmem_9$	$= --0-----$
$tagmem_{10}$	$= ------0-$
$tagmem_{11}$	$= --0-----$
$tagmem_{12}$	$= -----0--$
$tagmem_{13}$	$= ---0----$
$tagmem_{14}$	$= 0-------$
$tagmem_{15}$	$= 11111110$
$datmem_{15}$	$= 0100000000000000000000000000000000000000000000000000000000000000$

Fig. 16. A Weakest Satisfying Strengthening of Ass. (2) without extra assumptions on data-entries

5   Conclusion and Further Reading

We have presented an introduction to Symbolic Trajectory Evaluation, a powerful sim-ulation-based model-checking technique. When the right balance between X's and sym-bolic variables can be found, the capacity of STE goes far beyond what traditional model-checkers can accomplish. To help with finding the right abstraction, we have developed a tool called STAR.

However, even when the right abstraction level has been found, the high performance of STE comes not without a price. One of the main disadvantages of STE is the limited expressivess of STE assertions. It can be seen as a crippled form of LTL where only assertions over a finite amount of points of time can be made. The concept of initial state (and therefore reachable state) is completely absent.

One way to alleviate some of this restriction is to split up a desired property into a number of lower-level STE assertions that can be checked using an STE model-checker. An example is the following. Suppose we have a TEL formula B that we want to show holds for all reachable states. One way to do this using STE is to split this up into two STE assertions:

$$I \Longrightarrow B \quad \text{and} \quad B \Longrightarrow \mathbf{N}\, B$$

Here, I is a TEL formula characterizing the initial state of the design. Together, by using induction, the above two assertions imply that B must hold for all reachable states. However, it is quite easy to make a mistake in this kind of *meta-reasoning* that lies outside of STE. One solution to this is to use a theorem proving system to aid in this reasoning. Intel's in-house verification system Forte [4] has precisely that possibility. You can read more about it in [12].

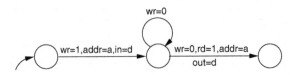

Fig. 17. GSTE specification of a memory

Another way to lift the expressiveness of STE is investigated in the work on *Generalized Symbolic Trajectory Evaluation* (GSTE) [16]. In GSTE, assertions are made in the form of graphs that can contain cycles. Informally, every path through the graph represents an STE assertion. For example, take a look at a GSTE specification of a memory in Fig. 17. We have symbolic variables a and d. The assertion says that if we write value d to address a, after which we spend an unspecified amount of cycles not writing, and then we read from address a, the result should be d. You can read more about GSTE in [16, 15].

Most STE model-checkers use BDDs to represent symbolic three-valued expressions. The disadvantage is that these tools can be sensitive to BDD blow-up. An alternative is to use a representation that is not canonical, and use a SAT-solver to check that the consequent is fulfilled. You can read more about that in [1, 14, 9, 8].

References

1. P. Bjesse, T. Leonard, and A. Mokkedem. Finding bugs in an Alpha microprocessor using satisfiability solvers. In *CAV 2001*, volume 2102 of *LNCS*. Springer-Verlag, 2001.
2. Randal E. Bryant. Graph-based algorithms for boolean function manipulation. *IEEE Trans. Comput.*, 35(8):677–691, 1986.
3. E.M. Clarke, O. Grumberg, and D.A. Peled. *Model Checking*. The MIT Press, 2001.
4. FORTE. http://www.intel.com/software/products/opensource/tools1/verification.
5. John Harrison. Marktoberdorf 2003 Page, 2003. http://www.cl.cam.ac.uk/users/jrh/marktoberdorf.
6. Thomas F. Melham and Robert B. Jones. Abstraction by symbolic indexing transformations. In Mark D. Aagaard and John W. O'Leary, editors, *Formal Methods in Computer-Aided Design (FMCAD)*, volume 2517 of *Lecture Notes in Computer Science*, pages 1–18. Springer-Verlag, 2002.
7. Manish Pandey, Richard Raimi, Randal E. Bryant, and Magdy S. Abadir. Formal verification of content addressable memories using symbolic trajectory evaluation. In *DAC'97*, 1997.
8. Jan-Willem Roorda. Symbolic trajectory evaluation using a satisfiability solver. Licentiate thesis, Computing Science, Chalmers University of Technology, 2005.
9. Jan-Willem Roorda and Koen Claessen. A new SAT-based Algorithm for Symbolic Trajectory Evaluation. In *Correct Hardware Design and Verification Methods (CHARME)*, volume 3725 of *LNCS*. Springer Verlag, 2005.
10. Jan-Willem Roorda and Koen Claessen. Explaining Symbolic Trajectory Evaluation by giving it a faithful semantics. In *Proc. of International Computer Science Symposium in Russia*, Lecture Notes in Computer Science. Springer Verlag, 2006.
11. Jan-Willem Roorda and Koen Claessen. SAT-based assistance in abstraction refinement for Symbolic Trajectory Evaluation. Technical Report 2006:5, Chalmers University of Technology, Göteborg, Sweden, 2006.

12. Carl Seger, Robert Jones, John O'Leary, Tom Melham, Mark Aagaard, Clark Barrett, and Don Syme. An industrially effective environment for hardware verification. *IEEE Transactions on Computer-Aided Design of Integrated Circuits and Systems*, 24(9):1381–1405, September 2005.

13. Carl-Johan H. Seger and Randal E. Bryant. Formal verification by symbolic evaluation of partially-ordered trajectories. *Formal Methods in System Design*, 6(2), 1995.

14. Jin Yang, Rami Gil, and Eli Singerman. satGSTE: Combining the abstraction of GSTE with the capacity of a SAT solver. In *Designing Correct Circuits (DCC'04)*, 2004.

15. Jin Yang and Amit Goel. GSTE through a case study. In *Proceedings of the 2002 IEEE/ACM international conference on Computer-aided design*, pages 534–541. ACM Press, 2002.

16. Jin Yang and C.-J. H. Seger. Introduction to generalized symbolic trajectory evaluation. In *IEEE International Conference on Computer Design: VLSI in Computers & Processors (ICCD '01)*, pages 360–367, Washington - Brussels - Tokyo, Sep 2001. IEEE.

BDD-Based Hardware Verification

Gianpiero Cabodi and Marco Murciano

Dip. di Automatica e Informatica, Politecnico di Torino, Turin, Italy
{gianpiero.cabodi, marco.murciano}@polito.it
http://fmgroup.polito.it/~{cabodi, murciano}

Abstract. This chapter overviewes Binary Decision Diagrams (BDDs) and their application in Formal Hardware Verification. BDDs are first described as a representation formalism for Boolean functions. BDDs are directed acyclic graphs, deriving their efficiency from canonicity, and from their ability to be exponentially more compact, in terms of node count, than alternative Boolean representations. The chapter introduces the main BDD operators, in terms of recursive graph manipulation functions. Some of the most succesful Formal Verification techniques, based on BDD engines, are then reported. The description is limited to Reduced Ordered BDDs (ROBDDs), which, albeight being just one among several decomposition types, are the most widely used and the most general one.

1 Introduction

Binary Decision Diagrams (BDDs[1]) are one of the most widely used core techniques in the field of Formal Verification. They are commonly used to implicitly represent large solution spaces in combinational and sequential problems, as they can provide effective implicit representations for Boolean functions depending on tens to hundreds of Boolean variables.

The interest in BDDs from the theoretical computer science community has largely been motivated by the practical importance and success of BDDs in formal hardware verification. Conversely, the growing industrial interest in formal hardware verification has largely been inspired by the effectiveness of BDD–based techniques in finding real bugs in practical, large–scale designs.

A BDD is a directed acyclic graph constructed in such a way that its directed paths represent objects of interest (such as subsets, clauses, minterms, etc.). A BDD is just a data structure for representing a Boolean function. Bryant [1] introduced the BDD in its current form, although the general ideas have been around for quite some time (e.g., as branching programs in the theoretical computer science literature [2, 3]).

BDDs may achieve an exponential compression rate, as the number of vertices and edges (graph size) is often exponentially lower than the number of paths (from root to leaves).

---

[1] Reduced Ordered BDDs (ROBDDs), or simply BDDs whenever no ambiguity arises.

M. Bernardo and A. Cimatti (Eds.): SFM 2006, LNCS 3965, pp. 78–107, 2006.

BDDs have several useful properties. First, many common functions have small BDDs. A BDD is a canonical representation for a Boolean function, i.e., every distinct Boolean function has exactly one unique BDD representation. Thus, comparing Boolean functions becomes just a pointer comparison. BDDs can be transformed by algorithms that visit all vertices and edges of the directed graph in some order. These algorithms take therefore polynomial time in the current size of the graph. Unfortunately, when new BDDs are created, some algorithms tend to significantly increase the number of vertices, potentially leading to exponential memory requirements. To reduce this drawback, variable reordering techniques have been introduced.

Choosing a good variable order is important. In general, the choice of variable order can make the difference between a linear size BDD and an exponential one. Variable order is usually chosen either statically, i.e., by pre–processing the input formula, or dynamically, i.e., by analyzing the outcome of previous steps.

Bryant [4] provides a detailed exposition on BDDs and surveys some applications and variations. BDDs have been adopted with success as a core technology for various formal verification approaches. Due to their canonicity and potential compactness, they are used

– To symbolically represent and manipulate Boolean functions generated at circuit (input, internal as well as output) nodes. In this chapter we will describe *combinational equivalence checking, symbolic simulation* and *symbolic trajectory evaluation*, three well known approaches in this general trend.
– To compute sets of states of sequential circuits modeled as Finite State Machines. BDD based symbolic traversals have represented the basic steps of both *model checking* and *sequential equivalence checking*, where BDDs are adopted to encode and manipulare chacteristic functions of state sets.

Among the above mentioned techniques, model checking probably represents the the main step towards fully automated formal verification. In contrast to theorem proving, model checking is completely automatic and fast, sometimes producing an answer in a matter of minutes.

Model checking is a technique that relies on building a finite model of a sequential system and checking that a desired property holds in that model. Roughly speaking, the check is performed as an exhaustive state space search, which is guaranteed to terminate since the model is finite.

Model checking can be used to check partial specifications, and so it can provide useful information about a system's correctness even if the system has not been completely specified. It produces counterexamples, which usually represent subtle errors in design, and thus can be used to aid in debugging.

The technical challenge in model checking is in devising algorithms and data structures that allow us to handle large search spaces. Model checking has been used primarily in hardware and protocol verification [5]; The main disadvantage of model checking is the *state explosion problem*. In 1987 McMillan used BDDs to represent state transition systems efficiently, thereby increasing the size of the systems that could be verified. Model checkers today are routinely expected to handle systems with between 100 and 200 state variables. They have checked interesting systems with 10^{20} reachable states [6], and by using appropriate abstraction techniques, they can check systems with an essentially unlimited number of states [7]. As a result, model checking is now powerful enough that it is becoming widely used in industry to aid in the verification of newly developed designs.

Space limits and memory explosion have always represented the main hurdle for a broader BDD exploitation with ever increasing circuit sizes. BDDs can in fact provide exponentially compact representations for Boolean functions of hundreds to thousands variables. Nonetheless, even after almost two decades of intensive research in the area, they have never been able to deal with the largest models and problem instances, and they are generally deemed to be effective up to a few hundred variables.

In the last decade, Boolean Satisfiability (SAT) Solvers [8] have generally beat BDDs in terms of scalability and attainable circuit sizes. SAT based verification tools are now able to work with larger circuits than BDD based tools, at least for bug hunting (debug) purposes. Still BDDs play important roles in most formal verification tools, either as stand–alone engines, or in mixed approaches, where they are combined, for instance, with non canonical Boolean function representations and SAT solvers. Furthermore, several alternative decomposition types ha ve been introduced, in order to overcome the limits of ROBDDs, either in terms of representation or symbolic manipulation power. Describin such extensions is outside the scope of this chapter.

In the sequel we first provide some preliminary informations about the general background and underlying theory (section 2). Section 3 concentrates on BDDs as a data structure with some of the most relevant implementation details. Section 4 overviewes recursive procedures implementing the main symbolic operators on BDDs We then move up to the applications on formal verification (section 5): we describe in that section the main classical verification frameworks exploiting the BDD technology, without going to deep engineering details and optimizations. We finally draw some concluding remarks in section 6. Some of the examples and figures presented are taken and/or inspired by the tutorial papers [9] and [10]

2   Background

Boolean Algebra forms a cornerstone of computer science and digital system design. Many problems in digital logic design and testing, artificial intelligence, and combinatorics can be expressed as a sequence of operations on Boolean functions. Such applications would benefit from efficient algorithms for representing and manipulating Boolean functions symbolically.

Unfortunately, many of the tasks one would like to perform with Boolean functions, such as testing whether there exists any assignment of input variables such that a given Boolean expression evaluates to 1 (satisfiability), or two Boolean expressions denote the same function (equivalence) require solutions to *NP–Complete* or *coNP–Complete* problems. Consequently, all known approaches to performing these operations require, in the worst case, an amount of computer time that grows exponentially with the size of the problem. This makes it difficult to compare the relative efficiencies of different approaches to representing and manipulating Boolean functions. In the worst case, all known approaches perform as poorly as the naive approach of representing functions by their truth tables and defining all of the desired operations in terms of their effect on truth table entries. In practice, by utilizing more clever representations and manipulation algorithms, we can often avoid these exponential computations.

2.1   Representations of Boolean Functions

A variety of methods have been developed for representing and manipulating Boolean functions. Those based on classical representations such as truth tables, Karnaugh maps, or canonical sum–of–products (SOP) forms are quite impractical as every function of n arguments has a representation of size 2^n or more. More practical approaches utilize representations that at least for many functions, are not of exponential size. Example representations include reduced sum of products, (or equivalently sets of prime cubes) and factorizations into unate functions. These representations suffer from several drawbacks. First, certain common functions still require representations of exponential size. For example, the even and odd parity functions serve as worst case examples in all of the above representations. Second, while a certain function may have a reasonable representation, performing a simple operation such as complementation could yield a function with an exponential representation. Finally, none of these representations are canonical forms, i.e. a given function may have many different representations. Consequently, testing for equivalence or satisfiability can be quite difficult.

2.2   Representations of (Combinational and Sequential) Circuits

Combinational circuits are generally represented by netlists of gates, each one modeled as a Boolean function. As far as we do not care about propagation delays, the overall input–output (functional) behavior of such circuits can be easily captured by Boolean functions, either in terms of a vector of functions (one for each circuit output) or as an overall Boolean relation, describing the legal correspondences of input and output values. Similar arguments apply to combinational parts of sequential circuits.

A bigger challenge comes from sequential circuits, where we need to model sequences of values over time. There are many kinds of system models to represent sequential systems. The models are Finite State Machines [11], Kripke Structures, ω–regular automata [12] [13], labeled transition systems [14] [15]. We refer in the sequel to FSMs and Kripke Structures.

Definition (Finite State Machine). A Finite State Machine is a 6–tuple, $(S, S_0, \Sigma, \lambda, T, O)$ where

- S is the set of states.
- $S_0 \subseteq S$ is the set of initial states.

- Σ is the input alphabet.
- λ is the output alphabet.
- $T \subseteq S \times \Sigma \times S$ is the transition relation between the states.
- $O \subseteq S \times \Sigma \times \lambda$ is the output relation.

Definition (Kripke Structure). A Kripke structure is defined as a 4–tuple $M = (S, S_0, T, L)$, where

- S is the set of states.
- $S_0 \subseteq S$ is the set of initial states.
- $T \subseteq S \times S$ is the transition relation between the states.
- $L : S \rightarrow 2^A$ is the function that labels each state with a set of atomic propositions.

The Kripke structure is a closed system and models all possible behaviors of the system. A Kripke structure can be derived from an FSM by taking a Cartesian product of S and Σ in the FSM as the set of states in the Kripke structure.

2.3   Temporal Logic

Temporal logic is a formalism to describe the ordering of events in time without introducing time explicitly. Therefore, temporal logics are very useful in verifying reactive systems. There are two main families of temporal logic and they are distinguished from each other by the capabilities to model *linear time systems*[2] or *branching time systems*[3].

In this chapter only *branching time systems* are taken into account because of the possibility to translate their underlaying structures into BDDs. The formalism used to specify properties in this set of applications is called **CTL**, to say, *Computation Tree Logic*.

There are four basic temporal operators in future tense logics:

- X - next time,
- F - eventually or in the future,
- G - always or globally,
- U - until.

Computation Tree Logic (CTL) was first proposed by Clarke and Emerson as a branching–time temporal logic [16]. CTL formulae are composed of path quantifiers and temporal operators. The path quantifiers are used to describe the branching structure in the computation tree. There are two path quantifiers:

---

[2] Systems that do not require branching time statements, for instance in *Bounded Model Checking* applications, where the system gets unrolled in order to check the desired property for a specified depth in transition relation evuolution.

[3] In which the transition relation is taken in his whole size and properties must be checked for all paths in a particular subgraph (often the entire tree). *Branching time structures* are hard to manipulate but give a warranty of completeness in verifying the model of the system against a set of properties that must hold always and everywhere.

- A - for all paths,
- E - there exists a path or some paths.

In CTL, every quantifier is followed by a temporal operator. Therefore, there are eight basic CTL operators:

- AX and EX
- AF and EF
- AG and EG
- AU and EU.

Sometimes another binary operator $(q\ R\ p)$ describes situations in which the raising of signal q *releases* the holding of signal p.

The path quantifiers and the temporal operators have the following relations:

- $F\phi \equiv True\ U\ \phi$
- $G\phi \equiv \neg F\neg\phi$
- $A\phi \equiv \neg E\neg\phi.$

Then, using these relations, each of the eight CTL operators can be expressed in terms of only three operators that are EX, EG, and EU:

- $AX\phi \equiv \neg EX\neg\phi$
- $EF\phi \equiv E[True\ U\ \phi]$
- $AG\phi \equiv \neg EF\neg\phi$
- $AF\phi \equiv \neg EG\neg\phi$
- $A[\phi\ U\ \psi] \equiv \neg E[\neg\psi\ U\ (\neg\phi \wedge \neg\psi)] \wedge \neg EG\neg\psi$

The syntax of CTL is defined with state formulas (*state_formulas*) and path formulas (*path_formulas*) [17].

$$
\begin{aligned}
state\_formula\ ::=\ &\langle atomic\_proposition\rangle\ |\\
&\langle state\_formula\rangle \wedge \langle state\_formula\rangle\ |\\
&\neg\langle state\_formula\rangle\ |\\
&E(\langle path\_formula\rangle)\ |\\
&A(\langle path\_formula\rangle)\\
\\
path\_formula\ ::=\ &X(\langle state\_formula\rangle)\ |\\
&(\langle state\_formula\rangle\ U\ \langle state\_formula\rangle)
\end{aligned}
$$

The notation $M, s \vDash \phi$ means that formula ϕ holds at state s in the Kripke structure M. Then, the semantics of CTL are as follows.

- $M, s \vDash \phi$ iff $\phi \in L(s)$
- $M, s \vDash \neg\phi$ iff $M, s \nvDash \phi$
- $M, s \vDash \phi \wedge \psi$ iff $M, s \vDash \phi$ and $M, s \vDash \psi$
- $M, s \vDash \phi\ U\ \psi$ iff $M, s \vDash \phi$ or $M, s \vDash \psi$
- $M, s \vDash E\phi$ iff $\exists\pi = (s, s_1, \ldots, s_n), M, \pi \vDash \phi$
- $M, s \vDash A\phi$ iff $\forall\pi = (s, s_1, \ldots, s_n), M, \pi \vDash \phi$

3   Introduction to BDDs

Binary Decision Diagrams (*BDDs*) are an alternative representation, proposing several advantages over previous approaches to Boolean function representation and manipulation.

BDDs have been introduced in their current form by Bryant [1], starting from the notations of Lee [2] and Akers [3], with further restrictions on the ordering of decision variables.

BDDs are directed acyclic graphs providing a canonical representation of Boolean functions. An Ordered BDD (*OBDD*) is a tree–like graph where Shannon (or Boole) decomposition is recursively applied at each node, following an ordered set of variables.

Let us denote by $f|_{v=1}$ ($f|_{v=0}$) the Boolean expression obtained by replacing v with 1 (0) in f. Let $v \to f_1, f_0$ be the *if–then–else* operator defined by

$$v \to f_1, f_0 = (v \land f_1) \lor (\neg v \land f_0)$$

then it is not hard to see that the following equivalence holds:

$$f = v \to f|_{v=1}, f|_{v=0} \tag{1}$$

This is known as the *Shannon expansion* of f with respect to v. The above simple equation has a lot of useful applications. The first one is to generate a canonical form from any expression f. All operators can easily be expressed using only *if–then–else* operators and then constants 0 and 1. Moreover, this can be done in such a way that all tests are performed only on (un–negated) variables and variables occur in no other places. Hence the operator gives rise to a new kind of normal form (INF: *If–then–else* Normal Form). If f contains no variables it is either equivalent to 0 or 1. Otherwise we form the Shannon expansion of f with respect to one of the variables v in f. Thus since $f|_{v=1}$ and $f|_{v=0}$ both contain one less variable than f, we can recursively find INFs for both of these; call them f_1 and f_0. An INF for f is now simply

$$v \to f_1, f_0$$

For example, $\neg x$ is $(x \to 0, 1)$, $x \Leftrightarrow y$ is $x \to (y \to 1, 0), (y \to 0, 1)$. Since variables must only occur in tests the Boolean expression x is respented as $x \to 1, 0$.

Example 1. Consider the Boolean expression $f = (x_1 \Leftrightarrow y_1) \land (x_2 \Leftrightarrow y_2)$. If we find an INF of f by selecting in order the variables x_1, y_1, x_2, y_2 on which to perform Shannon expansions, we get the expressions

$$f = x_1 \to f_1, f_0$$
$$f_0 = y_1 \to 0, f_{00}$$
$$f_1 = y_1 \to f_{11}, 0$$
$$f_{00} = x_2 \to f_{001}, f_{000}$$
$$f_{11} = x_2 \to f_{111}, f_{110}$$

$$f_{000} = y_2 \rightarrow 0, 1$$
$$f_{001} = y_2 \rightarrow 1, 0$$
$$f_{110} = y_2 \rightarrow 0, 1$$
$$f_{111} = y_2 \rightarrow 1, 0$$

Figure 1 shows the expression as a tree. Such a tree is also called a decision tree. A lot of the subexpressions are easily seen to be identical, so it is tempting to identify them. For example, instead of f_{110} we can use f_{000} and instead of f_{111} we can use f_{001}. If we substitute f_{000} for f_{110} in the righthand side of f_{11} and also f_{001} for f_{111}, we see that f_{00} and f_{11} are identical, and in f_1 we can replace f_{11} with f_{00}. If we identify all equal subexpressions we end up with what is known as a binary decision diagram (a BDD). It is no longer a tree of Boolean expressions but a directed acyclic graph (DAG).

Applying this idea of sharing, f can now be written as:

$$f = x_1 \rightarrow f_1, f_0$$
$$f_0 = y_1 \rightarrow 0, f_{00}$$
$$f_1 = y_1 \rightarrow f_{00}, 0$$
$$f_{00} = x_2 \rightarrow f_{001}, f_{000}$$
$$f_{000} = y_2 \rightarrow 0, 1$$
$$f_{001} = y_2 \rightarrow 1, 0$$

Each subexpression can be viewed as the node of a graph. Such a node is either terminal, in the case of the constants 0 and 1, or non-terminal. A non-terminal node has a low-edge corresponding to the *else–part* and a high-edge

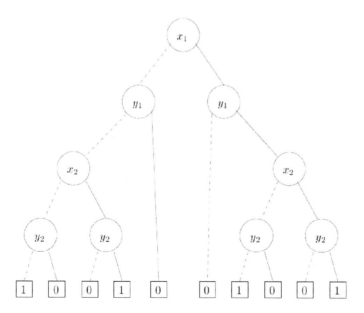

Fig. 1. A decision tree for $(x_1 \Leftrightarrow y_1) \wedge (x_2 \Leftrightarrow y_2)$. Dashed lines denote low–branches, solid lines high–branches.

corresponding to the *then-part* (see Figure 2). Notice that the number of nodes has decreased from 9 in the decision tree to 6 in the BDD. It is not hard to imagine that, if each of the terminal nodes were other big decision trees, the savings would be dramatic. Since we have chosen to consistently select variables in the same order in the recursive calls during the construction of the INF of f, the variables occur in the same order on all paths from the root of the BDD. In this situation the binary decision diagram is said to be ordered (an OBDD). Figure 2 shows a BDD that is also an OBDD.

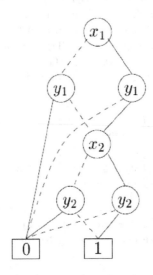

Fig. 2. A BDD for $(x_1 \Leftrightarrow y_1) \wedge (x_2 \Leftrightarrow y_2)$ with ordering $x_1 < y_1 < x_2 < y_2$. Dashed lines denote low–edges, solid lines high–edges.

Conceptually, we can construct the BDD for a Boolean function as follows (see Figure 3). First, build a decision tree for the desired function, obeying the restrictions that along any path from root to leaf, no variable appears more than once, and that along every path from root to leaf, the variables always appear in the same order (Figure 3 (a)). Next, generate a Reduced Ordered BDD (ROBDD), by applying the following two reduction rules as much as possible:

- *Merge* any duplicate (same label and same children) nodes, i.e., two isomorphic subgraphs are merged. The rule guarantees keeping a unique (canonical) representation (and BDD subgraph) for any given sub–function.
- *Delete* a node if both child pointers point to the same child, i.e. the node is redundant (Figure 3 (b)). The rule represents the fact that a given sub–function does not depend on the deleted variable.

The resulting directed, acyclic graph is the BDD for the function (Figure 3 (c)). In practice, BDDs are generated and manipulated in the fully reduced form, without ever building the decision tree. In a typical implementation, all BDDs in use by an application are merged as much as possible to maximize node sharing, so a

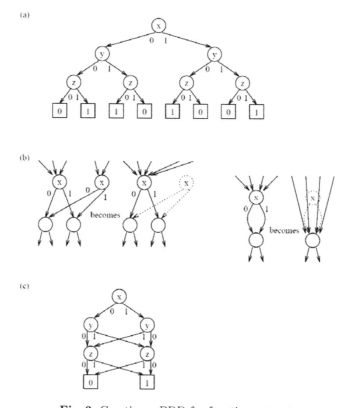

Fig. 3. Creating a BDD for function $x \oplus y \oplus z$

function is represented by a pointer to its root node. For example, in Figure 3 (c), the function (x) is represented by a pointer to the top node, whereas the function (y z) is represented by just a pointer to the leftmost node labeled y, rather than by copies of the nodes.

BDDs have several useful properties. First, many common functions have small BDDs. For example, generalizing the pattern in Figure 3(c), we see that the BDD for the parity of n variables requires $2n - 1$ nodes, whereas parity requires exponential size using, for instance, sum–of–products (SOP) form. A BDD is a canonical representation for a Boolean function, i.e., every distinct Boolean function has exactly one unique BDD representation. Thus, comparing Boolean functions becomes just a pointer comparison.

Example 2. Figure 4 and 5 shows the BDD for the function

$$f(x_1, x_2, x_3) = (x_1 \wedge (\neg x_2) \wedge x_3) \vee ((\neg x_1) \wedge x_2 \wedge x_3)$$

A solid (dashed) line indicates the 1 (0) value for the decision variable.

Figure 6 shows four OBDDs. Some of the tests (e.g., on x_2 in (b)) are redundant, since both the low– and high–branch lead to the same node. Such unnecessary

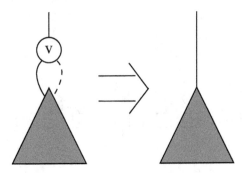

Fig. 4. BDD Deletion Rule. A BDD node with two equal outgoing edges is deleted.

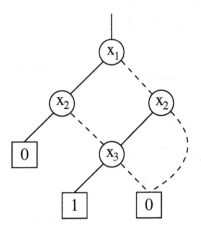

Fig. 5. An Example of BDD

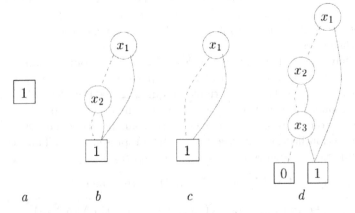

Fig. 6. Four OBBDs: a) And OBBD for 1; b) Another OBBD for 1 with two redundant tests; c) Same as (b) with one of the redundant tests removed; d) An OBDD for $x_1 \vee x_3$ with one redundant test

tests can be removed: any reference to the redundant node is simply replaced by a reference to its subnode. If all identical nodes are shared and all redundant tests are eliminated, the OBDD is said to be reduced (an ROBDD). ROBDDs have some very convenient properties centered around their canonicity (Often when people speak about BDDs they really mean ROBDDs). To summarize:

- A Binary Decision Diagram (BDD) is a rooted, directed acyclic graph with:
    1. one or two terminal nodes of outdegree zero labeled 0 or 1, and
    2. a set of variable nodes u of outdegree two. The two outgoing edges are given by two functions $low(u)$ and $high(u)$. (In pictures, these are shown as dotted and solid lines, respectively.) A variable $var(u)$ is associated with each variable node.
- A BDD is Ordered (OBDD) if on all paths through the graph the variables respect a given linear order $x_1 < x_2 < \ldots < x_n$. An (O)BDD is Reduced (R(O)BDD) if:
    1. (uniqueness) no two distinct nodes u and v have the same variable name and low– and high-successor, i.e.,
        $$var(u) = var(v), \; low(u) = low(v), \; high(u) = high(v) \text{ implies } u = v$$
    2. (nonredundant tests) no variable node u has identical low and highsuccessor, i.e.,
        $$low(u) \neq high(u)$$

The ordering and reducedness conditions are shown in Figure 7.

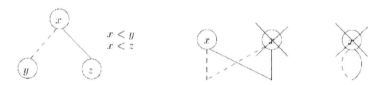

Fig. 7. The ordering and reduceness conditions of ROBDDs. Left: variables must be *ordered*. Middle: Nodes must be *unique*. Right: Only *non–redundant tests* should be present.

ROBDDs have some interesting properties. They provide compact representations of Boolean expressions, and there are efficient algorithms for performing all kinds of logical operations on ROBDDs. They are all based on the crucial fact that for any function $f : \mathbb{B}^n \to \mathbb{B}$ there is exactly one ROBDD representing it. This means, in particular, that there is exactly one ROBDD for the constant true (and constant false) function on $\mathbb{B}^n$: the terminal node 1 (and 0 in case of false). Hence, it is possible to test in constant time whether an ROBDD is constantly true or false. (Recall that for Boolean expressions this problem is *NP-complete*.)

Simple graph algorithms, working *depth–first* on BDDs, implement many operators. APPLY, ITE (*if–then–else*), and existential ($\exists$)/universal ($\forall$) quantifiers are well–known examples. BDDs have been widely used in verification problems to represent functions, as well as sets, by means of their characteristic functions. Operations on sets are efficiently implemented by Boolean operations on their characteristic functions.

4   Graph Algorithms on BDDs

In the previous section we saw how to construct an OBDD from a Boolean expression by a simple recursive procedure. The question arises now how do we construct a reduced OBDD? One way is to first construct an OBDD and then proceed by reducing it. Another more appealing approach, which we follow here, is to reduce the OBDD during construction.

To describe how this is done we will need an explicit representation of ROB-DDs. Nodes will be represented as numbers $\{0, 1, 2, \ldots\}$ with 0 and 1 reserved for the terminal nodes. The variables in the ordering $x_1 < x_2 < \ldots < x_n$ are represented by their indices $\{1, 2, \ldots, n\}$. The ROBDD is stored in a table $T : u \mapsto (i, l, h)$ which maps a node u to its three attributes $var(u) = i$, $low(u) = l$, and $high(u) = h$. Figure 8 shows the representation of the ROBDD from Figure 2 (with the variable names changed to $x_1 < x_2 < x_3 < x_4$).

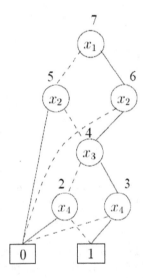

$$T : u \mapsto (i, l, h)$$

u	var	low	$high$
0	5		
1	5		
2	4	1	0
3	4	0	1
4	3	2	3
5	2	4	0
6	2	0	4
7	1	5	6

Fig. 8. Representing an OBDD with ordering $x_1 < x_2 < x_3 < x_4$. The numebers inside the vertices are the identities used in the representation. The numbers 0 and 1 are reserved for terminal nodes. The numbers to the right of the ROBBD shows the index of the variables in the ordering. The constants are assigned an index which is the number of variables in the ordering plus one (here $4 + 1 = 5$). This makes some subsequent algorithms easier to present. The low– and high–fields are unused for the terminal nodes.

Mk. In order to ensure that the OBDD being constructed is reduced, it is necessary to determine from a triple (i, l, h) whether there exists a node u with $var(u) = i$, $low(u) = l$, and $high(u) = h$. For this purpose we assume the presence of a table $H : (i, l, h) \mapsto u$ mapping triples (i, l, h) of variable indices i, and nodes l, h to nodes u. The table H is the "inverse" of the table T, i.e., for variable nodes u, $T(u) = (i, l, h)$, if and only if, $H(i, l, h) = u$. The operations needed on the two tables are:

$T : u \mapsto (i, l, h)$	
$\quad init(T)$	initialize T to contain only 0 and 1
$\quad u \leftarrow add(T, i, l, h)$	allocate a new node u with attributes (i, l, h)
$\quad var(u), low(u), high(u)$	lookup the attributes of u in T
$H : (i, l, h) \mapsto u$	
$\quad init(H)$	initialize H to be empty
$\quad b \leftarrow member(H, i, l, h)$	check if (i, l, h) is in H
$\quad u \leftarrow lookup(H, i, l, h)$	find H(i, l, h)
$\quad insert(H, i, l, h, u)$	make (i, l, h) map to u in H

We shall assume that all these operations can be performed in constant time, $O(1)$.

The function $\text{Mk}[T, H](i, l, h)$ (see Figure 9) searches the table H for a node with variable index i and low-, high-branches l, h and returns a matching node if one exists. Otherwise it creates a new node u, inserts it into H and returns the identity of it. The running time of Mk is $O(1)$ due to the assumptions on the basic operations on T and H. The OBDD is ensured to be reduced if nodes are only created through the use of Mk. In describing Mk and subsequent algorithms, we make use of the notation $[T, H]$ to indicate that Mk depends on the global data structures T and H, but we leave out the arguments when invoking it as part of other algorithms.

```
Mk[T, H](i, l, h) =
    if l = h then return l
    else if member(H, i, l, h) then
    return lookup(H, i, l, h)
    else u ← add(T, i, l, h)
    insert(H, i, l, h, u)
    return u
```

Fig. 9. The function $\text{Mk}[T, H](i, l, h)$

Build. The construction of an ROBDD from a given Boolean expression t proceeds as in the construction of an *if-then-else* normal form (INF) in section 2. An ordering of the variables $x_1 < \ldots < x_n$ is fixed. Using the Shannon expansion $t = x_1 \to t|_{x_1=1}, t|_{x_1=0}$, a node for t is constructed by a call to Mk, after the nodes for $t|_{x_1=0}$ and $t|_{x_1=1}$ have been constructed by recursion. The

$$\text{BUILD}[T, H](t) =$$
$$\text{function BUILD'}(t, i) =$$
$$\text{if } i > n \text{ then}$$
$$\text{if } t \text{ is false then return 0 else return 1}$$
$$\text{else } v_0 \leftarrow \text{BUILD'}(t|_{x_i=0}, i + 1)$$
$$v_1 \leftarrow \text{BUILD'}(t|_{x_i=1}, i + 1)$$
$$\text{return MK}(i, v_0, v_1)$$
$$\text{end BUILD'}$$

$$\text{return BUILD'}(t, 1)$$

Fig. 10. Algorithm for building an ROBDD from a Boolean expression t

algorithm is shown in Figure 10. The call BUILD'(t, i) constructs an ROBDD for a Boolean expression t with variables in $x_i, x_{i+1}, \ldots, x_n$. It does so by first recursively constructing ROBDDs v_0 and v_1 for $t|_{x_i=0}$ and $t|_{x_i=1}$ in lines 4 and 5, and then proceeding to find the identity of the node for t in line 6. Notice that if v_0 and v_1 are identical, or if there already is a node with the same i, v_0 and v_1 , no new node is created. An example of using BUILD to compute an ROBDD is shown in figure 10. The running time of BUILD is bad. It is easy to see that for a variable ordering with n variables there will always be generated on the order of 2^n calls.

Apply. All the binary Boolean operators on ROBDDs are implemented by the same general algorithm APPLY(op, u_1, u_2) that for two ROBDDs computes the ROBDD for the Boolean expression t^{u_1} op t^{u_2} . The construction of APPLY is based on the Shannon expansion (1):

$$\text{APPLY}[T, H](op, u_1, u_2) =$$
$$init(G)$$

$$\text{function APP}(u1, u2) =$$
$$\text{if } G(u_1, u_2) \neq \text{empty then return } G(u_1, u_2)$$
$$\text{else if } u_1 \in \{0, 1\} \text{ and } u_2 \in \{0, 1\} \text{ then } u \leftarrow op(u_1, u_2)$$
$$\text{else if } var(u_1) = var(u_2) \text{ then}$$
$$u \leftarrow \text{MK}(var(u_1), \text{APP}(low(u_1), low(u_2)), \text{APP}(high(u_1), high(u_2)))$$
$$\text{else if } var(u_1) < var(u_2) \text{ then}$$
$$u \leftarrow \text{MK}(var(u_1), \text{APP}(low(u_1), u_2), \text{APP}(high(u_1), u_2))$$
$$\text{else } (* \ var(u_1) > var(u_2) \ *)$$
$$u \leftarrow \text{MK}(var(u_2), \text{APP}(u_1, low(u_2)), \text{APP}(u_1, high(u_2)))$$
$$G(u_1, u_2) \leftarrow u$$
$$\text{return u}$$
$$\text{end APP}$$

$$\text{return APP}(u_1, u_2)$$

Fig. 11. The algorithm APPLY$[T, H](op, u_1, u_2)$

Observe that for all Boolean operators *op* the following holds:

$$(x \rightarrow f_1, f_2) \; op \; (x \rightarrow f_1', f_2') = x \rightarrow f_1 \; op \; f_1', f_2 \; op \; f_2' \qquad (2)$$

If we start from the root of the two ROBDDs we can construct the ROBDD of the result by recursively constructing the low and the highbranches and then form the new root from these. Again, to ensure that the result is reduced, we create the node through a call to MK. Moreover, to avoid an exponential blowup of recursive calls, dynamic programming is used. The algorithm is shown in Figure 11.

Dynamic programming is implemented using a table of results G. Each entry (i, j) is either empty or contains the earlier computed result of APP(i, j). The algorithm distinguishes between four different cases, the first of them handles the situation where both arguments are terminal nodes, the remaining three handle the situations where at least one argument is a variable node. If both u_1 and u_2 are terminal, a new terminal node is computed having the value of op applied

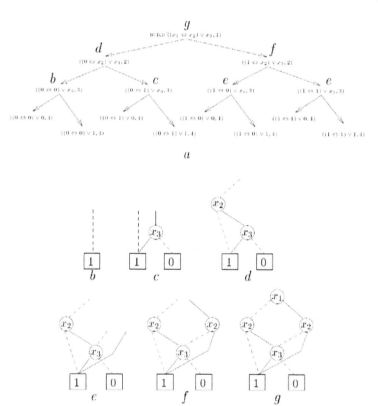

Fig. 12. Using BUILD on the expression $(x_1 \Leftrightarrow x_2) \vee x_3$. (a) The tree of calls to BUILD. (b) The ROBDD after the call BUILD'$((0 \Leftrightarrow 0) \vee x_3, 3)$. (c) After the call BUILD'$((0 \Leftrightarrow 1) \vee x_3, 3)$. (d) After the call BUILD'$((0 \Leftrightarrow x_2) \vee x_3, 2)$. (e) After the calls BUILD'$((1 \Leftrightarrow 0) \vee x_3, 3)$ and BUILD'$((1 \Leftrightarrow 1) \vee x_3, 3)$. (f) After the call BUILD'$((1 \Leftrightarrow x_2) \vee x_3, 2)$. (g) The final result.

RESTRICT[T, H]$(u, j, b) =$
    function RES(u) =
      if $var(u) > j$ then return u
      else if $var(u) < j$ then return MK($var(u)$, RES($low(u)$), RES($high(u)$))
      else (* $var(u) = j$ *) if $b = 0$ then return RES($low(u)$)
      else (* $var(u) = j, b = 1$ *) return RES($high(u)$)
    end RES
    return RES(u)

Fig. 13. The algorithm RESTRICT[T, H](u, j, b) which computes an ROBDD for $t^u[j/b]$

to the two truth values. (Recall, that terminal node 0 is represented by a node with identity 0 and similarly for 1).

If at least one of u_1 and u_2 are nonterminal, we proceed according to the variable index. If the nodes have the same index, the two lowbranches are paired and APP recursively computed on them. Similarly for the highbranches. This corresponds exactly to the case shown in equation (2). If they have different indices, we proceed by pairing the node with lowest index with the low and highbranches of the other. This corresponds to the equation

$$(x_i \rightarrow f_1, f_2) \ op \ t = x_i \rightarrow f_1 \ op \ t, f_2 \ op \ t \tag{3}$$

which holds for all t. Since we have taken the index of the terminals to be one larger than the index of the nonterminals, the last two cases, $var(u_1) < var(u_2)$ and $var(u_1) > var(u_2)$, take account of the situations where one of the nodes is a terminal.

Figure 12 shows an example of applying the algorithm on two small ROBDDs. Notice how pairs of nodes from the two ROBDDs are combined and computed.

To analyze the complexity of APPLY we let $| u |$ denote the number of nodes that can be reached from u in the ROBDD. Assume that G can be implemented with constant lookup and insertion times. (See section 5 for details on how to achieve this.) Due to the dynamic programming at most $| u_1 | \cdot | u_2 |$ calls to APPLY are generated. Each call takes constant time. The total running time is therefore $O(| u_1 | \cdot | u_2 |)$.

Restrict. The next operation we consider is the restriction of a ROBDD u. That is, given a truth assignment, for example $[x_3 = 0, x_5 = 1, x_6 = 1]$, we want to compute the ROBDD for t^u under this restriction, i.e., find the ROBDD for $t^u|_{x_3=0,x_5=1,x_6=1}$. As an example consider the ROBDD of Figure 12 (g) (repeated below to the left) representing the Boolean expression $(x_1 \Leftrightarrow x_2) \vee x_3$. Restricting it with respect to the truth assignment $[x_2 = 0]$ yields an ROBDD for $(\neg x_1 \vee x_3)$. It is constructed by replacing each occurrence of a node with label x_2 by its left branch yielding the ROBDD at the right:

The algorithm again uses MK to ensure that the resulting OBDD is reduced. Figure 13 shows the algorithm in the case where only singleton truth assignments $(x_j = b, b \in \{0, 1\})$ are allowed. Intuitively, in computing RESTRICT(u, j, b) we search for all nodes with $var = j$ and replace them by their low or highson depending on b. Since this might force nodes above the point of replacemen to become equal, it is followed by a reduction (through the calls to MK). Due to the two recursive calls in line 3, the algorithm has an exponential running time.

5   BDD-Based Applications

Let's now examine the basic algorithms for formal hardware verification using BDDs. We will start with conbinational equivalence checking and symbolic simulation, that basically require expressing Boolean functions of circuit nodes. Next we will consider sequential circuits, where BDDs are used to express/manipulate also states and state sets.

5.1   Combinational Equivalence

The most obvious application of BDDs is to check the equivalence of two combinational circuits.

   For example, we may want to verify that optimization or logic synthesis was done correctly by comparing the circuit before and after. The basic algorithm is, for each circuit, to build the BDDs for the outputs in terms of the primary inputs. Since BDDs are a canonical representation, the two combinational circuits implement the same function if and only if they have the same BDD. For example, let's consider verifying that the circuit in Figure 14 implements exclusive–OR. First, label the primary inputs with the BDDs for the variables y and z. Next, build the BDD for each gate output as a function of its inputs, labeling the OR gate with the BDD for $(y \lor z)$, the NAND gate with the BDD for $\neg(y \land z)$, and the AND gate with $(y \lor z) \land \neg(y \land z)$. For the specification circuit, we build the BDD for $(y \oplus z)$. Since these two expressions give the same Boolean function, they have the same BDD, which verifies that the circuit is indeed an exclusive–OR. In practice, this approach is limited by the size of the BDDs generated, which is highly sensitive to the function being verified and the variable order used. For pathological examples like multipliers, even 16–bits is too big to handle. Typically, circuits with up to a few hundred primary inputs can often be verified. For larger circuits, more sophisticated methods are needed.

5.2   Symbolic Simulation

Symbolic simulation [18] is a combination of the preceding ideas and a conventional logic simulator. The advantage of a conventional logic simulator is accuracy. Detailed timing models, hazards, and oscillatory behavior can all be simulated. The disadvantage of a conventional logic simulator is that only one simulation vector can be run at a time. In Figure 14, we would have had to run four simulations with the inputs equal to 00, 01, 10, and 11 to verify the circuit. A circuit with 20 inputs would have required over a million runs. Symbolic simulation adds two innovations to conventional logic simulation that give the effect of running large numbers of simulation vectors simultaneously. The first

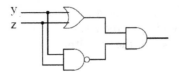

Fig. 14. A Simple Example: Is This XOR?

innovation is a third logic value X that represents an unknown value. This value is propagated through the circuit just as the 0 and 1 logic values are, although the X is always treated conservatively. For example, $0 \lor X$ is X, but $1 \land X$ is 1, since 1 is a controlling value for OR. Setting an input to X gives the effect of simulating the circuit for both the case where the inputwas 0 and the case where the input was 1, thereby cutting in half the number of simulation runs required. However, the X value loses information. In 14, setting one or both inputs to X yields an X at the output, a useless result for verification.

The more important innovation is the introduction of symbolic values, which avoids the information loss from using X values. The basic idea is to set an input to a symbolic value that can be either 0 or 1, rather than to a constant like 0, 1, or X. Alternatively, we can think of the symbolic value as remembering whether we assigned a 0 or 1 to a given input. Returning to Figure 3, suppose we set primary input y to 1 and primary input z to the symbolic value of a.

The symbolic simulator would then calculate that the OR gate will settle to 1 (since 1 OR anything is 1), that the NAND gate will settle to $\neg a$, and that the AND gate will settle to $\neg a$. Thus, we've effectively run two simulation vectors (yz equal to 10 and 11) at once, computing the output as a function of the symbolic values. To implement this idea, a conventional logic simulator is modified to use BDDs to represent the values on wires as a function of the symbolic values. In practice, the user must trade off using explicit 0s and 1s, the X value, and symbolic values. Setting an input to an explicit value gives conventional logic simulation. Setting an input to X halves the required number of simulation runs, but loses information so the simulation result might not be useful. Setting an input to a symbolic value halves the required number of simulation runs and does not lose information, but makes the BDDs representing the values on the wires larger. Too many symbolic values will make these BDDs too large to build.

5.3   Sequential Equivalence

Although symbolic simulation can be applied to sequential circuits as well as to combinational circuits, we would often like to reason about sequential circuits as finite state machines, rather than as just a bunch of gates. (This is analogous to the difference between cyclebased and eventdriven logic simulation.) A typical application would be comparing that two state machines have identical behavior, in order to verify the correctness of logic optimization, register retiming, state reencoding, etc. The problem of comparing two state machines can be converted into the problem of finding all of the reachable states of a state machine. Given two state machines to compare, tie the input lines together, send the outputs to a

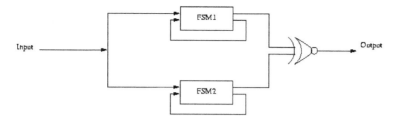

Fig. 15. A Product Machine: two FSMs are combined by sharing their Inputs and comparing their Outputs

comparator, and clock the two machines together in lockstep. This combination is just another, bigger state machine, known as *Product Machine* (see Figure 15). The original two machines have identical behavior if and only if the new machine indicates the outputs are equal for all reachable states. For example, consider the simple circuits in Figure 4. We have two small state machines: one with input i_0 , latch x_0 , and output out_0 ; the other with input i_1 , latches x_1 and x_2 , and output out_1 . To compare the two machines, we add the dotted lines, creating a new machine with input i, latches x_0 , x_1 , and x_2 , and output out.

Computing the set of reachable states using BDDs requires three basic ideas: representing sets of states using BDDs, computing images, and the reachability iteration. The first idea is to represent sets of states using BDDs. So far, we've been using BDDs to represent the logic function computed by a circuit. Now, we're going to use BDDs in a different manner. Basically, we can think of a BDD as representing a set of truth assignments: if the function the BDD represents is true for a given truth assignment, that assignment is in the set; if the function is false, that assignment is not in the set. For example, if we consider three Boolean variables x_0 , x_1 , and x_2 , the BDD for the function $x_0 \wedge x_1 \wedge \neg x_2$ represents the set containing only one truth assignment $\{110\}$; the BDD for $x_0 \wedge x_1$ represents the set of six truth assignments $\{100, 101, 110, 111, 010, 011\}$, and the BDD for 1 (the Boolean value True) represents the set of all eight truth assignments. If we associate a Boolean variable with each latch in a circuit, then these BDDs can be viewed as representing sets of states of the state machine. The next concept is image computation. Basically, if we have a BDD that represents a set of states of a state machine, the image of that BDD is a new BDD that represents the set of all possible states that the machine could be in exactly one clock tick later. For example, return to the state machine in Figure 16. The BDD for $\neg x_0 \wedge x_1 \wedge \neg x_2$ represents the single state where latches x_0, x_1, and x_2 are outputting 0, 1, and 0. Depending on the value of the input, the machine has two possible states at the next clock tick, so the image of this BDD is the BDD for $(\neg x_0 \wedge x_1 \wedge \neg x_2) \vee (x_0 \wedge \neg x_1 \wedge x_2)$. The simplest way to compute images is as follows:

First, build a BDD that represents the relationship between the present and next values of the latches. This BDD is called the transition relation. In our example, it would be the BDD for $(y_0 \equiv (x_0 \oplus i)) \wedge (y_1 \equiv (\neg i \wedge x_1) \vee (i \wedge x_2)) \vee (y_2 \equiv (\neg i \wedge x_2) \vee (i \wedge x_1))$. Next, AND the transition relation with the BDD whose

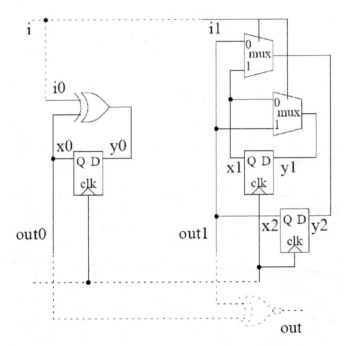

Fig. 16. Comparing Two State Machines

image you are computing. Then, existentially quantify 3 out the variables for the present state and the primary inputs. The final idea is an iteration using images to compute all reachable states. Basically, we start with the reset state and compute the image to get the set of states reachable in one more clock tick, i.e.,

$$R_0 := \text{BDD for reset state}$$
$$R_1 := R_0 \vee Image(R_0)$$
$$\dots$$
$$R_{i+1} := R_i \vee Image(R_i)$$

Intuitively, R_i is the set of all states reachable in i or fewer clock ticks from the reset state. This sequence will converge eventually, when $R_{i+1} = R_i$ (which is easy to test, since BDDs are canonical). In our example, the reset state $R_0 = \neg x_0 \wedge x_1 \wedge \neg x_2$, after one iteration $R_1 = (\neg x_0 \wedge x_1 \wedge \neg x_2) \vee (x_0 \wedge \neg x_1 \wedge x_2)$, and after two iterations $R_2 = R_1$, so we're done.

Reachability Analysis. The previously described technique is known as *Reachability Analysis* (or *Symbolic Traversal*). It is exploited, in one of its variants whenever we need to compute the states reachable by a FSM. Reachability analysis is, as a matter of fact, traversing an FSM to find all states that are reachable from initial states, and the unreachable states can be used as don't cares in model checking. The pseudocode of symbolic breadth–first traversal is shown in Figure 17. In the procedure, T is the transition relation of a system and I represents its initial states; both T and I are represented by BDDs. Reachability

```
FsmTraversal(T, S_0)
    New = Reached = Frontier = S_0
    repeat
        To = Img(T, Frontier)
        New = To − Reached
        if (New = 0)
            return Reached
        Frontier = bdd_between(New, Reached)
        Reached = Reached ∪ New
```

Fig. 17. BFS reachability analysis algorithm

analysis is a least fixpoint computation consisting of a series of image computations. Computing $Img(T, C)$ corresponds to finding all successor states of the constraint states represented by C. The procedure BDD_BETWEEN returns the smallest BDD in terms of nodes between New and $Reached$.

As with combinational verification, this approach is limited by the size of the BDDs generated, which is highly sensitive to the function being verified and the variable order used. Performance on any given circuit is extremely hard to predict. Nevertheless, as a very rough rule of thumb, the method described in this subsection can usually handle circuits with up to around one hundred latches. With more sophisticated enhancements, circuits with a few hundred latches are routinely verified, and occasionally practical circuits with thousands of latches can be verified. The original papers on using BDDs for sequential verification (e.g., [19] [20]) are excellent references for the basic algorithms, including image computation and the reachability iteration.

5.4 Model Checking

Two general approaches to model checking are used in practice today. The first, temporal model checking, is a technique developed independently in the 1980s by Clarke and Emerson [16] and by Queille and Sifakis [21]. In this approach specifications are expressed in a temporal logic [22] and systems are modeled as finite state transition systems. An efficient search procedure is used to check if a given finite state transition system is a model for the specification.

In the second approach, the specification is given as an automaton; then the system, also modeled as an automaton, is compared to the specification to determine whether or not its behavior conforms to that of the specification. Different notions of conformance have been explored, including language inclusion [23] [13], refinement orderings [24] [25] and observational equivalence [24] [26] [27]. Vardi and Wolper [28] showed how the temporal–logic model–checking problem could be recast in terms of automata, thus relating these two approaches.

Model checking is somehow related to the construction of a reference model with a set of properties that hold for a limited interval of time and that can be specified with a particular temporal logic before being automatically checked (e.g., one can say that a signal s_1 is raised after another one s_2 has lowed, or that finally the system signals an acknowledge (ack_i) once a request req_i is pending.

The Problem. The CTL model checking problem is as follows: Given a Kripke structure, $M = (S, S_0, T, L)$, and a CTL formula ϕ, checks whether

$$M, s \models \phi, \text{ for each } s \in S_0$$

This formulation is interpreted as *The structure M satisfies the property ϕ for each initial state in S_0*. The checking can be done by testing the containment of the initial states in the set of states that satisfy the property ϕ. 18 shows the pseudocode for CTL symbolic model checking. Since any CTL formula can be expressed in terms of only three operators $\{EX, EG, EU\}$, the procedure computes the satisfying set of states for only the three operators. The satisfying set of states for the three operators can be computed by the following fixpoint computations.

- $EX\phi = Pre(T, \phi)$
- $EG\phi = \nu Z.\ \phi \wedge EX(Z)$
- $E[\phi\ U\ \psi] = \mu Z.\ \psi\ U\ [(\phi \wedge EX(Z))$

where $Pre(T, \phi)$ is a *preimage computation* finding all predecessors of the states ϕ in one step; μ and ν are least and greatest fixpoint operators, respectively [29]. Notice that the preimage computation is the basic and key operation in model checking, and the model checking is performed by a series of preimage computations.

Model Checking Under Fairness Constraints. A fairness constraint is a set of states that must occur infinitely often along a computation path of the sysyem. When we have multiple fairness constraints, each fairness constraint must occur infinitely often along the computation path. We are often interested in verifying the correctness of the design only along *fair paths*. A fair path is a path along which each fairness constraint occurs infinitely often in the path.

In the presence of fairness constraints, we first compute the sets of states that lie along some fair paths and these states are called fair states. Since this fairness constraints are not expressible in CTL, we need to compute the satisfying states of CTL formulae in a different way by considering the fairness cosntraints. Using the sets of fair states, we can compute EG under fairness constraints as below.

$$\mathbf{E}_C\mathbf{G}_\phi = \nu Z.\phi \wedge EX(\bigvee_{c \in C} \mathbf{E}[Z\ \mathbf{U}\ (Z \wedge c)]) \tag{4}$$

where C is the sets of fair states and the subscript C in $E_C G$ indicates that the quantifiers are restricted to fair paths. We can also perform EX and EU computations under fairness constraints as below.

$$\mathbf{E}_C\mathbf{X}_\phi = \mathbf{EX}(\phi \wedge F)$$

```
MODELCHECK(T, f, S₀)
   if (S₀ ⊆ EVAL(T, f))
      return True
   else
      return False

EVAL(T, f)
   case
      f is an atomic proposition → return f
      f = ¬p → return ¬ EVAL(T, p)
      f = p ∨ q → return EVAL(T, p) ∨ EVAL(T, q)
      f = EXp → return EVALEX(T, EVAL(T, p))
      f = EGp → return EVALEG(T, EVAL(T, p))
      f = E(p U q) → return EVALEU(T, EVAL(T, p), EVAL(T, q), False)
   end case

EVALEX(T, p)
   return ∃ᵥ′.(T ∧ p′)

EVALEU(T, p, q, y)
   y′ = q ∨ (p∧ EVALEX(T, y))
   if (y′ = y)
      return y
   else
      return EVALEU(T, p, q, y′)

EVALEG(T, p, y)
   y′ = p∧ EVALEX(T, y)
   if (y′ = y)
      return y
   else
      return EVALEU(T, p, q, y′)
```

Fig. 18. Symbolic CTL model checking procedure

$$\mathbf{E}_C[\phi \, \mathbf{U} \, \psi] = \mathbf{E}[\phi \, \mathbf{U} \, (\psi \wedge F)]$$

where

$$F = \mathbf{E}_C G \, \mathbf{true}$$

Invariant Checking. Invariant checking can be thought of a special type of a model checking. It checks whether all reachable states are good states as determined by the invariant formulae. It does so by first finding the set of states that satisfy the invariant formulae, and then performing reachability analysis. At every image computation during the reachability analysis, it is checked whether there is any bad state in the current reached set. This also can be performed by $AG(p)$ in CTL model checking, where p is an atomic formula. The difference is that invariant checking is based on forward state traversal, whereas the $AG(p)$

model checking does not specify the type of search since the computation can be done in model checking by either forward or backward state traversal [30] [31].

5.5   Symbolic Trajectory Evaluation

Symbolic trajectory evaluation [32] is an attempt to combine the efficiency of symbolic simulation with a bit of the temporal expressiveness of model checking. The basic idea is that if we severely restrict the temporal logic used for specifying properties, we can verify the properties using symbolic simulation.

In symbolic trajectory evaluation, the property to be checked is written in the form $A \Rightarrow C$, which means that whenever the circuit behavior matches the pattern specified by A, it must also satisfy the pattern specified by C. The formulas A and C are written in a special form called "trajectory formulas". A trajectory formula only allows specifying the values of circuit nodes for a bounded number of events into the future (in contrast to CTL operators like EF that specify behavior arbitrarily far in the future).

Furthermore, trajectory formulas cannot express negation of a trajectory ("Match any pattern that doesn't look like...") or the OR of trajectories ("Match any pattern that looks like this or that."). In practice, the specfication language typically provides many features to ease writing trajectory formulas, but fundamentally, many properties that could be expressed in, say, CTL, simply cannot be expressed with trajectory formulas.

In exchange for this loss of expressiveness, though, comes a crucial property for efficiency: for any trajectory formula, there is a unique symbolic simulation vector (assignment of 0s, 1s, Xs, and symbolic values to the circuit inputs) that captures all behaviors that satisfy the trajectory formula. Verification, therefore, can be done with a single run of symbolic simulation — we symbolically simulate the vector for A, and after each simulation event, we check that the circuit state is consistent with the corresponding part of C . This algorithms is usually much faster than the iterations required for reachability and model checking. In practice, the main obstacle to symbolic trajectory evaluation is figuring out how to express the desired property using trajectory formulas that can be symbolically simulated efficiently. If the simulation vector has too many symbolic variables, the BDDs will become too big, just as in symbolic simulation.

The Evolution. The early Symbolic Trajectory Evaluators were limited in their analytical power since their symbolic manipulation methods were weak. Consequently, symbolic simulation for hardware verification did not evolve much further until more efficient methods of manipulating symbols emerged. The development of OBDDs for representing Boolean functions radically transformed symbolic simulation.

Since a symbolic simulator is based on a traditional logic simulator, it can use the same, quite accurate, electrical and timing models to compute the circuit behavior. For example, a detailed switch–level model, capturing charge sharing and subtle strengths phenomena, and a timing model, capturing bounded delay assumptions, are well within reach. Also — and of great significance — the switch–level circuit used in the simulator can be extracted automatically from the physical layout of the circuit. Hence, the correctness results can link the physical layout with some higher level of specification.

The first "pre–OBDD" symbolic simulators were simple extensions of traditional logic simulators [33]. In these symbolic simulators the input values could be Boolean variables rather than only 0's, 1's as in traditional logic simulators. Consequently, the results of the simulation were not single values but rather Boolean functions describing the behavior of the circuit for the set of all possible data represented by the Boolean variables. By representing these Boolean functions as OBDDs the task of comparing the results computed by the simulator and the expected results became straightforward for many circuits. Using these methods it has become possible to check many (combinational) circuits exhaustively.

It is important to realize that *if a circuit passes an exhaustive simulation suite, that does not necessarily mean that the circuit is formally verified correct.* In order to prove a correctness result, not only must all possible input values be simulated, all possible initial circuit states must also be taken into account. Hence, a verification strategy is needed as well as a sophisticated symbolic simulator. Bryant and Seger [34] developed a new generation of symbolic simulator based verifier. Since the method has departed quite far from traditional simulation, they called the approach Symbolic Trajectory Evaluation. Here a modified version of a simulator establishes the validity of formulas expressed in a very limited, but precisely defined, temporal logic.

This temporal logic allows the user to express properties of the circuit over trajectories: bounded–length sequences of circuit states. The verifier checks the validity of these formulas by a modified form of symbolic simulation. Further, by exploiting the 3–valued modeling capability of the simulator, where the third logic value X indicates an unknown or indeterminate value, the complexity of the symbolic manipulations is reduced considerably.

This verifier supports a verification methodology in which the desired behavior of the circuit is specified in terms of a set of assertions, each describing how a circuit operation modifies some component of the (finite) state or output. The temporal logic allows the user to define such interface details as the clocking methodology and the timing of input and output signals. The combination of timing and state transition information is expressed by an assertion over state trajectories giving properties the circuit state and output should obey at certain times whenever the state and inputs obey some constraints at earlier times. In addition to this abstract behavior specification, the user is also required to describe how the circuit realizes the abstract system state. This mapping is given as an encoding of the abstract state in terms of binary values on circuit nodes at different times in the clock cycle. This form of specification works well for circuits that are normally viewed as state transformation systems, i.e., where each operation is viewed as updating the circuit state. Examples of such systems include memories, data paths and processors. For such systems, the complex analysis permitted by model checkers is not required.

The Underlaying Theory. In this subsection we will highlight the underlying theory for STE. Although the general theory is equally applicable to hardware as software systems, here we will describe a somewhat specialized version tailored specifically to hardware verification. For the more general theory, the reader is referred to [32] and [34]. In symbolic trajectory evaluation the circuit is modeled as operating over logic levels 0, 1, and a third level X representing an undetermined or unknown level. These values can be partially ordered by their "information content" as $X \sqsubseteq 0$ and $X \sqsubseteq 1$, i.e., X conveys no information about the node value, while 0 and 1 are fully defined values. The only constraint placed on the circuit model — apart from the obvious requirement that it accurately represents the physical system — is monotonicity over the information ordering. Intuitively, changing an input from X to a binary value (i.e., 0 or 1) must not cause an observed node to change from a binary value to X or to the opposite binary value. In extending to symbolic simulation, the circuit nodes can take on arbitrary ternary functions over a set of Boolean variables $\mathcal{V}$.

Symbolic circuit evaluation can be thought of as computing circuit behavior for many different operating conditions simultaneously, with each possible assignment of 0 or 1 to the variables in $\mathcal{V}$ indicating a different condition. Formally, this is expressed by defining an assignment ϕ to be a particular mapping from the elements of $\mathcal{V}$ to binary values. A formula F in the logic expresses some property of the circuit in terms of the symbolic variables. It may hold for only a subset $\mathcal{D}$ of the possible assignments. Such a subset can be represented as a Boolean domain function d over $\mathcal{V}$ yielding 1 for precisely the assignments in $\mathcal{D}$. The constant functions 0 and 1, for example, represent the empty and universal sets, respectively. Properties of the system are expressed in a restricted form of temporal logic having just enough expressive power to describe both circuit timing and state transition properties, but remaining simple enough to be checked by an extension of symbolic simulation.

The basic decision algorithm checks only one basic form, the assertion, in the form of an implication $A \Rightarrow C$; the antecedent A gives the stimulus and current state, and the consequent C gives the desired response and state transition. System states and stimuli are given as trajectories over fixed length sequences of states. Each of these trajectories are described with a temporal formula. The temporal logic used here, however, is extremely limited. A formula in this logic is either:

1. UNC (unconstrained);
2. (a) $n = 1$ (a node is equal to 1);
   (b) $n = 0$ (a node is equal to 0),
3. $F_1 \wedge F_2$ (F_1 and F_2 must both hold);
4. $B \rightarrow F$ (the property represented by formula F needs only hold for those assignments satisfying Boolean expression B);
5. NF (F must hold in the following state).

The temporal logic supported by the evaluator is far weaker than that of other model checkers. It lacks such basic forms as disjunction and negation, along with temporal operators expressing properties of unbounded state sequences. The logic was designed as a compromise between expressive power and ease of evaluation. It is powerful enough to express the timing and state transition behavior of circuits, while allowing assertions to be verified by an extended form of symbolic simulation. The constraints placed on assertions make it possible to verify an assertion by a single evaluation of the circuit over a number of circuit states determined by the deepest nesting of the next–time operators. In essence, the circuit is simulated over the unique weakest (in information content) trajectory allowed by the antecedent, while checking that the resulting behavior satisfies the consequent. In this process a Boolean function OK is computed expressing those assignments for which the assertion holds. For a correct circuit, this function should equal 1; otherwise, the negation of the function provides counterexamples. The assertion syntax outlined above is very primitive. To facilitate generating more abstract notations, the specification language can be embedded in a general purpose programming language. When a program in this language is executed, it generates automatically the assertions and carries out the verification process.

6   Conclusions

In this chapter we have overviewed Binary Decision Diagrams and some of their main applications in Formal Hardware Verification. We have described the BDD structure, a graph based representation of Boolean function, and the recursive operators manipulating BDDs.

BDDs can be exponentially more compact than other formalisms, they are a canonical representation, providing constant time equality checks, and efficient symbolic recursive manipulations.

We have then introduced some of the most relevant verification frameworks exploiting BDDs, for combinational as well as sequential circuit verification.

After several years of active research and application within several achademic and industrial tools, BDDs show their main limitation in their potential memory blow-up, with increasing circuit sizes. Still they retain a powerful role for the analysis of abstract representations, or as a slave engine in mixed approaches, combined, for instance, with SAT solvers.

A realistic view of BDDs (and their role in formal hardware verification) is to consider them an essential formalism, and low level technology, for Boolean function representation and manipulation. The ability to provide compact representations for several practical cases, as well as to support state set representations in breadth–first traversals, both represent relevant aspects of BDD usage.

References

1. R. E. Bryant. Graph–Based Algorithms for Boolean Function Manipulation. *IEEE Trans. on Computers*, C–35(8):677–691, August 1986.
2. C. Y. Lee. Representation of Switching Circuits by Binary-Decision Programs. *Bell System Technical Journal*, 38:985–999, July 1959.

3. S. B. Akers. Binary Decision Diagram. *IEEE Trans. on Computers*, C–27(6):509–516, June 1978.
4. R. E. Bryant. Symbolic Boolean Manipulation with Ordered Binary–Decision Diagrams. *ACM Computing Surveys*, 24(3):293–318, September 1992.
5. E. Clarke and R. Kurshan. Computer-Aided Verification. *IEEE Spectrum*, 33(6):61–67, 1996.
6. J. R. Burch, E. M. Clarke, D. E. Long, K. L. McMillan, and D. L. Dill. Symbolic Model Checking for Sequential Circuit Verification. *IEEE Trans. on Computer-Aided Design*, 13(4):401–424, April 1994.
7. E. Clarke, O. Grumberg, and D. Long. Model Checking and Abstraction. In *Proc. ACM Symposium on Principles of Programming Languages*, New York, January 1992.
8. L. Zhang and S. Malik. The Quest for Efficient Boolean Satisfiability Solvers. In Ed Brinksma and Kim Guldstrand Larsen, editors, *Proc. Computer Aided Verification*, volume 2404 of *LNCS*, pages 17–36, Cophenagen, Denmark, 2002.
9. A. J. Hu. Formal Hardware Verification with BDDs: An Introduction. July 1999.
10. H. R. Andersen. An Introduction to Binary Decision Diagrams. In *www.itu.dk/people/hra/bdd97.ps*, October 1997.
11. E.F. Moore and C.E. Shannon. Reliable Circuits Using Less Reliable Relays I. *Journal Franklin Institute*, 262:191–208, September 1956.
12. W. Thomas. Automata on Infinite Objects. In *Handbook of Theoretical Computer Science*, volume B, pages 134–191, The Netherlands and Cambridge - Massachussets, September 1990. MIT Press and Elsevier Science Publishers.
13. R. P. Kurshan. Computer Aided Verification of Coordinating Processes. In *Princeton University Press*, Princeton, NJ, 1994.
14. C.A.R Hoare. Communicating sequential processes. In *Prentice-Hall International series in computer science*, Englewood Cliffs - New Jersey, 1985. Prentice Hall.
15. R. Milner. Communication and Concurrency. In *International Series in Computer Science*. Prentice-Hall International, 1989.
16. E. Clarke and M. Emerson. Synthesis of synchronization skeletons for branching time temporal logic. *Lecture Notes in Computer Science*, 131, May 1981.
17. E.A. Emerson. Temporal and modal logic. pages 997–1072, 1990.
18. R. E. Bryant. A Methodology for Hardware Verification Based on Logic Simulation. *Journal of the Association for Computing Machinery*, 38(2):299–328, 1991.
19. O. Coudert and J. C. Madre. A Unified Framework for the Formal Verification of Sequential Circuits. In *Proc. Int'l Conf. on Computer-Aided Design*, pages 126–129, San Jose, California, November 1990.
20. H. Touati, H. Savoj, B. Lin, R. K. Brayton, and A. Sangiovanni-Vincentelli. Implicit Enumeration of Finite State Machines Using BDDs. In *Proc. Int'l Conf. on Computer-Aided Design*, pages 130–133, San Jose, California, November 1990.
21. J. Queille and J. Sifakis. Specification and verification of concurrent systems in CAESAR. In *Proc. of Fifth ISP*, 1982.
22. A. Pnueli. A temporal logic of concurrent programs. *Theor. Comp. Sci.*, 13:45–60, 1981.
23. Z. Har'El and R. P. Kurshan. Software for analytical development of communications protocols. *AT&T Bell Laboratories Technical Journal*, 69(1):45–59, Jan.-Feb. 1990.
24. R. Cleaveland, J. Parrow, and B. Steffen. The Concurrency Workbench: A semantics-based tool for the verification of concurrent systems. *ACM TOPLAS*, 15(1):36–72, January 1993.

25. A. Roscoe. Model-checking CSP. In A. Roscoe Ed. In *A Classical Mind: Essays in Honour of C.A.R. Hoare*. Prentice-Hall, 1994.

26. J. A. Fernandez, J. Grant, and J. Minker. Model theoretic approach to view updates in deductive databases. *Journal of Automated Reasoning*, 17:171–197, 1996.

27. V. Roy and R. de Simone. Auto and autograph. In *Workshop on Computer Aided Verification*, pages 65–75, New-Brunswick - LNCS 531, June 1990. Spring-Verlag.

28. M. Vardi and P. Wolper. Automata-theoretic techniques for modal logics of programs. *Journal of Computer and Systems Science*, 32:183–221, 1986.

29. A. Tarski. Lattice-theoretic fixpoint theorem and its applications. *Journal Franklin Institute*, 5:285–309, 1955.

30. H. Iwashita, T. Nakata, and F. Hirose. CTL model checking based on forward state traversal. In *Proceedings of the International Conference on Computer-Aided Design*, pages 82–87, San Jose - CA, November 1996.

31. H. Iwashita and T. Nakata. Forward model checking techniques oriented to buggy designs. In *Proceedings of the International Conference on Computer-Aided Design*, pages 400–405, San Jose - CA, November 1997.

32. C.-J. H. Seger and R. E. Bryant. Formal Verification by Symbolic Evaluation of Partially-Ordered Trajectories. *Formal Methods in Systems Design*, 6(1):147–189, 1995.

33. R.E. Bryant. Symbolic Verification of MOS Circuits. *Chapel Hill Conference on VLSI*, pages 419–438, 1985.

34. R.E. Bryant and C-J. Seger. Formal Verification of Digital Circuits Using Symbolic Ternary System Models. *DIMAC Workshop on Computer-Aided Verification*, pages 183–221, June 1990.

SAT-Based Verification Methods and Applications in Hardware Verification

Aarti Gupta, Malay K. Ganai, and Chao Wang

NEC Laboratories America,
Princeton, USA
{agupta, malay, chaowang} at nec-labs dot com

Abstract. Verification methods based on *Boolean Satisfiability (SAT)* have emerged as a promising alternative to BDD-based symbolic model checking methods. This paper provides a tutorial on various SAT-based verification methods we have developed for verifying large hardware designs. We focus separately on methods for finding bugs and for finding proofs for correctness properties, along with highlighting the many common themes that benefit these methods. We also describe practical experiences with these methods implemented in our verification platform called *VeriSol* (formerly *DiVer*), which has been used successfully in industry practice.

1 Introduction

With the growing size and complexity of hardware designs, functional verification has become a bottleneck in the hardware and system development cycle. The cost of detecting bugs late in the design cycle is very high, both in terms of design re-spins and time lost to market. Simulation continues to be the primary workhorse for functional verification, primarily due to its scalability in performing dynamic analysis for a given testcase. However, its main problems are the prohibitive cost of exhaustive coverage and the practical difficulty in assessing good coverage. Formal verification techniques provide a complementary benefit to simulation, where static analysis is performed on a formal mathematical model of the given design, to check its correctness with respect to a given specification under all possible input scenarios. This provides exhaustive coverage, without any testcases, but at the expense of higher complexity of analysis.

Model checking is a formal verification technique for property checking, in which the design is typically modeled as a labeled state transition system, the correctness property is specified as a temporal logic formula, and verification is performed by checking whether the formula is true in the model provided by the design [1]. The practical application of model checking is limited by the state explosion problem, i.e. the state space to be searched grows exponentially with the number of state components in the design. Symbolic model checking techniques [2, 3] typically use methods based on Binary Decision Diagrams (BDDs) [4] to symbolically manipulate sets of states and transitions without explicit enumeration. Though this improves scalability to some degree, these techniques are unable to handle the large problems

M. Bernardo and A. Cimatti (Eds.): SFM 2006, LNCS 3965, pp. 108–143, 2006.

encountered in current industrial practice, mainly due to an explosion in memory requirements for BDDs. As an alternative, verification methods based on *Boolean Satisfiability (SAT)* have emerged as a promising solution. The success of SAT-based verification methods is due primarily to the many recent advances in SAT-solvers [5-8] that have enabled significantly larger problems to be solved in the last decade than ever before [9].

This paper provides a tutorial on the SAT-based verification methods we have developed for the purpose of verifying large scale industry designs. We focus mainly on property checking and model checking methods. (Sequential equivalence checking can be formulated in terms of model checking, and most of the methods described here can apply equally well in that context.) We describe the main technical ideas in relationship to SAT, along with pointers to related work. For a more comprehensive survey on SAT-based verification methods, the interested reader is referred to [10]; a discussion of SAT-based combinational equivalence checking techniques can be found in [11].

Our main classification is based on whether the methods are used for finding bugs (falsification) or for finding proofs (verification)[1]. In the former category, we discuss primarily Bounded Model Checking (BMC) [12] and its enhancements [13-15], while the latter category includes methods based on induction [16, 17], Unbounded Model Checking (UMC) [18-21], and proof-based iterative abstraction [22, 23]. In our experience, both falsification and verification methods are required for handling hardware verification problems in an industry setting. Furthermore, there are many common themes that benefit methods in both categories. In particular, we highlight the benefits of using an efficient circuit representation that supports on-the-fly simplifications [24]. We also exploit a hybrid SAT solver [25] that combines the benefits of circuit-based and CNF-based SAT solving techniques. It is useful for the circuit representation to also support symbolic manipulation through BDDs, and we describe many methods that combine SAT and BDDs to derive their complementary benefits in significantly enhancing the performance or scalability of the overall application. Another common theme is the use of bounded unrolling of the design (also called time frame expansion in related work on automatic test pattern generation [26]) to cast the associated problem as a SAT problem. This has been utilized by many falsification as well as verification methods. We use this feature most effectively for handling embedded memories, where our Embedded Memory Modeling (EMM) techniques abstract out the explicit memory elements, but add the data forwarding and other memory modeling constraints at each step of the unrolling [27]. This avoids the state space explosion of modeling the memory state, while preserving the accuracy of verification. Again, the EMM techniques have been used in both falsification [27] as well as verification methods [28].

We also describe practical experiences with these methods implemented in our verification platform called *VeriSol* (formerly *DiVer*), which has been used successfully in industry practice for the last four years to verify large hardware designs [29]. In addition to verifying correctness properties specified by a user on

---

[1] Although these categories correspond quite naturally to *bounded* and *unbounded* verification, respectively, we would like to avoid overloading the term *bounded*, since many verification methods we describe here use bounded design unrolling for unbounded verification.

RTL (Register Transfer Level) designs, it has also been used for checking automatically generated properties. Specifically, *VeriSol* has been integrated within a high level behavioral synthesis system called *Cyber* [30]. The *Cyber* system automatically generates RTL designs from high-level behavioral descriptions. In addition, it automatically generates correctness properties for these RTL designs also. The back-end property checking for *Cyber* can be performed by *VeriSol*. We have also added the capability of generating automatic correctness properties for typical Verilog RTL designs.

More recently, we have also used many of our SAT-based verification methods for performing the back-end verification in a system called *F-Soft*, which is targeted for verifying software programs [31, 32]. The *F-Soft* verification platform combines several recent advances in formal verification, including SAT-based verification, static analyses, and predicate abstraction. Basically, we accurately model the program behavior as a finite state symbolic model (under assumptions of finite data and control), use static analyses to reduce the size of the verification model, and perform back-end model checking using *VeriSol*. Although we will not describe the software verification applications in this paper, it is interesting to note that by adding several customized heuristics for software, our SAT-based methods in *VeriSol* could be applied successfully for verifying models generated from software programs.

Finally, we would like to note that there has been a lot of interest in applying SAT solver techniques to decision procedures for richer logics, such as quantifier-free fragments of first order logic [33, 34] . In our own work, we have proposed new solvers for difference logic, called SLICE [35] and SDSAT [36]. Since SAT solvers and such decision procedures provide essential components of many theorem provers, the SAT-based verification methods described here can be naturally extended to provide a bridge from model checking to theorem proving applications.

The paper is organized as follows. Section 2 briefly reviews the terminology and background for the basic SAT algorithms and model checking techniques. Section 3 describes the SAT-based verification methods, while their applications for hardware verification in a practical industry setting are described in Section 4. Finally, we conclude in Section 5.

2 Background

2.1 Boolean Satisfiability (SAT) Problem

The Boolean Satisfiability (SAT) problem is a well-known constraint satisfaction problem, with many applications in the fields of VLSI Computer-Aided Design (CAD) and Artificial Intelligence. Given a propositional formula, the Boolean Satisfiability problem is to determine whether there exists a variable assignment under which the formula evaluates to true. The SAT problem is known to be NP-Complete [37]. In practice, there has been tremendous progress in SAT solver technology over the years, summarized in a survey [9].

Most SAT solvers use a Conjunctive Normal Form (CNF) representation of the Boolean formula. In CNF, the formula is represented as a conjunction of clauses, each clause is a disjunction of literals, and a literal is a variable or its negation. Note that in order for the formula to be satisfied, each clause must also be satisfied, i.e., evaluate to true. A Boolean circuit can be encoded as a satisfiability equivalent CNF formula [38]. Alternatively, for SAT applications arising from the circuit domain, the SAT solver may be modified to work directly on the Boolean circuit representation.

```
SAT_Solve(P=1) { // Check if constraint P=1 satisfiable?
    while(Decide()=SUCCESS) //Selects a new variable
        while(Deduce()=CONFLICT)//BCP till conflict/no-conflict
            if (Diagnose()=FAILURE) //Add conflict learnt clause(s)
                return UNSAT;//Conflict found at decision level 0
    return SAT;} //No more decision to make
```

Fig. 1. DPLL style SAT Solver

Most modern SAT solvers are based on a DPLL-style [39] as shown in Figure 1 with three main engines: *decision, deduction,* and *diagnosis.* All these engines have seen remarkable progress in the last few years, e.g. the VSIDS decision heuristic and the lazy two-literal watching scheme for deduction in Chaff [6], and the conflict analysis and conflict-driven learning in Grasp [5]. Conflict-driven learning results in addition of *conflict clauses* to the SAT problem in order to prevent the same conflict from occurring again during the search. Additionally, information recorded during conflict analysis has been used very effectively to provide a proof when a formula is determined to be unsatisfiable by the SAT solver. This proof can be independently checked to verify the SAT solver itself [40, 41]. These techniques can also be easily adapted to identify a subset of clauses from the original problem, called the *unsatisfiable core* [40, 42], such that these clauses are sufficient for implying unsatisfiability. The use of such techniques in verification methods are described in more detail in Section 3.2.2.

2.2 Circuit-Based and Hybrid SAT Solvers

SAT has many applications in the logic circuit domain, such as automatic test pattern generation (ATPG), verification, timing analysis. The Boolean problem in these applications is typically derived from the circuit structure. This has also led to interest in circuit-based SAT solvers [43-45] that work directly on the circuit structure, and use circuit-specific heuristics to guide the search. In general, attempts to include circuit structure information into CNF-based SAT solvers have been unsuccessful due to their significant overhead.

Before we compare circuit-based and CNF-based SAT solvers, it is instructive to consider how each performs Boolean Constraint Propagation (BCP) which constitutes the core of most deduction engines, and typically consumes 80% of the SAT runtime. Circuit-based BCP is typically performed by using a lookup table for fast implication propagation [45]. Based on the current values of the inputs and output of the circuit node, the lookup table determines the next "state" of the gate where the state encapsulates any implied values and the next action to be taken for the node. The implication algorithm is iterated over the entire circuit graph. For each vertex, it determines new implied values and the direction for further processing. As an example, Figure 2 (from [45]) shows some cases from the implication lookup table for a two-input AND gate. Note that only one case, a logical *0* at the output of an AND vertex, requires a new case split to be scheduled for justification. All other cases either cause a conflict and backtracking, or further implications, or a return to process the next element to be justified. Due to its low overhead, this table lookup-based implication algorithm is very efficient in practice.

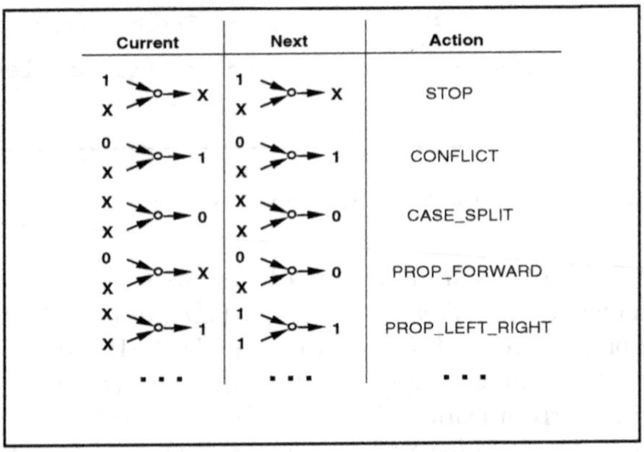

Fig. 2. Lookup Table for Fast Implication Propagation on a 2-input AND Gate

For CNF-based BCP, consider the *lazy two-literal watching scheme* proposed by Chaff [6] :

- For each clause, only two literals are monitored for state change.
- The clause state is updated lazily when a variable is assigned, i.e., only when the two monitored literals coincide.
- It does not require state change for clauses during the backtracking process, thus unassigning a variable takes constant time.

For clauses with many literals, this lazy update works significantly better than other BCP schemes like those in SATO [7], and GRASP [5]. It avoids unnecessary lookups for a clause, thereby significantly improving the underlying cache behavior and the resulting performance.

To get back to the comparison between circuit-based and CNF-based BCP, note that there is an inherent overhead built into the translation of circuit gates into clauses. A two-input gate translates to three clauses in the CNF approach, while in the circuit-based approach a gate is regarded as a monolithic entity. Therefore, in the circuit approach an implication across a gate requires a single table lookup, while in the CNF approach it requires processing multiple clauses. In addition, the CNF-based BCP in Chaff does not keep track of the clauses that have been satisfied in order to reduce overheads. However, there is an inherent cost associated with visiting the satisfied clauses. Specifically, even if a clause gets satisfied due to an assignment to some un-watched literal, the watched literal pointers could still get updated. Overall, for the generally small clauses arising from circuit gates, these differences translate to significant differences in BCP time, usually in favor of the circuit-based approach.

On the other hand, learned conflict clauses arising from conflict analysis are typically much larger than those arising from two-input gates. Adding a large learned clause as a gate tree can lead to a significant increase in the size of the circuit. This in turn, can increase the number of implications, thereby negating any potential gains obtained from circuit-based BCP. For such clauses, it is more useful to maintain them as monolithic clauses and take advantage of CNF-based two-literal watching and lazy update to process them efficiently.

Based on these observations, we proposed a hybrid SAT solver [25] to combine the relative benefits of CNF-based and circuit-based SAT solvers. In our scheme, the original circuit problem is represented as a gate-level netlist, while the learned conflict clauses are represented in CNF. The hybrid BCP engine consists of table lookups for the gates, and a Chaff-style two-literal watching scheme for the conflict clauses, thereby combining the advantages of both. Furthermore, a hybrid representation of the Boolean problem also allows exploitation of both circuit-based and CNF-based decision heuristics. In particular, we effectively exploit the justification frontier heuristic [43], which restricts the decision nodes to be those that justify the values on their fanout node. The use of this heuristic further improves performance in many practical instances of SAT problems arising in circuit applications. We typically obtained speedup by a factor of two, in comparison to a pure CNF-based approach. Since SAT is a core engine in many verification applications like equivalence checking and BMC, a consistent speedup can prove to be very significant in practice. Furthermore, any future improvements in the performance of circuit-based and CNF-based SAT solvers can directly translate into improvements of the hybrid SAT solver as well.

In related work, Kuehlmann et al. [46] used circuit-based SAT in combination with other useful techniques like BDD sweeping and dynamic circuit transformation for combinational equivalence checking. However, they did not propose any effective way to perform conflict-driven learning with conflict clauses represented as large OR-tree circuits. Other more recent efforts have also combined the advantages of multiple symbolic representations including circuit graphs, SAT, and BDDs [47, 48], and used these ideas along with additional conflict-driven learning, in order to improve the SAT solver performance [11].

2.3 Model Checking

In model checking [1], the design is typically modeled as a labeled state transition system, the property is specified as a temporal logic formula, and verification consists of checking whether the formula is true in that model. Temporal logics are very useful for specifying dynamic behavior over time. Different variants of temporal logics have become popular, such as Linear Temporal Logic (LTL) and Computation Tree Logic (CTL), depending on whether a linear or a branching view of time is considered, respectively. In this paper, we focus mainly on simple safety properties, denoted as AGp. This formula specifies that on $all(A)$ paths of a system, $globally (G)$ in each state of the path, the property p holds. Such properties can be verified by an exhaustive traversal of the state space to check that p holds in every reachable state. This state space traversal forms the computational core of most model checking techniques.

Explicit state model checkers, such as SPIN [49], use an explicit representation of the states and transitions in the system, and enumerate all reachable states explicitly. They utilize many additional techniques such as state hashing for compaction of state representations, and partial order methods to avoid exploring all interleavings of concurrent processes. The scalability issue in explicit state enumeration makes these checkers unsuitable for hardware designs, although they have found practical success in verification of controllers and software. In contrast, symbolic model checkers, such as SMV [3], avoid an explicit enumeration of the state space by using symbolic representations of sets of states and transitions. They typically use BDDs, which provide a canonical representation of Boolean formulas and efficient symbolic manipulation algorithms. For hardware designs, where these symbolic representations effectively capture the regularity in the state-space, symbolic model checking has significantly extended the ability to handle large state spaces.

The core steps in symbolic model checking are the *image/pre-image computations*, which compute the set of states reachable in one step from/to a given set of states via the transition relation, as follows:

$$Img(Y) = S_N(Y) = \exists X, W.\ S_C(X) \wedge T(X, Y, W) \tag{1}$$

$$PreImg\ (X) = S_C(X) = \exists Y, W.\ S_N(Y) \wedge T(X, Y, W) \tag{2}$$

Here, the variable sets X, Y, W, denote the present state, next state, and primary input variables, respectively; and S_C, S_N and T denote the next states, the current states, and the transition relation, respectively. When these state sets and the transition relation are represented symbolically as BDDs (or its variants), these computations can be performed symbolically by using the BDD-based operations for conjoining and existential quantification. However, for many large designs, these BDD-based operations can cause a blow up in memory size.

A basic algorithm for symbolic model checking simple safety properties can be formulated as shown in Figure 3. Let B be the set of bad states, in which property p does not hold, and I the set of initial states. It represents sets of states symbolically, and searches for bad states in breadth first order starting from the initial states.

```
1.  model-check(I,T,B)
2.      S_C =∅; S_N = I;
3.      while S_C ≠ S_N  do
4.          S_C = S_N ;
5.          if B ∩ S_C  ≠ ∅  then
6.              return ``found counter-example'';
7.          S_N = S_C ∪ Img(S_C);
8.      done;
9.  return ``no bad state reachable'';
```

Fig. 3. Forward model checking algorithm for simple safety properties

This forward model checking algorithm starts at the initial states and searches forward along the transition relation, relying on the symbolic image computation described earlier. Similarly, there are backward model checking algorithms, which search backward from the bad states, and rely on the symbolic pre-image computation.

3 SAT-Based Verification Methods

We start by describing methods specialized for finding bugs in hardware designs. Most of these are based on the Bounded Model Checking (BMC) framework proposed by Biere *et al.* [12]. In the second half of this section, we focus on methods targeted for finding proofs. Many of these use our efficient BMC framework and add techniques on top to provide completeness of verification. We also describe additional techniques for proof-based abstraction and unbounded model checking using SAT.

3.1 Methods for Finding Bugs

Despite the considerable benefits of symbolic model checking using BDDs, the basic *verification* approach of exhaustive analysis does not scale well in practice. An alternative is the use of *falsification* approaches which focus primarily on the search for finding bugs. One of the most popular falsification approaches is Bounded Model Checking (BMC) [12]. We describe the basic BMC framework, followed by various performance enhancements, and a distributed BMC framework useful for overcoming memory limitations of a single workstation environment. We also describe EMM techniques which allow efficient handling of embedded memories in hardware designs for BMC applications.

3.1.1 Bounded Model Checking (BMC)

In BMC, the problem of searching for a counter-example of length k is translated to a Boolean formula such that the formula is *satisfiable* if and only if there exists a counter-example of length k. Effectively, the translation to a Boolean formula is performed by unrolling the transition relation of the design for k time frames, and adding appropriate constraints due to the property. The satisfiability check is typically performed by using a Boolean SAT solver in the back-end.

In this paper, we consider the following notation and formulation of BMC. The design is described as a *Kripke* structure $M = (S, I, T, L)$, with a finite set of states S, a set of initial states I, a transition relation between states T, and a labeling L of states with atomic propositions. Let $T(x,y,w,z)$ denote the symbolic transition relation in terms of present state variables x, next state variables y, primary input variables w, and intermediate variables z. Let y_k denote the symbolic state (in terms of latch variables) after k time frames in the unrolled design. In addition, we can also consider environmental constraints on variables (signals) e in the design, which are required to hold in every time frame.

Definition 1. We use the following Boolean formula, denoted $BMC(M,f,k)$, to check the existence of a k-length witness for property f:

$$BMC(M, f, k) = I(y_0) \land {}_{1 \le j \le k} [\, T(x_j, y_j, w_j, z_j) \land (\, y_{j-1} = x_j \,)] \land {}_{0 \le j \le k} [Env(e_j)] \land \langle f \rangle_k$$

Here, the different sets of constraints are described as follows:

1. $I(y_0)$: Initial state constraints on initial state y_0
2. $T(x_j, y_j, w_j, z_j)$: Transition relation constraints for time frame j, $1 \leq j \leq k$
3. $(y_{j-1} = x_j)$: Latch interface propagation constraints, $1 \leq j \leq k$, which capture the propagation of latch inputs in one time frame to the latch outputs in the next time frame
4. $Env(e_j)$: Environmental constraints on signals e in each time frame j, $0 \leq j \leq k$
5. $\langle f \rangle_k$: Constraints due to property translation of formula f in time frames up to k

Verification typically proceeds by looking for witnesses or counter-examples (CE) of increasing length until some *completeness threshold* [12, 50] is reached. The overall algorithm of a SAT-based BMC procedure for checking (or falsifying) a simple safety property *AG p* is shown in Figure 4, where *Unroll* corresponds to an unrolling of the symbolic transition relation of the design, and *P* corresponds to the circuit representation of the proposition *p*. Note that the SAT problems generated by the BMC translation procedure grow bigger as k increases. Therefore, the practical efficiency of the backend SAT solver becomes critical in enabling deeper searches to be performed.

```
BMC(k,P){//Falsify safety property AG p within bound k
    for (int i=0; i<=k ; i++) {
        Pᵢ=Unroll(P,i);//Get property p at iᵗʰ unrolled frame
        if (SAT_Solve(Pᵢ=0)=SAT) return CE; //Try to falsify
    }
    return NO_CE; } //No counter-example found
```

Fig. 4. SAT-based BMC for Safety Property *AG p*

Since BMC was first proposed, several methods have improved upon the basic BMC framework described above. These include use of variable ordering techniques to guide the decision heuristics of the back-end SAT solver [51], use of incremental SAT solvers to exploit the learning across related problems in SAT-based BMC [52, 53], as well as improved techniques for finding completeness thresholds [54, 55]. We now describe in detail our BMC enhancements, along with related work.

3.1.2 Performance Enhancements for BMC

Circuit Simplification. In our BMC implementation, we use circuit simplification techniques to build the transition relation of the design and for unrolling it during the course of property checking. The main motivation is to simplify the generated SAT problems in order to reduce the overall verification time. Furthermore, we have found that circuit simplification techniques are more efficient in handling of constants, in comparison to constant propagation within CNF-based SAT decision procedures. Such constants arise due to initial state and environmental constraints involving constant values on flip-flops ($I(y_0)$ and $Env(e_j)$ constraints in Definition 1 above), and learned constant constraints added during property checking. Circuit simplification is achieved by using a non-canonical two-input AND/INVERTER graph representation [56], and an on-the-fly reduction algorithm [24, 45] on such a graph representation.

Hybrid SAT Solver. We also use a hybrid SAT solver (described in Section 2.2) as the back-end SAT solver for our BMC applications. In addition to the performance benefits, it also provides us memory savings, since it avoids the need for maintaining a separate CNF representation of the unrolled design. We have also implemented incremental SAT solving techniques in our hybrid SAT solver to take advantage of our incremental formlations of the BMC problem, described below.

Customized Property Translations. We use customized property translations for the LTL formulas ($\langle f \rangle_k$ constraints in Definition 1 above) [15]. Rather than generating a monolithic SAT formula as in standard BMC, our property translations can be viewed as building the SAT formula incrementally, by lazily indexing over the bounded conjunctions/disjunctions, terminating early when possible. Though the standard BMC procedure also partitions the overall problem into separate k-instances, in our customized translation we further partition each k-instance problem into multiple, smaller SAT sub-problems. To mitigate the overhead due to multiple problems, we use an incremental SAT solver in the back-end. Additionally, our property partitioning is formulated in a way that facilitates the following kinds of SAT-based learning:

- **Learning from shared constraints (L1):** Given two SAT instances S_1 and S_2, conflict clauses that are deduced solely from the set of constraints shared between S_1 and S_2 can be used as learned clauses while solving S_1 or S_2 [52, 57].
- **Learning from satisfiable results (L2):** Suppose $\{\varphi_1, ..., \varphi_n\}$ represents a series of SAT problems where problem φ_i is built incrementally by adding and removing constraints to and from φ_{i-1} respectively. The satisfying solution for φ_{i-1} (if it exists) can be used to guide SAT decision engine to solve φ_i [57].
- **Learning from unsatisfiable results (L3):** Let a SAT problem Φ be a disjunction of sub-problems $\{\varphi_1, ..., \varphi_n\}$. Instead of solving Φ as a monolithic problem, one can solve φ_i starting from $i=1$ with the additional constraint $C_i = \neg\varphi_1 \wedge ... \wedge \neg\varphi_{i-1}$ where each φ_j is unsatisfiable for all $j < i$. More benefit will be potentially obtained when the problem φ_i shares more with the additional constraint C_i, thereby, allowing $L1$ learning.

In a standard BMC procedure, there is a considerable overlap of circuit constraints due to unrolled transition relations between a k-instance and a $(k+1)$-instance of the BMC problem. Some researchers have applied L1 learning across k-instances [52, 57] while some researchers have used L3 learning for safety properties to reduce the overall verification time [58]. In our customized BMC translations, sharing occurs not just between the circuit constraints due to the unrolled transition relation, but also between the constraints arising from our property translations and between constraints learned from unsatisfiable SAT sub-problems. In order to take advantage of incremental SAT techniques, our property translations are geared toward an incremental formulation, i.e. reuse of variables and constraints wherever possible.

This allows use of incremental SAT learning techniques L1, L2 and L3 in the SAT solver very effectively. In contrast, the standard property translation in BMC does not provide such an incremental formulation of the property constraints.

Experimental Results. We briefly describe the results of some experiments (performed on a workstation with 2.8 GHz Xeon Processors with 4GB running Red Hat Linux 7.2) to show the benefits of our customized translation for checking liveness properties on industry designs D1-D3. These are bus core designs with multiple masters and slaves. The properties are of the type "request should be eventually followed by acknowledge or error". We compare various learning schemes i.e. NL (no learning), L1+L3, L2+L3, and L1+L2+L3 in our customized approach, called custom. We also compare them against standard BMC in VIS [59], called standard. For fair comparison, we use the same SAT heuristics in our SAT solver as those used in the backend SAT solver (zChaff [6]) in VIS BMC. We present the comparison results in Table 1. Columns 2-4 show the characteristics of the designs in Column 1, i.e., number of flip-flops, primary inputs and gates, respectively; Column 5 shows the length of counter example (CEX); Columns 6-9 and 10 report the time taken by (in seconds) our customized translation with different learning schemes, and the standard translation, respectively. Clearly, our customized translation is able to find counterexamples far quicker than the standard monolithic translation. Moreover, the various learning schemes improve the performance of BMC significantly.

Table 1. BMC Performance Improvements due to Customized Translations

D	#FF	#PI	#G	CEX (D)	Custom (DiVer)				Standard (VIS)
					NL	L1,3	L2,3	L1,2,3	
D1	2316	76	14655	19	2.3	2.2	2.3	2	77
D2	2563	88	16686	22	11.2	8.9	11.7	8	201
D3	2810	132	18740	28	730	290	862	240	2728

BDD Learning. As demonstrated by the recent SAT solvers, learned clauses play a crucial role in determining performance, both by pruning the search space, and by affecting the choice of decision variables.   In addition to the incremental SAT learning opportunities described above, we use an additional technique [13] for using learned clauses automatically generated from a BDD-based analysis. We call this BDD Learning. Essentially, a BDD is used to capture the relationship between Boolean variables of (a part of) the SAT problem, in the form of a characteristic function. In such a BDD, each path to a "0" (false) node denotes a conflict. A learned clause corresponding to this conflict is easily obtained by negating the literals that define the path. Since a BDD captures all paths to 0, i.e. all possible conflicts, the potential advantage is that multiple learned clauses can be generated and added to the SAT solver at the same time. In contrast, a SAT solver typically analyzes a single conflict at a time, thereby generating a single learned clause. An example with multiple learned clauses generated from a BDD is shown in Figure 5.

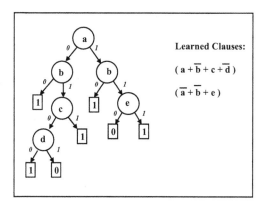

Fig. 5. Example of Learned Clauses from BDD Learning

In BMC, or any circuit-based application involving time frame expansion, the bulk of the constraints that define the SAT problem arise from the k-times unrolled transition relation of the design. Therefore, the transition relation is a natural candidate for the application of BDD Learning, i.e. BDDs are generated for "seed" nodes in the circuit structure graph corresponding to the transition relation (either before or after unrolling). At the same time, there is an overhead associated with the addition of each learned clause, e.g. during BCP. Due to this potential overhead of adding too many learned clauses, the choice of the seed nodes becomes crucial. To ensure a good tradeoff between the usefulness and the overheads of adding learned clauses, we experimented with the following kinds of learning:

- *Static learning*: seed nodes are selected using static information, and learned clauses are added statically, before the SAT solver starts the search.
- *Dynamic learning*: seed nodes are selected using dynamic SAT information, and learned clauses are added on-the-fly, during the SAT search.

In static learning, the seed selections will tend to reflect only the circuit structure information, while for dynamic learning they will also reflect the dynamic state of the SAT solver. Clearly, it is easier to integrate static learning with a SAT solver. On the other hand, we found that dynamic learning is crucial in attaining a good balance in the tradeoff between the usefulness and overhead of adding learned clauses. In our experimental results, we obtained up to 73% reduction in runtime, allowing us to perform deeper searches (with up to 45% more time frames) within the allotted time.

Additional Constraints from BDD-based Reachability Analysis. Another BDD-based technique that we have used very successfully with SAT-based methods is the addition of external constraints (not necessarily from conflicts) generated by performing BDD-based reachability analysis. While BDD-based reachability analysis provides a complete verification method, it works only on small models. On the other hand, SAT-based BMC can handle much larger models, but it is incomplete in practice. Conservative abstractions, i.e. abstractions that over-approximate the paths in concrete models, are the key in providing a link between the two. In particular, we use conservative approximations of reachable state sets, computed as BDDs, as additional constraints in BMC. Other related efforts have also used BDD-based enlarged targets [54], and BDD-based approximate reachability state sets [60], but only in searching for counterexamples with BMC. Our application of this idea in helping derive proofs by induction is described later in Section 3.2.1.

Since the BDD constraints for BMC are required to be over-approximations, we obtain "existential" abstractions of the design by considering some latches in the concrete design as pseudo-primary inputs. For example, we abstract away latches farther in the dependency closure of the property signals, identified by localization techniques [61]. Given a conservative abstract model, and a correctness property, we use exact or approximate symbolic model checking techniques to generate the BDD constraints. For example, for simple safety properties, we store the union of the state sets computed iteratively by the pre-image operation, backwards from the set of bad states, as shown in Figure 6 (a). We also store the union of the state sets in the forward reachability analysis, starting from the initial state, as shown in Figure 6 (b).

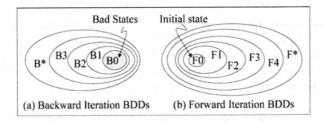

(a) Backward Iteration BDDs   (b) Forward Iteration BDDs

Fig. 6. Generation of BDD Reachability Constraints

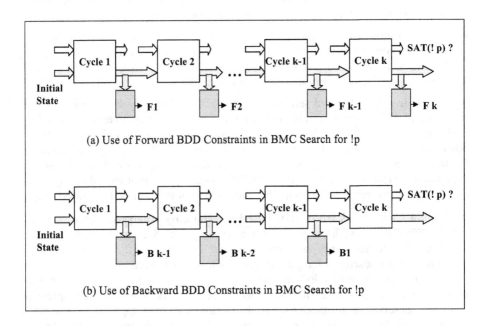

(a) Use of Forward BDD Constraints in BMC Search for !p

(b) Use of Backward BDD Constraints in BMC Search for !p

Fig. 7. Use of BDD Constraints in BMC

We convert each BDD to either a gate-level circuit or a CNF formula, where each internal BDD node is regarded as a multiplexor controlled by that node's variable. The size of the resulting circuit or CNF formula is linear in the size of the BDD, due to introduction of extra CNF variables for each BDD node. We use BDD reordering heuristics as well as over-approximation methods to keep down the BDD sizes. Finally, we use the BDD constraints as additional constraints on the state variables at each (or some) cycle of the unrolled design during BMC, as shown by dark boxes in Figure 7. Note that while these constraints are redundant, in practice they can improve the efficiency of the back-end SAT solver and allow deeper searches for bugs.

3.1.3 Distributed SAT and Distributed BMC

In SAT-based BMC the problems get larger as the depth of unrolling increases. Sometimes, the memory limitation of a single server, rather than SAT solver performance, can become a bottleneck for doing deeper BMC search for bugs. We have proposed methods for distributing SAT and distributing the BMC computation over a network of workstations (e.g. connected by Ethernet LAN) to overcome this memory limitation, albeit at increased communication cost and some performance overhead [14].

Our distributed methods use a master/client model where each client has an exclusive partition of the SAT problem and uses knowledge of the distributed partition topology to communicate with other clients. Due to the design unrolling, a BMC problem provides a natural linear partitioning of the overall SAT problem, thereby suggesting a linear topology for configuing the computing resources. An example topology using one master and several clients is shown in Figure 8. Each client C_i hosts a part of the unrolled design in BMC, e.g., from n_i+1 to an n_{i+1} where n_i represents the partition depth. Each C_i (except for the terminal clients) is connected to C_{i+1} and C_{i-1}. The master is connected to each of the clients. Using a linear topology, we can also distribute parts of the unrolled design dynamically over additional clients as and when memory resources on current clients get close to exhaustion.

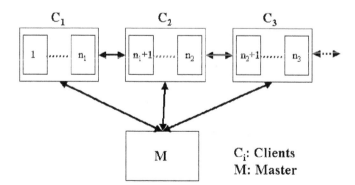

Fig. 8. Distributed BMC Configuration with Master/Clients

For distributed SAT, the master controls the overall execution between the parallelized decision, deduction, and diagnosis engines. The decision engine is distributed in a way such that each client selects a good local variable and the master then chooses the globally best variable to branch on. During the deduction phase, each client performs BCP on its exclusive local partitions, and communicates implications on the common variables to its neighboring clients. The master performs BCP on the global pool of learned conflict clauses, and also communicates the implications to all the clients. Diagnosis is performed by the master, and each client performs a local backtrack when requested by the master. Note that the master does not keep all problem clauses and variables; however, the master maintains the global assignment stack and the global state for diagnosis. This requires much less memory than the entire problem data.

Though this work is closely related to [62], there are some important differences. In that approach, although each client has a disjoint set of clauses, the variables are not shared in any set pattern. Therefore, each client broadcasts its implications to all other clients after completing the local BCP. In a communication network implementation like ours (unlike the application specific processor framework considered in [62]) broadcasting all these implications can be a significant overhead. In our improved distributed BCP, however, each client has knowledge of the topology of the SAT-problem partitioning, and uses it to communicate with other clients. This ensures that the receiving client has to never read a message that is not meant for it. To ensure proper execution of the parallel algorithm, each client is required to be synchronized. In addition, we use several optimization schemes to reduce the effect of communication overhead on performance in general-purpose networks by identifying and executing tasks in parallel while messages are in transit. For a large industry design with ~13K flip-flops and ~0.5Million gates, our distributed BMC approach enabled us to search up to a depth of 323 with only 30% communication overhead, while we could analyze only up to 120 time frames in a single workstation environment before running out of memory.

3.1.4 Efficient Memory Modeling (EMM) for Finding Bugs

Designs with large embedded memories have wide application in the industry. However, such designs add further complexity to formal verification tasks due to an exponential increase in the state space for each additional memory bit. For BMC, with each time frame unrolling of a design, the search space becomes prohibitively large to analyze beyond a reasonable depth. In order to make BMC more useful, it is important to have some abstraction of the memories. However, for finding real bugs, it is sufficient that the abstraction techniques capture the memory semantics [63] without explicitly modeling each memory bit.

To capture the memory semantics, Burch and Dill introduced the interpreted *read* and *write* operations in their logic of equality with un-interpreted functions (EUF) [63] instead of an un-interpreted abstraction of memories. These interpreted functions are used to represent the memory symbolically by creating nested *if-then-else* (ITE) expressions to record the history of writes to the memory. Such interpretated functions have also been exploited in later derivative verification efforts [64, 65]. More recently, Bryant *et al.* proposed the logic of Counter arithmetic with Lambda expressions and Un-interpreted functions (CLU) to model infinite-state systems and unbounded memory in the UCLID system [66]. Memory is modeled as a functional expression whose body changes with time step. Similar to [63], the memory is represented symbolically by creating nested ITE expressions, which are translated by the CLU decision procedure and handled by a back-end SAT solver.

Our EMM approach [27] is similar to the abstract interpretation of memory that captures its data forwarding semantics, i.e., a data read from a memory location is same as the most recent data written at the same location. We construct a BMC problem instance as follows. For our discussion, assume a single port memory with the following interface signals: Address Bus (*Addr*), Write Data Bus (*WD*), Read Data Bus (*RD*), Write Enable (*WE*), and Read Enable (*RE*). Assume that the *write* phase of the memory requires one clock cycle, i.e., in the current clock cycle when the data value is assigned to *WD* bus, write address location is assigned to *Addr* bus and *WE* signal is made active, then the new data is available in the next clock cycle. The *read* phase of memory is regarded as a same cycle event, i.e., when the read address location is assigned to *Addr* bus and the *RE* is made active, the read data is assigned to *RD* bus in the same clock cycle. Assume that we unroll the design up to depth k. Let S^j denote a memory interface signal variable S at time frame j. Let the Boolean variable E^{ij} denote the address comparison between time frames i and j, defined as $E^{ij}=(Addr^i=Addr^j)$. Then the forwarding semantics of the memory can be expressed as:

$$RD^k = \{WD^j \mid E^{jk}=1 \wedge WE^j=1 \wedge RE^k=1 \wedge \forall_{j<i<k}(E^{ik}=0 \vee WE^i=0)\}, \ where \ j<k \qquad (3)$$

In other words, data read at depth k equals the data written at depth j if memory addresses are equal at k and j, write enable is active at j, read enable is active at k, and for all depths i between j and k, either the address at i is different from that at k or the write enable at i is inactive.

Note that the BMC problem instance is generated by eliminating memory arrays but retaining the memory interface signals in the design, and adding memory-modeling constraints on those signals at every depth of unrolling to preserve the semantics of the memory. The additional novelty of our EMM approach is that the formulation of the memory-modeling constraints (not shown here) capture the exclusivity of a read and write pair explicitly, i.e., when a SAT-solver decides on a valid read and write pair, other pairs are *implied invalid immediately*, thereby reducing the SAT solve time. Furthermore, we use a hybrid circuit-based and CNF-based representation of these constraints, where their size depends linearly on the bus widths of memory interface signals and quadratically on the number of memory accesses. Since the unrolling depth of BMC bounds the number of memory accesses, the size of these constraints is significantly smaller than an explicit modeling of the memory state in BMC. We can also apply the EMM approach for handling multiple memories, with multiple read and write ports [28].

The modified BMC algorithm using EMM is shown in Figure 9. The memory modeling constraints are generated by the procedure *EMM_Constraints*, which is invoked after every unrolling. The updated constraints C^i in line 5 capture the forwarding semantics of the memory up to depth i very efficiently using hybrid symbolic representations, i.e., 2-input gates and CNF clauses, in order to improve the SAT solve time. We have experimented with our EMM method on a number of hardware and software designs with large embedded memories, where we have obtained at least an order of magnitude improvement (both in time and space) using our method over explicit modeling of each memory bit. We have also shown that the particular form of our memory modeling constraints boosts the performance of the SAT solver significantly, in comparison to the conventional way of modeling these constraints as nested *if-then-else* expressions [63, 66].

```
BMC-EMM (n, P) { // BMC with EMM
    C⁻¹=ϕ; // initialize memory modeling constraints
    for (int i=0; i<=n ; i++) {
        Pⁱ = Unroll(P,i); // get property node at iᵗʰ unrolling
        Cⁱ = Cⁱ⁻¹ ∪ EMM_Constraints(i); // update the constraints
        if (SAT_Solve(I∧¬Pⁱ∧Cⁱ)=SAT) return CE;}
    return NO_CE; } // no counter-example found
```

Fig. 9. SAT-based BMC with Efficient Memory Modeling (EMM)

3.2 Methods for Finding Proofs

In this section we describe SAT-based methods targeted for finding proofs. These methods can prove the correctness of a property on a design, as well as find counter-examples for failing properties. The method may or may not be complete, i.e. it may not be able to prove every correct property. We describe induction-based methods that have been found useful for proving safety properties. Next, we describe abstraction-refinement methods, where SAT-based BMC is used primarily for abstraction or refinement, and is supplemented by other techniques for obtaining proofs on the abstract models. We also describe the application of induction and proof-based abstraction in the context of our EMM approach, for finding proofs for embedded memory designs. Finally, we describe SAT-based methods that directly implement unbounded model checking. Many of these replace or supplement the use of BDDs by SAT solvers in traditional symbolic model checking techniques. In principle, completeness of verification can also be achieved by making the transition from SAT to solvers for Quantified Boolean Formulas (QBF) – we do not discuss QBF-based techniques here.

3.2.1 SAT-Based Induction

Induction with increasing depth k, and restriction to loop-free paths, provides a complete proof technique for safety properties and has been proposed for use with SAT solvers [16, 67]. Induction with depth k consists of the following two steps:

- Base step: to prove that the property holds on every k-length path starting from the initial state.

- Inductive step: to prove that if the property holds on a k-length path starting from any arbitrary state, then it also holds on all its extensions to a $(k+1)$-length path.

The restriction to loop-free paths imposes the constraints that no two states in a path are identical.

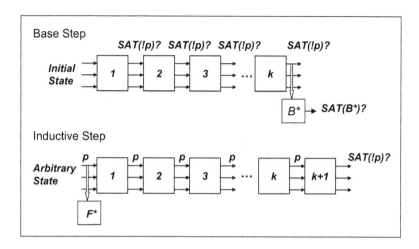

Fig. 10. Proof by Induction using SAT-based BMC (with BDD Constraints)

We use the BMC framework for performing a proof by induction, as shown pictorially in Figure 10 for the safety property AGp. (For the moment, disregard the boxes labeled $B*$ and $F*$.) For the base step, the satisfiability of *negated p* is checked at each cycle up to k, starting from the initial state. If it is satisfiable, then the property is proved to be false. If it is not, then the inductive step is carried out. For the inductive step, it is assumed that the property p holds at the first k cycles, starting from an arbitrary state, and satisfiability of *negated p* is checked at the $(k+1)^{th}$ cycle. If it is unsatisfiable, then the induction proof is complete, and the property is proved to be true. However, if it is satisfiable, then the verification is incomplete. In this case, the depth of induction (k) can be increased, and the proof steps repeated, until the longest loop-free paths have been examined.

Note that the base step includes use of the initial state constraint, but the inductive step does not. Therefore, the inductive step may search through unreachable states also. In practice, this may not allow the induction proof to go through at small depths, i.e. the proof may need stronger induction invariants than the property itself. In general, any circuit constraints known by the designers can be used to strengthen the induction invariant. We use BDD-based reachability constrains, described earlier in Section 3.1.2.

In our enhanced BMC method for induction [17], we use the BDD-based reachability constraints not as redundant constraints, but as additional constraints to the SAT problem in order to facilitate the proof by induction. This use is shown pictorially by the boxes labeled $B*$ and $F*$ in Figure 10. For the base step, after we have checked the unsatisfiability of the negated property at each cycle up to k cycles, we can additionally check the satisfiability of the $B*$ BDD constraint after k cycles. If it is unsatisfiable, then the property is proved to be true, without performing any more inductive steps by BMC. In a sense, the inductive step has been already performed by the BDD-based fixpoint operation on the abstract model. However, if $B*$ is satisfiable, we proceed with the inductive step. For the inductive step, we use the $F*$ BDD to constrain the arbitrary state at the start of the $k+1$ cycles. This provides an additional reachability invariant, which can potentially allow the inductive step to succeed with BMC. It is intructive to note that the base step of an induction proof proceeds in the forward direction, and therefore the $B*$ constraint derived from the backward BDD-based analysis complements BMC to provide completeness. In contrast, the inductive step constitutes a backward style of reasoning. Therefore, the $F*$ constraint derived from the forward BDD-based analysis complements BMC to provide completeness.

Experiment Results. Our results for using this technique for checking safety properties on some large industrial designs are shown in Table 2. Here, Columns 2 – 5 report the results for BDD-based analysis on the abstract model (number of flip-flops #FF, number of gates #G, the CPU time taken for traversal, the number of forward iterations, and the final size of the BDD $F*$, respectively). Columns 6 – 9 report the results for a BMC-based proof by induction on the concrete design, with use of the BDD constraints (the verification status, and the time and memory used by the BMC engine, respectively). We obtained the abstract models automatically from the unconstrained designs, by abstracting away latches farther in the dependency closure of the property variables. Due to the small size of the abstract models, we could keep the resource requirements for BDDs fairly low. The important observation is that despite gross approximations in the abstract models, the BDD reachability invariants were strong enough to let the induction proof go through successfully with BMC in each case. Though neither the BDD-based engine, nor the BMC engine, could individually prove these safety properties, their combination allowed the proof to be completed very easily (in less than a minute).

Table 2. Experimental Results for Proof by Induction using BDD-based Reachability Invariants

	BDD-based Abstract Model Analysis				Induction Proof with BDD Constraints on Concrete Design			
	#FF / #G	Time(s)	Depth	Size of F*	#FF / #G	Status	Time(s)	Mem(MB)
D1-p1	41 / 462	1.6	7	131	2198 / 14702	TRUE	0.07	2.72
D2-p2	115 / 1005	15.3	12	677	2265 / 16079	TRUE	0.11	2.84
D3-p3	63 / 1001	18.8	18	766	2204 / 16215	TRUE	0.1	2.85

3.2.2 Proof-Based Iterative Abstraction (PBIA)

In order to handle large designs, there has been a great deal of interest in the use of abstraction and refinement techniques for verification. Most efforts are refinement-based approaches, where starting from a small abstract model of the concrete design, counterexamples found on these models are used to refine the model iteratively until either a conclusive result is obtained by conservative model checking, or the resources are exhausted [61, 68]. In a separate development, resolution-based proof analysis techniques for SAT solvers [40, 42] can be used to identify a set of original clauses from an unsatisfiable SAT problem, called the *unsatisfiable core*, that are sufficient for implying unsatisfiability. These techniques have been independently used for verification applications also – counterexample guided refinement [69], proof-based abstraction [22, 42], unbounded model checking using interpolants [70]. Here we describe the details of our proof-based iterative abstraction (PBIA) technique [22, 23], based on our SAT-based BMC framework. It can be used to generate small abstract models, on which proofs can be derived using any unbounded verification methods. In the next section, we describe its use in conjunction with EMM techniques to find proofs for designs with embedded memories.

Proof-based Abstraction using SAT-based BMC. A proof-based abstraction technique works as follows. BMC is performed for increasing depths on the concrete design. Recall that when there is no counterexample at (or up to) a given depth of unrolling, the Boolean formula *BMC(M,f,k)* (Definition 1 in Section 3.1.1) is unsatisfiable. In this case, an unsatisfiable core consisting of a subset of constraints is identified using resolution-based proof analysis techniques. Then a latch-based [22] (or a gate-based [42]) abstraction is used to generate a conservative abstract model that is guaranteed to have more behaviors than the concrete design. In addition, due to the sufficiency property of the unsatisfiable core, the abstract model is guaranteed to preserve correctness of the related property up to the given depth. In many cases, the abstract model can also be proved correct for *all* depths, by using unbounded model checking techniques, such as those based on BDDs or SAT-based unbounded model checking. Since the abstract model has more behaviors than the concrete design, this also proves correctness for the concrete design. The usefulness of the proof-based abstractions stems from the empirical evidence that for typical verification applications, the unsatisfiable cores and the corresponding abstract models are much smaller than the concrete designs, thereby making it easier to apply unbounded verification methods for deriving proofs.

Proof-based Iterative Abstraction. We further use an iterative abstraction framework [22], where a proof-based abstraction is used in the inner loop (unlike other proof-based methods [42]). This is shown in Figure 11. Given a concrete model *M*, and an LTL formula *f* (negation of the given correctness property), the shown procedure either finds a true counterexample for the correctness property, or returns a final abstract model on which bounded or unbounded verification can be performed.

Starting from the concrete model, an outer loop indexed by *i* (line 3) performs BMC on increasingly more abstract models, denoted *M[i]*. In each iteration of the outer loop, BMC is performed on model *M[i]* for increasing bound *k* (line 6). If the BMC formula is satisfiable, the counterexample is checked to see if it is spurious. If it is not spurious, the correctness property is shown to be false. If it is spurious, a new model *M'* is derived, either by using proof-based refinement, or by deriving a proof-based abstraction from *M[i-1]* for a bound *d > k* (line 8). The current iteration is started again for the new model *M'* (line 10). On the other hand, if the BMC formula is unsatisfiable for bound *k*, an abstract model *A[k]* is derived by using a proof-based abstraction on the unsatisfiable core (line 14), e.g. the latch interface abstraction. If the abstract model is stable, e.g. if its size does not change over the last few time frames (indexed by *k*), then a new iteration is started with this model chosen as

M[i+1] (line 16). Otherwise, BMC is performed again on the current model *M[i]* after incrementing *k* (line 19). As shown here, the outer loop is iterated up to convergence of the size of the abstract model *M[i]* (line 21). Alternatively, unbounded verification can be attempted for any of the abstract models *M[i]*, where a true result is conclusive, while a counterexample is handled the same way as a satisfiable BMC formula (lines 6-12).

```
1   Proof_Based_Iterative_Abstraction (M,f) {
2     M[1] = M;  // start with concrete design
3     for (i=1; i; i++) { // multiple iterations
4       k = 1;
5       do {
6       if (BMC(M[i], f, k)_is_satisfiable)  // counterexample
7           if (counterexample_is_spurious) {
8               M' = get_refined_model(M[i], M[i-1], f, k);
9               M[i] = M';
10              k = 1; } // restart iteration i with model M'
11          else
12              return(property_is_false);
13      else {  // unsatisfiable BMC formula
14          A[k] = get_abstract_model(M[i], f, k);
15          if (model_A[k]_is_stable) {
16              M[i+1] = A[k];
17              break; } // out of do-while loop
18          else
19              k++; }
20      } while (1);
21      if (size(M[i+1]) == size(M[i]))
22          break; // out of loop on i
23  } // end of for loop
24  return(M[i]); // final abstract model for verification
25 }
```

Fig. 11. Pseudo-code for Iterative Abstraction

The overall flow in iterative abstraction is targeted at reducing the size of the abstract models across successive iterations. The potential benefit is that for properties that are false, BMC search for deeper counterexamples is performed on successively smaller models, thereby increasing the likelihood of finding them. For properties that are true, the successive iterations help to reduce the size of the abstract models, thereby increasing the likelihood of completing the proof by unbounded verification methods. We obtained typically two orders of magnitude reduction in the size of the abstract model across all iterations. In our experience, this reduction was crucial for successful verification of large industry designs.

Lazy Constraints in Proof-based Abstraction. We further proposed the idea of lazy constraints [23], where the main motivation is to delay propagating the effect of values implied by certain constraints, in order to derive smaller unsatisfiable cores for proof-based abstractions. In a standard DPLL-based SAT solver, the BCP procedure treats all constraints as eager constraints, i.e. implications due to the constraints are performed as soon as possible (modulo some ordering). Rather than modify the SAT solver, we change the CNF representation of certain single-literal constraints to achieve the desired lazy effect. This allows us to directly use, without any modification, the latest improvements in SAT solver technology. In particular, a 1-literal eager constraint (x) can be converted to a lazy constraint by replacing it with (x+y)(x+y'), where y is a fresh variable not appearing in the remaining formula.

We use lazy constraints in SAT-based BMC for handling initial state constraints for latches and for environmental constraints provided by the designer ($I(y_0)$ and $Env(e_j)$, respectively, in Definition 1, Section 3.1.1). Intuitively, lazy initial state constraints provide a way to get away from the "irrelevant" initial state values, which may otherwise get forced into the unsatisfiable core due to eager implication at the time of pre-processing in the SAT solver. Delaying such irrelevant implications (so that they potentially never take effect) can often lead to a much smaller invariant abstract model. Similarly, lazy constraints provide a way to delay enforcing "irrelevant" environmental constraints, potentially leading to a smaller set being actually used in the proof of unsatisfiability.

Experimental Results. Our experimental results for proof-based iterative abstraction are shown below in Table 3. The first three columns report the design name, the number of flip-flops and gates in the concrete design, respectively. The next three columns report the results for use of PBIA without lazy constraints, with number of flip-flops in the final abstract model, the number of iterations it took to derive the model, and the total time taken (in seconds), respectively. The last three columns report these data for use of PBIA with lazy constraints.

Note first that in all examples, the use of PBIA automatically generates much smaller abstract models than concrete designs. This greatly facilitates the use of unbounded verification methods on the abstract models to prove properties on the concrete design. With respect to use of lazy constraints, note that delaying implications by using lazy constraints can result in a performance penalty in some cases, since the efficiency of a SAT solver depends upon performing more implications in order to avoid search. On the other hand, it often results in further reduction in the sizes of the abstract models. In this sense, use of lazy constraints can be regarded as a heuristic targeted at deriving a smaller abstract model using proof-based abstraction. In practice, we also identify a *sufficient* set of environmental constraints for a given property, in order to generate smaller abstract models. In many cases, these techniques are crucial in being able to complete unbounded verification on the derived abstract models.

Table 3. Experimental Results for Proof-Based Iterative Abstraction (PBIA)

D	Concrete Model		Abstract Models from PBIA					
			No Lazy			With Lazy		
	#FF	# G	#FF	# I	T(s)	#FF	# I	T(s)
D1	3378	28384	522	9	60476	294	4	11817
D2	4367	36471	1223	8	80630	1119	9	64361
D3	910	13997	433	5	11156	166	10	29249
D4	12716	416182	369	4	1099	71	6	1310
D5	2714	77220	187	2	17	3	3	21
D6	1635	26059	228	6	5958	148	3	4102
D7	1635	26084	244	3	3028	155	5	2768
D8	1670	26729	149	3	25	148	3	28
D9	1670	26729	162	3	40	147	3	44
D10	1635	26064	159	2	12	146	3	30
D11	1670	26729	149	3	25	148	3	28
D12	1670	26729	183	4	2119	182	4	2376
D13	1670	26729	180	2	63	154	3	71
D14	1635	26085	190	3	1352	154	5	1480
D15	1635	26060	153	3	125	153	3	142

3.2.3 EMM for Finding Proofs

In this section, we describe extensions of our EMM method described earlier (for finding bugs, in Section 3.1.4), to providing correctness proofs for embedded memory systems. The novelties of our extended EMM approach [28] are:

- Modeling   an arbitrary memory state precisely, and thereby, providing the ability to derive induction proofs using SAT-based BMC
- Combining EMM with proof-based abstraction to find irrelevant memory modules/ports that do not affect correctness of a given property

Induction with EMM. To model a memory with an arbitrary initial state, we introduce new symbolic variables at every time frame. Note that for a k-depth analysis of a design, there can be at most k different memory read accesses from a read port; out of which at most k accesses can be to un-written memory locations. Therefore, in total we need to introduce k symbolic variables for the different data words in memory. However, these variables are not completely independent, and simply introducing new variables introduces spurious behaviors in the verification model. Therefore, we need to identify a sufficient set of constraints on these fresh variables that capture the arbitrary memory state precisely. This is done by identifying pairs of read operations from the same address, which should forward the same data, provided no other write operations have been performed on the same address in between the two reads. Again, we use a hybrid representation of these constraints and add them to the BMC problem at each depth of unrolling.

EMM with Proof-based Abstraction. Recall that EMM can significantly reduce the size of the verification model by eliminating explicit modeling of memory state. However, for checking the correctness of a given safety property, we may not require all the memory modules or the ports in the memory subsystem of a design. To further reduce the model, we can abstract out *irrelevant* memory modules or ports completely. In this case, we do not need to add the memory modeling constraints for the irrelevant memory modules or ports, thereby further reducing the BMC problem size.

For the purpose of automatically identifying irrelevant memory modules and ports, we use a technique combining EMM constraints with proof-based abstraction. We use SAT-based BMC with memory-modeling constraints added according to our EMM approach. Again, we derive an unsatisfiable core whenever the BMC problem is unsatisfiable at a given depth k. The latches appearing in the unsatisfiable core are accumulated over the depths in a set LR. If a latch in the control logic of a memory module (the logic driving its memory interface signals) does not appear in the set LR, we do not add the EMM modeling constraints for that memory module. In other words, since the correctness of the property does not depend on that memory module (up to depth k), we abstract it out completely. Note this corresponds to a conservative abstraction, i.e. a proof of correctness on the abstract model implies correctness on the original design. This reduction in the EMM constraints reduces the BMC problem size and significantly improves the performance in our experience.

4.2.4 SAT-Based Unbounded Model Checking (UMC)

Due to the success of SAT solvers in bounded model checking, there has been growing interest in their use for unbounded model checking as well. Here, the crucial non-trivial operation is quantifier elimination, which converts a QBF to a propositional Boolean formula. This is shown below for the image operation and pre-image operations, which form the computational core of symbolic model checking methods (also described in Section 2.3):

$$Img\ (Y) = S_N(Y) = \exists X, W, Z.\ S_C(X) \wedge T(X, Y, W, Z) \tag{4}$$

$$PreImg(X) = S_C(X) = \exists Y, W, Z.\ S_N(Y) \wedge T(X, Y, W, Z) \tag{5}$$

As before, the variable sets $X,\ Y,\ W,$ denote the present state, next state, and input variables respectively; and S_C, S_N and T denote the next states, the current states, and the transition relation, respectively. Note that there is an additional set of variables Z denoting the internal variables needed for a CNF representation of the transition relation. In addition to the issue of quantification of these additional variables, there is also the issue of what representation to use for the state sets. There have been many efforts with different approaches for handling these issues. We first discuss methods that use SAT in combination with other methods, and then methods that use purely SAT for symbolic model checking.

SAT with Other Symbolic UMC Methods. Symbolic model checking based on combining non-canonical decision diagrams like Reduced Boolean Circuits (RBCs) [71] and Boolean Expression Diagrams (BEDs) [72] with SAT-solvers were proposed to alleviate the problems seen in pure BDD-based approaches. However, the use of circuit-based existential quantification ($\exists xf = f_x + f_{x'}$) in pre-image/image computation results in a formula size that grows exponentially with the number of quantified variables, in spite of all heuristic attempts to mitigate the growth. These approaches are, therefore, limited to designs with a small number of primary inputs.

We have also proposed a combined method [18], which integrates BDD-based techniques tightly into the SAT decision procedure. We represent the transition relation T in CNF, and the set of states S_C and S_N as BDDs. For image computation, quantifier elimination is performed by using SAT techniques to enumerate all solutions to the CNF formula, and by projecting each solution on the set of image variables (Y). The search for solutions is constrained by the BDD for S_C, using a technique called *BDD Bounding*, whereby any partial solution in SAT which is inconsistent with the BDD is regarded as a conflict. This technique is also used effectively to avoid repeating image set solutions by bounding against the BDD representing the currently computed image set S_N.

Another novelty of our method is that in order to avoid enumeration of all solutions in SAT, we generate BDD-based subproblems on-the-fly for a partial assignment in SAT. The decision about when to generate a BDD subproblem is heuristically determined, e.g. when the number of assigned variables in SAT is some fraction of the total number of variables. The BDD subproblem corresponds to the transition relation cofactored with the current partial assignment in SAT. Indeed, each BDD subproblem is very similar to the standard BDD formulation of image computation, except that the CNF representation of the (cofactored) transition relation provides a much finer-grained conjunctive partition of the transition relation. This provides additional opportunities for early quantification of primary input variables. The overall image computation can be viewed as the SAT decision tree providing a disjunctive partitioning into multiple BDD subproblems at its leaves, as shown below in Figure 12. This combination of decision heuristics and implications provided by SAT, with the efficient computation of smaller subproblems using BDDs, is highly beneficial in handling large designs. We enhanced this basic image computation procedure by adding circuit structure information to the CNF formula of the transition relation, in order to dynamically detect and remove redundant clauses [19]. We also added partition-based SAT decision heuristics to further improve its performance [20].

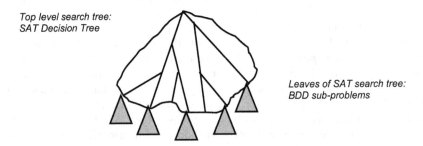

Top level search tree:
SAT Decision Tree

Leaves of SAT search tree:
BDD sub-problems

Fig. 12. Symbolic Image Computation Combining SAT and BDDs

Purely SAT-based UMC Methods. In purely SAT-based approaches, the transition relation is maintained in a conjunctive normal form (CNF) and a SAT procedure is used to enumerate all solutions for the required state set. Typically, the solution cubes are enumerated by the SAT solver for computing the pre-image state set [73, 74], and a blocking clause representing the negation of the enumerated state cube is added at each step in order to prevent repeating the solutions. In [73] a redrawing of the SAT solver's implication graph is carried out to enlarge the state cube. In [74], a two-level minimizer is used to compact the CNF formula after addition of new blocking clauses. Note that in both approaches, only a single state cube is captured at any enumeration step. Since the number of required enumerations is bounded below by the size of a two-level prime and irredundant cover of the solution set, quantifier elimination based on cube-by-cube enumeration tends to be expensive. In yet another approach [47], an ATPG solver is used as the search engine, and state cube enlargement is achieved using a separate justification procedure once a satisfying result is found by the SAT solver. This approach is also limited by its cube-wise enumeration strategy.

A different model checking approach based on use of SAT techniques and *Craig interpolants* has been proposed by McMillan [70]. Given an unsatisfiable Boolean problem, and a proof of unsatisfiability derived by a SAT solver, a Craig interpolant can be efficiently computed to characterize the interface between two partitions of the Boolean problem. In particular, when no counterexample exists for depth k, i.e., the SAT problem in BMC for depth k is found to be unsatisfiable, a Craig interpolant is used to obtain an over-approximation of the set of states reachable from the initial state in 1 step (or any fixed number of steps). This provides an approximate image operator, which can be used iteratively to compute an over-approximation of the set of reachable states, i.e., till a fixpoint is obtained. If at any point, the over-approximate reachable set is found to violate the given property, then the depth k is increased for BMC, till either a true counterexample is found, or the over-approximation converges without violating the property. The main advantage of the interpolant-based method is that it does not require an enumeration of satisfying assignments by the SAT solver. Indeed, the proof of unsatisfiability is used to efficiently compute the interpolant, which serves directly as an over-approximated state set. However, this approach can computes approximate reachable states, which are sufficient for proving safety properties, but are harder to apply for exact model checking.

Our SAT-based quantifier elimination method is considerably different from the other efforts. It dramatically reduces the number of enumerations of satisfying solutions in comparison to the cube-based approaches, thereby, significantly improving the performance of pre-image and fixed-point computation in SAT-based UMC [21]. Our SAT-based method is shown in Figure 13:

Note that we too use a SAT solver to enumerate solutions, but the novelty in our approach is that we use cofactoring after each enumeration, as follows:

- Get the satisfying assignment α, which could be a cube (line 4)
- Pick a satisfying input minterm m by choosing an assignment on the unassigned input variables in the satisfying cube α (line 5)
- Cofactor the function f with respect to the satisfying input minterm m (line 6)

Note that the cofactored function f_m is used to represent the set of satisfying states derived from a single solution enumerated by the SAT solver. In general, a cofactor can capture not just a single cube of the state solution set, but several cubes. Specifically, our cofactoring approach is *guaranteed* to contain the set of new states captured in each enumeration step by the cube-based approaches. Therefore, our approach is also guaranteed to require a smaller number of enumerations by the SAT solver. In our experience, cofactoring-based quantification greatly reduces the total number of solutions enumerated by the SAT solver, sometimes by several orders of magnitude, in comparison to cube-wise enumeration approaches. Furthermore, we do not require a redrawing of the implication graph [73], or an enlargement of the enumerated cube as a post-processing step [47].

```
SAT-EQuant(f,A,B) { // calculate ∃ₐ f(A,B)

  C = ∅; //initialize constraint

  while (SAT_Solve(f=1∧C=0) is SAT) {

    α = get_satisfying_cube();

    m = get_satisfying_input_minterm(α,B);

    fₘ = cofactor_cube(f, m);

    C = C ∨ fₘ; }

  return C; } // return when no more solution
```

Fig. 13. SAT-based existential quantification using Circuit Cofactoring

Additionally, we use circuit cofactoring techniques based on efficient circuit graphs [46] for representing the solution states, which is more robust in practice than CNF-based blocking clauses or BDD-based representations. We also use our hybrid SAT solver [25] to directly work on these representations. We also observed that the total number of enumerations depends, though less severely, on the choice of values chosen on the unassigned input variables in the satisfying cube assignment which determine the cofactor. We also proposed several SAT solver heuristics to choose an input minterm that enlarges the set represented by f_m.

Our circuit cofactoring-based quantification technique can be used to compute exact image/pre-image state sets, unlike the interpolant-based technique (described earlier), which computes approximate state sets. It has been used in SAT-based unbounded symbolic model checking to handle many difficult industry examples, which could not be handled by either BDDs or blocking-clause based SAT approaches. We have also used it in SAT-based UMC formulations (greatest fixed point, and least fixed point computations) for determining completeness bounds for liveness properties, which are then used in our customized translations with BMC to find proofs [15]. More recently, we have combined our SAT-based UMC technique with symmetry reduction [75] to obtain further performance improvements, due to both the reduced state space and simplification in the resulting SAT problems.

Experimental Results. We show experimental results on 102 examples for checking safety properties on designs from the VIS verification benchmark suite (VVB) [76] with a time limit of 1000s for each example. We present the comparison of our Circuit Cofactoring approach (CC) with the Blocking Clauses (BC) approach, and the BDD and BMC approaches in VIS, as scatter plots in Figure 14.

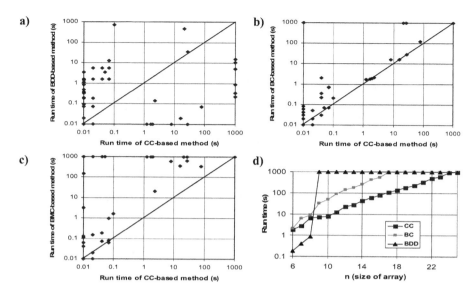

Fig. 14. Experimental Results for Circuit Cofactoring-based UMC Method (CC): (a) CC vs. BDD   (b) CC vs. BC   (c) CC vs. BMC   (d) Swap example results

As shown in the scatter plot of CC/BDD in Figure 14 (a), our approach performed better in 68 cases while BDD performed better in 16 cases. We observe here the complementary strengths of BDD-based and SAT-based approaches. As shown in the scatter plots of CC/BC and CC/BMC in Figure 14 (b) and 14 (c), respectively, our CC approach is almost always better than both BC and SAT-based BMC.

We also experimented on a design *swap* [73] that swaps non-deterministically consecutive elements in an array of length n. The correctness criterion is that all elements of the array are distinct. We compared our approach CC with BC and BDD (VIS) for varying n, each with a time limit of 1000s. The performance results are shown in Figure 14(d). Note that there is a time-out for BDDs for $n>8$ (also noted by others). With our CC approach, we can successfully analyze the design up to $n=24$, while with BC the analysis can complete only up to $n=16$. Note that our approach is about an order of magnitude faster than the *BC* approach on this example.

4   SAT-Based Applications in Hardware Verification

We have implemented our various SAT-based methods in a verification platform called *VeriSol* (formerly *DiVer*), targeted at verification of large scale hardware designs in the industry [29]. Due to an efficient and flexible infrastructure, *VeriSol* provides a very productive platform for research and development. A view of *VeriSol* as a "wheel of verification engines" is shown in Figure 15, where all these engines and their novel features have been described earlier in Section 3.

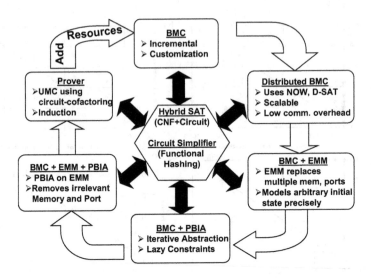

Fig. 15. Wheel of Verification Engines in *VeriSol*

In addition to the verification methods, *VeriSol* also has the ability to handle industry design features including multiple clocks, multiple phase and gated clocks, embedded memories with multiple read and write ports, environmental and fairness constraints. *VeriSol* has matured over the last four years, and has been used successfully by designers in our company to discover bugs that either could not have been found or were missed by functional simulation.

4.1 Selected Case Studies

Using selected case studies from the industry, we demonstrate the role of various engines in *VeriSol* at each step of the verification. It is interesting to note that without an interplay between the engines, we could not have verified any of these designs. The first two case studies do not contain large embedded memories, and use the verification flow shown in Figure 16(a). The next two case studies have large embedded memories and use the verification flow shown in Figure 16(b). All experiments were performed on a server with 2.8 GHz Xeon processors with 4GB running Red Hat Linux 7.2.

Industry Design I. The design has 13K flip-flops (FFs), ~0.5M gates in the cone of influence of a safety property. Using BMC, we showed that there was no witness up to depth 120 (in 1643s) before we run out of memory. Using d-BMC, we showed no witness up to depth 323 (in 8643s) using 5 workstations (configured as 1 Master and 4 Clients and connected with 1Gps Ethernet LAN), with a communication overhead of 30% and scalability factor of 0.1 (i.e, potentially we could do a 10 times deeper analysis than that on the single server.) We hypothesized that the property is correct. We used the PBIA engine to obtain an abstract model with 71 FFs and ~1K gates in 6 iterations taking ~1200s. By using standard BDD-based symbolic model checking on

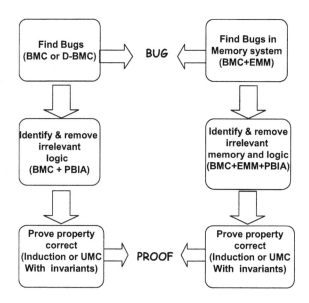

Fig. 16. (a) Standard Verification Flow   (b) Verification Flow with EMM

the conservative abstract model, we proved the property correct in 30s. This implied correctness on the original (much larger) design.

Industry Design II. The design with environmental constraints has 3.3K FFs and ~28K gates for a safety property. Using BMC, we showed there was no witness up to depth 113 (in ~3hr, 720MB). Again, we hypothesized the correctness of the property. We used PBIA to obtain an abstract model A1 with 163 FFs and ~2K gates in 4 iterations taking 9000s. Without the environmental constraints, the abstract model A2 has only 66 FFs and ~1K gates. We computed a reachability invariant on the A2 model (in ~4s) and used this invariant with SAT-based UMC on the A1 model to obtain a correctness proof in ~60s. Interestingly, for this example, none of the other UMC techniques (SAT-based induction, BDD-based symbolic model checking) was successful on the A1 model, even though the model was fairly small.

Industry Design III. The design has 756 FFs (excluding the memory registers), and ~15K gates. It has two memory modules, both having address width, AW = 10 and data width, DW = 8. Each memory module has 1 write and 1 read port, with the memory state initialized to 0. There are 216 reachability properties to be checked. Using BMC+EMM, we found witnesses for 206 of the 216 properties, taking ~400s and 50Mb. The maximum depth over all witnesses was 51. Using exact memory modeling of the state, we required 20540s (~6hrs) and 912Mb to find witnesses for all 206 properties. By using induction with BMC+EMM, we proved the remaining 10 properties in <1s (this took 25 s with exact modeling of the memory state).

Quicksort. A hardware implementation of this algorithm has two memory modules: an un-initialized array with AW=10, DW=32, 1 read and 1 write port; and an un-initialized stack (for implementing the recursive function calls) with AW=10, DW=24, 1 read and 1 write port. The design has 167 FFs (excluding memory registers), and ~9K gates for array size of 5. The correctness property states that after return from a recursive call, the program counter should go to a recursive call on the right partition or return to the parent on the recursion stack. Using BMC+EMM+PBIA, we reduced the model to 91 FFs and ~3K gates, and also identified that the array module was irrelevant for this property (since the array data does not affect the control structure of the algorithm). On this reduced model we proved correctness using forward induction (proof diameter = 59) in 2.3Ks, 116MB. Without the proof-based abstraction, the induction proof in BMC+EMM takes ~5Ks, 400MB. When modeling the exact memory state, however, we could obtain neither a proof nor an abstract model in 3 hours.

4.2   Integration of *VeriSol* with Hardware Design Methodology

Although checking properties on the hardware design can be made (almost) fully automatic, *VeriSol* relies on the designers or verification engineers to provide correctness properties. Properties must capture the design intent and at the same time be expressed in some kind of formal syntax [77]. This requires the users to have both detailed knowledge of the design and some background in formal methods. Despite the growing popularity of formal verification and assertion-based verification, many designers are often reluctant to specify properties due to lack of either interest or training. We believe this has been one of the major hurdles in the wider application of formal verification in hardware design

In terms of our efforts in this direction, *VeriSol* has been integrated within a high level behavioral synthesis system called *Cyber* [30] developed in NEC Japan, which is used in-house by many system design groups. The *Cyber* system automatically generates RTL designs from high-level behavioral descriptions. In addition, it also automatically generates correctness properties for these RTL designs. The back-end property checking for *Cyber* can be performed by *VeriSol*.

We have also added techniques to automatically generate verification properties from RTL Verilog designs. The properties include both simple Boolean assertions and temporal property checkers (those describing the behavior of the model over time). Although they are generated with absolutely no user effort, these properties often capture some important aspects of the design intent and cover corner case conditions that are critical for the design to be correct. *VeriSol* can be used to either formally verify these properties using its various SAT-based and BDD-based engines, or generate simulation monitors from these properties. Our automatic checker generation procedure targets properties in the categories of checking register usage (write before read, read before initialized), memory usage (unused, read-only, write-only, multiple drivers), full case / parallel case, unreachable or constant condition branches, etc.

Automatic property generation can significantly increase *VeriSol's* ability in capturing subtle corner case errors in early RTL design stages with absolutely no user effort, and significantly ease the burden that has traditionally been put solely on designers or verification engineers. Once the users start benefiting from these automatically generated properties, they can be motivated to start thinking of new properties to cover more subtle design errors. In this sense, it also helps in promoting formal verification techniques to a wider design community in real industry settings. Our target users include both designers using the *Cyber* design synthesis flow and designers using Verilog only. We have also developed an IDE (Integrated Design Environment) for *VeriSol* in the Verilog design flow, utilizing an Eclipse-based GUI and Icarus Verilog [78] in the tool front-end.

5 Conclusions

In this paper we have described SAT-based verification methods we have developed for verifying large hardware designs. Due to many recent advances in SAT solver technology, these methods have emerged as a promising alternative to the traditional BDD-based symbolic model checking methods. At the same time, we have found in our experience on industry designs that many of these methods need to be combined with each other, and also with other BDD-based and circuit-based methods, in order to successfully find bugs or proofs for correctness properties in practice.

While a lot of progress has been made, much remains to be done to make these methods more robust in order to apply them reliably to large scale industry designs. In terms of industry applications, there is also a need for more effort in integrating these methods and the related tools within practical design methodology flows, in order to more fully realize the potential of formal verification.

Acknowledgements

We would like to thank Pranav Ashar for his numerous and valuable contributions to the methods described here, and Kazutoshi Wakabayashi and Akira Mukaiyama for their contributions and help in applying them in an industry context.

References

1. E.M. Clarke, O. Grumberg, and D. Peled, *Model Checking*. 1999: MIT Press.
2. R. Burch, E.M. Clarke, D.E. Long, K.L. McMillan, and D. Dill, *Symbolic model checking for sequential circuit verification*. IEEE Transactions on Computer-Aided Design of Integrated Circuits and Systems, 1994. **13**(4): p. 401-424.
3. K.L. McMillan, *Symbolic Model Checking: An Approach to the State Explosion Problem*. 1993: Kluwer Academic Publishers.
4. R.E. Bryant, *Graph-based algorithms for Boolean function manipulation*. IEEE Transactions on Computers, 1986. **C-35**(8): p. 677-691.
5. J.P. Marques-Silva and K.A. Sakallah, *GRASP: A Search Algorithm for Propositional Satisfiability*. IEEE Transactions on Computers, 1999. **48**: p. 506-521.
6. M. Moskewicz, C. Madigan, Y. Zhao, L. Zhang, and S. Malik, *Chaff: Engineering an Efficient SAT Solver*, in *Proceedings of Design Automation Conference*. 2001.
7. H. Zhang, *SATO: An efficient propositional prover*, in *Proceedings of International Conference on Automated Deduction*. 1997. p. 272-275.
8. E. Goldberg and Y. Novikov, *BerkMin: A Fast and Robust SAT-Solver*, in *Proceedings of Conference on Design Automation & Test Europe (DATE)*. 2002. p. 142-149.

9. L. Zhang and S. Malik, *The Quest for Efficient Boolean Satisfiability Solvers*, in *Proceedings of the International Conference on Computer Aided Verification*. 2002, Springer. p. 17-36.

10. M. Prasad, A. Biere, and A. Gupta, *A survey of recent advances in SAT-based formal verification*. Software Tools for Technology Transfer, 2005. **7**(2): p. 156-173.

11. F. Lu, L.-C. Wang, K.-T. Cheng, J. Moondanos, and Z. Hanna, *A signal correlation guided ATPG solver and its applications for solving difficult industrial cases*, in *Proceedings of the Design Automation Conference*. 2003. p. 436-441.

12. A. Biere, A. Cimatti, E.M. Clarke, and Y. Zhu, *Symbolic Model Checking without BDDs*, in *Proceedings of Tools and Algorithms for Analysis and Construction of Systems (TACAS)*. 1999.

13. A. Gupta, M. Ganai, C. Wang, Z. Yang, and P. Ashar. *Learning from BDDs in SAT-based bounded model checking*. in *Design Automation Conference*. 2003.

14. M. Ganai, A. Gupta, Z. Yang, and P. Ashar, *Efficient distributed SAT and SAT-based distributed bounded model checking*, in *Proceedings of the Conference on Correct Hardware Design and Verification Methods (CHARME)*. 2003. p. 334-347.

15. M. Ganai, A. Gupta, and P. Ashar, *Beyond safety: Customized SAT-based model checking*, in *Proceedings of the Design Automation Conference*. 2005. p. 738-743.

16. M. Sheeran, S. Singh, and G. Stalmarck, *Checking Safety Properties using Induction and a SAT Solver*, in *Proceedings of Conference on Formal Methods in Computer-Aided Design*. 2000.

17. A. Gupta, M. Ganai, C. Wang, Z. Yang, and P. Ashar, *Abstraction and BDDs Complement SAT-based BMC in DiVer*, in *Proceedings of International Conference on Computer Aided Verification*. 2003.

18. A. Gupta, Z. Yang, P. Ashar, and A. Gupta, *SAT-based Image Computation with Application in Reachability Analysis*, in *Proceedings of Conference on Formal Methods in Computer-Aided Design*. 2000. p. 354-371.

19. A. Gupta, A. Gupta, Z. Yang, and P. Ashar, *Dynamic detection and removal of inactive clauses in SAT with application in image computation*, in *Proceedings of Design Automation Conference*. 2001.

20. A. Gupta, Z. Yang, P. Ashar, L. Zhang, and S. Malik, *Partition-Based Decision Heuristics for Image Computation using SAT and BDDs*, in *Proceedings of International Conference on Computer-Aided Design*. 2001.

21. M. Ganai, A. Gupta, and P. Ashar, *Efficient SAT-based unbounded symbolic model checking using circuit cofactoring*, in *Proceedings of the International Conference on Computer-Aided Design*. 2004. p. 510-517.

22. A. Gupta, M. Ganai, J. Yang, and P. Ashar, *Iterative Abstraction using SAT-based BMC with Proof Analysis*, in *Proceedings of International Conference on Computer Aided Design (ICCAD)*. 2003.

23. A. Gupta, M. Ganai, and P. Ashar, *Lazy constraints and SAT heuristics for proof-based abstraction*, in *Proceedings of the International Conference on VLSI Design*. 2005. p. 183-188.

24. M. Ganai and A. Kuehlmann, *On-the-fly compression of logical circuits*, in *Proceedings of International Workshop on Logic Synthesis*. 2000.

25. M. Ganai, L. Zhang, P. Ashar, and A. Gupta, *Combining Strengths of Circuit-based and CNF-based Algorithms for a High Performance SAT Solver*, in *Proceedings of the Design Automation Conference*. 2002.

26. M. Abramovici, M.A. Breuer, and A.D. Friedman, *Digital Systems Testing and Testable Design*. 1990: Computer Science Press.

27. M. Ganai, A. Gupta, and P. Ashar, *Efficient modeling of embedded memories in bounded model checking*, in *Proceedings of the International Conference on Computer Aided Verification*. 2004, Springer. p. 440-452.

28. M. Ganai, A. Gupta, and P. Ashar, *Verification of embedded memory systems using efficient memory modeling*, in *Proceedings of Design Automation and Test Europe (DATE)*. 2005. p. 1096-1101.

29. M. Ganai, A. Gupta, and P. Ashar, *DiVer: SAT-based model checking platform for verifying large scale systems*, in *Proceedings of Tools and Algorithms for the Construction and Analysis of Systems (TACAS)*. 2005, Springer. p. 575-580.

30. K. Wakabayashi, *Cyber: High level synthesis system from software into ASIC*, in *High Level VLSI Synthesis*, R. Camposano and W. Wolf, Editors. 1991, Kluwer Academic Publishers. p. 127-151.

31. F. Ivancic, J. Yang, M. Ganai, A. Gupta, I. Shlyakhter, and P. Ashar, *F-Soft: Software Verification Platform*, in *Proceedings of the International Conference on Computer Aided Verification*. 2005, Springer. p. 301-306.

32. F. Ivancic, I. Shlyakhter, A. Gupta, M. Ganai, V. Kahlon, C. Wang, and Z. Yang, *Model checking C programs using F-Soft*, in *Proceedings of the International Conference on Computer Design*. 2005. p. 297-308.

33. C. Barrett, D. Dill, and A. Stump, *Checking satisfiability of first-order formulas by incremental translation to SAT*, in *Proceedings of the International Conference on Computer Aided Verification*. 2002. p. 236-249.

34. S. Seshia, S. Lahiri, and R.E. Bryant. *A hybrid SAT-based decision procedure for separation logic with uninterpreted functions*. in *Design Automation Conference*. 2003.

35. C. Wang, F. Ivancic, M. Ganai, and A. Gupta, *Deciding separation logic formulae by SAT and incremental negative cycle elimination*, in *Proceedings of Logic for Programming, Artificial Intelligence and Reasoning*. 2005. p. 322-336.

36. M. Ganai, M. Talupur, and A. Gupta, *SDSAT: Tight integration of small domain encoding and lazy approaches in a separation logic solver*, in *Proceedings of Tools and Algorithms for the Construction and Analysis of Systems*. 2006.

37. M.R. Garey and D.S. Johnson, *Computers and Intractability: A guide to the theory of NP-Completeness*. 1979: W. H. Freeman and Co.

38. T. Larrabee, *Test pattern generation using Boolean Satisfiability*. IEEE Transactions on Computer-Aided Design of Integrated Circuits and Systems, 1992. **11**(1): p. 4-15.

39. M. Davis, G. Longeman, and D. Loveland, *A Machine Program for Theorem Proving*. Communications of the ACM, 1962. **5**: p. 394-397.

40. L. Zhang and S. Malik, *Validating SAT Solvers Using an Independent Resolution-Based Checker: Practical Implementations and Other Applications*, in *Proceedings of Conference on Design Automation & Test Europe (DATE)*. 2003.

41. E. Goldberg and Y. Novikov, *Verification of Proofs of Unsatisfiability for CNF Formulas*, in *Proceedings of Conference on Design Automation & Test Europe (DATE)*. 2003.

42. K.L. McMillan and N. Amla, *Automatic Abstraction Without Counterexamples*, in *Proceedings of Tools for Algorithms for Construction and Analysis of Systems (TACAS)*. 2003.

43. H. Fujiwara and T. Shimono, *On the Acceleration of Test Generation Algorithms*. IEEE Transactions on Computers, 1983. **C-32**(12): p. 265-272.

44. P. Goel, *An implicit enumeration algorithm to generate tests for Combinational circuits*. IEEE Transactions on Computers, 1981. **C-30**(3): p. 215-222.

45. A. Kuehlmann, M. Ganai, and V. Paruthi, *Circuit-based Boolean Reasoning*, in *Proceedings of Design Automation Conference*. 2001.

46. A. Kuehlmann, V. Paruthi, F. Krohm, and M. Ganai, *Robust Boolean Reasoning for Equivalence Checking and Functional Property Verification.* IEEE Transactions on Computer-Aided Design of Integrated Circuits and Systems, 2002. **21**(12): p. 1377-1394.

47. M. Iyer, G. Parthasarthy, and K.-T. Cheng, *SATORI -- A fast sequential SAT engine for circuits*, in *Proceedings of the International Conference on Computer-Aided Design*. 2003. p. 320-325.

48. H.S. Jin, M. Awedh, and F. Somenzi, *CirCUs: A satisfiability solver geared toward bounded model checking*, in *Proceedings of the International Conference on Computer Aided Verification*. 2004, Springer. p. 519-522.

49. G.J. Holzmann, *The Model Checker SPIN.* IEEE Transactions of Software Engineering, 1997. **23**(5): p. 279-295.

50. D. Kroening and O. Strichman, *Efficient Computation of Recurrence Diameters*, in *Proceedings of the 4th International Conference on Verification, Model Checking, and Abstract Interpretation*. 2003, Springer Verlag.

51. O. Shtrichman, *Tuning SAT Checkers for Bounded Model Checking*, in *Proceedings of International Conference on Computer-Aided Verification*. 2000.

52. O. Shtrichman, *Pruning Techniques for the SAT-based bounded model checking*, in *Proceedings of Workshop on Tools and Algorithms for the Analysis and Construction of Systems (TACAS)*. 2001.

53. N. Een and N. Sorensson, *Temporal induction by incremental SAT solving*, in *Proceedings of the First International Workshop on Bounded Model Checking (BMC)*. 2003, Elsevier.

54. J. Baumgartner, A. Kuehlmann, and J. Abraham, *Property Checking via Structural Analysis*, in *Proceedings of CAV*. 2002.

55. M. Mneimneh and K. Sakallah. *SAT-based sequential depth computation.* in *Proceedings of the First International Workshop on Constraints in Formal Verification*. 2002.

56. A. Kuehlmann and F. Krohm, *Equivalence Checking using Cuts and Heaps*, in *Proceedings of Design Automation Conference*. 1997.

57. J. Whittemore, J. Kim, and K. Sakallah, *SATIRE: A new incremental SAT engine*, in *Proceedings of the Design Automation Conference*. 2001.

58. M. Ganai and A. Aziz, *Improved SAT-based Bounded Reachability Analysis*, in *Proceedings of VLSI Design Conference*. 2002.

59. R. Brayton, F. Somenzi, and others, *VIS: Verification Interacting with Synthesis*, http://vlsi.colorado.edu/~vis. 2002.

60. Cabodi, S. Nocco, and S. Quer, *Improving SAT-based bounded model checking by means of BDD-based approximate traversals*, in *Proceedings of Design Automation and Test Europe*. 2003. p. 898-903.

61. R.P. Kurshan, *Computer-Aided Verification of Co-ordinating Processes: The Automata-Theoretic Approach*. 1994: Princeton University Press.

62. Y. Zhao, *Accelerating Boolean Satisfiability through Application Specific Processing*, in *Electrical Engineering*. 2001, Princeton University.

63. J.R. Burch and D. Dill, *Automatic verification of pipelined microprocessor control*, in *Proceedings of the International Conference on Computer Aided Verification*. 1994.

64. R.E. Bryant, S. German, and M.N. Velev, *Processor verification using efficient reductions of the logic of uninterpreted functions to propositional logic*, in *Proceedings of the International Conference on Computer Aided Verification*. 1999.

65. M.N. Velev, *Automatic abstraction of memories in the formal verification of superscalar microprocessors*, in *Proceedings of Tools and Algorithms for the Construction and Analysis of Systems (TACAS)*. 2001.

66. R.E. Bryant, S. Lahiri, and S. Seshia, *Modeling and Verifying Systems using a Logic of Counter Arithmetic with Lambda Expressions and Uninterpreted Functions*, in *Proceedings of Conference on Computer Aided Verification*. 2002.

67. P. Bjesse and K. Claessen, *SAT-based verification without state space traversal*, in *Proceedings of Conference on Formal Methods in Computer-Aided Design*. 2000.

68. E.M. Clarke, O. Grumberg, S. Jha, Y. Lu, and H. Veith, *Counterexample-guided abstraction refinement*, in *Proceedings of Conference on Computer Aided Verification*. 2000. p. 154-169.

69. P. Chauhan, E.M. Clarke, J. Kukula, S. Sapra, H. Veith, and D. Wang, *Automated Abstraction Refinement for Model Checking Large State Spaces using SAT based Conflict Analysis*, in *Proceedings of Conference on Formal Methods in CAD (FMCAD)*. 2002.

70. K.L. McMillan, *Interpolation and SAT-based Model Checking*, in *Proceedings of Conference on Computer-Aided Verification*. 2003.

71. P.A. Abdulla, P. Bjesse, and N. Een, *Symbolic Reachability Analysis based on {SAT}-Solvers*, in *Proceedings of Workshop on Tools and Algorithms for the Analysis and Construction of Systems (TACAS)*. 2000.

72. P. Williams, A. Biere, E.M. Clarke, and A. Gupta, *Combining Decision Diagrams and SAT Procedures for Efficient Symbolic Model Checking*, in *Proceedings of International Conference on Computer-Aided Verification*. 2000. p. 124-138.

73. K.L. McMillan, *Applying SAT methods in unbounded symbolic model checking*, in *Proceedings of the International Conference on Computer Aided Verification*. 2002, Springer.

74. H.-J. Kang and I.-C. Park, *SAT-based unbounded symbolic model checking*, in *Proceedings of the Design Automation Conference*. 2003.

75. D. Tang, S. Malik, A. Gupta, and N. Ip, *Symmetry reduction in SAT-based model checking*, in *Proceedings of the International Conference on Computer Aided Verification*. 2005. p. 125-138.

76. *VIS Home page. http://www-cad.eecs.berkeley.edu/~vis*.

77. A. Gupta, A.A. Bayazit, and Y. Mahajan, *Verification Languages*, in *The Industrial Information Technology Handbook*. 2005, CRC Press.

78. S. Williams, *Icarus Verilog. http://www.icarus.com/eda/verilog*.

Building Efficient Decision Procedures on Top of SAT Solvers

Alessandro Cimatti[1] and Roberto Sebastiani[2]

[1] ITC-IRST, Povo, Trento, Italy
cimatti@itc.it
[2] DIT, Università di Trento, Italy
rseba@dit.unitn.it

Abstract. Many verification problems can be naturally represented as satisfiability problems in some decidable fragments of first order logic. Efficient decision procedures for such problems can be obtained by combining technology for propositional satisfiability and solvers able to deal with the theory component.

We provide a unifying and abstract, theory-independent perspective on the various integration schemas and techniques. Within this framework, we survey, analyze and classify the most effective integration techniques and optimizations for the development of decision procedures. We also discuss the relative benefits and drawbacks of the various techniques, and we analyze the features for SAT solvers and theory-specific solvers which make them more suitable for an integration.

1 Introduction

In the last decade we have witnessed an impressive advance in the efficiency of propositional satisfiability techniques (SAT henceforth), which has brought large and previously intractable problems at the reach of state-of-the-art SAT solvers (see, e.g., [86]). As a consequence, some hard real-world problems have been successfully solved by encoding them into SAT. SAT solvers are now a fundamental tool in most formal verification design flows for hardware systems, both for equivalence, property checking, and ATPG [16, 61, 75]. Other application areas include the verification of safety critical systems [42, 18], and AI planning in its classical formulation [56], and in its extensions to nondeterministic domains [29, 53].

However, the formalism of boolean logic is not expressive enough for representing many other real-world problems, including the verification of pipelined microprocessors, of real-time and hybrid control systems, and the analysis of proof obligations in software verification. In other cases, such as the verification of RTL designs or assembly-level code, even if boolean logic is expressive enough to encode the verification problem, it does not seem to be the most effective level of abstraction — for instance, words in the data path are typically treated as collections of unrelated boolean variables. Such problems are naturally expressible in decidable fragments of first order logics (quantifier-free first-order theories, or simply "theories" henceforth), and decision procedures have been developed that allow to evaluate the satisfiability of first order formulae with respect to such theories. Decision procedures have been conceived

M. Bernardo and A. Cimatti (Eds.): SFM 2006, LNCS 3965, pp. 144–175, 2006.

in different communities, like, e.g., automated theorem proving, AI planning, formal verification, and address several theories, including

- *separation logic* $(\mathcal{DL})^1$ [2, 4, 60, 77, 3, 66],
- *linear arithmetic on* $\mathbb{Q}$ $(\mathcal{LA}(\mathbb{Q}))$ *or on* $\mathbb{Z}$ $(\mathcal{LA}(\mathbb{Z}))^2$ [82, 40, 4, 10, 37, 41, 21],
- *logic of equality and uninterpreted functions* $(\mathcal{EUF})$ [81, 40, 10, 71, 43],
- *logics of bit-vectors* $(\mathcal{BV}(\mathbb{Z}))$ [40, 10, 78],
- *logic of arrays* $(\mathcal{AR}(\mathbb{Z}))$ [40, 10, 78, 41].

Most effort has been concentrated in producing ad hoc procedures of increasing expressiveness and efficiency, and in combining them in the most efficient way [64, 73, 40, 12, 72, 37, 20]. In many such communities, however, the importance of dealing efficiently with the *boolean component* of the problem has been been recognized and investigated only recently. This has lead to the development of new techniques for integrating efficient boolean reasoning within theory-specific decision procedures, producing big performance improvements when applied (see, e.g., [49, 55, 68, 2, 44, 34, 10]). Nearly all such results have been produced by building decision procedures on top of SAT procedures[3]. Most procedures are based on variants of the DPLL algorithm [33, 32, 74, 15, 63, 51, 39]. In addition to the improvements in SAT technology, the above results rely on a clever integration between SAT solvers and theory-specific decision procedures.

In this chapter we survey, analyze and classify the most effective integration techniques and optimizations for the development of decision procedures which have been proposed in the various communities. Our goal is to provide a unifying and abstract, theory-independent perspective on the various integration schemas and techniques. We also discuss the relative benefits and drawbacks of the various techniques, and we analyze the features for SAT solvers and theory-specific solvers which make them more suitable for an integration.

We briefly mention here an alternative, translational approach to the development of decision procedures [77, 71]. The idea is to generate a propositional formula that is equisatisfiable to the original problem of satisfiability with respect to a given theory, and then decide it by means of a propositional SAT solver. This approach, often referred to as *eager* (to contrast it with the *lazy* approaches described in this chapter), relies even more on the improvement of SAT solvers method, since huge propositional formulae may result from the translation.

The chapter is organized as follows. In §2 we provide some theoretical background, and we recall some basic concepts about SAT procedures. In §3 we introduce some general integration schemata, and discuss the features of SAT solvers and theory-specific decision procedures which make them more suitable for integration.

---

[1] Also called *difference logic*.

[2] By "linear arithmetic" here we mean "boolean combinations of linear equalities and inequalities on $\mathbb{Q}$ or $\mathbb{Z}$" (and boolean propositions).

[3] Notice that the idea of building decision procedures on top of a SAT procedure, and many techniques for maximizing the benefits of this idea, have been conceived first in the domain of modal and description logics [48, 49, 55, 68, 44], and they have been imported into the domain of first-order theories only lately.

In §4 we survey and analyze the various integration techniques and optimizations. In §5, we discuss the case of combined theories. In §6 we overview the some application domains, and in §7 we conclude, highlighting the main research directions and challenges.

2 Background

In this section we recall some basic theoretical concepts, mostly from [50, 70, 5], providing the background for investigating the integration of SAT and decision procedures within our theory-independent perspective. We assume that the reader is familiar with the basic concepts and terminology in logic, theorem proving and SAT.

2.1 Basic Definitions and Results

We abstract away the information specifically related to the theories, and we consider a generic decidable theory $\mathcal{T}$, with the standard semantics of boolean connectives. Notationally, we will often use the prefix "$\mathcal{T}$-" to denote "in the theory $\mathcal{T}$". (E.g., we call a "$\mathcal{T}$-model" a model in $\mathcal{T}$, and so on.)

Given a generic theory $\mathcal{T}$, we consider the $\mathcal{T}$-formulas built on atomic $\mathcal{T}$-formulas ($\mathcal{T}$-atoms) and closed under boolean connectives: a $\mathcal{T}$-atom is a $\mathcal{T}$-formula; if φ_1, φ_2 are $\mathcal{T}$-formulas, then $\neg\varphi_1$ and $(\varphi_1 \wedge \varphi_2)$ are $\mathcal{T}$-formulas; nothing else is a $\mathcal{T}$-formula (e.g., no external quantifiers) [4]. We use the standard boolean abbreviations: "$\varphi_1 \vee \varphi_2$" for "$\neg(\neg\varphi_1 \wedge \neg\varphi_2)$", "$\varphi_1 \rightarrow \varphi_2$" for "$\neg(\varphi_1 \wedge \neg\varphi_2)$", "$\varphi_1 \leftrightarrow \varphi_2$" for "$\neg(\varphi_1 \wedge \neg\varphi_2) \wedge \neg(\varphi_2 \wedge \neg\varphi_1)$", "$\top$" (resp. "$\bot$") for the true (resp. false) constant.

We generically call $\mathcal{T}$-atom any $\mathcal{T}$-formula that cannot be decomposed propositionally, that is, any $\mathcal{T}$-formula whose main connective is not a boolean operator. A $\mathcal{T}$-literal is either an atom (a *positive* literal) or its negation (a *negative* literal). The exact definition of $\mathcal{T}$-atoms and $\mathcal{T}$-literals depends on the theory $\mathcal{T}$ addressed. Examples of $\mathcal{T}$-literals in different theories are,

- A_1 and $\neg A_2$ (boolean),
- $(x - y \leq 6)$ and $\neg(z - y \leq 2)$ $(\mathcal{DL})$,
- $(x_1 + 5 \leq 2x_3)$ and $\neg(2x_1 + x_2 + 4x_3 = 5)$ $(\mathcal{LA}(\mathbb{Z}))$,
- $(c = f(g(a,b)))$ and $\neg(c = g(f(b), h(a)))$ $(\mathcal{EUF})$.

Notationally we use the Greek letters φ, ψ to represent $\mathcal{T}$-formulas, the capital letters A_i's and B_i's to represent boolean atoms, and the Greek letters α, β, γ to represent $\mathcal{T}$-atoms, the letters l_i's to represent $\mathcal{T}$-literals. If l is a negative $\mathcal{T}$-literal $\neg\beta$, then by "$\neg l$" we conventionally mean β rather than $\neg\neg\beta$. We denote by $Atoms(\varphi)$ the set of $\mathcal{T}$-atoms which occur in φ. (For simplicity, henceforth we will sometimes omit the "$\mathcal{T}$-" prefix from "atom" and "literal" when not necessary.)

---

[4] Notice that many theories of practical interest are quantifier-free sub-cases of first order theories, so that the variables are implicitly existentially quantified, and hence equivalent to Skolem constants.

For better readability, in all the examples of this chapter we will use the theory of linear arithmetic on rational number $\mathcal{LA}(\mathbb{Q})$, because of its intuitive semantics. Nevertheless, analogous examples can be built with many other theories of interest.

We call a *total truth assignment* μ for a $\mathcal{T}$-formula φ a set of $\mathcal{T}$-literals

$$\mu = \{\alpha_1, \ldots, \alpha_N, \neg\beta_1, \ldots, \neg\beta_M, A_1, \ldots, A_R, \neg A_{R+1}, \ldots, \neg A_S\}, \qquad (1)$$

such that every $\mathcal{T}$-atom in $Atoms(\varphi)$ occurs as a either positive or negative literal in μ. A *partial truth assignment* μ for φ is a subset of a total truth assignment for φ. If $\mu_2 \subseteq \mu_1$, then we say that μ_1 *extends* μ_2 and that μ_2 *subsumes* μ_1. Notationally, we use the Greek letters μ, η to represent truth assignments.

A total truth assignment μ is interpreted as a truth value assignment to all the atoms of φ: $\alpha_i \in \mu$ means that α_i is assigned to true, $\neg\beta_i \in \mu$ means that β_i is assigned to false. Syntactically identical instances of the same $\mathcal{T}$-atom are always assigned identical truth values; syntactically different $\mathcal{T}$-atoms, e.g., $(t_1 \geq t_2)$ and $(t_2 \leq t_1)$, are treated differently and may thus be assigned different truth values. To this extent, we introduce a bijective function $\mathcal{T2B}$ ("Theory-to-Boolean") and its inverse $\mathcal{B2T} := \mathcal{T2B}^{-1}$ ("Boolean-to-Theory"), s.t. $\mathcal{T2B}$ maps boolean atoms into themselves, $\mathcal{T}$-atoms into fresh boolean atoms —so that two atom instances in φ are mapped into the same boolean atom iff they are syntactically identical— and distributes with sets and boolean connectives. $\mathcal{T2B}$ and $\mathcal{B2T}$ are also called *boolean abstraction* and *refinement* respectively.

We say that a total truth assignment μ for φ *propositionally* $\mathcal{T}$-satisfies φ, written $\mu \models_p \varphi$, if and only if it makes φ evaluate to true, that is, for all sub-formulas φ_1, φ_2 of φ:

$$\begin{aligned}
\mu &\models_p \varphi_1, \ \varphi_1 \in Atoms(\varphi) &&\Longleftrightarrow \varphi_1 \in \mu, \\
\mu &\models_p \neg\varphi_1 &&\Longleftrightarrow \mu \not\models_p \varphi_1, \\
\mu &\models_p \varphi_1 \wedge \varphi_2 &&\Longleftrightarrow \mu \models_p \varphi_1 \text{ and } \mu \models_p \varphi_2.
\end{aligned}$$

We say that a partial truth assignment μ *propositionally* $\mathcal{T}$-satisfies φ if and only if all the total truth assignments for φ which extend μ propositionally $\mathcal{T}$-satisfy φ. (Henceforth, if not specified, when dealing with propositional $\mathcal{T}$-satisfiability we do not distinguish between total and partial assignments.)

Intuitively, if we consider a $\mathcal{T}$-formula φ as a propositional formulas in its atoms, then $\models_p$ is the standard satisfiability in propositional logic, i.e., $\mu \models_p \varphi \Longleftrightarrow \mathcal{T2B}(\mu) \models \mathcal{T2B}(\varphi)$. Thus, for every φ_1 and φ_2, we say that $\varphi_1 \models_p \varphi_2$ if and only if $\mu \models_p \varphi_2$ for every μ s.t. $\mu \models_p \varphi_1$. We say that φ is *propositionally* $\mathcal{T}$-*satisfiable* if and only if there exist an assignment μ s.t. $\mu \models_p \varphi$. We also say that $\models_p \varphi$ (φ is *propositionally valid*) if and only if $\mu \models_p \varphi$ for every assignment μ for φ. Thus $\varphi_1 \models_p \varphi_2$ if and only if $\models_p \varphi_1 \rightarrow \varphi_2$, and $\models_p \varphi$ iff $\neg\varphi$ is propositionally $\mathcal{T}$-unsatisfiable. Notice that $\models_p$ is stronger than $\models_{\mathcal{T}}$, that is, if $\varphi_1 \models_p \varphi_2$, then $\varphi_1 \models_{\mathcal{T}} \varphi_2$, but not vice versa. E.g., $(x_1 \leq x_2) \wedge (x_2 \leq x_3) \models_{\mathcal{T}} (x_1 \leq x_3)$, but $(x_1 \leq x_2) \wedge (x_2 \leq x_3) \not\models_p (x_1 \leq x_3)$.

Example 1. Consider the following $\mathcal{LA}(\mathbb{Q})$-formula φ:

$$\varphi = \{\neg(2x_2 - x_3 > 2) \lor A_1\} \land$$
$$\{\neg A_2 \lor (x_1 - x_5 \le 1)\} \land$$
$$\{(3x_1 - 2x_2 \le 3) \lor A_2\} \land$$
$$\{\neg(2x_3 + x_4 \ge 5) \lor \neg(3x_1 - x_3 \le 6) \lor \neg A_1\} \land$$
$$\{A_1 \lor (3x_1 - 2x_2 \le 3)\} \land$$
$$\{(x_2 - x_4 \le 6) \lor (x_5 = 5 - 3x_4) \lor \neg A_1\} \land$$
$$\{A_1 \lor (x_3 = 3x_5 + 4) \lor A_2\}$$

The partial truth assignment μ given by the underlined literals above is:

$$\{\neg(2x_2 - x_3 > 2), \neg A_2, (3x_1 - 2x_2 \le 3), \neg(3x_1 - x_3 \le 6), (x_2 - x_4 \le 6), (x_3 = 3x_5 + 4)\}.$$

(Notice that the two occurrences of $(3x_1 - 2x_2 \le 3)$ in rows 3 and 5 of φ are both assigned true.) μ is a partial assignment which propositionally $\mathcal{T}$-satisfies φ, as it assigns to true one literal of every disjunction in φ, so that every total assignment which extends μ propositionally $\mathcal{T}$-satisfies φ. Notice that μ is not $\mathcal{T}$-satisfiable, as its sub-assignment

$$\{(3x_1 - 2x_2 \le 3), \neg(2x_2 - x_3 > 2), \neg(3x_1 - x_3 \le 6)\} \tag{2}$$

(rows 3, 1 and 4 in φ) is inconsistent.

We say that a collection $\mathcal{M} = \{\mu_1, \ldots, \mu_n\}$ of partial assignments propositionally $\mathcal{T}$-satisfying φ is *complete* if and only if, for every *total* assignment η s.t. $\eta \models_p \varphi$, there exists $\mu_j \in \mathcal{M}$ s.t. $\mu_j \subseteq \eta$. $\mathcal{M}$ thus represents the set of all total assignments propositionally satisfying φ.

Proposition 1. *Let φ be a $\mathcal{T}$-formula and let $\mathcal{M} = \{\mu_1, \ldots, \mu_n\}$ be a complete collection of truth assignments propositionally satisfying φ. Then, φ is $\mathcal{T}$-satisfiable if and only if μ_j is $\mathcal{T}$-satisfiable for some $\mu_j \in \mathcal{M}$.*

We also notice the following fact.

Proposition 2. *Let α be a non-boolean atom occurring only positively [resp. negatively] in φ. Let $\mathcal{M}$ be a complete set of assignments satisfying φ, and let*

$$\mathcal{M}' := \{\mu_j \setminus \{\neg\alpha\} \mid \mu_j \in \mathcal{M}\} \quad [\text{resp. } \{\mu_j \setminus \{\alpha\} \mid \mu_j \in \mathcal{M}\}].$$

Then (i) for every $\eta' \in \mathcal{M}'$, $\eta' \models_p \varphi$, and (ii) φ is satisfiable if and only if there exist a satisfiable $\eta' \in \mathcal{M}'$.

By proposition 1, $\mathcal{T}$-satisfiability of φ can be decomposed into two orthogonal components: a *purely boolean* one, consisting in searching for (up to a complete set of) propositional models μ's propositionally satisfying φ, and a *purely theory-dependent* one, consisting in checking the $\mathcal{T}$-consistence of μ (that is, for the set of $\mathcal{T}$-literals in μ). This suggests that a decision procedure for a theory $\mathcal{T}$ can be seen as a combination of two basic ingredients: a *Truth Assignment Enumerator* and a *Theory Solver* for $\mathcal{T}$.

We call a *Truth Assignment Enumerator* (ENUMERATOR henceforth) a total function which takes as input a $\mathcal{T}$-formula φ and returns a complete collection $\mathcal{M} :=$ $\{\mu_1, \ldots, \mu_n\}$ of assignments propositionally satisfying φ.

We call a *Theory Solver* for $\mathcal{T}$ ($\mathcal{T}$-SOLVE henceforth) a total function which takes as input a set of $\mathcal{T}$-literals μ and decides whether μ is $\mathcal{T}$-satisfiable; optionally, it can return a $\mathcal{T}$-model satisfying μ, or *Null* if there is none. (It can return also some other information, which we will discuss in §3.2.)

Examples of calls to $\mathcal{T}$-SOLVE for different theories $\mathcal{T}$ are:

- ($\mathcal{EUF}$): $\mathcal{EUF}$-SOLVE($\{a = b, b = f(c), \neg(g(a) = g(f(c)))\}$) returns "unsat";
- ($\mathcal{DL}$): $\mathcal{DL}$-SOLVE($\{(x - y \leq 3), (y - z \leq 4), \neg(x - z \leq 8)\}$) returns "unsat";
- ($\mathcal{LA}(\mathbb{Q})$): $\mathcal{DL}$-SOLVE($\{(x - 2y \leq 3), (4y - 2z < 9), \neg(x - z \leq 7)\}$) returns "sat";
- ($\mathcal{LA}(\mathbb{Z})$): $\mathcal{DL}$-SOLVE($\{(x - 2y \leq 3), (4y - 2z < 9), \neg(x - z \leq 7)\}$) returns "unsat".

Notice that $\mathcal{T}$ can be a combination of sub-theories, and hence $\mathcal{T}$-SOLVE be a combined solver, as in [64, 73, 40, 12, 72].

2.2 Basics on SAT and Boolean Reasoning

A SAT solver is a procedure which decides whether an input boolean formula φ is satisfiable, returning a satisfying assignment if this is the case. (Notice the difference between a SAT solver and a truth assignment enumerator: the former has to find *only one* satisfying assignment —or to decide there is none— while the latter has to find a *complete collection* of satisfying assignments.)

Most state-of-the-art SAT procedures are variants of the DPLL procedure [33, 32]. The "classic" recursive schema of DPLL is described in Figure 1. (For simplicity, we assume here that the input formulas are given in CNF; to see how to use a DPLL with non-CNF formulas see, e.g., [47, 79].) The function SAT takes in input a boolean formula φ and returns a truth value asserting whether φ is satisfiable or not. SAT invokes DPLL passing as arguments φ and (by reference) an empty assignment μ. DPLL tries to build recursively a truth assignment μ satisfying φ, according to the following steps:

- (base) If $\varphi == \top$, then μ satisfies φ. Thus DPLL returns *Sat*.
- (backtrack) If $\varphi == \bot$, then μ has lead to a contradiction. Thus DPLL returns *Unsat* and backtracks.
- (unit propagation) If a literal l occurs in φ as a unit clause, then l must be assigned to true. To obtain this, DPLL is invoked recursively with arguments the formula returned by $assign(l, \varphi)$ and the assignment obtained by adding l to μ. $assign(l, \varphi)$ substitutes every occurrence of l in φ with $\top$ and propositionally simplifies the result.
- (pure literal) If a literal l occurs only positively in φ, then l must be assigned to true. In this case DPLL behaves as with unit propagation.
- (split) If none of the above situations occurs, then *choose-literal(φ)* returns an unassigned literal l according to some heuristic criterion. Then DPLL is first invoked recursively with arguments $assign(l, \varphi)$ and $\mu \cup \{l\}$. If the result is *Sat*, then such value is returned. If the result is *Unsat*, then DPLL is invoked with arguments $assign(\neg l, \varphi)$ and $\mu \cup \{\neg l\}$.

function SAT(*Bool formula* φ)
  return DPLL(φ, {});

function DPLL(*Bool formula* φ, *assignment* & μ)
  if (φ == ⊤)   /* base   */
    then return *Sat*;
  if (φ == ⊥)   /* backtrack */
    then return *Unsat*;
  if {l occurs in φ as a unit clause}   /* unit prop. */
    then return DPLL(*assign*(l, φ), μ ∪ {l});
  if {l occurs only positively in φ}   /* pure literal */
    then return DPLL(*assign*(l, φ), μ ∪ {l});
  l := *choose-literal*(φ);   /* split   */
  if (DPLL(*assign*(l, φ), μ ∪ {l}) == *Sat*)
    then return *Sat*;
    else return DPLL(*assign*(¬l, φ), μ ∪ {¬l});

Fig. 1. The basic recursive schema of DPLL

In current SAT solvers, the pure literal rule is rarely implemented, because its benefits do not balance its overheads.

DPLL can be used as truth assignment enumerator as well, by modifying the "base" step so that it stores the assignment μ and backtracks, and by dropping the pure literal step ([49, 50]). The resulting collection of assignments is complete [70].

In order to keep our explanation as simple as possible, in this chapter we will adopt the basic recursive representation of DPLL of Figure 1. We notice, however, that this schema is, to many extents, over-simplified. Modern DPLL implementation are non-recursive, and are based on very efficient, destructive data structures to handle boolean formulas and assignments. They benefit of sophisticated search techniques (e.g., back-jumping, learning, restarts [74, 15, 52]), smart splitting heuristics (e.g., [63, 51, 39]), highly-engineered data structures and implementation tricks (e.g., the two-watched literal scheme [63]), and advanced preprocessing techniques [24, 8, 38].

In particular, modern DPLL implementations perform *conflict analysis* on failed assignments μ's, which detect the *reason* of each failure, that is, a (typically much smaller) subset μ' of μ which alone causes the failure. When this happens, the procedure

- adds the negation of μ' as a new clause to the formula, so that no assignment containing μ' will be ever investigated again. This technique is called *learning*;
- backtracks to the highest point in the stack where one literal l in the learned clause ¬μ' is not assigned, it unit propagates l, and it proceeds with the search. This technique is called *backjumping*.

Backjumping and learning are of great interest in our discussion, as it will be made clear in §4. The other enhancements come for free by using state-of-the-art SAT solvers and they are substantially orthogonal to our discussion, so that they will not be discussed here.

3   Integrating DPLL and Theory-Specific Solvers

The basic schema of a decision procedure for $\mathcal{T}$-satisfiability, which we generically call "$\mathcal{T}$-SAT" henceforth, is reported in Figure 2. $\mathcal{T}$-SAT takes as input a $\mathcal{T}$-formula φ, and builds its boolean abstraction $\varphi^p \doteq \mathcal{T2B}(\varphi)$. (Notationally, we use the superscript ^{p} to denote boolean abstractions: given a $\mathcal{T}$-expression e, we write e^p to denote $\mathcal{T2B}(e)$. Similarly, we write e to denote $\mathcal{B2T}(e^p)$.) Notice that both $\mathcal{T2B}$ and $\mathcal{B2T}$ can be implemented so that to require constant time to map a literal from one representation to the other.

φ^p is given in input to ENUMERATOR, which enumerates all the assignments in a complete collection $\{\mu_1^p, .., \mu_n^p\}$ for φ^p. Each time a new μ^p is generated, its corresponding list of $\mathcal{T}$-literals μ is fed to the theory solver $\mathcal{T}$-SOLVE ($\mathcal{T}$-SOLVE can be invoked also on intermediate assignments during their constructions, as it will be made clear in §4.) If μ is found $\mathcal{T}$-satisfiable, then the procedure ends and returns "Sat". If not, a new assignment is generated by ENUMERATOR, and so on. The process is repeated until either one $\mathcal{T}$-satisfiable assignment is found, or no more assignments are generated by ENUMERATOR. In the former case φ is $\mathcal{T}$-satisfiable, in the latter case it is not.

3.1   The Online and Offline Integration Schemata

A DPLL-based $\mathcal{T}$-SAT solver ($\mathcal{T}$-DPLL henceforth) is a variant of the DPLL procedure, modified to work as an enumerator of assignments, whose $\mathcal{T}$-satisfiability is checked by $\mathcal{T}$-SOLVE, in accordance with the paradigm of Figure 2.

In Figure 3 we propose a representation of $\mathcal{T}$-DPLL, following the simplified schema of DPLL given in Figure 1. (The reader may refer, e.g., to [23] for a more realistic representation of a modern $\mathcal{T}$-DPLL engine.) Like DPLL, $\mathcal{T}$-DPLL gets as input a boolean formula, which is the result of applying $\mathcal{T2B}$ to the input $\mathcal{T}$-formula, and by reference, an empty assignment μ. The $\mathcal{T}$-DPLL schema differs from that of DPLL only by two steps. (We temporarily ignore the "early pruning" step in $\mathcal{T}$-DPLL, which will be discussed in §4.)

The first is the "base" case: when DPLL finds an assignment μ which propositionally satisfies the input formula, simply returns "Sat". $\mathcal{T}$-DPLL instead, whenever an assignment μ has been found, has to check the $\mathcal{T}$-satisfiability of the corresponding set of $\mathcal{T}$-literals by invoking $\mathcal{T}$-SOLVE($\mathcal{B2T}(\mu)$). If the latter returns "Sat", then the whole formula is satisfiable and $\mathcal{T}$-DPLL returns "Sat" as well; otherwise, $\mathcal{T}$-DPLL backtracks and looks for the next assignment, and so on.

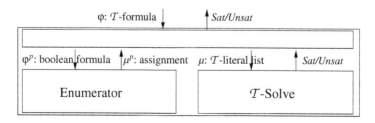

Fig. 2. Basic schema of an integrated procedure

```
function T-SAT(T-formula φ)
   return T-DPLL(T2B(φ), {});

function T-DPLL(Bool formula φ, assignment & μ)
   if (φ == ⊤)                              /* base       */
      then return T-SOLVE(B2T(μ)) ;
   if (φ == ⊥)                              /* backtrack */
      then return Unsat;
   if {l occurs in φ as a unit clause}      /* unit prop. */
      then return T-DPLL(assign(l, φ), μ ∪ {l});
   if (T-SOLVE(B2T(μ)) == Unsat)            /* early pruning */
      then return Unsat;
   l := choose-literal(φ);                  /* split      */
   if ( T-DPLL(assign(l, φ), μ ∪ {l}) == Sat )
      then return Sat;
      else return T-DPLL(assign(¬l, φ), μ ∪ {¬l});
```

Fig. 3. The basic schema of a DPLL-based satisfiability procedure for T.

The second is in the fact that the pure literal step is removed in T-DPLL. In fact the sets of assignments generated by DPLL with pure literal rule may be incomplete and cause incorrect results, as shown by the following example.

Example 2. Let φ be the following T-formula:

$$((x-y \leq 1) \vee A_1) \wedge ((y-z \leq 2) \vee A_2) \wedge (\neg(x-z \leq 4) \vee A_2) \wedge (\neg A_2 \vee A_3) \wedge (\neg A_2 \vee \neg A_3).$$

φ is T-satisfiable, because $\mu = \{A_1, \neg A_2, (y-z \leq 2), \neg(x-z \leq 4)\}$ is a consistent assignment propositionally satisfying φ. It is easy to see that no satisfiable assignment propositionally satisfying φ contains $(x-y \leq 1)$. Unfortunately, as $(x-y \leq 1)$ occurs only positively in φ, DPLL with the pure literal rule may assign $(x-y \leq 1)$ to true as first step, which leads the procedure to return the incorrect value "Unsat".

An alternative way of integrating DPLL and T-SOLVE is that independently proposed in [10] and in [35]. In its naivest form, the idea works as follows. The propositional abstraction of the input formula φ ($T2B(\varphi)$ in our notation) is given as input to a SAT solver, which either decides that $T2B(\varphi)$ is unsatisfiable, and hence φ is T-unsatisfiable, or it returns a satisfying assignment μ; in the latter case, μ is mapped back to the domain T ($B2T(\mu)$ in our notation), and $B2T(\mu)$ is given as input to T-SOLVE. If $B2T(\mu)$ is found T-consistent, then φ is T-consistent. If not, the negation of $B2T(\mu)$ is added as a clause to φ, and the SAT solver is *restarted from scratch* on (the boolean abstraction of) the resulting formula. The proposed schema can be improved when T-SOLVE is able to return the subset η which caused the T-inconsistency of $B2T(\mu)$ (see §4).

Following [41], we call *offline* integration schemata those in which DPLL is used as a SAT solver, and thus is reinvoked from scratch each time an assignment is found T-unsatisfiable (e.g., [10, 35]); we call *online* integration schema(s) those in which DPLL is *customized* to be used directly as an enumerator, that is, in which each time it continues the boolean search from the point the checked assignment was found (e.g., [48, 55, 82, 2, 4, 23]). An extreme case of online approach is that of the tool DPLL(T) described in [43, 66], where a DPLL enumerator is implemented ad-hoc, so that to embed some theory-specific reasoning steps within the SAT solver.

An alternative way of describing DPLL-based decision procedures is proposed by [80, 67], who introduced rule-based logical frameworks for representing both DPLL and of DPLL-based procedures, which are thus represented as control strategies applied to a set of formal rules. This framework allows for expressing and formally reasoning about most known variants of both DPLL and DPLL-based decision procedures (see also [43, 66]).

3.2 Features of Theory Solvers

We now discuss some features for $\mathcal{T}$-SOLVE, which can be extremely useful to maximize the benefits of the interaction between $\mathcal{T}$-SOLVE and ENUMERATOR, in particular when the latter is a DPLL solver.

Incrementality and Backtrackability. It is often the case that $\mathcal{T}$-SOLVE is invoked sequentially on *incremental* assignments, in a stack-based manner, like in the following trace (left column first, then right) [21]:

$\mathcal{T}$-SOLVE(μ_1)	$\Longrightarrow$ *Sat*	Undo μ_4, μ_3, μ_2	
$\mathcal{T}$-SOLVE$(\mu_1 \cup \mu_2)$	$\Longrightarrow$ *Sat*	$\mathcal{T}$-SOLVE$(\mu_1 \cup \mu_2')$	$\Longrightarrow$ *Sat*
$\mathcal{T}$-SOLVE$(\mu_1 \cup \mu_2 \cup \mu_3)$	$\Longrightarrow$ *Sat*	$\mathcal{T}$-SOLVE$(\mu_1 \cup \mu_2' \cup \mu_3')$	$\Longrightarrow$ *Sat*
$\mathcal{T}$-SOLVE$(\mu_1 \cup \mu_2 \cup \mu_3 \cup \mu_4)$	$\Longrightarrow$ *Unsat*	...	

Thus, a key efficiency issue of $\mathcal{T}$-SOLVE is that of being *incremental* and *backtrackable*. Incremental means that $\mathcal{T}$-SOLVE "remembers" its computation status from one call to the other, so that, whenever it is given in input an assignment $\mu_1 \cup \mu_2$ such that μ_1 has just been proved $\mathcal{T}$-satisfiable, it avoids restarting the computation from scratch by restarting the computation from the previous status. Backtrackable[5] means that it is possible to efficiently undo previous additions and return to a previous status on the stack.

For instance, there are incremental and backtrackable versions of the congruence closure algorithm for $\mathcal{EUF}$ logic [65], of the Belman-Ford algorithm for $\mathcal{DL}$ [30, 66], and of the Simplex LP procedure for $\mathcal{LA}(\mathbb{Q})$ [9].

Conflict set generation. Given a $\mathcal{T}$-unsatisfiable assignment μ, we call a *conflict set*[6] any $\mathcal{T}$-unsatisfiable sub-assignment $\mu' \subseteq \mu$; we say that μ' is a *minimal* conflict set if all strict subsets of μ' are $\mathcal{T}$-consistent. (E.g., in Example 1, (2) is a minimal conflict set for μ.) A key efficiency issue for $\mathcal{T}$-SOLVE, whenever it is invoked on an $\mathcal{T}$-inconsistent assignment μ, is its ability to produce the (possibly minimal) conflict set of μ which has caused its inconsistency.

For instance, there exist conflict-set-producing variants for the Belman-Ford algorithm for $\mathcal{DL}$ [30], for the Simplex LP procedures for $\mathcal{LA}(\mathbb{Q})$ [9] and for the congruence closure algorithm for $\mathcal{EUF}$ [65].

---

[5] The word *resettable* is used in other contests (e.g., [64]) to indicate the same feature.

[6] Conflict sets are sometimes referred to as *reasons* or *proofs*.

Deduction. For some theories it is possible to implement $\mathcal{T}$-SOLVE so that some call to $\mathcal{T}$-SOLVE(μ) returning "Sat" can also perform a set of deductions in the form $\mu' \models_{\mathcal{T}} l$, s.t. $\mu' \subseteq \mu$ and l is a literal on a not-yet-assigned atom in φ. We say that $\mathcal{T}$-SOLVE is *deduction-complete* if it can perform all possible such deductions. [7]

Example 3. Consider the $\mathcal{T}$-formula φ in Example 1, and suppose $\mathcal{T}$-SOLVE is called on $\{\neg(2x_2 - x_3 > 2), \neg(3x_1 - x_3 \leq 6), (x_3 = 3x_5 + 4)\}$ (1st, 4th and 7th rows in φ); then $\mathcal{T}$-SOLVE returns "Sat" and may perform and return the deduction

$$\{\neg(2x_2 - x_3 > 2), \neg(3x_1 - x_3 \leq 6)\} \models_{\mathcal{T}} \neg(3x_1 - 2x_2 \leq 3). \tag{3}$$

For instance, for $\mathcal{EUF}$, the computation of congruence closure allows for efficiently deducing positive equalities, like $\{(a = b), (b = g(c))\} \models_{euf} (f(a) = f(g(c)))$ [65]. For $\mathcal{DL}$, a very efficient implementation of a deduction-complete $\mathcal{T}$-SOLVE has been presented by [66]. For $\mathcal{LA}(\mathbb{Q})$ and $\mathcal{LA}(\mathbb{Z})$ the task is much harder. A very partial form of deduction is that of [4], which computes equivalence classes on variables and performs substitutions in the unassigned atoms.

Notice that, in principle, every $\mathcal{T}$-SOLVE has deduction capabilities, as it is always possible to call $\mathcal{T}$-SOLVE$(\mu \cup \{\neg l\})$ for every unassigned literal l. This technique, called *plunging* [37], is in practice very inefficient, unless applied in some particular applications [2].

4   Efficient Integration Techniques

The basic integration schemata of §3.1 are rather naive, as $\mathcal{T}$-DPLL interacts with $\mathcal{T}$-SOLVE in a blind way, without exchanging any information with $\mathcal{T}$-SOLVE about the semantics of the $\mathcal{T}$-atoms to which it is assigning boolean values. This may cause an excessive number of calls to $\mathcal{T}$-SOLVE on assignments which are obviously $\mathcal{T}$-inconsistent, or whose inconsistency could have been easily derived from that of previously checked assignments.

In this section we describe the most effective integration techniques and optimizations which have been proposed in various communities, for the theories listed in §1. Such techniques have been collected from a large and very heterogeneous bibliography, "cleaned up" of any information related to the theory $\mathcal{T}$, renamed and grouped according to the form of interaction between the boolean and the theory-specific components of reasoning. To this extent, we remark a few facts.

First, we focus on the interaction between boolean reasoning and theory-specific reasoning. Therefore techniques and optimizations focused only on pure boolean reasoning (e.g., *boolean preprocessing* [24, 8, 38] or *restarts* [52]) or on pure theory-specific reasoning (e.g., *layering* [4, 21]) are not considered here.

Second, the techniques and optimizations described here may have been called different names in their source papers, so that the names used here may differ from those

---

[7] Notice the difference between the deduction of generic unassigned literal, which must occur in φ, and that performed by theory solvers in Nelson-Oppen style tools (e.g., [64, 73, 40, 12, 72]), which deduce equalities in the form $x = y$ which do not necessarily occur in φ.

used by some of the authors. (E.g., *Theory-driven deduction* (see §4.6) is called *forward reasoning* in [2], *enhanced early pruning* in [4], *theory propagation* in [67, 66], *theory-driven deduction or $\mathcal{T}$-deduction* in [21].)

Third, we may present as separate techniques which some authors present as one technique (but some other authors do not). (E.g., *early pruning* (§4.3) and *theory-driven deduction* (§4.6) are often described as only one technique (e.g., in [43]).)

Finally, and more generally, due to the effort of collecting and describing from a unified perspective techniques which have been presented by a variety of authors in different domains, the description of some technique may differ significantly from that given by some of the authors. (E.g., [67, 43, 66] describe their procedures in terms of inference rules and control strategies, whilst most authors instead prefer a pseudo-code description.)

We coarsely distinguish four main categories of integration techniques and optimizations.

Preprocessing. Rewrite the input $\mathcal{T}$-formula φ into an equivalent or equivalently satisfiable one which is supposedly easier to solve for $\mathcal{T}$-DPLL. Among them we have *normalizing $\mathcal{T}$-atoms* and *static learning*.

Look-ahead. Analyze the current status of the search and get from it as much information as possible which is useful to prune the remaining search space. Among them we have *early pruning, theory-driven deduction*, and *branching heuristics*.

Look-back. When recovering from a failure, try to understand the cause of that failure and use such an information to improve future search. Among them we have *theory-driven backjumping* and *theory-driven learning*.

Assignment simplification. $\mathcal{T}$-DPLL can provide useful information to make the assignment smaller and/or simpler for $\mathcal{T}$-SOLVE. Among them we have *clustering, reduction of assignments to prime implicants, pure literal filtering* and *theory literal filtering*.

4.1 Normalizing $\mathcal{T}$-Atoms

The idea of normalizing the $\mathcal{T}$-atoms was first suggested by [48] for their DPLL-based procedure for modal logics; similar idea were then introduced for description logics in [55, 68], and for $\mathcal{LA}(\mathbb{Z})$ in [4].

One potential source of inefficiency for $\mathcal{T}$-DPLL is the fact that semantically equivalent but syntactically different atoms are not recognized to be identical [resp. one the negation of the other] and thus they may be assigned different [resp. identical] truth values. For instance, syntactically different atoms may be equivalent modulo reordering or associativity of operators, or may be one the negation of the other. This causes the undesired generation of a potentially very big amount of intrinsically $\mathcal{T}$-unsatisfiable assignments (for instance, up to $2^{Atoms(\varphi)-2}$ assignments of the kind $\{(x_1 < x_2), (x_1 \geq x_2), ...\}$).

To avoid these problems, it is wise to preprocess atoms so that to map semantically equivalent atoms into syntactically identical ones. Some typical rewriting steps are:

- *Rewrite dual operators*. E.g., $(x_1 < x_2), (x_1 \geq x_2) \implies \neg(x_1 \geq x_2), (x_1 \geq x_2)$.
- *Exploit associativity of operators*. E.g., $(x_1 + (x_2 + x_3) = 1), ((x_1 + x_2) + x_3) = 1 \implies (x_1 + x_2 + x_3 = 1)$.

- *Sort.* E.g., $(x_1 + x_2 - x_3 \leq 1)$, $(x_2 + x_1 - 1 \leq x_3) \Longrightarrow (x_1 + x_2 - x_3 \leq 1))$.
- *Exploiting specific properties of $\mathcal{T}$.* E.g., in $\mathcal{LA}(\mathbb{Z})$, $(x_1 \leq 3)$, $(x_1 < 4) \Longrightarrow (x_1 \leq 3)$.

Of course, the applicability and effectiveness of these mappings depend on the theory addressed. Although rather straightforward, normalizing atoms is an essential step which may drastically reduce the global amount of search (see, e.g., [48]).

4.2   Static Learning

The following idea was proposed by [2] for their procedure $\mathcal{DL}$. Similar such techniques were generalized and used in [7, 58, 21].

On some specific kind of problems, it is possible to quickly detect a priori short and "obviously $\mathcal{T}$-inconsistent" assignments of $\mathcal{T}$-atoms occurring in the original formula (typically pairs or triplets). Some examples are:

- *incompatible value assignments* (e.g., $\{x = 0, x = 1\}$),
- *congruence constraints* (e.g., $\{(x_1 = y_1), (x_2 = y_2), \neg(f(x_1, x_2) = f(y_1, y_2))\}$),
- *incompatible difference constraints* (e.g., $\{(x - y = 2), (y - z \leq 4), \neg(x - z \leq 5)\}$),
- *equivalence constraints* ($\{(x = y), (2x - 3z \leq 3), \neg(2y - 3z \leq 3)\}$).

If so, the clauses obtained by negating the assignments (e.g., $\neg(x = 0) \vee \neg(x = 1)$) can be added a priori to the formula before the search starts. Thus, whenever all but one of the literals in the inconsistent assignment are assigned, the negation of the remaining one is deterministically assigned by unit propagation, which prevents the solver generating any assignment including the inconsistent one. This technique may drastically prune the boolean search space, and thus produce very relevant speed-ups [2, 7, 21].

Notice that, unlike the extra clauses added in [77, 71], the clauses added by static learning refer only to atoms which *already occur in the original formula*, so that no new atom is added. This means that the boolean search space is not enlarged. Furthermore, we remark that, unlike with [77, 71], these added clauses are not needed for correctness and completeness, but rather they are only used for reducing the boolean search space.

4.3   Early Pruning

The following enhancement to the basic integration schema of Figure 3, here called *early pruning*[8], was introduced by [48] in procedures for modal and description logics; [82, 4, 10, 43] developed similar ideas in procedures for $\mathcal{LA}(\mathbb{Q})$, $\mathcal{LA}(\mathbb{Z})$, $\mathcal{EUF}$, $\mathcal{BV}(\mathbb{Z})$, $\mathcal{AR}(\mathbb{Z})$ and inductive datatypes.

Typically most assignments found by $\mathcal{T}$-DPLL are "trivially" $\mathcal{T}$-unsatisfiable, in the sense that their $\mathcal{T}$-unsatisfiability is caused by much smaller subsets (conflict sets). If an assignment μ' is $\mathcal{T}$-unsatisfiable, then all its extensions are $\mathcal{T}$-unsatisfiable. If the unsatisfiability of an assignment μ' is detected during its construction, then this prevents checking the $\mathcal{T}$-satisfiability of all the up to $2^{|Atoms(\varphi)| - |\mu'|}$ total truth assignments which extend μ'.

This suggests to introduce an intermediate $\mathcal{T}$-satisfiability test on intermediate assignments before each decision (in Figure 3, just before the "split" step). If $\mathcal{T}$-SOLVE(μ) returns *Unsat*, then all possible extensions of μ are unsatisfiable, and therefore $\mathcal{T}$-DPLL returns *Unsat* and backtracks, avoiding a possibly big amount of useless search.

---

[8] Also called *intermediate assignment checking* [48] and *eager notification* [10].

Example 4. Consider the formula φ of Example 1. Suppose that, after four decisions, $\mathcal{T}$-DPLL builds the intermediate assignment:

$$\mu' = \{\neg(2x_2 - x_3 > 2), \neg A_2, (3x_1 - 2x_2 \le 3), \neg(3x_1 - x_3 \le 6)\}, \qquad (4)$$

(rows 1, 2, 3 and 5, 4 of φ respectively). If $\mathcal{T}$-SOLVE is invoked on μ', it returns *Unsat*, and $\mathcal{T}$-DPLL backtracks without exploring any extension of μ'.

In theory, the introduction of an intermediate consistency check before *every* split could negatively affect the global worst-case performance. In practice, it is sufficient an average pruning of one split per branch to make the intermediate consistency check worth doing[9]. (E.g., in the worst-case in which no intermediate test causes backtracking, the number of $\mathcal{T}$-SOLVE calls doubles.) Notice that the overhead of intermediate calls in early pruning reduces drastically if $\mathcal{T}$-SOLVE is incremental (see §3.2).

Some variants of early pruning have been proposed in the literature.

Selective or intermittent early pruning. Some heuristic criteria can be introduced to reduce the number of redundant calls to $\mathcal{T}$-SOLVE in early pruning steps. One way is not to invoke $\mathcal{T}$-SOLVE when it is very unlikely that, since last call, the new literals added to μ' can cause inconsistency. For instance, this is the case when they are added only literals which either are purely-propositional [48] or contain new variables [4].

Another way is to call $\mathcal{T}$-SOLVE every k branching steps, k being an user-defined integer parameter [3].

Weakened early pruning. In order to further reduce the overhead due to early pruning, another idea is to use, for intermediate checks only, *weaker* but *faster* versions of $\mathcal{T}$-SOLVE [22]. This is possible because intermediate checks are not necessary to the correctness and completeness of the procedure. The notion of "weaker $\mathcal{T}$-SOLVE" depends on the theory we are dealing with. Some general ideas are:

- in case of "Sat" response, avoid reconstructing the satisfying assignments and models (which are non-informative in intermediate checks);
- check only easier-to-check sub-assignments of μ. E.g., as $\mathcal{DL}$ is much easier than $\mathcal{LA}$, if μ is $\{(x - y \le 4), (z - x \le -6), (z - y = 0), (x - y = z - w)\}$, then one can test only the sub-assignment dealing with $\mathcal{DL}$ terms (e.g., the first three literals in μ, which are inconsistent) and backtrack if this is inconsistent[10];
- check μ only on some easier theory $\mathcal{T}'$ s.t., if φ is inconsistent in $\mathcal{T}'$ then φ is inconsistent in $\mathcal{T}$. For example, as $\mathcal{LA}(\mathbb{Z})$ is way harder than $\mathcal{LA}(\mathbb{Q})$ (see [17]), we may want to check the consistency of an assignment on $\mathbb{R}$ rather than on $\mathbb{Z}$, and backtrack if $\mathcal{T}$-SOLVE return "Unsat".

On the whole, there is a tradeoff between the benefits of reducing the overhead and the drawbacks of reducing the pruning effect.

---

[9] In fact, in a binary tree the number of internal nodes equals the number of leaves minus one.

[10] This situation is the very frequent in the domain of bounded model checking for timed systems, where we have a big majority of $\mathcal{DL}$ literals, and only very few $\mathcal{LA}$ literals [7].

Eager early pruning. Some DPLL-based procedures for various theories (e.g., [82, 78, 43, 66]) perform a more *eager* form of early pruning, in which the theory solver is invoked every time a new $\mathcal{T}$-atom is added to the assignment (including those added by unit propagation). In the schema of Figure 3, this corresponds to move the early pruning step before the unit propagation one. The eager approach benefits of a more aggressive pruning due to $\mathcal{T}$-inconsistencies, but pays for extra overhead.

4.4   Theory-Driven Backjumping

This technique, which generalizes that of backjumping in standard DPLL, was introduced by [55] and [68] for description logics; [82, 4, 35, 78] proposed the same idea for many other theories.

As for early pruning, the rationale of Theory-driven backjumping ($\mathcal{T}$-backjumping henceforth) it to avoid investigating parts of the boolean search tree under an intermediate branch which is $\mathcal{T}$-inconsistent. Suppose a satisfying assignment μ is found and $\mathcal{T}$-SOLVE is invoked on μ, which is found $\mathcal{T}$-inconsistent; suppose also that $\mathcal{T}$-SOLVE is able to return also a conflict set $\eta \subseteq \mu$ causing the $\mathcal{T}$-unsatisfiability of the input assignment μ, as discussed in §3.2. If so, $\mathcal{T}$-DPLL can jump back in its search to the most recent branching point s.t. at least one literal $l \in \eta$ is not assigned; in fact, all subbranches of the branch below that point contain the conflict set η, so that there is no need to explore them. This allows for pruning all these subbranches from the search tree[11].

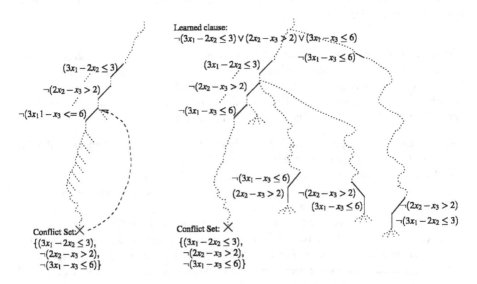

Fig. 4. Example of search trees: left: with theory-driven backjumping; right: with theory-driven learning

---

[11] In more modern implementations, $\mathcal{T}$-DPLL can jump back in its search to the highest point where only one literal $l \in \eta$ is not assigned, unit-propagate $\neg l$, and proceed with the search.

Example 5. Consider the formula φ and the assignment μ of Example 1, and suppose that φ is a small subpart of a much bigger formula φ', and that μ is a small subpart of an assignment μ' propositionally satisfying it. Assume the literals in μ have been assigned in order. Consider the following scenario, depicted in the search schema of Figure 4, left: $\mathcal{T}$-SOLVE is invoked on μ', and returns the conflict set (2) in Example 1; thus $\mathcal{T}$-DPLL can jump back directly to the most recent branching point where at least one literal in the conflict set is not assigned (say $\neg(3x_1 - x_3 \leq 6)$), because all subbranches below that point would lead to assignment containing the conflict set, and can thus be skipped. (E.g., no need to try to assign negative values to $(x_2 - x_4 \leq 6)$ and $(x_3 = 3x_5 + 4)$).

$\mathcal{T}$-backjumping is very similar to standard DPLL backjumping. The main difference is in the notion of conflict set used: here a conflict set is an assignment which is *intrinsically inconsistent in $\mathcal{T}$*, rather than an assignment which forces propositional inconsistency if added to φ.

In general, the benefits of $\mathcal{T}$-backjumping depend on the "quality" of the conflict set returned by $\mathcal{T}$-SAT. To this extent, techniques to force $\mathcal{T}$-SOLVE to return "better" or "best" conflict sets have been proposed in [83, 3] for different theories.

4.5 Theory-Driven Learning

This technique, which generalizes that of learning in standard DPLL procedures, was introduced by [82] for $\mathcal{LA}(\mathbb{Q})$; [4, 35, 78, 41] proposed the same idea for many other theories.

The rationale of theory-driven learning ($\mathcal{T}$-learning henceforth) is that, when $\mathcal{T}$-SOLVE returns a conflict set η, the clause $\neg\eta$ can be added in conjunction to φ. Since then, $\mathcal{T}$-DPLL will never again generate any branch containing η. In fact, as soon as $|\eta| - 1$ literals in η are assigned to true, the remaining literal will be immediately assigned to false by unit propagation.

Example 6. Consider the formula φ of Example 1. As in Examples 5, suppose $\mathcal{T}$-SOLVE returns the conflict set (2). Then the clause

$$\neg(3x_1 - 2x_2 \leq 3) \vee (2x_2 - x_3 > 2) \vee (3x_1 - x_3 \leq 6)$$

is added in conjunction to φ. Thus, in all future branches, whenever a branch contains two elements of the conflict set, then $\mathcal{T}$-DPLL will immediately assign the third to false by unit propagation (Figure 4, right).

As for $\mathcal{T}$-backjumping, the only difference wrt. standard DPLL learning is in the notion of conflict set used, which is an assignment intrinsically inconsistent in $\mathcal{T}$. To this extent, notice that, whilst for $\mathcal{T}$-backjumping the best conflict set is that which forces the highest jump in the stack, for $\mathcal{T}$-learning the best conflict set is the one which causes the pruning of most future branches. In practice, these are the shortest conflict sets and those containing most atoms occurring in future branches (relevant atoms). To this extent, techniques to force $\mathcal{T}$-SOLVE to return shorter conflict sets have been proposed in [83, 3, 36] for different theories.

Like all learning techniques, $\mathcal{T}$-learning must be used with some care, because it may cause an explosion in size of φ. To avoid this, one has to introduce techniques for discarding learned clauses when necessary [15]. Luckily, by using one modern DPLL implementation from the shelf, one gets this feature for free.

As with static learning, the clauses added by $\mathcal{T}$-learning refer only to atoms which already occur in the original formula, so that no new atom is added. [41] proposed an interesting generalization of $\mathcal{T}$-learning, in which at each consistency check more than one clause may be added, which may contain also new atoms. To overcome the consequent enlargement of the search space, they proposed to restrict splitting to the original atoms. [20, 23] used a similar idea to improve the efficiency of Delayed Theory Combination (see §5).

4.6 Theory-Driven Deduction of Unassigned Literals

Theory-driven deduction of unassigned literals —$\mathcal{T}$-deduction henceforth [12]— was introduced in its simplest form (plunging) by [2] for $\mathcal{DL}$; [4], [80], [14] proposed similar or improved techniques for other theories; however, the technique showed its full potential in [43, 66], where solvers for $\mathcal{EUF}$ and $\mathcal{DL}$ have been presented, which apply $\mathcal{T}$-deduction aggressively, obtaining impressive performances. Remarkably, the latter paper introduced also a general technique for exploiting the use of deduction-complete theory solvers.

As discussed in §3.2, for some theories it is possible to implement $\mathcal{T}$-SOLVE so that any call to $\mathcal{T}$-SOLVE(μ) returning "Sat" can also perform a set of deductions in the form $\mu' \models_{\mathcal{T}} l$, s.t. $\mu' \subseteq \mu$ and l is a literal on a not-yet-assigned atom in φ. If this is the case, then $\mathcal{T}$-SOLVE can return l, which is unit-propagated away by $\mathcal{T}$-DPLL. This may induce new literals to be assigned, new calls to $\mathcal{T}$-SOLVE, new assignments deduced, and so on, possibly causing a beneficial loop between $\mathcal{T}$-deduction and unit propagation [13].

The effects of $\mathcal{T}$-deduction can be used also for learning. Whenever $\mathcal{T}$-SOLVE deduces a literal l as a $\mathcal{T}$-consequence of $\{l_1, ..., l_k\}$, the clause $\bigvee_{i=1}^{k} \neg l_i \vee l$ can be learned, with benefits analogous to those of $\mathcal{T}$-learning. (Again, one must take into account the problem of the potential explosion of φ, as hinted in §4.5.)

Example 7. Consider the following scenario with the $\mathcal{T}$-formula φ in Example 1: $\mathcal{T}$-SOLVE is called on $\{\neg(2x_2 - x_3 > 2), \neg(3x_1 - x_3 \leq 6), (x_3 = 3x_5 + 4)\}$ (1st, 4th and 7th rows in φ); then $\mathcal{T}$-SOLVE returns "Sat" and deduces $\{\neg(3x_1 - 2x_2 \leq 3)\}$ (3rd and 5th rows) as a consequence of the first two literals. This forces unit-propagating A_1 and A_2, and hence $(x_1 - x_5 \leq 1)$ (2nd row); then $\mathcal{T}$-SOLVE is invoked on the resulting assignment:

$$\{\neg(2x_2 - x_3 > 2), \underline{\neg(3x_1 - x_3 \leq 6)}, (x_3 = 3x_5 + 4), \neg(3x_1 - 2x_2 \leq 3), \underline{(x_1 - x_5 \leq 1)}\}$$

---

[12] Also called *forward reasoning* in [2], *enhanced early pruning* in [4], *theory propagation* in [67, 66].

[13] As an implementation remark, implementing this technique on top of a modern DPLL implementation can be tricky, as the deduction mechanism may interfere with the "reason" in the construction of the implication graph [74] of DPLL. [43] show how to tackle these problems.

which is inconsistent because of the 2nd, 3rd and 5th literals, so that the whole procedure backtracks, learning the corresponding conflict clause. The deduction step allows
for learning also the clause

$$(2x_2 - x_3 > 2) \vee (3x_1 - x_3 \leq 6) \vee \neg(3x_1 - 2x_2 \leq 3),$$

which is the same as in Example 6, and will thus produce the benefits described there.

As $\mathcal{T}$-deduction is performed during the intermediate calls to $\mathcal{T}$-SOLVE, it is always
related to early pruning. Like with early pruning, $\mathcal{T}$-deduction can be applied either in
a lazy way, before any new branching [4], or, more eagerly, every time a new $\mathcal{T}$-atom is
added to the assignment (including those added by unit propagation) [2, 13, 80, 14, 43].
As with early pruning, the eager approach benefits of a more aggressive pruning, but
pays for extra overhead.

4.7   Clustering

This technique was proposed in [21] for $\mathcal{EUF}$, $\mathcal{LA}(\mathbb{Q})$ and $\mathcal{LA}(\mathbb{Z})$.

At the beginning of the search, the set of $\mathcal{T}$-atoms of φ is partitioned into a set
of disjoint *clusters* $C_1 \cup \cdots \cup C_k$, s.t. atoms which do not interfere to each-other's $\mathcal{T}$-
satisfiability belong to different clusters. Consequently, every assignment μ can be partitioned into k disjoint sub-assignments μ_i, one for each cluster, so that μ is $\mathcal{T}$-satisfiable
iff each μ_i is. Based on this idea, instead of having a single, monolithic solver, $\mathcal{T}$-
SOLVE is instantiated (up to) k different times: each is responsible for the handling of
the reasoning within a single cluster.

The advantage of this "divide-and-conquer" approach is manifold. First, k solvers
running on k disjoint problems are typically faster then running one solver monolithi-
cally on the union of the problems. Second, the solvers can be activated in a lazy way: if
one returns "Unsat", there is no need to call the others. Third, the construction of smaller
conflict sets becomes easier, and this may result in significant gain in the overall search.

4.8   Reduction of Assignments to Prime Implicants

The following technique was recently proposed for $\mathcal{DL}$ [3].

Let μ be an assignment propositionally satisfying the input formula φ. Sometimes
μ may not be a *prime implicant* for φ, that is, some of the literals in μ may be unnecessary to propositionally satisfy φ (i.e., $\mu \setminus \{l\} \models_p \varphi$ for some $l \in \mu$). The typical case
is when more than two literals in the same clause are satisfied by μ. Thus $\mathcal{T}$-SOLVE
may eliminate such literals l's from μ. There are a couple of potential benefits for this
behavior. Let μ' be the reduced version of μ. First, μ' might be $\mathcal{T}$-satisfiable despite μ is
$\mathcal{T}$-unsatisfiable. If so, $\mathcal{T}$-DPLL can stop. Second, if both μ' and μ are $\mathcal{T}$-unsatisfiable,
checking the consistency of μ' rather than that of μ can be faster and cause smaller
conflict sets, so that to improve the effectiveness of $\mathcal{T}$-backjumping and $\mathcal{T}$-learning.

Example 8. Consider the following scenario with the $\mathcal{T}$-formula φ in Example 1:
$\mathcal{T}$-DPLL generates the following assignment μ, which propositionally satisfies φ:

$$\{\neg(2x_2 - x_3 > 2), \neg A_2, (3x_1 - 2x_2 \le 3), \neg(3x_1 - x_3 \le 6), \neg A_1, (x_3 = 3x_5 + 4)\}.$$

If $\mathcal{T}$-SOLVE is invoked on μ without reduction, then it will return "Unsat" due to the conflict set $\{\neg(2x_2 - x_3 > 2), (3x_1 - 2x_2 \le 3), \neg(3x_1 - x_3 \le 6)\}$. We notice that the literal $\neg(3x_1 - x_3 \le 6)$ is unnecessary for satisfying φ, because the 4th clause is 'satisfied also by $\neg A_1$. Thus, if we drop it from μ, we obtain a $\mathcal{T}$-satisfiable assignment μ' s.t. $\mu' \models_p \varphi$, so that $\mathcal{T}$-DPLL can return "Sat" without further backtracking.

4.9   Pure Literal Filtering

This technique, which we call *pure literal filtering*,[14] was implicitly proposed by [82] and then generalized by [45, 4, 22].

The idea is that, if we have non-boolean $\mathcal{T}$-atoms occurring only positively [resp. negatively] in the input formulas, we can drop any negative [resp. positive] occurrence of them from the assignment to be checked by $\mathcal{T}$-SOLVE. (The correctness of this process is a consequence of Proposition 2.)

We notice first that this techniques has the same two benefits a described for reduction to prime implicants in §4.8. Moreover, this technique is particularly useful in some situations. For instance, in mathematical reasoning many solvers cannot handle efficiently disequalities (e.g., $(x_1 - x_2 \neq 3)$), so that they are forced to split them into the disjunction of strict inequalities $(x_1 - x_2 > 3) \vee (x_1 - x_2 < 3)$. In many problems its very frequent that an equality like $(x_1 - x_2 = 3)$ occurs with positive polarity only. If so, and if it is assigned to false by $\mathcal{T}$-DPLL, then the technique described avoids adding to μ the corresponding disequality $(x_1 - x_2 \neq 3)$ [82, 4].

4.10   Theory Literal Filtering

This technique has been recently proposed by [22] to further reduce the amount of $\mathcal{T}$-literals given to $\mathcal{T}$-SOLVE.

Let $C = l_1 \vee \cdots \vee l_n$ be a theory-learned clause, that is, a clause resulting from either static learning (§4.2), or theory-driven learning (§4.5), or theory-driven deduction (§4.6). By construction, $\{\neg l_1, \ldots, \neg l_n\}$ is $\mathcal{T}$-unsatisfiable, so that, all interpretations that satisfy all $\neg l_1, \ldots, \neg l_{i-1}, \neg l_{i+1}, \ldots, \neg l_n$ must satisfy the literal l_i, for every $i \in [1...n]$. Thus, if the current assignment μ contains the literals $\neg l_1, \ldots, \neg l_{i-1}, \neg l_{i+1}, \ldots, \neg l_n$, and hence l_i is forced to true by unit propagation on the clause C, then there is no need to pass l_i to $\mathcal{T}$-SOLVE as μ is $\mathcal{T}$-satisfiable iff $\mu \cup \{l_i\}$ is. In order to detect these cases, the theory-deduced clauses can be marked with a flag.

Combining the filtering methods requires some care, as $\neg l_1, \ldots, \neg l_{i-1}, \neg l_{i+1}, \ldots, \neg l_n$ in the current truth assignment must have been passed to $\mathcal{T}$-SOLVE (i.e. not filtered) in order to apply theory-deduced literal filtering to l_i. Moreover, also combining one or both literal filtering method(s) with $\mathcal{T}$-deduction requires some care, in order to prevent $\mathcal{T}$-SOLVE to perform useless $\mathcal{T}$-deductions of literals which have been filtered away. In fact, if both $\mathcal{T}$-deduction and some form of literal filtering is implemented, then it is advisable that the filtered atoms are dropped not only from the assignment, but also from the list of atoms which can be $\mathcal{T}$-deduced.

---

[14] Also called *triggering* [82, 4].

4.11   Branching Heuristics

In the efficiency of standard DPLL algorithms, a key role is played by the heuristic adopted for selecting the literal to branch on (the function *"choose-literal"* in the schema of Figure 3). Traditionally, most heuristics were variants of the so-called MOMS schema: pick the literal occurring **m**ost **o**ften in the **m**inimal **s**ize clauses (see, e.g., [54]); others select a candidate set of literals, perform explicitly unit propagation on all of them in turn, and choose the choice leading to the smaller clause set [59]; more recent ones privilege literals occurring in clauses which have been learned most recently [63, 51, 39]. Moreover, when formulas derive from the encoding of some specific problem, it is often useful to allow the encoder to provide to the DPLL solver a list of "privileged" variables on which to branch on first (e.g., action variables in SAT-based planning [46], primary inputs in bounded model checking [76], transition variables for verification of timed automata [7]).

In general, good splitting heuristics for "pure" DPLL are not necessary good for $\mathcal{T}$-DPLL-like procedures as well. First, a heuristic which is good to search for *one* assignment is not necessary good for enumerating up to a complete collection of them. More importantly, traditional DPLL heuristics are "blind", in the sense that they do not take into account the $\mathcal{T}$-semantics of the literals.

Despite some interesting attempts (e.g., DLP has a heuristic aiming at maximizing the benefits of $\mathcal{T}$-backjumping [68]) so far there seem to be no really satisfactory proposals in this direction, and most tool simply use standard DPLL heuristics.

One of the main reason for this fact may be that the problem of taking into account the semantics of $\mathcal{T}$-atoms in splitting is trickier then one would expect. In fact, to be effective, the heuristic should not only take into account the semantics of the literal chosen, but also that of *all* the literals that are assigned as a deterministic consequence (unit propagation, $\mathcal{T}$-deduction) of that choice. (For instance, with some problems it is often the case that boolean literals are better choices than others, because they cause longer chains of unit propagations [48, 49, 7].)

Example 9. Consider the $\mathcal{T}$-formula φ in Example 1. Branching on the boolean literal $\neg A_1$ causes the assignment of $\neg(2x_2 - x_3 > 2)$ and $(3x_1 - 2x_2 \leq 3)$ by unit propagation (rows 1, 5 and hence 3) and hence of $(3x_1 - x_3 \leq 6)$ by $\mathcal{T}$-deduction.

Unfortunately, the whole sets of deterministic consequences of a branch choice are difficult to predict a priori. One possible direction, is to perform all propagations explicitly on all the candidate literals in turn as in [59], but this is likely to be extremely expensive. Another direction is, as with the pure boolean case, to provide to $\mathcal{T}$-DPLL solver a list of "privileged" variables on which to branch on first [7].

4.12   Discussion

For most of the integration techniques described in §4, the applicability and the benefits of their application depend on many factors.

First, some integration techniques require as necessary conditions some of the specific features of $\mathcal{T}$-SOLVE described in §3.2. For instance, $\mathcal{T}$-backjumping and $\mathcal{T}$-learning can not be applied if the theory solver is not capable of producing (good enough) conflict sets; similarly, the benefits of $\mathcal{T}$-deduction depend only on the deduction capabilities of $\mathcal{T}$-SOLVE, and on their efficiency.

Second, the effects of the different integration techniques are not mutually independent, and are thus difficult to evaluate as stand-alone ones. Some techniques can share part of their benefits: for instance, $\mathcal{T}$-learning and $\mathcal{T}$-deduction may learn the same clauses, as in Examples 6 and 7. Some other can interact negatively: pure literal filtering can reduce the pruning power of early pruning, because it may drop literals causing $\mathcal{T}$-inconsistencies, and thus some pruning of the boolean search. Finally, some other techniques are pairwise related: for instance, $\mathcal{T}$-deduction is associated with early pruning; both $\mathcal{T}$-backjumping and $\mathcal{T}$-learning benefit of the conflict sets generated by $\mathcal{T}$-SOLVE, and are thus implemented together in most solvers.

We also remark that the benefits of many integration techniques, like early pruning and $\mathcal{T}$-deduction, depend on the theory $\mathcal{T}$ addressed and, in particular, on the tradeoff between the cost of $\mathcal{T}$-solving and the benefits of reducing boolean search space. [15] For some theories $\mathcal{T}$-solving is extremely cheap, so that it is typically worth performing extra calls to $\mathcal{T}$-SOLVE if this allows for pruning the boolean search. E.g., the satisfiability of sets of constraints in $\mathcal{EUF}$ and $\mathcal{DL}$ can be solved respectively in $O(n\log(n))$ and $O(n^2)$ time, and very fast algorithms are available [30, 65, 66]. For some other theories, $\mathcal{T}$-solving is expensive, so that trading $\mathcal{T}$-SOLVE calls for boolean search reduction is not always a good deal.

Thus, with very few exceptions, there is no universal, theory-independent recipe for choosing the right integration techniques to apply.

5   Decision Procedures for Combined Theories

In many practical applications, the theory $\mathcal{T}$ is a combination of two (or more) theories $\mathcal{T}_1$ and $\mathcal{T}_2$. For instance, an atom of the form $f(x + 3y) = g(2x - y)$, that combines uninterpreted function symbols (from $\mathcal{EUF}$) with arithmetic functions (from $\mathcal{LA}(\mathbb{Q})$), could be used to naturally model in a uniform setting the abstraction of some functional blocks in an arithmetic circuit. Other relevant examples of combination include, for instance, $\mathcal{DL}$ and $\mathcal{EUF}$, and $\mathcal{LA}(\mathbb{Z})$ and $\mathcal{EUF}$. In the following, we discuss two approaches to the development of $\mathcal{T}$-decision procedures, where $\mathcal{T}$ is the combination of two different theories.

We first provide some additional background notions. A theory $\mathcal{T}$ is *stably-infinite* iff every quantifier-free $\mathcal{T}$-satisfiable formula is satisfiable in an infinite model of $\mathcal{T}$. Notice that $\mathcal{EUF}$, $\mathcal{DL}$, $\mathcal{LA}(\mathbb{Q})$, $\mathcal{LA}(\mathbb{Z})$ are stably-infinite, whilst e.g. bit-vector theories typically are not. In what follows, we shall assume to deal only with stably-infinite theories with disjoint signatures.

$\mathcal{T}$ is *convex* iff, for every set $l_1, ..., l_k, l', l''$ of literals in $\mathcal{T}$ s.t. l', l'' are in the form $(x = y)$, x, y being variables, we have that

$$\{l_1, ..., l_k\} \models_{\mathcal{T}} (l' \vee l'') \iff \{l_1, ..., l_k\} \models_{\mathcal{T}} l' \text{ or } \{l_1, ..., l_k\} \models_{\mathcal{T}} l''.$$

---

[15] Notice that "reducing the boolean search" means not only reducing the time spent on boolean reasoning but also, and much more importantly, reducing the size of the boolean search tree and consequently the number of calls to $\mathcal{T}$-SOLVE.

Notice that $\mathcal{EUF}$, $\mathcal{DL}$, $\mathcal{LA}(\mathbb{Q})$ are convex, whilst $\mathcal{LA}(\mathbb{Z})$ is not.

Let now $\mathcal{T}_1$ and $\mathcal{T}_2$ be two theories with equality and disjoint signatures Σ_1, Σ_2. An atom ψ is i-pure if only $=$, variables and symbols from Σ_i occur in ψ. We say ψ is *strictly i-pure* if at least one symbol from Σ_i occurs in ψ. A formula φ is pure iff every atom in φ is i-pure for some $i \in \{1, 2\}$. Every non-pure $\mathcal{T}_1 \cup \mathcal{T}_2$ formula φ can be converted into an equivalently satisfiable pure formula φ', by recursively labeling terms t with fresh variables v_t, and by adding the atom $(v_t = t)$. For instance, $f(x + 3y) = g(2x - y)$ can be transformed into $(w = x + 3y) \wedge (t = 2x - y) \wedge (f(w) = g(t))$. This process, called *purification*, is linear in the size of the input formula. Without loss of generality, in the following we assume that all input formulas $\varphi \in \mathcal{T}_1 \cup \mathcal{T}_2$ are pure.

If φ is a pure $\mathcal{T}_1 \cup \mathcal{T}_2$ formula, then a variable v is an *interface variable* for φ iff it occurs in both strictly 1-pure and 2-pure atoms of φ. An equality $(v_i = v_j)$ is an *interface equality* for φ iff v_i, v_j are interface variables for φ.

Henceforth we denote the interface equality $(v_i = v_j)$ by "e_{ij}"; we call e_{ij}-*deduction* every deduction in the form $\mu \models_{\mathcal{T}} (\bigvee_j e_j)$ s.t. all e_j's are interface equalities; we say that a $\mathcal{T}$-conflict set η is $\neg e_{ij}$-*minimal* iff $\eta \setminus \{\neg e_{ij}\}$ is $\mathcal{T}$-satisfiable, for every negated interface equality $\neg e_{ij} \in \eta$.

5.1 Nelson-Oppen Combination

The first approach we discuss is conceptually very simple: we instantiate the approach proposed in Figure 3 to the case where the theory solver for the theory $\mathcal{T}_1 \cup \mathcal{T}_2$ is obtained by means of the Nelson-Oppen's combination schema [64], in the following referred to as NO.

Given two signature-disjoint stably infinite theories $\mathcal{T}_1$ and $\mathcal{T}_2$, NO allows for solving the satisfiability problem for $\mathcal{T}_1 \cup \mathcal{T}_2$ (i.e. the problem of checking the $\mathcal{T}_1 \cup \mathcal{T}_2$-satisfiability of sets of $\Sigma_1 \cup \Sigma_2$-literals) by using the satisfiability procedures for $\mathcal{T}_1$ and $\mathcal{T}_2$. The decision procedure is based a structured interchange of information inferred from either theory, and propagated to the other, until convergence is reached. The schema requires the exchange of information, the kind of which depends on the *convexity* of the involved theories. In the case of convex theories, the two solvers communicate to each other single interface equalities. In the case of non-convex theories, the NO schema becomes more complicated, because the two solvers need to exchange *arbitrary disjunctions of interface equalities*, which have to be managed within the decision procedure by means of case splitting and of *backtrack* search. In the latter case, the NO schema performs a number of *branches* to check the consistency of a set of literals which depends on how many disjunctions of equalities are exchanged at each step: if the current set of literals is μ, and one of the $\mathcal{T}_i$-solver sends the disjunction $\bigvee_{k=1}^n (e_{ij})_k$ to the other, the latter must further investigate up to n branches to check the consistency of each of the $\mu \cup \{(e_{ij})_k\}$ sets separately.

We notice that the ability to carry out deductions is crucial for efficiency: each solver must be able to derive the (disjunctions of) interface equalities e_{ij} entailed by its current facts φ. If the $\mathcal{T}_i$-solver is always capable of doing this, we say that it is e_{ij}-*deduction complete*. When this capability is not available, it must be replaced by "guessing" followed by a satisfiability check with respect to $\mathcal{T}_i$. In what follows we shall assume that all the $\mathcal{T}_i$-solver's used in a NO schema are e_{ij}-deduction complete.

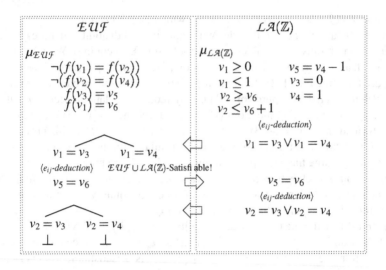

Fig. 5. Representation of the NO search tree for the formula of Example 10

Hereafter, we denote with $\mu_{\mathcal{T}_i}$ the subassignment of μ containing only i-pure literals.

Example 10. Consider the following $\mathcal{EUF} \cup \mathcal{LA}(\mathbb{Z})$ formula φ

$$\mathcal{EUF} : \ \neg(f(v_1) = f(v_2)) \wedge \neg(f(v_2) = f(v_4)) \wedge (f(v_3) = v_5) \wedge (f(v_1) = v_6) \wedge$$
$$\mathcal{LA}(\mathbb{Z}) : (v_1 \geq 0) \wedge (v_1 \leq 1) \wedge (v_5 = v_4 - 1) \wedge (v_3 = 0) \wedge (v_4 = 1) \wedge \qquad (5)$$
$$(v_2 \geq v_6) \wedge (v_2 \leq v_6 + 1).$$

Here all the variables $(v_1, \ldots, v_6)$ are interface ones. φ contains only unit clauses, so after the first run of unit propagations, DPLL generates the assignment μ which is simply the set of literals in φ. The NO combination schema then runs as depicted in Fig. 5.

First, the sub-assignment $\mu_{\mathcal{EUF}}$ is given to the $\mathcal{EUF}$ solver, which reports its consistency and deduces no interface equality. Then, the sub-assignment $\mu_{\mathcal{LA}(\mathbb{Z})}$ is given to the $\mathcal{LA}(\mathbb{Z})$ solver, which reports its consistency and deduces the disjunction $(v_1 = v_3) \vee (v_1 = v_4)$. Next, there is a case-splitting and the two equalities $(v_1 = v_3)$ and $(v_1 = v_4)$ are passed to the $\mathcal{EUF}$ solver. The first branch, corresponding to selecting $(v_1 = v_3)$, is opened: then the set $\mu_{\mathcal{EUF}} \cup \{(v_1 = v_3)\}$ is $\mathcal{EUF}$-consistent, and the equality $(v_5 = v_6)$ is deduced. After that, the assignment $\mu_{\mathcal{LA}(\mathbb{Z})} \cup \{(v_5 = v_6)\}$ is passed to the $\mathcal{LA}(\mathbb{Z})$ solver, that reports its consistency and deduces another disjunction, $(v_2 = v_3) \vee (v_2 = v_4)$. At this point, another case-splitting is needed in the $\mathcal{EUF}$ solver, resulting in the two branches $\mu_{\mathcal{EUF}} \cup \{(v_1 = v_3), (v_2 = v_3)\}$ and $\mu_{\mathcal{EUF}} \cup \{(v_1 = v_3), (v_2 = v_4)\}$. Both of them are found inconsistent, so the whole branch previously opened by the selection of $(v_1 = v_3)$ is found inconsistent.

At this point, the other case of the branch (i.e. the equality $(v_1 = v_4)$) is selected, and since the assignment $\mu_{\mathcal{EUF}} \cup \{(v_1 = v_4)\}$ is $\mathcal{EUF}$-consistent and no new interface equality is deduced, the Nelson-Oppen method reports the $\mathcal{EUF} \cup \mathcal{LA}(\mathbb{Z})$-satisfiability of φ under the whole assignment μ.

function Bool+$\mathcal{T}_1$+$\mathcal{T}_2$ (φ_i: *quantifier-free formula*)

1      $\varphi \longleftarrow purify(\varphi_i)$
2      $\mathcal{A}^p \longleftarrow \mathcal{T}2\mathcal{B}(Atoms(\varphi) \cup interface\_equalities(\varphi))$
3      $\varphi^p \longleftarrow \mathcal{T}2\mathcal{B}(\varphi)$
4   **while** Bool-*solver* (φ^p) **do**
5          $\mu_1^p \wedge \mu_2^p \wedge \mu_e^p = \mu^p \longleftarrow pick\_total\_assign(\mathcal{A}^p, \varphi^p)$
6          $(\rho_1, \pi_1) \longleftarrow \mathcal{T}_1\text{-solver}(\mathcal{B}2\mathcal{T}(\mu_1^p \wedge \mu_e^p))$
7          $(\rho_2, \pi_2) \longleftarrow \mathcal{T}_2\text{-solver}(\mathcal{B}2\mathcal{T}(\mu_2^p \wedge \mu_e^p))$
8   **if** $(\rho_1 = \text{sat} \wedge \rho_2 = \text{sat})$ **then return** sat **else**
9   **if** $\rho_1 = \text{unsat}$ **then** $\varphi^p \longleftarrow \varphi^p \wedge \neg \mathcal{T}2\mathcal{B}(\pi_1)$
10   **if** $\rho_2 = \text{unsat}$ **then** $\varphi^p \longleftarrow \varphi^p \wedge \neg \mathcal{T}2\mathcal{B}(\pi_2)$
11   **end while**
12   **return** unsat
end function

Fig. 6. The Delayed Theory Combination procedure for $SMT(\mathcal{T}_1 \cup \mathcal{T}_2)$

5.2   Delayed Theory Combination

The Delayed Theory Combination (DTC, [20, 23]) schema tackles the $SMT(\mathcal{T}_1 \cup \mathcal{T}_2)$ problem in a different way. Instead of using the Nelson-Oppen schema to combine two decision procedures for $\mathcal{T}_1$ and $\mathcal{T}_2$ by exchange of (disjunctions of) interface equalities, each of the two $\mathcal{T}_i$ solvers only interacts with the boolean enumeration level: there is no direct exchange of information between the theory solvers. Their mutual consistency is ensured by augmenting the input problem with all interface equalities e_{ij}, even if these do not occur in the original problem. The enumerated assignments include not only the atoms in the formula, but also the interface equalities e_{ij}. Both theory solvers receive, from the boolean level, the same truth assignment μ_e for e_{ij}: under such conditions, the two "partial" models found by each decision procedure can be merged into a model for the input formula.

Notationally, we call "*new*" e_{ij}'s all the interface equalities e_{ij}'s which do not occur in any clause of the input formula φ (including all the clauses learned). Moreover, in the following we often write sets of literals $\{l_1, ..., l_n\}$ as conjunctions $l_1 \wedge ... \wedge l_n$, and we often write clauses $(\bigvee_i l_i) \vee (\bigvee_j l_j)$ as implications: $(\bigwedge_i \neg l_i) \rightarrow (\bigvee_j l_j)$.

A simplified view of the algorithm is presented in Fig. 6. Initially (lines 1–3), the formula is purified, the *new* e_{ij}'s are created and added to the set of propositional symbols $\mathcal{A}^p$, and the propositional abstraction φ^p of φ is created. Then, the main loop is entered (lines 4–11): while φ^p is propositionally satisfiable (line 4), a satisfying truth assignment μ^p is selected (line 5). It is important to stress that truth values are associated not only to atoms in φ, but also to the e_{ij} atoms, even though they do not occur in φ. μ^p is then (implicitly) separated into $\mu_1^p \wedge \mu_e^p \wedge \mu_2^p$, where $\mathcal{B}2\mathcal{T}(\mu_i^p)$ is a set of i-pure literals and $\mathcal{B}2\mathcal{T}(\mu_e^p)$ is a set of e_{ij}-literals. The relevant part of μ^p are checked for consistency against each theory (lines 6–7); $\mathcal{T}_i$-solver($\mu_i \wedge \mu_e$) returns a pair (ρ_i, π_i), where ρ_i is unsat iff μ is unsatisfiable in $\mathcal{T}_i$, and sat otherwise. If both calls to $\mathcal{T}_i$-solver return sat, then the formula is satisfiable. Otherwise, when ρ_i is unsat, then π_i is a theory conflict set, i.e. $\pi_i \subseteq \mu$ and π_i is $\mathcal{T}_i$-unsatisfiable. Then, φ^p is strengthened to exclude truth assignments which may fail in the same way (line 9–10), and the loop is resumed.

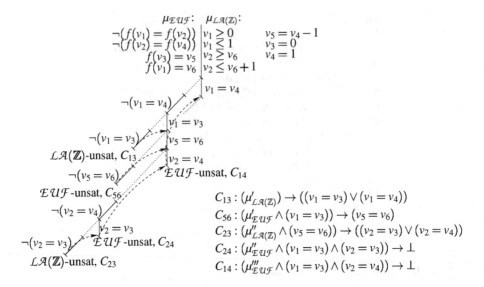

Fig. 7. DTC execution of Example 11 on $\mathcal{LA}(\mathbb{Z}) \cup \mathcal{EUF}$, with no e_{ij}-deduction

Unsatisfiability is returned (line 12) when the loop is exited without having found a model.

Practical implementations of DTC are based on a DPLL engine, that exploits unit-propagation, early pruning, $\mathcal{T}$-backjumping and $\mathcal{T}$-learning.

Example 11. Consider the $\mathcal{EUF} \cup \mathcal{LA}(\mathbb{Z})$ formula φ (5) and the assignment μ of Example 10. We assume here that both the $\mathcal{EUF}$- and $\mathcal{LA}(\mathbb{Z})$-solver's have no e_{ij}-deduction capabilities, but that they always return $\neg e_{ij}$-minimal conflict sets. A session of DTC is depicted in Fig. 7. (We adopt here a strategy for DTC which is described in detail in [26].)

Initially, both $\mu_{\mathcal{LA}(\mathbb{Z})}$ and $\mu_{\mathcal{EUF}}$ are found consistent in each of the theories by the respective solvers. Then DTC starts selecting new $\neg e_{ij}$'s, and proceeds without causing conflicts, until it selects $\neg(v_1 = v_4)$ and $\neg(v_1 = v_3)$, which cause a $\mathcal{LA}(\mathbb{Z})$ conflict. The branch is in the form $\mu \cup \bigcup_j \neg e_j$, so that, the $\neg e_{ij}$-minimal conflict set η_{13} returned is in the form $\mu'_{\mathcal{LA}(\mathbb{Z})} \cup \{\neg(v_1 = v_3), \neg(v_1 = v_4)\}$. [16] DTC learns the corresponding clause C_{13}, and backjumps up to the highest point which allows for unit-propagating $(v_1 = v_3)$ on C_{13}, and performs such unit propagation. Then DTC selects a chain of new $\neg e_{ij}$'s without causing conflicts, until it selects $\neg(v_5 = v_6)$, which causes a $\mathcal{EUF}$ conflict. As $\mathcal{EUF}$ is convex, $\neg(v_5 = v_6)$ is the only $\neg e_{ij}$ occurring in the conflict set, so that DTC learns clause C_{56}, backtracks over the last chain of $\neg e_{ij}$'s and unit-propagates $(v_5 = v_6)$.

Again, DTC selects a chain of new $\neg e_{ij}$'s without causing conflicts, until it selects $\neg(v_2 = v_4)$ and $\neg(v_2 = v_3)$, which cause a $\mathcal{LA}(\mathbb{Z})$ conflict. As before, it learns clause C_{23}, and backjumps to the highest point where it can unit-propagate $(v_2 = v_3)$ on C_{23}. Performing the latter unit propagation causes a $\mathcal{EUF}$ conflict, with conflict-

---

[16] Hereafter, $\mu'_{\mathcal{T}}, \mu''_{\mathcal{T}}, \mu'''_{\mathcal{T}}$ will denote generic subsets of $\mu_{\mathcal{T}}$, $\mathcal{T} \in \{\mathcal{EUF}, \mathcal{LA}(\mathbb{Q}), \mathcal{LA}(\mathbb{Z})\}$.

ing clause C_{24}. By resolving on literal $(v_2 = v_3)$ the conflicting clause C_{24} with the clause C_{23} (which caused the unit-propagation of $(v_2 = v_3)$), DTC may obtain a clause $C'_{24} : (\mu''_{\mathcal{LA}(\mathbb{Z})} \wedge \mu''_{\mathcal{EUF}} \wedge (v_5 = v_6) \wedge (v_1 = v_3)) \rightarrow (v_2 = v_4)$, which allows for backjumping over all the remaining $\neg e_{ij}$'s of the current chain and unit-propagating $(v_2 = v_4)$. [17]

The latter causes a new $\mathcal{EUF}$ conflict represented by the conflicting clause C_{14}. Then C_{14} is resolved with the clauses C'_{24}, C_{56}, C_{13} (which caused the unit-propagation of $(v_2 = v_4)$, $(v_5 = v_6)$, $(v_1 = v_3)$ respectively), obtaining thus the new conflict clause $C'_{14} : (\mu'_{\mathcal{LA}(\mathbb{Z})} \wedge \mu''_{\mathcal{LA}(\mathbb{Z})} \wedge \mu'_{\mathcal{EUF}} \wedge \mu''_{\mathcal{EUF}} \wedge \mu'''_{\mathcal{EUF}}) \rightarrow (v_1 = v_4)$, which allows for backjumping up to μ and for unit-propagating $(v_1 = v_4)$.

Finally, DTC selects a sequence of $\neg e_{ij}$'s (possibly unit-propagating some value due to the clauses learned) without generating conflicts, so that to conclude that the formula is $\mathcal{T}_1 \cup \mathcal{T}_2$-satisfiable.

Unlike NO, DTC allows for using $\mathcal{T}_i$-solver's with partial or no e_{ij}-deduction capability, as part of all the e_{ij}-deduction is played by the SAT solver. Moreover, in DTC the SAT solver is aware a priori of the e_{ij}'s, so that DTC can learn clauses containing e_{ij}'s, which can be used in subsequent branches to prune search and avoid redoing the same search/deductions from scratch. We refer the reader to [20, 23, 26] for a more detailed description of DTC and for an analytical comparison with NO.

6 Decision Procedures for Formal Verification

Decision procedures have been applied in different domains in verification. In particular, the well known techniques based on SAT solvers [16, 61] can be generalized from the propositional case to analyze transition systems whose dynamics can be represented as $\mathcal{T}$-formulae in some theory $\mathcal{T}$. The verification subproblems are then reduced to checking the satisfiability of $\mathcal{T}$-formulae representing the unrolling of the transition relation over multiple steps of exectuion.

This approach has been proposed for timed systems, hybrid systems, and also for the analysis of abstractions of extemely large or infinite state spaces (see for instance [7, 6, 57]).

In the following, we concentrate on the potential application of decision procedures to the formal checking at Register-Transfer Level (RTL), that is currently a fundamental step in the design of hardware circuits. A number of techniques and tools have been developed, able to carry out equivalence checking and property checking of combinational and sequential circuits. Most tools for formal checking, however, work at the boolean level, which is not expressive enough to capture the abstract, high level (e.g., structural, word level) information of RTL designs. Tools for formal checking are thus confronted with problems which are "flattened" down to boolean level (e.g., integer

---

[17] In building the conflict clause, a literal l which has been assigned by unit-propagation on a previously learned clause C_l can be eliminated from the conflicting clause C by resolving the latter with C_l. This is a standard technique implemented in most SAT solvers in order to traverse backward the implication graph and to build the boolean conflict clauses [85], and which can be used for building $\mathcal{T}$-conflict clauses as well.

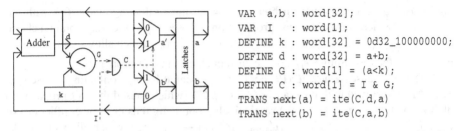

```
VAR  a,b : word[32];
VAR  I   : word[1];
DEFINE k : word[32] = 0d32_100000000;
DEFINE d : word[32] = a+b;
DEFINE G : word[1] = (a<k);
DEFINE C : word[1] = I & G;
TRANS next(a) = ite(C,d,a)
TRANS next(b) = ite(C,a,b)
```

Fig. 8. RTL representation of a simple sequential circuit (left) and the corresponding representations in bit-vectors (right). Solid lines represent 32-bit datapath lines (words), whilst dashed lines represent control lines (single bits).

data values are encoded and manipulated as arrays of booleans), so that a predominant part of their computational effort is wasted in performing useless boolean search on the bitwise encoding of integer data and arithmetical operations (e.g., up to a 2^{32} factor in the amount of boolean search for a 32-bit integer value).

This phenomenon is particularly hard in the presence of mathematical reasoning. In fact, boolean solvers are "bad at mathematics", in the sense that reasoning on the boolean encoding of arithmetical operations (e.g., sums) causes a blowup of the computational effort.

The problem of RTL verification trying to avoid *bit-blasting*, i.e. the uniform reduction to a problem of propositional satisfiability, has received significant attention in the last years. The approaches proposed in [25, 84] are based on the encoding of bits, bit-vectors and their operators into integer linear programming (ILP) expressions. An ILP procedure is then used to solve the problem. The main difference with respect to the approaches described in this chapter is that single bits and relative operators are also handled within the ILP rather than with efficient SAT solving techniques.

In [28, 62, 31, 11], the decision procedure is engineered to be a component of more general reasoning frameworks. For this reason, they rely on various combination schemata (e.g. Nelson-Oppen, Shostak). Another remarkable difference is that the decision procedures described in [62, 31] extend Binary Decision Diagrams [27].

A completely different approach is followed in [71, 1]: abstract representations of an RTL circuit are generated by abstracting away information on the datapath, and the resulting encoding is then fed into propositional SAT tools. The approach in [1] is subject to loss of information, and iterative refinement may be required.

In [19] an alternative approach is proposed, where RTL constructs are encoded into formulae in $\mathcal{LA}(\mathbb{Z})$ or in $\mathcal{EUF} \cup \mathcal{LA}(\mathbb{Z})$. Such formulae can be handled by decision procedures *directly*, without flattening to boolean level, so that to reduce the computational effort. The main assumption is that an RTL circuit can be partitioned into *control* and *datapath* components. The former can be directly encoded int boolean *formulas*, and can be handled by the SAT solver embedded in the decision procedure. The latter is encoded (as much as possible) into *terms* in $LA(\mathbb{Z})$, so that to be handled directly by the $LA(\mathbb{Z})$ solver, thus avoiding bit-blasting as much as possible.

Example 12. The transition relation of the circuit of Figure 8 can be encoded into a $LA(\mathbb{Z})$ formula as follows:

$$\langle Range(\{\mathsf{a},\mathsf{a}',\mathsf{b},\mathsf{b}',\mathsf{d}\})\rangle : (0 \leq a) \wedge (a < 2^{32}) \wedge \ldots \wedge (0 \leq d) \wedge (d < 2^{32}) \wedge$$

DEFINE k : $\qquad (k = 100000000) \wedge$

$>$: $\qquad\qquad (G \leftrightarrow (a < k)) \wedge$

and : $\qquad\quad (C \leftrightarrow (G \wedge I)) \wedge$

ite : $\qquad\qquad (C \to (a' = d)) \wedge (\neg C \to (a' = a)) \wedge$

ite : $\qquad\qquad (C \to (b' = a)) \wedge (\neg C \to (b' = b)) \wedge$

$\langle Adder\ \mathsf{d} := \mathsf{a} + \mathsf{b}\rangle : \quad (d = a + b - o \cdot 2^{32}) \wedge (0 \leq o) \wedge (o \leq 1).$

In general, the verification of RTL circuit design may involve different theories, like $\mathcal{EUF}$, linear arithmetic on $\mathbb{Z}$, theory of arrays, theory of bitvectors, which may be used both alone or in combination.

7 Conclusions and Future Perspectives

We have presented a survey of the techniques for the development of decision procedures based on an integration of efficient boolean reasoning, DPLL in particular, and dedicated theory solvers. For their ability to deal efficiently with fragments of first-order logic that are interesting from the practical view point, decision procedures have been devoted a substantial effort in the last few years.

In fact, the area of decision procedures is extremely active. A remarkable initiative is STM-LIB [69], whose goal is to establish a standard language and a library of benchmarks for satisfiability with respect to background theories.

Yet, many research challenges remain open. A primary goal is to devise new algorithms and techniques that will enable decision procedures to deal effectively on problems of practical relevance with the same strength of SAT solvers. Key issues to be investigated are theory-dependent splitting heuristics, finding a balance between the amount of effort spent in boolean reasoning and in theory reasoning, and developing effective incremental and backtrackabile theory solving algorithms. Other important features appear to be the ability to enumerate all models (i.e. to carry out a form of quantifier elimination), to produce explanations (i.e. proofs of unsatisfiability), and to optimize specific cost functionals over the space of all solutions.

References

1. Z. S. Andraus and K. A. Sakallah. Automatic abstraction and verification of verilog models. In *Proc. DAC '04*. ACM Press, 2004.
2. A. Armando, C. Castellini, and E. Giunchiglia. SAT-based procedures for temporal reasoning. In *Proc. European Conference on Planning, CP-99*, 1999.
3. A. Armando, C. Castellini, E. Giunchiglia, and M. Maratea. A SAT-based Decision Procedure for the Boolean Combination of Difference Constraints. In *SAT'04 - The Seventh International Conference on Theory and Applications of Satisfiability Testing*, Vancouver, BC, Canada, 2004. Presented at SAT 2004.
4. G. Audemard, P. Bertoli, A. Cimatti, A. Korniłowicz, and R. Sebastiani. A SAT Based Approach for Solving Formulas over Boolean and Linear Mathematical Propositions. In *Proc. CADE'2002.*, volume 2392 of *LNAI*. Springer, July 2002.

5. G. Audemard, P. Bertoli, A. Cimatti, A. Korniłowicz, and R. Sebastiani. Integrating boolean and mathematical solving: Foundations, basic algorithms and requirements. In *Proc. AISC-Calculemus 2002*, volume 2385 of *LNAI*, pages 231–245. Springer, 2002.

6. G. Audemard, M. Bozzano, A. Cimatti, and R. Sebastiani. Verifying Industrial Hybrid Systems with MathSAT. In *Proc. CAV'04 Workshop on Bounded Model Checking (BMC'04)*, volume 89 of *ENTCS*. Elsevier, 2004.

7. G. Audemard, A. Cimatti, A. Korniłowicz, and R. Sebastiani. SAT-Based Bounded Model Checking for Timed Systems. In *Proc. FORTE'02.*, volume 2529 of *LNCS*. Springer, November 2002.

8. F. Bacchus and J. Winter. Effective Preprocessing with Hyper-Resolution and Equality Reduction. In *Proc. Sixth International Symposium on Theory and Applications of Satisfiability Testing*, 2003.

9. G. J. Badros and A. Borning. The Cassowary Linear Arithmetic Constraint Solving Algorith. *ACM Transactions on Computer Human Interaction*, 8(4):267–306, december 2001.

10. C. Barrett, D. Dill, and A. Stump. Checking Satisfiability of First-Order Formulas by Incremental Translation to SAT. In *14th International Conference on Computer-Aided Verification*, 2002.

11. C. W. Barrett, D. L. Dill, and J. R. Levitt. A decision procedure for bit-vector arithmetic. In *Proc. DAC '98*. ACM Press, 1998.

12. C. W. Barrett, D. L. Dill, and A. Stump. A generalization of Shostak's method for combining decision procedures. In *Frontiers of Combining Systems (FROCOS)*, LNAI. Springer, April 2002. S. Margherita Ligure, Italy.

13. P. Baumgartner. FDPLL - A First Order Davis-Putnam-Longeman-Loveland Procedure. In *Proceedings of CADE-17*, pages 200–219. Springer, 2000.

14. P. Baumgartner and C. Tinelli. The Model Evolution Calculus. In F. Baader, editor, *Proc. CADE-19*, number 2741 in LNAI, pages 350–364. Springer, 2003.

15. R. J. Bayardo and R. C. Schrag. Using CSP Look-Back Techniques to Solve Real-World SAT instances. In *Proc. AAAI'97*, pages 203–208. AAAI Press, 1997.

16. A. Biere, A. Cimatti, E. Clarke, and Y. Zhu. Symbolic model checking without BDDs. In *Proc. CAV'99*, 1999.

17. A. Bockmayr and V. Weispfenning. Solving Numerical Constraints. In *Handbook of Automated Reasoning*, pages 751–842. MIT Press, 2001.

18. A. Borälv. A Fully Automated Approach for Proving Safety Properties in Interlocking Software Using Automatic Theorem-Proving. In S. Gnesi and D. Latella, editors, *Proceedings of the Second International ERCIM Workshop on Formal Methods for Industrial Critical Systems*, Pisa, Italy, July 1997.

19. M. Bozzano, R. Bruttomesso, A. Cimatti, A. Franzén, Z. Hanna, Z. Khasidashvili, A. Palti, and R. Sebastiani. Encoding RTL Constructs for MathSAT: a Preliminary Report. In *Proc. 3rd Workshop of Pragmatics on Decision Procedure in Automated Reasoning, PDPAR'05*, ENTCS. Elsevier, 2006. To appear.

20. M. Bozzano, R. Bruttomesso, A. Cimatti, T. Junttila, P.van Rossum, S. Ranise, and R. Sebastiani. Efficient Satisfiability Modulo Theories via Delayed Theory Combination. In *Proc. Int. Conf. on Computer-Aided Verification, CAV 2005.*, volume 3576 of *LNCS*. Springer, 2005.

21. M. Bozzano, R. Bruttomesso, A. Cimatti, T. Junttila, P.van Rossum, S. Schulz, and R. Sebastiani. An incremental and Layered Procedure for the Satisfiability of Linear Arithmetic Logic. In *Proc. TACAS'05*, volume 3440 of *LNCS*. Springer, 2005.

22. M. Bozzano, R. Bruttomesso, A. Cimatti, T. Junttila, P.van Rossum, S. Schulz, and R. Sebastiani. MathSAT: A Tight Integration of SAT and Mathematical Decision Procedure. *Journal of Automated Reasoning*, 2006. To appear.

23. M. Bozzano, R. Bruttomesso, A. Cimatti, T. Junttila, P. van Rossum, S. Ranise, and R. Sebastiani. Theory Combination via Boolean Search. *Information and Computation*, 2006. To appear.

24. R. Brafman. A simplifier for propositional formulas with many binary clauses. In *Proc. IJCAI01*, 2001.

25. R. Brinkmann and R. Drechsler. RTL-datapath verification using integer linear programming. In *Proc. ASP-DAC 2002*, pages 741–746. IEEE, 2002.

26. R. Bruttomesso, A. Cimatti, A. Franzèn, A. Griggio, and R. Sebastiani. Delayed Theory Combination vs. Nelson-Oppen for Satisfiability Modulo Theories: a Comparative Analysis. Submitted for pubblication., March 2006.

27. R. E. Bryant. Graph-Based Algorithms for Boolean Function Manipulation. *IEEE Transactions on Computers*, C-35(8):677–691, August 1986.

28. J. R. Burch and D. L. Dill. Automatic Verification of Pipelined Microprocessor Control. In *Proc. CAV '94*, volume 818 of *LNCS*. Springer, 1994.

29. C. Castellini, E. Giunchiglia, and A. Tacchella. Sat-based planning in complex domains: Concurrency, constraints and nondeterminism. *Artificial Intelligence*, 147(1-2):85–117, 2003.

30. B. V. Cherkassky and A. V. Goldberg. Negative-cycle detection algorithms. *Mathematical Programming*, 85(2):277–311, 1999.

31. D. Cyrluk, M. Oliver Möller, and H. Ruess. An efficient decision procedure for the theory of fixed-sized bit-vectors. In *Proceedings of CAV'97*, pages 60–71, 1997.

32. M. Davis, G. Longemann, and D. Loveland. A machine program for theorem proving. *Journal of the ACM*, 5(7), 1962.

33. M. Davis and H. Putnam. A computing procedure for quantification theory. *Journal of the ACM*, 7:201–215, 1960.

34. L. de Moura, H. Rueß, and M. Sorea. Lazy theorem proving for bounded model checking over infinite domains. In *Proc. of the 18th International Conference on Automated Deduction*, volume 2392 of *LNCS*, pages 438–455. Springer, July 2002.

35. L. de Moura, H. Rueß, and M. Sorea. Lemmas on Demand for Satisfiability Solvers. Presented at the Fifth International Symposium on the Theory and Applications of Satisfiability Testing (SAT'02), Cincinnati, USA, 15 May 2002, May 2002.

36. L. deMoura, H. Ruess, and N. Shankar. Justifying Equality. In *Proc. PDPAR'04*, volume 68 (5) of *ENTCS*. Elsevier, 2004.

37. D. Detlefs, G. Nelson, and J. Saxe. Simplify: A theorem prover for program checking, 2003. Technical Report HPL-2003-148, HP Labs, Palo Alto, CA. http://www.hpl.hp.com/techreports/2003/HPL-2003-148.ps.

38. N. Een and A. Biere. Effective Preprocessing in SAT Through Variable and Clause Elimination. In *proc. SAT'05*, volume 3569 of *LNCS*. Springer, 2005.

39. N. Eén and N. Sörensson. An extensible SAT-solver. In *Theory and Applications of Satisfiability Testing (SAT 2003)*, volume 2919 of *LNCS*, pages 502–518. Springer, 2004.

40. J.-C. Filliâtre, S. Owre, H. Rueß, and N. Shankar. ICS: Integrated Canonizer and Solver. Proc. CAV'2001, 2001.

41. C. Flanagan, R. Joshi, X. Ou, and J. B. Saxe. Theorem Proving Using Lazy Proof Explication. In *Proc. CAV 2003*, LNCS. Springer, 2003.

42. G. Stålmarck and M. Säflund. Modelling and Verifying Systems and Software in Propositional Logic. *Ifac SAFECOMP'90*, 1990.

43. H. Ganzinger, G. Hagen, R. Nieuwenhuis, A. Oliveras, and C. Tinelli. DPLL(T): Fast Decision Procedures. In *Proc. CAV'04*, volume 3114 of *LNCS*. Springer, 2004.

44. E. Giunchiglia, F. Giunchiglia, R. Sebastiani, and A. Tacchella. SAT vs. Translation based decision procedures for modal logics: a comparative evaluation. *Journal of Applied Non-Classical Logics*, 10(2):145–172, 2000.

45. E. Giunchiglia, F. Giunchiglia, and A. Tacchella. SAT Based Decision Procedures for Classical Modal Logics. Journal of Automated Reasoning. Special Issue: Satisfiability at the start of the year 2000, 2001.

46. E. Giunchiglia, A. Massarotto, and R. Sebastiani. Act, and the Rest Will Follow: Exploiting Determinism in Planning as Satisfiability. In *Proc. AAAI'98*, pages 948–953, 1998.

47. E. Giunchiglia and R. Sebastiani. Applying the Davis-Putnam procedure to non-clausal formulas. In *Proc. AI*IA'99*, volume 1792 of *LNAI*. Springer, 1999.

48. F. Giunchiglia and R. Sebastiani. Building decision procedures for modal logics from propositional decision procedures - the case study of modal K. In *CADE-13*, LNAI, New Brunswick, NJ, USA, August 1996. Springer Verlag.

49. F. Giunchiglia and R. Sebastiani. A SAT-based decision procedure for ALC. In *Proc. of the 5th International Conference on Principles of Knowledge Representation and Reasoning - KR'96*, Cambridge, MA, USA, November 1996.

50. F. Giunchiglia and R. Sebastiani. Building decision procedures for modal logics from propositional decision procedures - the case study of modal K(m). *Information and Computation*, 162(1/2), October/November 2000.

51. E. Goldberg and Y. Novikov. BerkMin: A Fast and Robust SAT-Solver. In *Proc. DATE '02*, page 142, Washington, DC, USA, 2002. IEEE Computer Society.

52. C. P. Gomes, B. Selman, and H. Kautz. Boosting combinatorial search through randomization. In *Proceedings of the Fifteenth National Conference on Artificial Intelligence (AAAI'98)*, pages 431–437, Madison, Wisconsin, 1998.

53. J. Hoffmann and R. I. Brafman. Contingent planning via heuristic forward search witn implicit belief states. In *Proceedings of the Fifteenth International Conference on Automated Planning and Scheduling (ICAPS 2005)*, pages 71–80. AAAI, 2005.

54. J. N. Hooker and V. Vinay. Branching Rules for Satisfiability. *Journal of Automated Reasoning*, 15(3):359–383, 1995.

55. I. Horrocks. The FaCT system. In H. de Swart, editor, *Proc. TABLEAUX-98*, volume 1397 of *LNAI*, pages 307–312. Springer, 1998.

56. H. Kautz, D. McAllester, and B. Selman. Encoding Plans in Propositional Logic. In *Proc. KR'96*, 1996.

57. S. K. Lahiri and R. E. Bryant. Deductive verification of advanced out-of-order microprocessors. In *Proceedings of CAV*, pages 341–353, 2003.

58. T. Latvala, A. Biere, K. Heljanko, and T. Junttila. Simple Bounded LTL Model Checking. In *Proc. FMCAD'04*, volume 3312 of *LNCS*. Springer, 2004.

59. C. M. Li and Anbulagan. Heuristics based on unit propagation for satisfiability problems. In *Proceedings of the 15th International Joint Conference on Artificial Intelligence (IJCAI-97)*, pages 366–371, 1997.

60. M. Mahfoudh, P. Niebert, E. Asarin, and O. Maler. A Satisfiability Checker for Difference Logic. In *Proceedings of SAT-02*, pages 222–230, 2002.

61. K. McMillan. Applying SAT Methods in Unbounded Symbolic Model Checking. In *Proc. CAV '02*, number 2404 in LNCS. Springer, 2002.

62. M. O. Möller and H. Ruess. Solving bit-vector equations. In *Proceedings of FMCAD'98*, pages 36–48, 1998.

63. M. W. Moskewicz, C. F. Madigan, Y. Z., L. Zhang, and S. Malik. Chaff: Engineering an efficient SAT solver. In *Design Automation Conference*, 2001.

64. G. Nelson and D.C. Oppen. Simplification by Cooperating Decision Procedures. *ACM Trans. on Programming Languages and Systems*, 1(2):245–257, 1979.

65. R. Nieuwenhuis and A. Oliveras. Congruence closure with integer offsets. In *In 10th Int. Conf. Logic for Programming, Artif. Intell. and Reasoning (LPAR)*, volume 2850 of *LNAI*, pages 78–90. Springer, 2003.

66. R. Nieuwenhuis and A. Oliveras. DPLL(T) with Exhaustive Theory Propagation and its Application to Difference Logic. In *Proc. CAV'05*, volume 3576 of *LNCS*. Springer, 2005.

67. R. Nieuwenhuis, A. Oliveras, and C. Tinelli. Abstract DPLL and Abstract DPLL Modulo Theories. In *Proc. LPAR'04*, volume 3452 of *LNCS*. Springer, 2005.

68. P. F. Patel-Schneider. DLP system description. In *Proc. DL-98*, pages 87–89, 1998.

69. S. Ranise and C. Tinelli. The SMT-LIB Standard. Available at http://combination.cs.uiowa.edu/smtlib/.

70. R. Sebastiani. Integrating SAT Solvers with Math Reasoners: Foundations and Basic Algorithms. ITC-IRST Technical report., November 2001.

71. S. A. Seshia, S. K. Lahiri, and R. E. Bryant. A Hybrid SAT-Based Decision Procedure for Separation Logic with Uninterpreted Functions. In *Proc. DAC'03*, 2003.

72. N. Shankar and H. Rueß. Combining shostak theories. Invited paper for Floc'02/RTA'02, 2002.

73. R. Shostak. A Pratical Decision Procedure for Arithmetic with Function Symbols. *Journal of the ACM*, 26(2):351–360, 1979.

74. J. P. M. Silva and K. A. Sakallah. GRASP - A new Search Algorithm for Satisfiability. In *Proc. ICCAD'96*, 1996.

75. P. Stephan, R. Brayton, and A. Sangiovanni-Vincentelli. Combinational Test Generation Using Satisfiability. *IEEE Transactions on Computer-Aided Design of Integrated Circuits and Systems*, 15:1167–1176, 1996.

76. O. Strichman. Tuning SAT checkers for Bounded Model Checking. In *Proc. CAV00*, volume 1855 of *LNCS*, pages 480–494. Springer, 2000.

77. O. Strichman, S. Seshia, and R. Bryant. Deciding separation formulas with SAT. In *Proc. of Computer Aided Verification, (CAV'02)*, LNCS. Springer, 2002.

78. A. Stump, C. W. Barrett, and D. L. Dill. CVC: A Cooperating Validity Checker. In *Proc. CAV'02*, number 2404 in LNCS. Springer Verlag, 2002.

79. C. Thiffault, F. Bacchus, and T. Walsh. Solving Non-clausal Formulas with DPLL Search. In *proc. 7th Int. Conference on Theory and Applications of Satisfiability Testing (SAT 2004*, LNCS. Springer, 2004.

80. C. Tinelli. A DPLL-based Calculus for Ground Satisfiability Modulo Theories. In *Proc. JELIA-02*, volume 2424 of *LNAI*, pages 308–319. Springer, 2002.

81. M. Velev and R. E. Bryant. Exploiting Positive Equality and Partial Non-Consistency in the Formal Verification of Pipelined Microprocessors. In *Design Automation Conference*, pages 397–401, 1999.

82. S. Wolfman and D. Weld. The LPSAT Engine & its Application to Resource Planning. In *Proc. IJCAI*, 1999.

83. S. Wolfman and D. Weld. Combining linear programming and satisfiability solving for resource planning. *Knowledge Engineering Review*, 2000.

84. Z. Zeng, P. Kalla, and M. Ciesielski. LPSAT: a unified approach to RTL satisfiability. In *Proc. DATE '01*. IEEE Press, 2001.

85. L. Zhang, C. F. Madigan, M. H. Moskewicz, and S. Malik. Efficient conflict driven learning in a boolean satisfiability solver. In *Proc. ICCAD '01*, pages 279–285. IEEE Press, 2001.

86. L. Zhang and S. Malik. The quest for efficient boolean satisfiability solvers. In *Proc. CAV'02*, number 2404 in LNCS, pages 17–36. Springer, 2002.

Refinement and Theorem Proving[*]

Panagiotis Manolios

College of Computing,
Georgia Institute of Technology,
Atlanta, GA, 30318
manolios@cc.gatech.edu

1 Introduction

In this chapter, we describe the ACL2 theorem proving system and show how it can be used to model and verify hardware using refinement.

This is a timely problem, as the ever-increasing complexity of microprocessor designs and the potentially devastating economic consequences of shipping defective products has made functional verification a bottleneck in the microprocessor design cycle, requiring a large amount of time, human effort, and resources [1, 58]. For example, the 1994 Pentium FDIV bug cost Intel $475 million and it is estimated that a similar bug in the current generation Intel Pentium processor would cost Intel $12 billion [2].

One of the key optimizations used in these designs is pipelining, a topic that has received a fair amount of interest from the research community. In this chapter, we show how to define a pipelined machine in ACL2 and how to use refinement to verify that it correctly implements its instruction set architecture. We discuss how to automate such proofs using theorem proving, decision procedures, and hybrid approaches that combine these two methods. We also outline future research directions.

2 The ACL2 Theorem Proving System

"ACL2" stands for "A Computational Logic for Applicative Common Lisp." It is the name of a programming language, a first-order mathematical logic based on recursive functions, and a mechanical theorem prover for that logic.

ACL2 is an industrial-strength version of the Boyer-Moore theorem prover [5] and was developed by Kaufmann and Moore , with early contributions by Robert Boyer; all three developers were awarded the 2005 ACM Software System Award for their work. Of special note is its "industrial-strength": as a programming language, it executes so efficiently that formal models written in it have been used as simulation platforms for pre-fabrication requirements testing; as a theorem prover, it has been used to prove the largest and most complicated theorems ever proved about commercially designed digital artifacts. In this section we give an informal overview of the ACL2 system.

---

[*] This research was funded in part by NSF grants CCF-0429924, IIS-0417413, and CCF-0438871.

The sources for ACL2 are freely available on the Web, under the GNU General Public License. The ACL2 homepage is http://www.cs.utexas.edu/users/-moore/acl2 [26]. Extensive documentation, including tutorials, a user's manual, workshop proceedings, and related papers are available from the ACL2 homepage. ACL2 is also described in a textbook by Kaufmann, Manolios, and Moore [23]. There is also a book of case studies [22]. Supplementary material for both books, including all the solutions to the exercises (over 200 in total) can be found on the Web [25, 24].

We recently released ACL2s [13], a version of ACL2 that features a modern graphical integrated development environment in Eclipse, levels appropriate for beginners through experts, state-of-the-art enhancements such as our recent improvements to termination analysis [45], etc. ACL2s is available at http://www.cc.gatech.edu/home/manolios/acl2s and is being developed with the goal of making formal reasoning accessible to the masses, with an emphasis on building a tool that any undergraduate can profitably use in a short amount of time. The tool includes many features for streamlining the learning process that are not found in ACL2. In general, the goal is to develop a tool that is "self-teaching," *i.e.*, it should be possible for an undergraduate to sit down and play with it and learn how to program in ACL2 and how to reason about the programs she writes.

ACL2, the language, is an applicative, or purely functional programming language. The ACL2 data types and expressions are presented in sections 2.1 and 2.2, respectively. A consequence of the applicative nature of ACL2 is that the rule of Leibniz, *i.e.*, $x = y \Rightarrow f.x = f.y$, written in ACL2 as (implies (equal x y) (equal (f x) (f y))), is a theorem. This effectively rules out side effects. Even so, ACL2 code can be made to execute efficiently. One way is to compile ACL2 code, which can be done with any Common Lisp [59] compiler. Another way is to use stobjs, single-threaded objects. Logically, stobjs have applicative semantics, but syntactic restrictions on their use allow ACL2 to produce code that *destructively* modifies stobjs. Stobjs have been very useful when efficiency is paramount, as is the case when modeling complicated computing systems such as microprocessors. For example, Hardin, Wilding, and Greve compare the speeds of a C model and an ACL2 model of the JEM1 (a silicon Java Virtual Machine designed by Rockwell Collins). They found that the ACL2 model runs at about 90% of the speed of the C model [16].

ACL2, the logic, is a first-order logic. The logic can be extended with *events*; examples of events are function definitions, constant definitions, macro definitions, and theorems. Logically speaking, function definitions introduce new axioms. Since new axioms can easily render the theory unsound, ACL2 has a definitional principle which limits the kinds of functions one can define. For example, the definitional principle guarantees that functions are *total*, *i.e.*, that they terminate. ACL2 also has macros, which allow one to customize the syntax. In section 2.3 we discuss the issues.

We give a brief overview of how the theorem prover works in section 2.4. We also describe encapsulation, a mechanism for introducing constrained functions,

functions that satisfy certain constraints, but that are otherwise undefined. We end section 2.4 by describing books in section 2.4. Books are files of events that often contain libraries of theorems and can be loaded by ACL2 quickly, without having to prove theorems.

In section 2.5 we list some of the applications to which ACL2 has been applied. We end in section 2.6, by showing, in detail, how to model hardware in ACL2. We do this by defining a simple, but not trivial, pipelined machine and its instruction set architecture.

2.1   Data Types

The ACL2 universe consists of *atoms* and *conses*. Atoms are atomic objects and include the following.

1. *Numbers* includes integers, rationals, and complex rationals. Examples include -1, 3/2, and #c(-1 2).
2. *Characters* represent the ASCII characters. Examples include #\2, #\a, and #\Space.
3. *Strings* are finite sequences of characters; an example is "Hello World!".
4. *Symbols* consist of two strings: a *package name* and a *symbol name*. For example, the symbol FOO::BAR has package name "FOO" and symbol name "BAR". ACL2 is case-insensitive with respect to symbol and package names. If a package name is not given, then the current package name is used, *e.g.*, if the current package is "FOO", then BAR denotes the symbol FOO::BAR. The symbols t and nil are used to denote **true** and **false**, respectively.

Conses are ordered pairs of objects. For example, the ordered pair consisting of the number 1 and the string "A" is written (X . "X"). The left component of a cons is called the *car* and the right component is called the *cdr*. You can think of conses as binary trees; the cons (X . "X") is depicted in figure 1(a). Of special interest are a class of conses called *true lists*. A true list is either the symbol nil, which denotes the empty list and can be written (), or a cons whose cdr is a true list. For example, the true list containing the numbers 0 and $\frac{1}{2}$, written (0 1/2), is depicted in figure 1(b). Also of interest are *association lists* or *alists*. An alist is a true list of conses and is often used to represent a mapping that associates the car of an element in the list with its cdr. The alist ((X . 3) (Y . 2)) is shown in figure 1(c).

2.2   Expressions

Expressions, which are also called terms, represent ACL2 programs and evaluate to ACL2 objects. We give an informal overview of expressions in this section. This allows us to suppress many of the details while focusing on the main ideas. Expressions depend on what we call a *history*, a list recording events. One reason for this dependency is that it is possible to define new functions (see section 2.3 on page 182) and these new functions can be used to form new expressions. User interaction with ACL2 starts in what we call the *ground-zero* history which

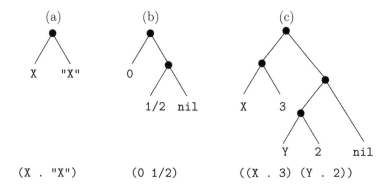

Fig. 1. Examples of conses

includes an entry for the built-in functions. As new events arise, the history is extended, *e.g.*, a function definition extends the history with an entry, which includes the name of the function and its arity. We are now ready to discuss expressions. Essentially, given history h, an expression is:

- A constant symbol, which includes the symbols `t`, `nil`, and symbols in the package `"KEYWORD"`; constant symbols evaluate to themselves.
- A constant expression, which is a number, a character, a string, or a *quoted constant*, a single quote (`'`) followed by an object. Numbers, characters, and strings evaluate to themselves. The value of a quoted constant is the object quoted. For example, the values of `1`, `#\A`, `"Hello"`, `'hello`, and `'(1 2 3)` are `1`, `#\A`, `"Hello"`, (the symbol) `hello`, and (the list) `(1 2 3)`, respectively.
- A variable symbol, which is any symbol other than a constant symbol. The value of a variable symbol is determined by an environment.
- A function application, $(f\ e_1\ \ldots\ e_n)$, where f is a function expression of arity n in history h and e_i, for $1 \leq i \leq n$, is an expression in history h. A function expression of arity n is a symbol denoting a function of arity n (in history h) or a lambda expression of the form `(lambda` $(v_1 \ldots v_n)$ *body*`)`, where $v_1, \ldots, v_n$ are distinct, *body* is an expression (in history h), and the only variables occurring freely in *body* are $v_1, \ldots, v_n$. The value of the expression is obtained by evaluating function f in the environment where the values of $v_1, \ldots, v_n$ are $e_1, \ldots, e_n$, respectively.

ACL2 contains many built-in, or primitive, functions. For example, `cons` is a built-in function of two arguments that returns a cons whose left element is the value of the first argument and whose right element is the value of the second argument. Thus, the value of the expression (`cons 'x 3`) is the cons (`x . 3`) because the value of the quoted constant `'x` is the symbol `x` and the value of the constant `3` is itself. Similarly, the value of expression (`cons (cons nil '(cons a 1)) (cons 'x 3)`) is `((nil . (cons a 1)) . (x . 3))`. There are built-in functions for manipulating all of the ACL2 data types. Some of the built-in functions are described in table 1.

Table 1. Some built-in function symbols and their values

Expression	Value
(equal x y)	T if the value of x equals the value of y, else nil
(if x y z)	The value of z if the value of x is nil, else the value of y
(implies x y)	T if the value of x is nil or the value of y is not nil, else nil
(not x)	T if the value of x is nil, else nil
(acl2-numberp x)	T if the value of x is a number, else nil
(integerp x)	T if the value of x is an integer, else nil
(rationalp x)	T if the value of x is a rational number, else nil
(atom x)	T if the value of x is an atom, else nil
(endp x)	Same as (atom x)
(zp x)	T if the value of x is 0 or is not a natural number, else nil
(consp x)	T if the value of x is a cons, else nil
(car x)	If the value of x is a cons, its left element, else nil
(cdr x)	If the value of x is a cons, its right element, else nil
(cons x y)	A cons whose car is the value of x and whose cdr is the value of y
(binary-append x y)	The list resulting from concatenating the value of x and the value of y
(len x)	The length of the value of x, if it is a cons, else 0

Table 2. Some commonly used macros and their values

Expression	Value
(caar x)	The car of the car of x
(cadr x)	The car of the cdr of x
(cdar x)	The cdr of the car of x
(cddr x)	The cdr of the cdr of x
(first x)	The car of x
(second x)	The cadr of x
(append x1 ... xn)	The binary-append of x1 ... xn
(list x1 ... xn)	The list containing x1 ... xn
(+ x1 ... xn)	Addition
(* x1 ... xn)	Multiplication
(- x y)	Subtraction
(and x1 ... xn)	Logical conjunction
(or x1 ... xn)	Logical disjunction

Comments are written with the use of semicolons: anything following a semicolon, up to the end of the line on which the semicolon appears, is a comment. Notice that an expression is an (ACL2) object and that an object is the value of some expression. For example, the object (if (consp x) (car x) nil) is the value of the expression '(if (consp x) (car x) nil).

Expressions also include *macros*, which are discussed in more detail in section 2.3. Macros are syntactic sugar and can be used to define what seem to be functions of arbitrary arity. For example, + is a macro that can be used as if it is a function of arbitrary arity. We can write (+), (+ x), and (+ x y z) which evaluate to 0, the value of x, and the sum of the values of x, y, and z, respectively. The way this works is that `binary-+` is a function of two arguments and expressions involving `+` are abbreviations for expressions involving 0 or more occurrences of `binary-+`, e.g., `(+ x y z)` is an abbreviation for `(binary-+ x (binary-+ y z))`.

Commonly used macros include the ones listed in table 2.

An often used macro is `cond`. `Cond` is a generalization of `if`. Instead of deciding between two expressions based on one test, as happens with `if`, one can decide between any number of expressions based on the appropriate number of tests. Here is an example.

```
(cond (test₁  exp₁)
      ...
      (testₙ  expₙ)
      (t  expₙ₊₁))
```

The above `cond` is an abbreviation for the following expression.

```
(if test₁  exp₁
    ...
       (if testₙ  expₙ
               expₙ₊₁) ... )
```

Another important macro is `let`. `Let` expressions are used to (simultaneously) bind values to variables and expand into lambdas. For example

```
(let ((v₁  e₁)
      ...
      (vₙ  eₙ))
  body)
```

is an abbreviation for

```
((lambda (v₁ ... vₙ)
    body)
 e₁ ... eₙ)
```

Consider the expression `(let ((x '(1 2)) (y '(3 4))) (append x y))`. It is an abbreviation for `((lambda (x y) (binary-append x y)) '(1 2) '(3 4))`, whose value is the list `(1 2 3 4)`.

Finally, `let*` is a macro that is used to sequentially bind values to variables and can be defined using `let`, as we now show.

```
(let* ((v₁  e₁)
       ...
       (vₙ  eₙ))
  body)
```

is an abbreviation for

```
(let ((v₁  e₁))
   (let* (...
             (vₙ  eₙ))
          body))
```

2.3   Definitions

In this section, we give an overview of how one goes about defining new functions and macros in ACL2.

Functions. Functions are defined using `defun`. For example, we can define the successor function, a function of one argument that increments its argument by 1, as follows.

```
(defun succ (x)
  (+ x 1))
```

The form of a `defun` is $(\texttt{defun}\ f\ doc\ dcl_1\ldots dcl_m\ (x_1\ldots x_n)\ body)$, where:

- $x_1\ldots x_n$ are distinct variable symbols
- the free variables in *body* are in $x_1\ldots x_n$
- *doc* is a documentation string and is optional
- $dcl_1\ldots dcl_m$ are declarations and are optional
- functions, other than f, used in *body* have been previously introduced
- *body* is an expression in the current history, extended to allow function applications of f
- if f is recursive we must prove that it terminates

A common use of declarations is to declare *guards*. Guards are used to indicate the expected domain of a function. Since ACL2 is a logic of *total* functions, all functions, regardless of whether there are guard declarations or not, are defined on all ACL2 objects. However, guards can be used to increase efficiency because proving that guards are satisfied allows ACL2 to directly use the underlying Common Lisp implementation to execute functions. For example, `endp` and `eq` are defined as follows.

```
(defun endp (x)
  (declare (xargs :guard (or (consp x) (equal x nil))))
  (atom x))

(defun eq (x y)
  (declare (xargs :guard (if (symbolp x) t (symbolp y))))
  (equal x y))
```

Both `endp` and `eq` are logically equivalent to `atom` and `equal`, respectively. The only difference is in their guards, as `atom` and `equal` both have the guard `t`. If `eq` is only called when one of its arguments is a symbol, then it can be implemented more efficiently than `equal`, which can be called on anything, including conses, numbers, and strings. Guard verification consists of proving that defined functions respect the guards of the functions they call. If guards are verified, then ACL2 can use efficient versions of functions.

Another common use of declarations is to declare the measure used to prove termination of a function. Consider the following function definition.

```
(defun app (x y)
  (declare (xargs :measure (len x)))
```

```
(if (consp x)
    (cons (car x) (app (cdr x) y))
  y))
```

App is a recursive function that can be used to concatenate lists x and y. Such a definition introduces the axiom (app x y) = *body* where *body* is the body of the function definition. The unconstrained introduction of such axioms can render the theory unsound, *e.g.*, consider the "definition" (defun bad (x) (not (bad x))). The axiom introduced, namely, (bad x) = (not (bad x)) allows us to prove nil (**false**). To guarantee that function definitions are meaningful, ACL2 has a definitional principle which requires that the we prove that the function terminates. This requires exhibiting a *measure*, an expression that decreases on each recursive call of the function. For many of the common recursion schemes, ACL2 can guess the measure. In the above example, we explicitly provide a measure for function app using a declaration. The measure is the length of x. Notice that app is called recursively only if x is a cons and it is called on the cdr of x, hence the length of x decreases. For an expression to be a measure, it must evaluate to an ACL2 ordinal on any argument. ACL2 ordinals correspond to the ordinals up to ϵ_0 in set theory [43, 41, 42, 44]. They allow one to use many of the standard well-founded structures commonly used in termination proofs, *e.g.*, the lexicographic ordering on tuples of natural numbers [42].

Macros. Macros are really useful for creating specialized notation and for abbreviating commonly occurring expressions. Macros are functions on ACL2 objects, but they differ from ACL2 functions in that they map the objects given as arguments to expressions, whereas ACL2 functions map the values of the objects given as arguments to objects. For example, if m is a macro then $(m\ x_1\ \ldots\ x_n)$ may evaluate to an expression obtained by evaluating the function corresponding to the macro symbol m on arguments $x_1, \ldots, x_n$ (not their values, as happens with function evaluation), obtaining an expression *exp*. *Exp* is the *immediate expansion* of $(m\ x_1\ \ldots\ x_n)$ and is then further evaluated until no macros remain, resulting in the *complete expansion* of the term. The complete expansion is then evaluated, as described previously.

Suppose that we are defining recursive functions whose termination can be shown with measure (len x), where x is the first argument to the function. Instead of adding the required declarations to all of the functions under consideration, we might want to write a macro that generates the required defun. Here is one way of doing this.

```
(defmacro defunm (name args body)
  `(defun ,name
     ,args
     (declare (xargs :measure (len ,(first args))))
     ,body))
```

Notice that we define macros using defmacro, in a manner similar to function definitions. Notice the use of what is called the *backquote* notation. The value of a backquoted list is a list that has the same structure as the backquoted list except that expressions preceded by a comma are replaced by their values. For example, if the value of name is app, then the value of `(defun ,name) is (defun app).

We can now use defunm as follows.

```
(defunm app (x y)
  (if (consp x)
      (cons (car x) (app (cdr x) y))
    y))
```

This expands to the following.

```
(defun app (x y)
  (declare (xargs :measure (len x)))
  (if (consp x)
      (cons (car x) (app (cdr x) y))
    y))
```

When the above is processed, the result is that the function app is defined. In more detail, the above macro is evaluated as follows. The macro formals name, args, and body are bound to app, (x y), and (if (consp x) (cons (car x) (app (cdr x) y)) y), respectively. Then, the macro body is evaluated. As per the discussion on the backquote notation, the above expansion is produced.

We consider a final example to introduce ampersand markers. The example is the list macro and its definition follows.

```
(defmacro list (&rest args)
  (list-macro args))
```

Recall that (list 1 2) is an abbreviation for (cons 1 (cons 2 nil)). In addition, list can be called on an arbitrary number of arguments; this is accomplished with the use of the &rest ampersand marker. When this marker is used, it results in the next formal, args, getting bound to the list of the remaining arguments. Thus, the value of (list 1 2) is the value of the expression (list-macro '(1 2)). In this way, an arbitrary number of objects are turned into a single object, which is passed to the function list-macro, which in the above case returns the expression (cons 1 (cons 2 nil)).

2.4   The Theorem Prover

The ACL2 theorem prover is an integrated system of ad hoc proof techniques that include simplification, generalization, induction and many other techniques.

Simplification is, however, the key technique. The typewriter font keywords below refer to online documentation topics accessible from the ACL2 online user's manual [26]. The simplifier includes the use of (1) evaluation (i.e., the explicit computation of constants when, in the course of symbolic manipulation, certain variable-free expressions, like (expt 2 32), arise), (2) conditional rewrite rules (derived from previously proved lemmas), cf. rewrite, (3) definitions (including recursive definitions), cf. defun, (4) propositional calculus (implemented both by the normalization of if-then-else expressions and the use of

BDDs), cf. bdd, (5) a linear arithmetic decision procedure for the rationals (with extensions to help with integer problems and with non-linear problems [17]), cf. linear-arithmetic, (6) user-defined equivalence and congruence relations, cf. equivalence, (7) user-defined and mechanically verified simplifiers, cf. meta, (8) a user-extensible type system, cf. type-prescription, (9) forward chaining, cf. forward-chaining, (10) an interactive loop for entering proof commands, cf. proof-checker, and (11) various means to control and monitor these features including heuristics, interactive features, and user-supplied functional programs.

The induction heuristic, cf. induction, automatically selects an induction based on the recursive patterns used by the functions appearing in the conjecture or a user-supplied hint. It may combine various patterns to derive a "new" one considered more suitable for the particular conjecture. The chosen induction scheme is then applied to the conjecture to produce a set of new subgoals, typically including one or more base cases and induction steps. The induction steps typically contain hypotheses identifying a particular non-base case, one or more instances of the conjecture to serve as induction hypotheses, and, as the conclusion, the conjecture being proved. The system attempts to select an induction scheme that will provide induction hypotheses that are useful when the function applications in the conclusion are expanded under the case analysis provided. Thus, while induction is often considered the system's *forte*, most of the interesting work, even for inductive proofs, occurs in the simplifier.

We now discuss how to prove theorems with ACL2. All of the system's proof techniques are sensitive to the database of previously proved rules, included in the *logical world* or *world* and, if any, user-supplied hints. By proving appropriate theorems (and tagging them in pragmatic ways) it is possible to make the system expand functions in new ways, replace one term by another in certain contexts, consider unusual inductions, add new known inequalities to the linear arithmetic procedure, restrict generalizations, etc.

The command for submitting theorems to ACL2 is defthm. Here is an example.

```
(defthm app-is-associative
  (equal (app (app x y) z)
         (app x (app y z))))
```

ACL2 proves this theorem automatically, given the definition of app, but with more complicated theorems ACL2 often needs help. One way of providing help is to prove lemmas which are added to the world and can then be used in future proof attempts. For example, ACL2 does not prove the following theorem automatically.

```
(defthm app-is-associative-with-one-arg
  (equal (app (app x x) x)
         (app x (app x x))))
```

However, if app-is-associative is in the world, then ACL2 recognizes that the above theorem follows (it is a special case of app-is-associative). Another way of providing help is to give explicit hints, *e.g.*, one can specify what induction scheme to use, or what instantiations of previously proven theorems to use, and so on. More generally, the form of a `defthm` is

```
(defthm name formula
  :rule-classes (class₁ ... classₙ)
  :hints ...)
```

where both the `:rule-classes` and `:hints` parts are optional.

Encapsulation. ACL2 provides a mechanism called *encapsulation* by which one can introduce constrained functions. For example, the following event can be used to introduce a function that is constrained to be associative and commutative.

```
(encapsulate
  (((ac * *) => *))
  (local (defun ac (x y) (+ x y)))
  (defthm ac-is-associative
    (equal (ac (ac x y) z)
           (ac x (ac y z)))))
  (defthm ac-is-commutative
    (equal (ac x y)
           (ac y x))))
```

This event adds the axioms `ac-is-associative` and `ac-is-commutative`. The sole purpose of the local definition of `ac` in the above encapsulate form is to establish that the constraints are satisfiable. In the world after admission of the encapsulate event, the function `ac` is undefined; only the two constraint axioms are known.

There is a derived rule of inference called *functional instantiation* that is used as follows. Suppose f is a constrained function with constraint ϕ and suppose that we prove theorem ψ. Further suppose that g is a function that satisfies the constraint ϕ, with f replaced by g, then replacing f by g in ψ results in a theorem as well. That is, any theorem proven about f holds for any function satisfying the constraints on f. For example, we can prove the following theorem about `ac`. Notice that we had to provide hints to ACL2.

```
(defthm commutativity-2-of-ac
  (equal (ac y (ac x z))
         (ac x (ac y z)))
  :hints (("Goal"
           :in-theory (disable ac-is-associative)
           :use ((:instance ac-is-associative)
                 (:instance ac-is-associative
                            (x y) (y x)))))))
```

We can now use the above theorem and the derived rule of inference to show that any associative and commutative function satisfies the above theorem. For example, here is how we show that `*` satisfies the above theorem.

```
(defthm commutativity-2-of-*
  (equal (* y (* x z))
         (* x (* y z)))
  :hints (("Goal"
             :by (:functional-instance
                   commutativity-2-of-ac
                   (ac (lambda (x y) (* x y)))))))
```

ACL2 generates and establishes the necessary constraints, that * is associative and commutative.

Encapsulation and functional instantiation allow quantification over functions and thus have the flavor of a second order mechanism, although they are really first-order. For the full details see [4, 29].

Books. A *book* is a file of ACL2 events analogous to a library. The ACL2 distribution comes with many books, including books for arithmetic, set theory, data structures, and so on. The events in books are *certified* as admissible and can be loaded into subsequent ACL2 sessions without having to replay the proofs. This makes it possible to structure large proofs and to isolate related theorems into libraries. Books can include *local* events that are not included when books are *included*, or loaded, into an ACL2 session.

2.5   Applications

ACL2 has been applied to a wide range of commercially interesting verification problems. We recommend visiting the ACL2 home page [26] and inspecting the links on Tours, Demo, Books and Papers, and for the most current work, The Workshops and Related Meetings. See especially [22]. ACL2 has been used on various large projects, including the verification of floating point [48, 50, 52, 51, 53], microprocessor verification [18, 19, 7, 20, 56, 57, 54, 15, 14, 16, 8], and programming languages [47, 3]. There are various papers describing aspects the internals of ACL2, including single-threaded objects [6], encapsulation [29], and the base logic [27].

2.6   Modeling Hardware

In this section, we show how to model a simple machine both at the instruction set architecture (ISA) level and at the microarchitecture (MA) level. The MA machine is roughly based on Sawada's simple machine [55, 54] and the related machines appearing in [30, 31]. It contains a three-stage pipeline and in the sequel, we will be interested in verifying that it "correctly" implements the ISA machine.

The ISA machine has instructions that are four-tuples consisting of an opcode, a target register, and two source registers. The MA machine is a pipelined machine with three stages. A pipeline is analogous to an assembly line. The pipeline consists of several stages each of which performs part of the computation required to complete an instruction. When the pipeline is full many instructions are in various degrees of completion. A diagram of the MA machine

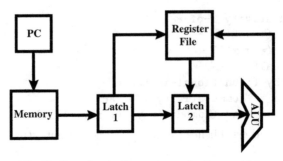

Fig. 2. Our simple three-stage pipeline machine

appears in Fig. 2. The three stages are fetch, set-up, and write. During the fetch stage, the instruction pointed to by the PC (program counter) is retrieved from memory and placed into latch 1. During the set-up stage, the contents of the source registers (of the instruction in latch 1) are retrieved from the register file and sent to latch 2 along with the rest of the instruction in latch 1. During the write stage, the appropriate ALU (arithmetic logic unit) operation is performed and the result is used to update the value of the target register.

Let us consider a simple example where the contents of memory are as follows.

Inst				
0	add	rb	ra	ra
1	add	ra	rb	ra

When this simple two-line code fragment is executed on the ISA and MA machines, we get the following traces, where we only show the value of the program counter and the contents of registers ra and rb.

Clock	ISA	MA	Inst 0	Inst 1
0	$\langle 0, \langle 1, 1 \rangle \rangle$	$\langle 0, \langle 1, 1 \rangle \rangle$		
1	$\langle 1, \langle 1, 2 \rangle \rangle$	$\langle 1, \langle 1, 1 \rangle \rangle$	Fetch	
2	$\langle 2, \langle 3, 2 \rangle \rangle$	$\langle 2, \langle 1, 1 \rangle \rangle$	Set-up	Fetch
3		$\langle 2, \langle 1, 2 \rangle \rangle$	Write	Stall
4		$\langle \_, \langle 1, 2 \rangle \rangle$		Set-up
5		$\langle \_, \langle 3, 2 \rangle \rangle$		Write

The rows correspond to steps of the machines, *e.g.*, row Clock 0 corresponds to the initial state, Clock 1 to the next state, and so on. The ISA and MA columns contain the relevant parts of the state of the machines: a pair consisting of the PC and the register file (itself a pair consisting of registers ra and rb). The final two columns indicate what stage the instructions are in (only applicable to the MA machine).

In the initial state (in row Clock 0) the PCs of the ISA and MA machines contain the value 0 (indicating that the next instruction to execute is Inst 0) and both registers have the value 1. In the next ISA state (in row Clock 1), the PC is incremented and the add instruction performed, *i.e.*, register rb is updated with the value ra + ra = 2. The final entry in the ISA column contains the state of the ISA machine after executing Inst 1.

After one step of the MA machine, Inst 0 completes the fetch phase and the PC is incremented to point to the next instruction. After step 2 (in row Clock 2), Inst 0 completes the set-up stage, Inst 1 completes the fetch phase, and the PC is incremented. After step 3, Inst 0 completes the write-back phase and the register file is updated for the first time with rb set to 2. However, Inst 1 is stalled during step 3 because one of its source registers is rb, the target register of the previous instruction. Since the previous instruction has not completed, the value of rb is not available and Inst 1 is stalled for one cycle. In the next cycle, Inst 1 enters the set-up stage and Inst 2 enters the fetch stage (not shown). Finally, after step 5, Inst 1 is completed and register ra is updated.

ISA Definition. We now consider how to define the ISA and MA machines using ACL2. The first machine we define is ISA. The main function is ISA-step, a function that steps the ISA machine, *i.e.*, it takes an ISA state and returns the next ISA state. The definition of ISA-step follows.

```
(defun ISA-step (ISA)
  (let ((inst (g (g :pc ISA) (g :imem ISA))))
    (let ((op (g :opcode inst))
          (rc (g :rc    inst))
          (ra (g :ra    inst))
          (rb (g :rb    inst)))
      (case op
        (add (ISA-add rc ra rb ISA))
          ;; REGS[rc] := REGS[ra] + REGS[rb]
        (sub (ISA-sub rc ra rb ISA))
          ;; REGS[rc] := REGS[ra] - REGS[rb]
        (mul (ISA-mul rc ra rb ISA))
          ;; REGS[rc] := REGS[ra] * REGS[rb]
        (load (ISA-load rc ra ISA))
          ;; REGS[rc] := MEM[ra]
        (loadi (ISA-loadi rc ra ISA))
          ;; REGS[rc] := MEM[REGS[ra]]
        (store (ISA-store ra rb ISA))
          ;; MEM[REGS[ra]] := REGS[rb]
        (bez (ISA-bez ra rb ISA))
          ;; REGS[ra]=0 -> pc:=pc+REGS[rb]
        (jump (ISA-jump ra ISA))
          ;; pc:=REGS[ra]
        (otherwise (ISA-default ISA))))))) 
```

The ISA-step function uses a book (library) for reasoning about records. One of the functions exported by the records books is g (get), where (g f r) gets the value of field f from record r. Therefore, ISA-step fetches the instruction in the instruction memory (the field :imem of ISA state ISA) referenced by the program counter (the field :pc of ISA state ISA) and stores this in inst, which itself is a record consisting of fields :opcode, :rc, :ra, and :rb. Then, based on the opcode, the appropriate action is taken. For example, in the case of an add instruction, the next ISA state is (ISA-add rc ra rb ISA), where ISA-add provides the semantics of add instructions. The definition of ISA-add is given below

```
(defun ISA-add (rc ra rb ISA)
  (seq-isa nil
            :pc    (1+ (g :pc ISA))
            :regs (add-rc ra rb rc (g :regs ISA))
            :imem (g :imem ISA)
            :dmem (g :dmem ISA)))

(defun add-rc (ra rb rc regs)
  (seq regs rc (+ (g ra regs)
                  (g rb regs))))
```

The macro seq-isa is used to construct an ISA state whose four fields have the given values. Notice that the program counter is incremented and the register file is updated by setting the value of register rc to the sum of the values in registers ra and rb. This happens in fuction add-rc, where seq is a macro that given a record, r, and a collection of field/value pairs, updates the fields in r with the given values and returns the result.

The other ALU instructions are similarly defined. We now show how to define the semantics of the rest of the instructions (ifix forces its argument to be an integer).

```
(defun ISA-loadi (rc ra ISA)
  (let ((regs (g :regs ISA)))
    (seq-isa nil
              :pc    (1+ (g :pc ISA))
              :regs (load-rc (g ra regs) rc regs (g :dmem ISA))
              :imem (g :imem ISA)
              :dmem (g :dmem ISA))))

(defun load-rc (ad rc regs dmem)
  (seq regs rc (g ad dmem)))

(defun ISA-load (rc ad ISA)
  (seq-isa nil
            :pc    (1+ (g :pc ISA))
            :regs (load-rc  ad rc (g :regs ISA) (g :dmem ISA))
            :imem (g :imem ISA)
            :dmem (g :dmem ISA)))

(defun ISA-store (ra rb ISA)
  (seq-isa nil
```

```
           :pc   (1+ (g :pc ISA))
           :regs (g :regs ISA)
           :imem (g :imem ISA)
           :dmem (store ra rb (g :regs ISA) (g :dmem ISA))))

(defun store (ra rb regs dmem)
  (seq dmem (g ra regs) (g rb regs)))

(defun ISA-jump (ra ISA)
  (seq-isa nil
           :pc (ifix (g ra (g :regs ISA)))
           :regs (g :regs ISA)
           :imem (g :imem ISA)
           :dmem (g :dmem ISA)))

(defun ISA-bez (ra rb ISA)
  (seq-isa nil
           :pc (bez ra rb (g :regs ISA) (g :pc ISA))
           :regs (g :regs ISA)
           :imem (g :imem ISA)
           :dmem (g :dmem ISA)))

(defun bez (ra rb regs pc)
  (if (equal 0 (g ra regs))
      (ifix (+ pc (g rb regs)))
    (1+ pc)))

(defun ISA-default (ISA)
  (seq-isa nil
           :pc (1+ (g :pc ISA))
           :regs (g :regs ISA)
           :imem (g :imem ISA)
           :dmem (g :dmem ISA)))
```

MA Definition. ISA is the specification for MA, a three stage pipelined machine, which contains a program counter, a register file, a memory, and two latches. The first latch contains a flag which indicates if the latch is valid, an opcode, the target register, and two source registers. The second latch contains a flag as before, an opcode, the target register, and the values of the two source registers. The definition of MA-step follows.

```
(defun MA-step (MA)
  (seq-ma nil
          :pc    (step-pc MA)
          :regs  (step-regs MA)
          :dmem  (step-dmem MA)
          :imem  (g :imem MA)
```

```
:latch1 (step-latch1 MA)
:latch2 (step-latch2 MA)))
```

MA-step works by calling functions that given one of the MA components return the next state value of that component. Note that this is very different from ISA-step, which calls functions, based on the type of the next instruction, that return the complete next ISA state.

Below, we show how the register file is updated. If latch2 is valid, then if we have an ALU instruction, the output of the ALU is used to update register rc. Otherwise, if we have a load instruction, then we update register rc with the appropriate word from memory.

```
(defun step-regs (MA)
  (let* ((regs     (g :regs MA))
         (dmem     (g :dmem MA))
         (latch2   (g :latch2 MA))
         (validp   (g :validp latch2))
         (op       (g :op latch2))
         (rc       (g :rc latch2))
         (ra-val   (g :ra-val latch2))
         (rb-val   (g :rb-val latch2)))
    (if validp
        (cond ((alu-opp op)
               (seq regs rc (ALU-output op ra-val rb-val)))
              ((load-opp op)
               (seq regs rc (g ra-val dmem)))
              (t regs))
      regs)))

(defun alu-opp (op)
  (in op '(add sub mul)))

(defun load-opp (op)
  (in op '(load loadi)))

(defun in (x y)
  (if (endp y)
      nil
    (or (equal x (car y))
        (in x (cdr y)))))

(defun ALU-output (op val1 val2)
  (cond ((equal op 'add)
         (+ val1 val2))
        ((equal op 'sub)
         (- val1 val2))
        (t (* val1 val2))))
```

We now show how to update latch2. If latch1 is not valid or if it will be stalled, then latch2 is invalidated. Othewise, we copy the `:op` and `:rc` fields from latch1 and read the contents of registers `:rb` and `:ra`, except for `load` instructions. The `:pch` field is a history variable: it does not affect the computation of the machine and is used only to aid the proof process. We use one more history variable in latch1. Both history variables serve the same purpose: they are used to record the address of the instruction with which they are associated.

```
(defun step-latch2 (MA)
  (let* ((latch1 (g :latch1 MA))
         (l1op   (g :op latch1)))
    (if (or (not (g :validp latch1))
            (stall-l1p MA))
        (seq-12 nil :validp nil)
      (seq-12 nil
              :validp t
              :op     l1op
              :rc     (g :rc latch1)
              :ra-val (if (equal l1op 'load)
                          (g :ra latch1)
                        (g (g :ra latch1) (g :regs MA)))
              :rb-val (g (g :rb latch1) (g :regs MA))
              :pch    (g :pch latch1)))))
```

We update latch1 as follows. If it will be stalled then, it stays the same. If it will be invalidated, then it is. Otherwise, we fetch the next instruction from memory and store it in the register (and record the address of the instruction in the history variable `:pch`). Latch1 is stalled exactly when it and latch2 are valid and latch2 contains an instruction that will modify one of the registers latch1 depends on. Latch1 is invalidated if it contains any branch instruction (because the jump address cannot be determined yet) or if latch2 contains a **bez** instruction (again, the jump address cannot be determined for **bez** instructions until the instruction has made its way through the pipeline, whereas the jump address for **jump** instructions can be computed during the second stage of the machine).

```
(defun step-latch1 (MA)
  (let ((latch1 (g :latch1 MA))
        (inst   (g (g :pc MA) (g :imem MA))))
    (cond ((stall-l1p MA)
           latch1)
          ((invalidate-l1p MA)
           (seq-l1 nil :validp nil))
          (t (seq-l1 nil
                     :validp t
                     :op     (g :opcode inst)
                     :rc     (g :rc inst)
```

```
                         :ra     (g :ra inst)
                         :rb     (g :rb inst)
                         :pch    (g :pc MA))))))

(defun stall-l1p (MA)
  (let* ((latch1   (g :latch1 MA))
         (l1validp (g :validp latch1))
         (latch2   (g :latch2 MA))
         (l1op     (g :op latch1))
         (l2op     (g :op latch2))
         (l2validp (g :validp latch2))
         (l2rc     (g :rc latch2))
         (l1ra     (g :ra latch1))
         (l1rb     (g :rb latch1)))
    (and l2validp l1validp
         (rc-activep l2op)
         (or (equal l1ra l2rc)
             (and (uses-rbp l1op)
                  (equal l1rb l2rc))))))

(defun rc-activep (op)
  (or (alu-opp op)
      (load-opp op)))

(defun uses-rbp (op)
  (or (alu-opp op)
      (in op '(store bez))))

(defun uses-rbp (op)
  (or (alu-opp op)
      (in op '(store bez))))

(defun invalidate-l1p (MA)
  (let* ((latch1   (g :latch1 MA))
         (l1op     (g :op latch1))
         (l1validp (g :validp latch1))
         (latch2   (g :latch2 MA))
         (l2op     (g :op latch2))
         (l2validp (g :validp latch2)))
    (or (and l1validp
             (in l1op '(bez jump)))
        (and l2validp
             (equal l2op 'bez)))))
```

Memory is updated only when we have a store instruction, in which case we update the memory appropriately.

```
(defun step-dmem (MA)
  (let* ((dmem    (g :dmem MA))
         (latch2  (g :latch2 MA))
         (l2validp (g :validp latch2))
         (l2op    (g :op latch2))
         (l2ra-val (g :ra-val latch2))
         (l2rb-val (g :rb-val latch2)))
    (if (and l2validp (equal l2op 'store))
        (seq dmem l2ra-val l2rb-val)
      dmem)))
```

Finally, the program counter is updated as follows. If latch1 will stall, then the program counter is not modified. Otherwise, if latch1 will be invalidated, then if this is due to a bez instruction in latch2, the jump address can be now be determined, so the program counter is updated as per the semantics of the bez instruction. Otherwise, if the invalidation is due to a jump instruction in latch1, the jump address can be computed and the program counter is set to this address. The only other possibility is that the invalidation is due to a bez instruction in latch1; in this case the jump address has not yet been determined, so the pc is not modified. Note, this simple machine does not have a branch predictor. If the invalidate signal does not hold, then we increment the program counter unless we are fetching a branch instruction.

```
(defun step-pc (MA)
  (let* ((pc       (g :pc MA))
         (inst     (g (g :pc MA) (g :imem MA)))
         (op       (g :opcode inst))
         (regs     (g :regs MA))
         (latch1   (g :latch1 MA))
         (l1op     (g :op latch1))
         (latch2   (g :latch2 MA))
         (l2op     (g :op latch2))
         (l2validp (g :validp latch2))
         (l2ra-val (g :ra-val latch2))
         (l2rb-val (g :rb-val latch2)))
    (cond ((stall-l1p MA)
           pc)
          ((invalidate-l1p MA)
           (cond ((and l2validp
                       (equal l2op 'bez))
                  (if (equal 0 l2ra-val)
                      (ifix (ALU-output 'add pc l2rb-val))
                    (1+ pc)))
                 ((equal l1op 'jump)
                  (ifix (g (g :ra latch1) regs)))
                 (t pc)))
```

```
                    ;;; must be bez instruction
          ((in op '(jump bez))
           pc)
          (t (1+ pc)))))
```

This ends the description of the ISA and MA machines. To summarize, we can use ACL2 to define machines models at any level of abstraction we like. What we wind up with are simulators for the machines, which we can execute. For example, consider the following program to multiply x and y (without using the mul instruction). The data memory contains the constants 0, 1, 4, and 6 in memory locations 0, 1, 4, and 6, respectively. It also contains x and y in memory locations 2 and 3.

```
(defun mul-dmem (x y)
  (seq nil 0 0 1 1 2 x 3 y 4 4 6 6))
```

The instruction memory contains the following code.

```
(defun inst (op rc ra rb)
  (seq nil :opcode op :rc rc :ra ra :rb rb))
```

```
(defun mul-imem ()
  (seq nil
       0 (inst 'load 0 1 nil)
       1 (inst 'load 1 2 nil)
       2 (inst 'load 2 3 nil)
       3 (inst 'load 3 0 nil)
       4 (inst 'load 4 4 nil)
       5 (inst 'load 6 6 nil)
       6 (inst 'bez nil 1 4)
       7 (inst 'sub 1 1 0)
       8 (inst 'add 3 3 2)
       9 (inst 'jump nil 6 nil)))
```

The code works by adding x copies of y in register 3. For example (isa-run (isa-state 0 nil (mul-imem) (mul-dmem 3 4)) 19) is an ISA state whose :pc is 10 (indicating exit from the loop) and with a value of 12 in register 3. Similarly, (ma-run (ma-state 0 nil (mul-imem) (mul-dmem 3 4) nil nil) 30) is the corresponding MA state.

3   Refinement

In the previous section, we saw how one can model a pipelined machine and its instruction set architecture in ACL2. We now discuss how to verify such machines. Consider the partial traces of the ISA and MA machines on the simple two-line code fragment from the previous section (add rb ra ra followed by add ra rb ra). We are only showing the value of the program counter and the contents of registers ra and rb.

ISA	MA		MA		MA
$\langle 0, \langle 1,1 \rangle \rangle$	$\langle 0, \langle 1,1 \rangle \rangle$		$\langle 0, \langle 1,1 \rangle \rangle$		$\langle 0, \langle 1,1 \rangle \rangle$
$\langle 1, \langle 1,2 \rangle \rangle$	$\langle 1, \langle 1,1 \rangle \rangle$		$\langle 0, \langle 1,1 \rangle \rangle$		$\langle 1, \langle 1,2 \rangle \rangle$
$\langle 2, \langle 3,2 \rangle \rangle$	$\langle 2, \langle 1,1 \rangle \rangle$	$\longrightarrow$	$\langle 0, \langle 1,1 \rangle \rangle$	$\longrightarrow$	$\langle 2, \langle 3,2 \rangle \rangle$
	$\langle 2, \langle 1,2 \rangle \rangle$	Commit	$\langle 1, \langle 1,2 \rangle \rangle$	Remove	
	$\langle \text{-}, \langle 1,2 \rangle \rangle$	PC	$\langle 1, \langle 1,2 \rangle \rangle$	Stutter	
	$\langle \text{-}, \langle 3,2 \rangle \rangle$		$\langle 2, \langle 3,2 \rangle \rangle$		

Notice that the PC differs in the two traces and this occurs because the pipeline, initially empty, is being filled and the PC points to the next instruction to fetch. If the PC were to point to the next instruction to commit (*i.e.*, the next instruction to complete), then we would get the trace shown in column 3. Notice that in column 3, the PC does not change from 0 to 1 until Inst 0 is committed in which case the next instruction to commit is Inst 1. We now have a trace that is the same as the ISA trace except for stuttering; after removing the stuttering we have, in column 4, the ISA trace.

We now formalize the above and start with the notion of a *refinement map*, a function that maps MA states to ISA states. In the above example we mapped MA states to ISA states by transforming the PC. Proving correctness amounts to relating MA states with the ISA states they map to under the refinement map and proving a WEB (Well-founded Equivalence Bisimulation). Proving a WEB guarantees that MA states and related ISA states have related computations up to finite stuttering. This is a strong notion of equivalence, *e.g.*, a consequence is that the two machines satisfy the same $\text{CTL}^* \setminus \text{X}$ properties.[1] This includes the class of next-time free safety and liveness (including fairness) properties, *e.g.*, one such property is that the MA machine cannot deadlock (because the ISA machine cannot deadlock).

Why "up to finite stuttering"? Because we are comparing machines at different levels of abstraction: the pipelined machine is a low-level implementation of the high-level ISA specification. When comparing systems at different levels of abstraction, it is often the case that the low-level system requires several steps to match a single step of the high-level system.

Why use a refinement map? Because there may be components in one system that do not appear in the other, *e.g.*, the MA machine has latches but the ISA machine does not. In addition, data can be represented in different ways, *e.g.*, a pipelined machine might use binary numbers whereas its instruction set architecture might use a decimal representation. Yet another reason is that components present in both systems may have different behaviors, as is the case with the PC above. Notice that the refinement map affects how MA and ISA states are related, not the behavior of the MA machine.

The theory of refinement we present is based on transition systems (TSs). A TS, $\mathcal{M}$, is a triple $\langle S, \dashrightarrow, L \rangle$, consisting of a set of states, S, a left-total transition relation, $\dashrightarrow \subseteq S^2$, and a labeling function L whose domain is S and where $L.s$ (we sometimes use an infix dot to denote function application) corresponds to

---

[1] CTL^* is a braching-time temporal logic; $\text{CTL}^* \setminus \text{X}$ is CTL^* without the next-time operator X.

what is "visible" at state s. Clearly, the ISA and MA machines can be thought of as transition systems (TS).

Our notion of refinement is based on the following definition of stuttering bisimulation [9], where by $fp(\sigma, s)$ we mean that σ is a fullpath (infinite path) starting at s, and by $match(B, \sigma, \delta)$ we mean that the fullpaths σ and δ are equivalent sequences up to finite stuttering (repetition of states).

Definition 1. $B \subseteq S \times S$ *is a stuttering bisimulation (STB) on TS* $\mathcal{M} = \langle S, \dashrightarrow, L \rangle$ *iff* B *is an equivalence relation and for all* s, w *such that* sBw:

(Stb1) $L.s = L.w$

(Stb2) $\langle \forall \sigma : fp(\sigma, s) : \langle \exists \delta : fp(\delta, w) : match(B, \sigma, \delta) \rangle \rangle$

Browne, Clarke, and Grumberg have shown that states that are stuttering bisimilar satisfy the same next-time-free temporal logic formulas [9].

Lemma 1. *Let* B *be an STB on* $\mathcal{M}$ *and let* sBw. *For any* CTL$^* \setminus$ X *formula* f, $\mathcal{M}, w \models f$ *iff* $\mathcal{M}, s \models f$.

We note that stuttering bisimulation differs from weak bisimulation [46] in that weak bisimulation allows infinite stuttering. Stuttering is a common phenomenon when comparing systems at different levels of abstraction, *e.g.*, if the pipeline is empty, MA will require several steps to complete an instruction, whereas ISA completes an instruction during every step. Distinguishing between infinite and finite stuttering is important, because (among other things) we want to distinguish deadlock from stutter.

When we say that MA refines ISA, we mean that in the disjoint union ($\uplus$) of the two systems, there is an STB that relates every pair of states w, s such that w is an MA state and $r(w) = s$.

Definition 2. *(STB Refinement) Let* $\mathcal{M} = \langle S, \dashrightarrow, L \rangle$, $\mathcal{M}' = \langle S', \dashrightarrow', L' \rangle$, *and* $r : S \to S'$. *We say that* $\mathcal{M}$ *is a STB refinement of* $\mathcal{M}'$ *with respect to refinement map* r, *written* $\mathcal{M} \approx_r \mathcal{M}'$, *if there exists a relation*, B, *such that* $\langle \forall s \in S :: sBr.s \rangle$ *and* B *is an STB on the TS* $\langle S \uplus S', \dashrightarrow \uplus \dashrightarrow', \mathcal{L} \rangle$, *where* $\mathcal{L}.s = L'.s$ *for* s *an* S' *state and* $\mathcal{L}.s = L'(r.s)$ *otherwise.*

STB refinement is a generally applicable notion. However, since it is based on bisimulation, it is often too strong a notion and in this case refinement based on stuttering *simulation* should be used (see [32, 33]). The reader may be surprised that STB refinement theorems can be proved in the context of pipelined machine verification; after all, features such as branch prediction can lead to non-deterministic pipelined machines, whereas the ISA is deterministic. While this is true, the pipelined machine is related to the ISA via a refinement map that hides the pipeline; when viewed in this way, the nondeterminism is masked and we can prove that the two systems are stuttering bisimilar (with respect to the ISA visible components).

A major shortcoming of the above formulation of refinement is that it requires reasoning about infinite paths, something that is difficult to automate [49].

In [32], WEB-refinement, an equivalent formulation is given that requires only local reasoning, involving only MA states, the ISA states they map to under the refinement map, and their successor states.

Definition 3. *Well-Founded Equivalence Bisimulation (WEB [34, 49]) B is a well-founded equivalence bisimulation on TS* $M = \langle S, \dashrightarrow, L \rangle$ *iff:*

1. *B is an equivalence relation on* S; *and*
2. $\langle \forall s, w \in S : sBw : L.s = L.w \rangle$; *and*
3. *There exists function* $erank : S \times S \to W$, *with* $\langle W, \prec \rangle$ *well-founded, and*
    $\langle \forall s, u, w \in S : sBw \ \land \ s \dashrightarrow u :$
    $\qquad \langle \exists v : w \dashrightarrow v : uBv \rangle \ \lor$
    $\qquad (uBw \ \land \ erank(u, u) \prec erank(s, s)) \ \lor$
    $\qquad \langle \exists v : w \dashrightarrow v : sBv \ \land \ erank(u, v) \prec erank(u, w) \rangle \rangle$

We call a pair $\langle rank, \langle W, \prec \rangle \rangle$ satisfying condition 3 in the above definition, a *well-founded witness*. The third WEB condition guarantees that related states have the same computations up to stuttering. If states s and w are in the same class and s can transit to u, then one of the following holds.

1. The transition can be matched with no stutter, in which case, u is matched by a step from w.
2. The transition can be matched but there is stutter on the left (from s), in which case, u and w are in the same class and the rank function decreases (to guarantee that w is forced to take a step eventually).
3. The transition can be matched but there is stutter on the right (from w), in which case, there is some successor v of w in the same class as s and the rank function decreases (to guarantee that u is eventually matched).

To prove a relation is a WEB, note that reasoning about single steps of $\dashrightarrow$ suffices. In addition we can often get by with a rank function of one argument.

Note that the notion of WEB refinement is independent of the refinement map used. For example, we can use the standard flushing refinement map [11], where MA states are mapped to ISA states by executing all partially completed instructions without fetching any new instructions, and then projecting out the ISA visible components. In previous work, we have explored the use of other refinement maps, *e.g.*, in [39, 38, 21], we present new classes of refinement maps that can provide several orders of magnitude improvements in verification times over the standard flushing-based refinement maps. In this paper, however, we use the commitment refinement map, introduced in [30].

A very important property of WEB refinement is that it is compositional, something that we have exploited in several different contexts [40, 37].

Theorem 1. *(Composition) If* $\mathcal{M} \approx_r \mathcal{M}'$ *and* $\mathcal{M}' \approx_q \mathcal{M}''$ *then* $\mathcal{M} \approx_{r;q} \mathcal{M}''$.

Above, $r; q$ denotes composition, *i.e.*, $(r; q)(s) = q(r.s)$.

From the above theorem we can derive several other composition results; for example:

Theorem 2. *(Composition)*

$$\frac{\begin{array}{c} \text{MA} \approx_r \cdots \approx_q \text{ISA} \\ \text{ISA} \parallel P \vdash \varphi \end{array}}{\text{MA} \parallel P \vdash \varphi}$$

In this form, the above rule exactly matches the compositional proof rules in [12]. The above theorem states that to prove MA $\parallel$ P $\vdash$ φ (that MA, the pipelined machine, executing program P satisfies property φ, a property over the ISA visible state), it suffices to prove MA $\approx$ ISA and ISA $\parallel$ P $\vdash$ φ: that MA refines ISA (which can be done using a sequence of refinement proofs) and that ISA, executing P, satisfies φ. That is, we can prove that code running on the pipelined machine is correct, by first proving that the pipelined machine refines the instruction set architecture and then proving that the software running on the instruction set—not on the pipelined machine—is correct.

4   Pipelined Machine Verification

In this section, we show how to use ACL2 to prove the correctness of the pipelined machine we have defined, using WEB-refinement. We start, in section 4.1 by discussing how we deal with quantification in ACL2. We then discuss how the refinement maps are defined, in section 4.2. Finally, in section 4.3, we discuss the proof of correctness.

4.1   Quantification

The macro defun-sk is used to implement quantification in ACL2 by introducing witness functions and constraints. For example, the quantified formula $\langle \exists x :: P(x, y) \rangle$ is expressed in ACL2 as the function EP with the constraints (P x y) $\Rightarrow$ (EP y) and (EP y) = (P (W y) y). To see that this corresponds to quantification, notice that the first constraint gives us one direction of the argument: it says that if any value of x makes (P x y) true (*i.e.*, if $\langle \exists x :: P(x, y) \rangle$) then (EP y) is true. This constraint allows us to establish an existentially quantified formula by exhibiting a witness, but the constraint can be satisfied if EP always returns t. The second constraint gives us the other direction. It introduces the witness function W and requires that (EP y) is true iff (P (W y) y) is true. As a result, if (EP y) is true, then some value of x makes (P x y) true. As is mentioned in the ACL2 documentation [26], this idea was known to Hilbert.

We wish to use quantification and encapsulation in the following way. We prove that a set of constrained functions satisfy a quantified formula. We then use functional instantiation to show that a set of functions satisfying these constraints also satisfy the (analogous) quantified formula. We want this proof obligation to be generated by macros but have found that the constraints generated by the quantified formulas complicate the design of such macros. The following observation has allowed us to simplify the process. The quantified formulas are established using witness functions, as is often the case. Therefore, only the first constraint generated by `defun-sk` is required for the proof. We defined the macro `defun-weak-sk` which generates only this constraint, *e.g.*, the following

```
(defun-weak-sk E (y)
  (exists (x) (P x y)))
```

leads only to the constraint that $(P\ x\ y) \Rightarrow (E\ y)$. By functional instantiation, any theorem proved about E also holds when E is replaced by EP (since EP satisfies the constraint on E). We use `defun-weak-sk` in our scripts and at the very end we prove the `defun-sk` versions of the main results by functional instantiation (a step taken to make the presentation of the final result independent of our macros).

4.2   Refinement Map Definitions

To prove that MA is a correct implementation of ISA, we prove a WEB on the (disjoint) union of the machines, with MA states labeled by the appropriate refinement map. Once the required notions are defined, the macros implementing our proof methodology can be used to prove correctness without any user supplied theorems. In this section, we present the definitions which make the statement of correctness precise.

The following function is a recognizer for "good" MA states.

```
(defun good-MA (ma)
  (and (integerp (g :pc MA))
       (let* ((latch1 (g :latch1 MA))
              (latch2 (g :latch2 MA))
              (nma (committed-ma ma)))
         (cond ((g :validp latch2)
                (equiv-ma (ma-step (ma-step nma)) ma))
               ((g :validp latch1)
                (equiv-ma (ma-step nma) ma))
               (t t)))))
```

First, we require that `pc`, the program counter, is an integer. Such type restrictions are common. Next, we require that MA states are reachable from clean states (states with invalid latches). The reason for this restriction is that otherwise MA states can be inconsistent (unreachable), *e.g.*, consider an MA state whose first latch contains an add instruction, but where there are no add instructions in memory. We check for this by stepping the *committed state*, the state obtained by invalidating all partially completed instructions and altering the program counter so that it points to the next instruction to commit.

```
(defun committed-MA (MA)
  (let* ((pc       (g :pc MA))
         (latch1   (g :latch1 MA))
         (latch2   (g :latch2 MA)))
    (seq-ma nil :pc    (committed-pc latch1 latch2 pc)
                :regs  (g :regs MA)
                :dmem  (g :dmem MA)
```

```
:imem    (g :imem MA)
:latch1 (seq-l1 nil)
:latch2 (seq-l2 nil))))
```

The program counter of the committed state is obtained from the history variable of the first valid latch.

```
(defun committed-pc (l1 l2 pc)
  (cond ((g :validp l2)
         (g :pch l2))
        ((g :validp l1)
         (g :pch l1))
        (t pc)))
```

Finally, we note that `equiv-MA` relates two MA states if they have the same pc, regs, memories, and if their latches match, *i.e.*, they have equivalent latch 1s or both states have an invalid latch 1 and similarly with latch 2.

Note that `committed-MA` invalidates pending instructions and adjusts the program counter accordingly. To make sure that a state is not inconsistent, we check that it is reachable from the corresponding committed state. Now that we have made precise what the MA states are, the refinement map is:

```
(defun MA-to-ISA (MA)
  (let ((MA (committed-MA MA)))
    (seq-isa nil :pc   (g :pc MA)
                 :regs (g :regs MA)
                 :dmem (g :dmem MA)
                 :imem (g :imem MA))))
```

The final definition required is that of the well-founded witness. The function `MA-rank` serves this purpose by computing how long it will take an MA state to commit an instruction. An MA state will commit an instruction in the next step if its second latch is valid. Otherwise, if its first latch is valid it will be ready to commit an instruction in one step. Otherwise, both latches are invalid and it will be ready to commit an instruction in two steps.

```
(defun MA-rank (MA)
  (let ((latch1 (g :latch1 MA))
        (latch2 (g :latch2 MA)))
    (cond ((g :validp latch2)
           0)
          ((g :validp latch1)
           1)
          (t 2))))
```

4.3   Proof of Correctness

To complete the proof we have to define the machine corresponding to the disjoint union of ISA and MA, define a WEB that relates a (good) MA state s to (MA-to-ISA s), define the well-founded witness, and prove that indeed the purported WEB really is a WEB. We have implemented macros which automate this. The macros are useful not only for this example, but have also been used to verification many other machines, including machines defined at the bit level. (Non-deterministic versions have also been developed that can be used to reason about machines with interrupts [31, 30].) The proof of correctness is completed with the following three macro calls.

```
(generate-full-system isa-step isa-p ma-step ma-p
                      ma-to-isa good-ma ma-rank)

(prove-web isa-step isa-p ma-step ma-p ma-to-isa ma-rank)

(wrap-it-up isa-step isa-p ma-step ma-p good-ma
            ma-to-isa ma-rank)
```

The first macro, **generate-full-system**, generates the definition of B, the purported WEB, as well as R, the transition relation of the disjoint union of the ISA and MA machines. The macro translates to the following. (Some declarations and forward-chaining theorems used to control the theorem prover have been elided.)

```
(progn
  (defun wf-rel (x y)
    (and (ISA-p x)
         (MA-p y)
         (good-MA y)
         (equal x (MA-to-ISA y))))

  (defun B (x y)
    (or (wf-rel x y)
        (wf-rel y x)
        (equal x y)
        (and (MA-p x)
             (MA-p y)
             (good-MA x)
             (good-MA y)
             (equal (MA-to-ISA x) (MA-to-ISA y)))))

  (defun rank (x)
    (if (MA-p x) (MA-rank x) 0))

  (defun R (x y)
    (cond ((ISA-p x) (equal y (ISA-step x)))
          (t (equal y (MA-step x))))))
```

What is left is to prove that B—the reflexive, symmetric, transitive closure of **wf-rel**—is a WEB with well-founded witness **rank**. We do this in two steps. First, the macro **prove-web** is used to prove the "core" theorem (as well as some "type" theorems not shown).

```
(defthm B-is-a-wf-bisim-core
  (let ((u (ISA-step s))
```

```
          (v (MA-step w)))
   (implies (and (wf-rel s w)
                 (not (wf-rel u v)))
            (and (wf-rel s v)
                 (o< (MA-rank v) (MA-rank w))))))))
```

Comparing B-is-a-wf-bisim-core with the definition of WEBs, we see that
B-is-a-wf-bisim-core does not contain quantifiers and it mentions neither B
nor R. This is on purpose as we use "domain-specific" information to construct
a simplified theorem that is used to establish the main theorem. To that end
we removed the quantifiers and much of the case analysis. For example, in the
definition of WEBs, u ranges over successors of s and v is existentially quantified
over successors of w, but because we are dealing with deterministic systems, u
and v are defined to be *the* successors of s and w, respectively. Also, wf-rel is
not an equivalence relation as it is not reflexive, symmetric, or transitive. Finally,
we ignore the second disjunct in the third condition of the definition of WEBs
because ISA does not stutter. The justification for calling this the "core" theorem
is that we have proved in ACL2 that a constrained system which satisfies a
theorem analogous to B-is-a-wf-bisim-core (and some "type" theorems) also
satisfies a WEB. Using functional instantiation we can now prove MA correct.
The use of this domain-specific information makes a big difference, *e.g.*, when
we tried to prove the theorem obtained by a naive translation of the WEB
definition (sans quantifiers), ACL2 ran out of memory after many hours, yet the
above theorem is now proved in about 1,000 seconds.

The final macro call generates the events used to finish the proof. We present the
generated events germane to this discussion below. The first step is to show that B
is an equivalence relation. This theorem is proved by functional instantiation.

```
(defequiv B
  :hints (("goal" :by (:functional-instance
                       encap-B-is-an-equivalence ...))))
```

The second WEB condition, that related states have the same label, is taken
care of by the refinement map. We show that rank is a well-founded witness.

```
(defthm rank-well-founded
  (o-p (rank x)))
```

We use functional instantiation and B-is-a-wf-bisim-core as described
above to prove the following.

```
(defun-weak-sk exists-w-succ-for-u-weak (w u)
  (exists (v) (and (R w v) (B u v))))
```

```
(defun-weak-sk exists-w-succ-for-s-weak (w s)
  (exists (v)
    (and (R w v)
         (B s v)
         (o< (rank v) (rank w)))))
```

```
(defthm B-is-a-wf-bisim-weak
  (implies (and (B s w)
                (R s u))
           (or (exists-w-succ-for-u-weak w u)
               (and (B u w)
                    (o< (rank u) (rank s)))
               (exists-w-succ-for-s-weak w s)))
  :hints
  (("goal" :by (:functional-instance
                  B-is-a-wf-bisim-sk ...)))
  :rule-classes nil)
```

We use `defun-weak-sk` for these definitions for the reasons outlined in Section 4.1. Stating the result in terms of the built-in macro `defun-sk` involves a trivial functional instantiation (since the single constraint generated by `defun-weak-sk` is one of the constraints generated by `defun-sk`).

```
(defun-sk exists-w-succ-for-u (w u)
  (exists (v) (and (R w v) (B u v))))

(defun-sk exists-w-succ-for-s (w s)
  (exists (v)
    (and (R w v)
         (B s v)
         (o< (rank v) (rank w)))))

(defthm B-is-a-wf-bisim
  (implies (and (B s w)
                (R s u))
           (or (exists-w-succ-for-u w u)
               (and (B u w)
                    (o< (rank u) (rank s)))
               (exists-w-succ-for-s w s)))
  :hints
  (("goal"
    :by
    (:functional-instance b-is-a-wf-bisim-weak
       (exists-w-succ-for-u-weak exists-w-succ-for-u)
       (exists-w-succ-for-s-weak exists-w-succ-for-s))))
  :rule-classes nil))
```

5   Verifying Complex Machines

While the proof of the pipelined machine defined in this paper required little more than writing down the correctness statement, unfortunately, using theorem proving to verify more complicated machines requires heroic effort [54]. The second major approach to the pipeline machine verification problem is based on decision procedures such as UCLID [10]. UCLID is a tool that decides the CLU logic, a logic containing the boolean connectives, uninterpreted functions and predicates, equality, counter arithmetic, ordering, and restricted lambda expressions. This approach is very automatic, *e.g.*, in a carefully constructed experiment, problems that took ACL2 days took seconds with UCLID [36]. Unfortunately, this approach has several problems. For example, pipelined machines that exceed the complexity threshold of the tools used, which happens rather easily, cannot be analyzed. Another serious limitation is that the pipelined machine models used are term-level models: they abstract away the datapath, implement a small subset of the instruction set, require the use of numerous abstractions, and are far from executable. Nonetheless, one can automatically handle much more complex machines with decision procedures than one can handle with general purpose theorem provers. In this section, we discuss some of our current work on this topic, as well as directions for future work.

5.1   Automating Verification of Term-Level Machines

In [35], it is shown how to automate the refinement proofs in the context of term-level pipelined machine verification. The idea is to strengthen, thereby simplifying, the refinement proof obligation; the result is the CLU-expressible formula, where *rank* is a function that maps states of MA into the natural numbers. MA $\approx_r$ ISA if:

$$\langle \forall w \in \text{MA} :: \quad s = r.w \quad \wedge \quad u = \text{ISA-step}(s) \quad \wedge$$
$$v = \text{MA-step}(w) \quad \wedge \quad u \neq r.v$$
$$\implies \quad s = r.v \quad \wedge \quad rank.v < rank.w \rangle$$

In the formula above s and u are ISA states, and w and v are MA states; ISA-step is a function corresponding to stepping the ISA machine once and MA-step is a function corresponding to stepping the MA machine once. It may help to think of the first conjunct of the consequent ($s = r.v$) as the safety component of the proof and the second conjunct $rank.v < rank.w$ as the liveness component.

5.2   Compositional Reasoning

We have developed a compositional reasoning framework based on refinement that consists of a set of convenient, easily-applicable, and complete compositional proof rules [37]. Our framework greatly extends the applicability of decision procedures, *e.g.*, we were able to verify, in seconds, a complex, deeply pipelined machine that state-of-the-art tools cannot currently handle. Our framework can be added to the design cycle, which is also compositional. In addition, one of the most important benefits of our approach over current methods is that the counterexamples generated tend to be much simpler, in terms of size and number of simulation steps involved and can be generated much more quickly.

5.3   Combining ACL2 and UCLID

The major problem with approaches based on decision procedures is that they only work for abstract term-level models and do not provide a firm connection with RTL models. In order to be industrially useful, we need both automation and a connection to the RTL level. As an initial step towards verifying RTL-level designs, we have combined ACL2 and UCLID in order to verify pipelined machine models with bit-level interfaces [40]. We use ACL2 to reduce the proof that an executable, bit-level machine refines its instruction set architecture to a proof that a term level abstraction of the bit-level machine refines the instruction set architecture, which is then handled automatically by UCLID. The amount of effort required is about 3-4 times the effort required to prove the term-level model correct using only UCLID. This allows us to exploit the strengths of ACL2 and UCLID to prove theorems that are not possible to even state using UCLID and that would require prohibitively more effort using just ACL2.

5.4   Conclusion and Future Perspectives

We view our work on compositional reasoning and on combining ACL2 and UCLID as promising first steps. Clearly, compositional reasoning will be needed to allow us to handle the verification problems one component at a time. With regard to RTL-level reasoning, our work has shown that we can automate the problem to within a small constant factor of what can be done for term-level models, but it will be important to change the factor to $1 + \varepsilon$. Several ideas for doing this include: developing a pattern database that with some intelligent search that can automatically decompose verification problems, automating some of the simpler refinement steps we currently perform, using counter-example guided abstraction-refinement to automatically abstract RTL designs to term-level designs, automating the handling of memories and register files, improved decision procedures, and creating analyses that work directly on hardware description languages.

References

[1] B. Bentley. Validating the Intel Pentium 4 microprocessor. In *38th Design Automation Conference*, pages 253–255, 2001.

[2] B. Bentley. Validating a modern microprocessor, 2005. See URL `http://-www.cav2005.inf.ed.ac.uk/bentley_CAV_07_08_2005.ppt`.

[3] P. Bertoli and P. Traverso. Design verification of a safety-critical embedded verifier. In Kaufmann et al. [22], pages 233–245.

[4] R. S. Boyer, D. M. Goldschlag, M. Kaufmann, and J. S. Moore. Functional instantiation in first order logic. In V. Lifschitz, editor, *Artificial Intelligence and Mathematical Theory of Computation: Papers in Honor of John McCarthy*, pages 7–26. Academic Press, 1991.

[5] R. S. Boyer and J. S. Moore. *A Computational Logic Handbook*. Academic Press, second edition, 1997.

[6] R. S. Boyer and J. S. Moore. Single-threaded objects in ACL2, 1999. See URL `http://www.cs.utexas.edu/users/moore/publications/-acl2-papers.html#Foundations`.

[7] B. Brock and W. A. Hunt, Jr. Formally specifying and mechanically verifying programs for the Motorola complex arithmetic processor DSP. In *1997 IEEE International Conference on Computer Design*, pages 31–36. IEEE Computer Society, Oct. 1997.

[8] B. Brock, M. Kaufmann, and J. S. Moore. ACL2 theorems about commercial microprocessors. In M. Srivas and A. Camilleri, editors, *Formal Methods in Computer-Aided Design (FMCAD'96)*, pages 275–293. Springer-Verlag, 1996.

[9] M. Browne, E. M. Clarke, and O. Grumberg. Characterizing finite Kripke structures in propositional temporal logic. *Theoretical Computer Science*, 59, 1988.

[10] R. E. Bryant, S. K. Lahiri, and S. Seshia. Modeling and verifying systems using a logic of counter arithmetic with lambda expressions and uninterpreted functions. In E. Brinksma and K. Larsen, editors, *Computer-Aided Verification–CAV 2002*, volume 2404 of *LNCS*, pages 78–92. Springer-Verlag, 2002.

[11] J. R. Burch and D. L. Dill. Automatic verification of pipelined microprocessor control. In *Computer-Aided Verification (CAV '94)*, volume 818 of *LNCS*, pages 68–80. Springer-Verlag, 1994.

[12] E. M. Clarke, O. Grumberg, and D. Peled. *Model Checking*. MIT Press, 1999.

[13] P. Dillinger, P. Manolios, J. S. Moore, and D. Vroon. ACL2E homepage. See URL http://www.cc.gatech.edu/home/manolios/acl2s.

[14] D. Greve, M. Wilding, and D. Hardin. High-speed, analyzable simulators. In Kaufmann et al. [22], pages 113–135.

[15] D. A. Greve. Symbolic simulation of the JEM1 microprocessor. In *Formal Methods in Computer-Aided Design – FMCAD*, LNCS. Springer-Verlag, 1998.

[16] D. Hardin, M. Wilding, and D. Greve. Transforming the theorem prover into a digital design tool: From concept car to off-road vehicle. In A. J. Hu and M. Y. Vardi, editors, *Computer-Aided Verification – CAV '98*, volume 1427 of *LNCS*. Springer-Verlag, 1998. See URL http://pobox.com/users/hokie/docs/-concept.ps.

[17] W. Hunt, R. Krug, and J. S. Moore. The addition of non-linear arithmetic to ACL2. In D. Geist, editor, *Proceedings of CHARME 2003*, volume 2860 of *Lecture Notes in Computer Science*, pages 319–333. Springer Verlag, 2003.

[18] W. A. Hunt, Jr. Microprocessor design verification. *Journal of Automated Reasoning*, 5(4):429–460, 1989.

[19] W. A. Hunt, Jr. and B. Brock. A formal HDL and its use in the FM9001 verification. *Proceedings of the Royal Society*, 1992.

[20] W. A. Hunt, Jr. and B. Brock. The DUAL-EVAL hardware description language and its use in the formal specification and verification of the FM9001 microprocessor. *Formal Methods in Systems Design*, 11:71–105, 1997.

[21] R. Kane, P. Manolios, and S. K. Srinivasan. Monolithic verification of deep pipelines with collapsed flushing. In *Design Automation and Test in Europe, DATE'06*, 2006.

[22] M. Kaufmann, P. Manolios, and J. S. Moore, editors. *Computer-Aided Reasoning: ACL2 Case Studies*. Kluwer Academic Publishers, June 2000.

[23] M. Kaufmann, P. Manolios, and J. S. Moore. *Computer-Aided Reasoning: An Approach*. Kluwer Academic Publishers, July 2000.

[24] M. Kaufmann, P. Manolios, and J. S. Moore. Supporting files for "Computer-Aided Reasoning: ACL2 Case Studies". See the link from URL http://www.cs.-utexas.edu/users/moore/acl2, 2000.

[25] M. Kaufmann, P. Manolios, and J. S. Moore. Supporting files for "Computer-Aided Reasoning: An Approach". See the link from URL http://www.cs.-utexas.edu/users/moore/acl2, 2000.

[26] M. Kaufmann and J. S. Moore. ACL2 homepage. See URL `http://www.cs.-utexas.edu/users/moore/acl2`.

[27] M. Kaufmann and J. S. Moore. A precise description of the ACL2 logic. Technical report, Department of Computer Sciences, University of Texas at Austin, 1997. See URL `http://www.cs.utexas.edu/users/moore/publications/-acl2-papers.html#Foundations`.

[28] M. Kaufmann and J. S. Moore, editors. *Proceedings of the ACL2 Workshop 2000*. The University of Texas at Austin, Technical Report TR-00-29, November 2000.

[29] M. Kaufmann and J. S. Moore. Structured theory development for a mechanized logic. *Journal of Automated Reasoning*, 26(2):161–203, February 2001.

[30] P. Manolios. Correctness of pipelined machines. In W. A. Hunt, Jr. and S. D. Johnson, editors, *Formal Methods in Computer-Aided Design–FMCAD 2000*, volume 1954 of *LNCS*, pages 161–178. Springer-Verlag, 2000.

[31] P. Manolios. Verification of pipelined machines in ACL2. In Kaufmann and Moore [28].

[32] P. Manolios. *Mechanical Verification of Reactive Systems*. PhD thesis, University of Texas at Austin, August 2001. See URL `http://www.cc.gatech.edu/-~manolios/publications.html`.

[33] P. Manolios. A compositional theory of refinement for branching time. In D. Geist and E. Tronci, editors, *12th IFIP WG 10.5 Advanced Research Working Conference, CHARME 2003*, volume 2860 of *LNCS*, pages 304–318. Springer-Verlag, 2003.

[34] P. Manolios, K. Namjoshi, and R. Sumners. Linking theorem proving and model-checking with well-founded bisimulation. In N. Halbwachs and D. Peled, editors, *Computer-Aided Verification–CAV '99*, volume 1633 of *LNCS*, pages 369–379. Springer-Verlag, 1999.

[35] P. Manolios and S. Srinivasan. Automatic verification of safety and liveness for XScale-like processor models using WEB-refinements. In *Design Automation and Test in Europe, DATE'04*, pages 168–175, 2004.

[36] P. Manolios and S. Srinivasan. A suite of hard ACL2 theorems arising in refinement-based processor verification. In M. Kaufmann and J. S. Moore, editors, *Fifth International Workshop on the ACL2 Theorem Prover and Its Applications (ACL2-2004)*, November 2004. See URL `http://www.cs.utexas.edu/users/-moore/acl2/workshop-2004/`.

[37] P. Manolios and S. Srinivasan. A complete compositional reasoning framework for the efficient verification of pipelined machines. In *ICCAD-2005, International Conference on Computer-Aided Design*, 2005.

[38] P. Manolios and S. Srinivasan. A computationally efficient method based on commitment refinement maps for verifying pipelined machines models. In *ACM-IEEE International Conference on Formal Methods and Models for Codesign*, pages 189–198, 2005.

[39] P. Manolios and S. Srinivasan. Refinement maps for efficient verification of processor models. In *Design Automation and Test in Europe, DATE'05*, pages 1304–1309, 2005.

[40] P. Manolios and S. Srinivasan. Verification of executable pipelined machines with bit-level interfaces. In *ICCAD-2005, International Conference on Computer-Aided Design*, 2005.

[41] P. Manolios and D. Vroon. Algorithms for ordinal arithmetic. In F. Baader, editor, *19th International Conference on Automated Deduction – CADE-19*, volume 2741 of *LNAI*, pages 243–257. Springer–Verlag, July/August 2003.

[42] P. Manolios and D. Vroon. Ordinal arithmetic in ACL2. In M. Kaufmann and J. S. Moore, editors, *Fourth International Workshop on the ACL2 Theorem Prover and Its Applications (ACL2-2003)*, July 2003. See URL http://www.cs.utexas.edu/users/moore/acl2/workshop-2003/.

[43] P. Manolios and D. Vroon. Integrating reasoning about ordinal arithmetic into ACL2. In *Formal Methods in Computer-Aided Design: 5th International Conference – FMCAD-2004*, LNCS. Springer–Verlag, November 2004.

[44] P. Manolios and D. Vroon. Ordinal arithmetic: Algorithms and mechanization. *Journal of Automated Reasoning*, 2006. to appear.

[45] P. Manolios and D. Vroon. Termination analysis with calling context graphs, 2006. Submitted.

[46] R. Milner. *Communication and Concurrency*. Prentice-Hall, 1990.

[47] J. S. Moore. *Piton : A Mechanically Verified Assembly-Level Language*. Kluwer Academic Press, Dordrecht, The Netherlands, 1996.

[48] J. S. Moore, T. Lynch, and M. Kaufmann. A mechanically checked proof of the AMD5$_K$86 floating-point division program. *IEEE Trans. Comp.*, 47(9):913–926, September 1998.

[49] K. S. Namjoshi. A simple characterization of stuttering bisimulation. In *17th Conference on Foundations of Software Technology and Theoretical Computer Science*, volume 1346 of *LNCS*, pages 284–296, 1997.

[50] D. M. Russinoff. A mechanically checked proof of correctness of the AMD5$_K$86 floating-point square root microcode. *Formal Methods in System Design Special Issue on Arithmetic Circuits*, 1997.

[51] D. M. Russinoff. A mechanically checked proof of IEEE compliance of a register-transfer-level specification of the AMD-K7 floating-point multiplication, division, and square root instructions. *London Mathematical Society Journal of Computation and Mathematics*, 1:148–200, December 1998.

[52] D. M. Russinoff. A mechanically checked proof of correctness of the AMD-K5 floating-point square root microcode. *Formal Methods in System Design*, 14:75–125, 1999.

[53] D. M. Russinoff and A. Flatau. RTL verification: A floating-point multiplier. In Kaufmann et al. [22], pages 201–231.

[54] J. Sawada. *Formal Verification of an Advanced Pipelined Machine*. PhD thesis, University of Texas at Austin, Dec. 1999. See URL http://www.cs.utexas.edu/users/sawada/dissertation/.

[55] J. Sawada. Verification of a simple pipelined machine model. In Kaufmann et al. [22], pages 137–150.

[56] J. Sawada and W. A. Hunt, Jr. Trace table based approach for pipelined microprocessor verification. In *Computer Aided Verification (CAV '97)*, volume 1254 of *LNCS*, pages 364–375. Springer-Verlag, 1997.

[57] J. Sawada and W. A. Hunt, Jr. Processor verification with precise exceptions and speculative execution. In A. J. Hu and M. Y. Vardi, editors, *Computer Aided Verification (CAV '98)*, volume 1427 of *LNCS*, pages 135–146. Springer-Verlag, 1998.

[58] International technology roadmap for semiconductors, 2004. See URL http://public.itrs.net/.

[59] G. L. Steele, Jr. *Common Lisp The Language, Second Edition*. Digital Press, Burlington, MA, 1990.

Floating-Point Verification Using Theorem Proving

John Harrison

Intel Corporation, JF1-13,
2111 NE 25th Avenue,
Hillsboro OR 97124
johnh@ichips.intel.com

Abstract. This chapter describes our work on formal verification of floating-point algorithms using the HOL Light theorem prover.

1   Introduction

Representation of real numbers on the computer is fundamental to much of applied mathematics, from aircraft control systems to weather forecasting. Most applications use floating-point approximations, though this raises significant mathematical difficulties because of rounding and approximation errors. Even if rounding is properly controlled, "bugs" in software using real numbers can be particularly subtle and insidious. Yet because real-number programs are often used in controlling and monitoring physical systems, the consequences can be catastrophic. A spectacular example is the destruction of the Ariane 5 rocket shortly after takeoff in 1996, owing to an uncaught floating-point exception. Less dramatic, but very costly and embarrassing to Intel, was an error in the FDIV (floating-point division) instruction of some early Intel® Pentium® processors in 1994 [45]. Intel set aside approximately \$475M to cover costs arising from this issue.

So it is not surprising that a considerable amount of effort has been applied to formal verification in the floating-point domain, not just at Intel [44, 34], but also at AMD [40, 50] and IBM [51], as well as in academia [33, 5]. Floating-point algorithms are in some ways an especially natural and appealing target for formal verification. It is not hard to come up with widely accepted formal specifications of how basic floating-point operations *should* behave. In fact, many operations are specified almost completely by the IEEE Standard governing binary floating-point arithmetic [32]. This gives a clear specification that high-level algorithms can rely on, and which implementors of instruction sets and compilers need to realize.

In some other respects though, floating-point operations present a difficult challenge for formal verification. In many other areas of verification, significant success has been achieved using highly automated techniques, usually based on a Boolean or other finite-state model of the state of the system. For example, efficient algorithms for propositional logic [7, 15, 53] and their aggressively efficient implementation [41, 19] have made possible a variety of techniques ranging from

M. Bernardo and A. Cimatti (Eds.): SFM 2006, LNCS 3965, pp. 211–242, 2006.

simple Boolean equivalence checking of combinational circuits to more advanced symbolic simulation or model checking of sequential systems [10, 47, 8, 52].

But it is less easy to verify non-trivial floating-point arithmetic operations using such techniques. The natural specifications, including the IEEE Standard, are based on real numbers, not bit-strings. While simple adders and multipliers can be specified quite naturally in Boolean terms, this becomes progressively more difficult when one considers division and square root, and seems quite impractical for transcendental functions. So while model checkers and similar tools are of great value in dealing with low-level details, at least some parts of the proof must be constructed in general theorem proving systems that enable one to talk about high-level mathematics.

There are many theorem proving programs,[1] and quite a few have been applied to floating-point verification, including at least ACL2, Coq, HOL Light and PVS. We will concentrate later on our own work using HOL Light [23], but this is not meant to disparage other important work being done at Intel and elsewhere in other systems.

2   Architectural Context

Most of the general points we want to make here are independent of particular low-level details. Whether certain operations are implemented in software, microcode or hardware RTL, the general verification problems are similar, though the question of how they fit into the low-level design flow can be different. Nevertheless, in order to appreciate the examples that follow, the reader needs to know that the algorithms are mainly intended for software implementation on the Intel® Itanium® architecture, and needs to understand something about IEEE floating-point numbers and the special features of the Itanium floating-point architecture.

2.1   The IEEE-754 Floating Point Standard

The IEEE Standard 754 for Binary Floating-Point Arithmetic [32] was developed in response to the wide range of incompatible and often surprising behaviours of floating-point arithmetic on different machines. In the 1970s, this was creating serious problems in porting numerical programs from one machine to another, with for example VAX, IBM/360 and Cray families all having different formats for floating point numbers and incompatible ways of doing arithmetic on them. Practically all of the arithmetics displayed peculiarities that could ensnare inexperienced programmers, for example $x = y$ being false but $x - y = 0$ true. The sudden proliferation of microprocessors in the 1970s promised to create even more problems, and was probably a motivating factor in the success of the IEEE standardization effort. Indeed, before the Standard was ratified, Intel had

---

[1] See   http://www.cs.ru.nl/~freek/digimath/index.html   for   a   list,   and   http://www.cs.ru.nl/~freek/comparison/index.html   for   a   comparison   of the formalization of an elementary mathematical theorem in several.

produced the 8087 math coprocessor to implement it, and other microprocessor makers followed suit. Since that time, practically every new microprocessor floating-point architecture has conformed to the standard.

Floating point numbers, at least in the conventional binary formats considered by the IEEE Standard 754,[2] are those of the form:

$$\pm 2^e k$$

with the *exponent* e subject to a certain bound, and the *fraction* (also called significand or mantissa) k expressible in a binary positional representation using a certain number p of bits:

$$k = k_0 \cdot k_1 k_2 \cdots k_{p-1}$$

The bound on the exponent range $E_{min} \leq e \leq E_{max}$, together with the allowed *precision* p determines a particular floating point *format*. The novel aspect of the IEEE formats, and by far the most controversial part of the whole Standard, consists in allowing k_0 to be zero even when other k_i's are not. In the model established by most earlier arithmetics, the number $2^{E_{min}} 1.00 \cdots 0$ is the floating point number with smallest nonzero magnitude. But the IEEE-754 Standard allows for a set of smaller numbers $2^{E_{min}} 0.11 \cdots 11$, $2^{E_{min}} 0.11 \cdots 10$, ..., $2^{E_{min}} 0.00 \cdots 01$ which allow a more graceful underflow. Note that the above presentation enumerates some values redundantly, with for example $2^{e+1} 0 \cdot 100 \cdots 0$ and $2^e 1 \cdot 000 \cdots 0$ representing the same number. For many purposes, we consider the *canonical* representation, where $k_0 = 0$ only if $e = E_{min}$. Indeed, when it specifies how some floating point formats (single and double precision) are encoded as bit patterns, the Standard uses an encoding designed to avoid redundancy. Note, however, that the Standard specifies that the floating point representation must maintain the distinction between a positive and negative zero.

Floating point numbers cover a wide range of values from the very small to the very large. They are evenly spaced except that at the points 2^j the interval between adjacent numbers doubles. (Just as in decimal the gap between 1.00 and 1.01 is ten times the gap between 0.999 and 1.00, where all numbers are constrained to three significant digits.) The intervals $2^j \leq x \leq 2^{j+1}$, possibly excluding one or both endpoints, are often called *binades* (by analogy with 'decades'), and the numbers 2^j *binade boundaries*. The following diagram illustrates this.

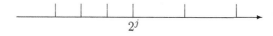

In the IEEE Standard, the results of the basic algebraic operations (addition, subtraction, multiplication, division, remainder and square root) on finite

---

[2] The IBM/360 family, for example, used a hexadecimal not a binary system. Exotic formats such as those proposed in [11] depart even more radically from the Standard.

operands[3] are specified in a simple and uniform way. According to the standard (section 5):

> ...each of these operations shall be performed as if it first produced an intermediate result correct to infinite precision and unbounded range and then coerced this intermediate result to fit in the destination's format.

In non-exceptional situations (no overflow etc.) the coercion is done using a simple and natural form of *rounding*, defined in section 4 of the standard. Rounding essentially takes an arbitrary real number and returns another real number that is its best floating point approximation. Which particular number is considered 'best' may depend on the *rounding mode*. In the usual mode of *round to nearest*, the representable value closest to the exact one is chosen. If two representable values are equally close, i.e. the exact value is precisely the midpoint of two adjacent floating point numbers, then the one with its least significant bit zero is delivered. (See [48] for a problem caused by systematically truncating rather than rounding to even in such cases).

Other rounding modes force the exact real number to be rounded to the representable number closest to it yet greater or equal ('round toward $+\infty$' or 'round up'), less or equal ('round toward $-\infty$' or 'round down') or smaller or equal in magnitude ('round toward 0'). The following diagram illustrates some IEEE-correct roundings; y is assumed to be exactly a midpoint, and rounds to 2^j because of the round-to-even preference.

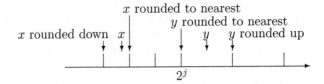

2.2   The Intel® Itanium® Floating Point Architecture

The Intel® Itanium® architecture is a 64-bit computer architecture jointly developed by Hewlett-Packard and Intel. In an attempt to avoid some of the limitations of traditional architectures, it incorporates a unique combination of features, including an instruction format encoding parallelism explicitly, instruction predication, and speculative/advanced loads [17]. However, we will not need to discuss general features like this, but only the special features of its floating-point architecture.

The centerpiece of the Intel® Itanium® floating-point architecture is the fma (floating point multiply-add or fused multiply-accumulate) instruction. This computes $xy + z$ from inputs x, y and z with a single rounding error. Except for subtleties over signed zeros, floating point addition and multiplication are just

---

[3] In other words, those representing ordinary floating point numbers, rather than infinities or 'NaN's (NaN = not a number).

degenerate cases of fma, $1y + z$ and $xy + 0$, so do not need separate instructions. However, there are variants of the fma to switch signs of operands: fms computes $xy - z$ while fnma computes $z - xy$. While the IEEE standard does not explicitly address fma-type operations, the main extrapolation is obvious and natural: these operations behave as if they rounded an exact result, $xy + z$ for fma. The fact that there is only *one* rounding at the end, with no intermediate rounding of the product xy, is crucial in much of what follows.

It needs a little more care to specify the signs of zero results in IEEE style. First, the interpretation of addition and multiplication as degenerate cases of fma requires some policy on the sign of $1 \times -0 + 0$. More significantly, the fma leads to a new possibility: $a \times b + c$ can round to zero even though the exact result is nonzero. Out of the operations in the standard, this can occur for multiplication or division, but in this case the rules for signs are simple and natural. A little reflection shows that this cannot happen for pure addition, so the rule in the standard that 'the sign of a sum ... differs from at most one of the addend's signs' is enough to fix the sign of zeros when the exact result is nonzero. For the fma this is not the case, and fma-type instructions guarantee that the sign correctly reflects the sign of the exact result in such cases. This is important, for example, in ensuring that the algorithms for division that we consider later yield the correctly signed zeros in all cases without special measures.

The Intel® Itanium® architecture supports several different IEEE-specified or IEEE-compatible floating point formats. For the four most important formats, we give the conventional name, the precision, and the minimum and maximum exponents.

Format name	p	E_{min}	E_{max}
Single	24	-126	127
Double	53	-1022	1023
Double-extended	64	-16382	16383
Register	64	-65534	65535

The single and double formats are mandated and completely specified in the Standard. The double-extended format (we will often just call it 'extended') is recommended and only partially specified by the Standard; the particular version used in Intel® Itanium® is the one introduced by on the 8087.[4] The register format has the same precision as extended, but allows greater exponent range, helping to avoid overflows and underflows in intermediate calculations. In a sense, the register format is all-inclusive, since its representable values properly include those of all other formats.

Most operations, including the fma, take arguments and return results in some of the 128 floating point registers provided for by the architecture. All the formats are mapped into a standard bit encoding in registers, and any value

---

[4] A similar format was supported by the Motorola 68000 family, but now it is mainly supported by Intel processors.

represented by a floating point register is representable in the 'Register' floating point format.[5] By a combination of settings in the multiple status fields and completers on instructions, the results of operations can be rounded in any of the four rounding modes and into any of the supported formats.

In most current computer architectures, in particular Intel IA-32 (x86) currently represented by the Intel® Pentium® processor family, instructions are specified for the floating point division and square root operations. In the Itanium architecture, the only instructions specifically intended to support division and square root are initial approximation instructions. The `frcpa` (floating point reciprocal approximation) instruction applied to an argument a gives an approximation to $1/a$, while the `frsqrta` (floating point reciprocal square root approximation) instruction gives an approximation to $1/\sqrt{a}$. (In each case, the approximation may have a relative error of approximately $2^{-8.8}$ in the worst case, so they are far from delivering an exact result. Of course, special action is taken in some special cases like $a = 0$.) There are several reasons for relegating division and square root to software.

- In typical applications, division and square root are not extremely frequent operations, and so it may be that die area on the chip would be better devoted to something else. However they are not so infrequent that a grossly inefficient software solution is acceptable, so the rest of the architecture needs to be designed to allow reasonably fast software implementations. As we shall see, the `fma` is the key ingredient.
- By implementing division and square root in software they immediately inherit the high degree of pipelining in the basic `fma` operations. Even though these operations take several clock cycles, new ones can be started each cycle while others are in progress. Hence, many division or square root operations can proceed in parallel, leading to much higher throughput than is the case with typical hardware implementations.
- Greater flexibility is afforded because alternative algorithms can be substituted where it is advantageous. First of all, any improvements can quickly be incorporated into a computer system without hardware changes. Second, it is often the case that in a particular context a faster algorithm suffices, e.g. because the ambient IEEE rounding mode is known at compile-time, or even because only a moderately accurate result is required (e.g. in some graphics applications).

3   HOL Light

Theorem provers descended from Edinburgh LCF [22] reduce all reasoning to formal proofs in something like a standard natural deduction system. That is, everything must be proved in detail at a low level, not simply asserted, nor even claimed on the basis of running some complex decision procedure. However, the

---

[5] However, that for reasons of compatibility, there are bit encodings used for extended precision numbers but not register format numbers.

user is able to write arbitrary programs in the metalanguage ML to automate patterns of inferences and hence reduce the tedium involved. The original LCF system implemented Scott's Logic of Computable Functions (hence the name LCF), but as emphasized by Gordon [20], the basic LCF approach is applicable to any logic, and now there are descendents implementing a variety of higher order logics, set theories and constructive type theories.

In particular, members of the HOL family [21] implement a version of simply typed λ-calculus with logical operations defined on top, more or less following Church [9]. They take the LCF approach a step further in that all theory developments are pursued 'definitionally'. New mathematical structures, such as the real numbers, may be defined only by exhibiting a model for them in the existing theories (say as Dedekind cuts of rationals). New constants may only be introduced by definitional extension (roughly speaking, merely being a shorthand for an expression in the existing theory). This fits naturally with the LCF style, since it ensures that all extensions, whether of the deductive system or the mathematical theories, are consistent per construction. HOL Light [23] is our own version of the HOL prover. It maintains most of the general principles underlying its ancestors, but attempts to be more logically coherent, simple and elegant. It is written entirely in a fairly simple and mostly functional subset of Objective CAML [57, 14], giving it advantages of portability and efficient resource usage compared with its ancestors, which are based on LISP or Standard ML.

Like other LCF provers, HOL Light is in essence simply a large OCaml program that defines data structures to represent logical entities, together with a suite of functions to manipulate them in a way guaranteeing soundness. The most important data structures belong to one of the datatypes `hol_type`, `term` and `thm`, which represent types, terms (including formulas) and theorems respectively. The user can write arbitrary programs to manipulate these objects, and it is by creating new objects of type `thm` that one proves theorems. HOL's notion of an 'inference rule' is simply a function with return type `thm`.

In order to guarantee logical soundness, however, all these types are encapsulated as abstract types. In particular, the only way of creating objects of type `thm` is to apply one of HOL's 10 very simple inference rules or to make a new term or type definition. Thus, whatever the circuitous route by which one arrives at it, the validity of any object of type `thm` rests only on the correctness of the rather simple primitive rules (and of course the correctness of OCaml's type checking etc.). For example, one of HOL's primitives is the rule of transitivity of equality:

$$\frac{\Gamma \vdash s = t \quad \Delta \vdash t = u}{\Gamma \cup \Delta \vdash s = u} \text{ TRANS}$$

This allows one to make the following logical step: if under assumptions Γ one can deduce $s = t$ (that is, s and t are equal), and under assumptions Δ one can deduce $t = u$, then one can deduce that from all the assumptions together, $\Gamma \cup \Delta$, that $s = u$ holds. If the two starting theorems are bound to the names th1 and th2, then one can apply the above logical step in HOL and bind the result to th3 via:

```
let th3 = TRANS th1 th2;;
```

One doesn't normally use such low-level rules much, but instead interacts with HOL via a series of higher-level derived rules, using built-in parsers and printers to read and write terms in a more natural syntax. For example, if one wants to bind the name th6 to the theorem of real arithmetic that when $|c - a| < e$ and $|b| \leq d$ then $|(a + b) - c| < d + e$, one simply does:

```
let th6 = REAL_ARITH
  'abs(c - a) < e ∧ abs(b) <= d
    ⟹ abs((a + b) - c) < d + e';;
```

If the purported fact in quotations turns out not to be true, then the rule will fail by raising an exception. Similarly, any bug in the derived rule (which represents several dozen pages of code written by the present author) would lead to an exception.[6] But we can be rather confident in the truth of any theorem that is returned, since it must have been created via applications of primitive rules, even though the precise choreographing of these rules is automatic and of no concern to the user. What's more, users can write their own special-purpose proof rules in the same style when the standard ones seem inadequate — HOL is fully programmable, yet retains its logical trustworthiness when extended by ordinary users.

Among the facilities provided by HOL is the ability to organize proofs in a mixture of forward and backward steps, which users often find more congenial. The user invokes so-called *tactics* to break down the goal into more manageable subgoals. For example, in HOL's inbuilt foundations of number theory, the proof that addition of natural numbers is commutative is written as follows (the symbol ∀ means 'for all'):

```
let ADD_SYM = prove
  ('∀m n. m + n = n + m',
   INDUCT_TAC THEN
   ASM_REWRITE_TAC[ADD_CLAUSES]);;
```

The tactic INDUCT_TAC uses mathematical induction to break the original goal down into two separate goals, one for $m = 0$ and one for $m + 1$ on the assumption that the goal holds for m. Both of these are disposed of quickly simply by repeated rewriting with the current assumptions and a previous, even more elementary, theorem about the addition operator. The identifier THEN is a so-called *tactical*, i.e. a function that takes two tactics and produces another tactic, which applies the first tactic then applies the second to any resulting subgoals (there are two in this case).

---

[6] Or possibly to a true but different theorem being returned, but this is easily guarded against by inserting sanity checks in the rules.

For another example, we can prove that there is a unique x such that $x = f(g(x))$ if and only if there is a unique y with $y = g(f(y))$ using a single standard tactic MESON_TAC, which performs model elimination [36] to prove theorems about first order logic with equality. As usual, the actual proof under the surface happens by the standard primitive inference rules.

```
let WISHNU = prove
 (`(∃!x. x = f (g x)) ⇔ (∃!y. y = g(f y))`,
  MESON_TAC[]);;
```

These and similar higher-level rules certainly make the construction of proofs manageable whereas it would be almost unbearable in terms of the primitive rules alone. Nevertheless, we want to dispel any false impression given by the simple examples above: nontrivial proofs, as are carried out in the work described here, often require long and complicated sequences of rules. The construction of these proofs often requires considerable persistence. Moreover, the resulting proof scripts can be quite hard to read, and in some cases hard to modify to prove a slightly different theorem. One source of these difficulties is that the proof scripts are highly procedural — they are, ultimately, OCaml programs, albeit of a fairly stylized form. Perhaps in the future a more declarative style for proof scripts will prove to be more effective, but the procedural approach has its merits [24], particularly in applications like this one where we program several complex specialized inference rules.

In presenting HOL theorems below, we will use standard symbols for the logical operators, as we have in the above examples, but when actually interacting with HOL, ASCII equivalents are used:

Standard symbol	ASCII version	Meaning
$\bot$	F	falsity
$\top$	T	truth
$\neg p$	~p	not p
$p \wedge q$	p /\ q	p and q
$p \vee q$	p \/ q	p or q
$p \Longrightarrow q$	p ==> q	if p then q
$p \Leftrightarrow q$	p <=> q	p if and only if q
$\forall x. p$	!x. p	for all x, p
$\exists x. p$	?x. p	there exists x such that p
$\varepsilon x. p$	@x. p	some x such that p
$\lambda x. t$	\x. t	the function $x \mapsto t$
$x \in s$	x IN s	x is a member of set s

For more on the fundamentals of the HOL logic, see the appendix of our PhD dissertation [25], or actually download the system and its documentation from:

```
http://www.cl.cam.ac.uk/users/jrh/hol-light/index.html
```

Our thesis [25] also gives extensive detail on the definition of real numbers in HOL and the formalization of mathematical analysis built on this foundation. In what follows, we exploit various results of pure mathematics without particular comment. However, it may be worth noting some of the less obvious aspects of the HOL symbolism when dealing with numbers:

HOL notation	Standard symbol	Meaning
m EXP n	m^n	Natural number exponentiation
&	(none)	Natural map $\mathbb{N} \to \mathbb{R}$
--x	$-x$	Unary negation of x
inv(x)	x^{-1}	Multiplicative inverse of x
abs(x)	$|x|$	Absolute value of x
x pow n	x^n	Real x raised to natural number power n

HOL's type system distinguishes natural numbers and reals, so & is used to map between them. It's mainly used as part of real number constants like &0, &1 etc. Note also that while one might prefer to regard 0^{-1} as 'undefined' (in some precise sense), we set inv(&0) = &0 by definition.

4   Application Examples

We will now give a brief overview of some of our verification projects using HOL Light at Intel. For more details on the various parts, see [26, 28, 29, 27].

4.1   Formalization of Floating Point Arithmetic

The first stage in all proofs of this kind is to formalize the key floating point concepts and prove the necessary general lemmas. We have tried to provide a generic, re-usable theory of useful results that can be applied conveniently in these and other proofs. In what follows we will just discuss things in sufficient detail to allow the reader to get the gist of what follows.

Floating point numbers can be stored either in floating point registers or in memory, and in each case we cannot always assume the encoding is irredundant (i.e. there may be several different encodings of the same real value, even apart from IEEE signed zeros). Thus, we need to take particular care over the distinction between values and their floating point encodings.[7] Systematically making this separation nicely divides our formalization into two parts: those that are concerned only with real numbers, and those where the floating point encodings with the associated plethora of special cases (infinities, NaNs, signed zeros etc.) come into play. Most of the interesting issues can be considered at the level of real numbers, and we will generally follow this approach here. However there are certainly subtleties over the actual representations that we need to be aware of, e.g. checking that zero results have the right sign and characterizing the situations where exceptions can or will occur.

---

[7] In the actual standard (p7) 'a bit-string is not always distinguished from a number it may represent'.

Floating point formats. Our formalization of the encoding-free parts of the standard is highly generic, covering an infinite collection of possible floating point formats, even including absurd formats with zero precision (no fraction bits). It is a matter of taste whether the pathological cases should be excluded at the outset. We sometimes need to exclude them from particular theorems, but many of the theorems turn out to be degenerately true even for extreme values.

Section 3.1 of the standard parametrizes floating point formats by precision p and maximum and minimum exponents E_{max} and E_{min}. We follow this closely, except we represent the fraction by an integer rather than a value $1 \leq f < 2$, and the exponent range by two nonnegative numbers N and E. The allowable floating point numbers are then of the form $\pm 2^{e-N} k$ with $k < 2^p$ and $0 \leq e < E$. This was not done because of the use of biasing in actual floating point encodings (as we have stressed before, we avoid such issues at this stage), but rather to use nonnegative integers everywhere and carry around fewer side-conditions. The cost of this is that one needs to remember the bias when considering the exponents of floating point numbers. We name the fields of a format triple as follows:

```
|- exprange (E,p,N) = E

|- precision (E,p,N) = p

|- ulpscale (E,p,N) = N
```

and the definition of the set of real numbers corresponding to a triple is:[8]

```
|- format (E,p,N) =
    { x | ∃s e k. s < 2 ∧ e < E ∧ k < 2 EXP p ∧
                  x = --(&1) pow s * &2 pow e * &k / &2 pow N}
```

This says exactly that the format is the set of real numbers representable in the form $(-1)^s 2^{e-N} k$ with $e < E$ and $k < 2^p$ (the additional restriction $s < 2$ is just a convenience). For many purposes, including floating point rounding, we also consider an analogous format with an exponent range unbounded above. This is defined by simply dropping the exponent restriction $e < E$. Note that the exponent is still bounded *below*, i.e. N is unchanged.

```
|- iformat (E,p,N) =
    { x | ∃s e k. s < 2 ∧ k < 2 EXP p ∧
                  x = --(&1) pow s * &2 pow e * &k / &2 pow N}
```

Ulps. The term 'unit in the last place' (ulp) is only mentioned in passing by the standard on p. 12 when discussing binary to decimal conversion. Nevertheless, it

---

[8] Recall that the ampersand denotes the injection from $\mathbb{N}$ to $\mathbb{R}$, which HOL's type system distinguishes. The function **EXP** denotes exponentiation on naturals, and **pow** the analogous function on reals.

is of great importance for later proofs because the error bounds for transcendental functions need to be expressed in terms of ulps. Doing so is quite standard, yet there is widespread confusion about what an ulp is, and a variety of incompatible definitions appear in the literature [43]. Given a particular floating-point format and a real number x, we define an ulp in x as the distance between the two closest *straddling* floating point numbers a and b, i.e. those with $a \leq x \leq b$ and $a \neq b$ assuming an unbounded exponent range.

This seems to convey the natural intuition of units in the last place, and preserves the important mathematical properties that rounding to nearest corresponds to an error of $0.5ulp$ and directed roundings imply a maximum error of $1ulp$. The actual HOL definition is explicitly in terms of binades, and defined using the Hilbert choice operator ε:[9]

```
|- binade(E,p,N) x =
      εe. abs(x) <= &2 pow (e + p) / &2 pow N ∧
          ∀e'. abs(x) <= &2 pow (e' + p) / &2 pow N ⟹ e <= e'

|- ulp(E,p,N) x = &2 pow (binade(E,p,N) x) / &2 pow N
```

After a fairly tedious series of proofs, we eventually derive the theorem that an ulp does indeed yield the distance between two straddling floating point numbers.

Rounding. Floating point rounding takes an arbitrary real number and chooses a floating point approximation. Rounding is regarded in the Standard as an operation mapping a real to a member of the extended real line $\mathbb{R} \cup \{+\infty, -\infty\}$, not the space of floating point numbers itself. Thus, encoding and representational issues (e.g. zero signs) are not relevant to rounding. The Standard defines four rounding modes, which we formalize as the members of an enumerated type:

```
roundmode = Nearest | Down | Up | Zero
```

Our formalization defines rounding into a given format as an operation that maps into the corresponding format *with an exponent range unbounded above*. That is, we do not take any special measures like coercing overflows back into the format or to additional 'infinite' elements; this is defined separately when we consider operations. While this separation is not quite faithful to the letter of the Standard, we consider our approach preferable. It has obvious technical convenience, avoiding the formally laborious adjunction of infinite elements to the real line and messy side-conditions in some theorems about rounding. Moreover, it avoids duplication of closely related issues in different parts of the Standard. For example, the rather involved criterion for rounding to $\pm\infty$ in round-to-nearest mode in sec. 4.1 of the Standard ('an infinitely precise result with magnitude at least $E_{max}(2 - 2^{-p})$ shall round to ∞ with no change of sign') is not needed. In our setup we later consider numbers that round to values outside the range-restricted format as overflowing, so the exact same condition is implied. This

---

[9] Read '$\varepsilon e. \ldots$' as 'the e such that $\ldots$'.

approach in any case *is* used later in the Standard 7.3 when discussing the raising of the overflow exception ('...were the exponent range unbounded').

Rounding is defined in HOL as a direct transcription of the Standard's definition. There is one clause for each of the four rounding modes:

```
|- (round fmt Nearest x =
        closest_such (iformat fmt) (EVEN o decode_fraction fmt) x) ∧
   (round fmt Down x = closest {a | a ∈ iformat fmt ∧ a <= x} x) ∧
   (round fmt Up x = closest {a | a ∈ iformat fmt ∧ a >= x} x) ∧
   (round fmt Zero x =
        closest {a | a ∈ iformat fmt ∧ abs a <= abs x} x)
```

For example, the result of rounding x down is defined to be the closest to x of the set of real numbers a representable in the format concerned (a ∈ iformat fmt) and no larger than x (a <= x). The subsidiary notion of 'the closest member of a set of real numbers' is defined using the Hilbert ε operator. As can be seen from the definition, rounding to nearest uses a slightly elaborated notion of closeness where the result with an even fraction is preferred.[10]

```
|- is_closest s x a ⇔
        a ∈ s ∧ ∀b. b ∈ s ⟹ abs(b - x) >= abs(a - x)

|- closest s x = εa. is_closest s x a

|- closest_such s p x =
        εa. is_closest s x a ∧ (∀b. is_closest s x b ∧ p b ⟹ p a)
```

In order to derive useful consequences from the definition, we then need to show that the postulated closest elements always exist. Actually, this depends on the format's being nontrivial. For example, if the format has nonzero precision, then rounding up behaves as expected:

```
|- ¬(precision fmt = 0)
    ⟹ round fmt Up x ∈ iformat fmt ∧
      x <= round fmt Up x ∧
      abs(x - round fmt Up x) < ulp fmt x ∧
      ∀c. c ∈ iformat fmt ∧ x <= c
          ⟹ abs(x - round fmt Up x) <= abs(x - c)
```

The strongest results for rounding to nearest depend on the precision being at least 2. This is because in a format with $p = 1$ nonzero normalized numbers all have fraction 1, so 'rounding to even' no longer discriminates between adjacent floating point numbers in the same way.

---

[10] Note again the important distinction between real values and encodings. The canonical fraction is used; the question of whether the actual floating point value has an even fraction is irrelevant. We do not show all the details of how the canonical fraction is defined.

The $(1 + \epsilon)$ lemma. The most widely used lemma about floating point arithmetic, often called the '$(1 + \epsilon)$' property, is simply that the result of a floating point operation is the exact result, perturbed by a relative error of bounded magnitude. Recalling that in our IEEE arithmetic, the result of an operation is the rounded exact value, this amounts to saying that x rounded is always of the form $x(1 + \epsilon)$ with $|\epsilon|$ bounded by a known value, typically 2^{-p} where p is the precision of the floating point format. We can derive a result of this form fairly easily, though we need sideconditions to exclude the possibility of underflow (not overflow, which we consider separately from rounding). The main theorem is as follows:

```
|- ¬(losing fmt rc x) ∧ ¬(precision fmt = 0)
   ⟹ ∃e. abs(e) <= mu rc / &2 pow (precision fmt - 1) ∧
        round fmt rc x = x * (&1 + e)
```

This essentially states exactly the '$1 + \epsilon$' property, and the bound on ϵ depends on the rounding mode, according to the following auxiliary definition of mu:

```
|- mu Nearest = &1 / &2 ∧
   mu Down = &1 ∧
   mu Up = &1 ∧
   mu Zero = &1
```

The theorem has two sideconditions, the second being the usual nontriviality hypothesis, and the first being an assertion that the value x does not *lose precision*, in other words, that the result of rounding x would not change if the lower exponent range were extended. We will not show the formal definition [26] here, since it is rather complicated. However, a simple and usually adequate sufficient condition is that the exact result lies in the normal range (or is zero):

```
|- normalizes fmt x ⟹ ¬(losing fmt rc x)
```

where

```
|- normalizes fmt x ⟺
      x = &0 ∨
      &2 pow (precision fmt - 1) / &2 pow (ulpscale fmt) <= abs(x)
```

In a couple of places, however, we need a sharper criterion for when the result of an fma operation will not lose precision. The proof of the following result merely observes that either the result is in the normalized range, or else the result will cancel so completely that the result will be exactly representable; however the technical details are non-trivial.

```
|- ¬(precision fmt = 0) ∧
   a ∈ iformat fmt ∧
   b ∈ iformat fmt ∧
   c ∈ iformat fmt ∧
   &2 pow (2 * precision fmt - 1) / &2 pow (ulpscale fmt) <= abs(c)
   ⟹ ¬(losing fmt rc (a * b + c))
```

Lemmas about exactness. The '$(1 + \epsilon)$' property allows us to ignore most of the technical details of floating point rounding, and step back into the world of exact real numbers and straightforward algebraic calculations. Many highly successful backward error analyses of higher-level algorithms [59] often rely essentially only on this property. Indeed, for most of the operations in the algorithms we are concerned with here, '$(1 + \epsilon)$' is the only property needed for us to verify what we require of them.

However, in lower-level algorithms like the ones considered here and others that the present author is concerned with verifying, a number of additional properties of floating point arithmetic are sometimes exploited by the algorithm designer, and proofs of them are required for verifications. In particular, there are important situations where floating point arithmetic is exact, i.e. results round to themselves. This happens if and only if the result is representable as a floating point number:

```
|- a ∈ iformat fmt ⟹ round fmt rc a = a

|- ¬(precision fmt = 0) ⟹ (round fmt rc x = x ⟺ x ∈ iformat fmt)
```

There are a number of situations where arithmetic operations are exact. Perhaps the best-known instance is subtraction of nearby quantities; cf. Theorem 4.3.1 of [54]:

```
|- a ∈ iformat fmt ∧ b ∈ iformat fmt ∧ a / &2 <= b ∧ b <= &2 * a
   ⟹ (b - a) ∈ iformat fmt
```

The availability of an fma operation leads us to consider generalization where results with higher intermediate precision are subtracted. The following is a direct generalization of the previous theorem, which corresponds to the case $k = 0$.[11]

```
|- ¬(p = 0) ∧
   a ∈ iformat (E1,p+k,N) ∧
   b ∈ iformat (E1,p+k,N) ∧
   abs(b - a) <= abs(b) / &2 pow (k + 1)
   ⟹ (b - a) ∈ iformat (E2,p,N)
```

Another classic result [39, 16] shows that we can obtain the sum of two floating point numbers exactly in two parts, one a rounding error in the other, by performing the floating point addition then subtracting both summands from the result, the larger one first:

```
|- x ∈ iformat fmt ∧
   y ∈ iformat fmt ∧
   abs(x) <= abs(y)
   ⟹ (round fmt Nearest (x + y) - y) ∈ iformat fmt ∧
       (round fmt Nearest (x + y) - (x + y)) ∈ iformat fmt
```

---

[11] With an assumption that a and b belong to the same binade, the (k + 1) can be strengthened to k.

Once again, we have devised a more general form of this theorem, with the above being the $k = 0$ case.[12] It allows a laxer relationship between x and y if the smaller number has k fewer significant digits:

```
|- k <= ulpscale fmt ∧
   x ∈ iformat fmt ∧
   y ∈ iformat(exprange fmt,precision fmt - k,ulpscale fmt - k) ∧
   abs(x) <= abs(&2 pow k * y)
   ⟹ (round fmt Nearest (x + y) - y) ∈ iformat fmt ∧
      (round fmt Nearest (x + y) - (x + y)) ∈ iformat fmt
```

The `fma` leads to a new result of this kind, allowing us to obtain an exact product in two parts:[13]

```
|- a ∈ iformat fmt ∧ b ∈ iformat fmt ∧
   &2 pow (2 * precision fmt - 1) / &2 pow (ulpscale fmt) <= abs(a * b)
   ⟹ (a * b - round fmt Nearest (a * b)) ∈ iformat fmt
```

A note on floating point axiomatics. The proofs of many of the above lemmas, and other more specialized results used in proofs, are often quite awkward and technical. In particular, they often require us to return to the basic definitions of floating point numbers and expand them out as sign, exponent and fraction before proceeding with some detailed bitwise or arithmetical proofs. This state of affairs compares badly with the organization of material in much of pure mathematics. For example the HOL theory of abstract real numbers proves from the definitions of reals (via a variant of Cauchy sequences) some basic 'axioms' from which all of real analysis is developed; once the reals have been constructed, the details of how the real numbers were constructed are irrelevant.

One naturally wonders if there is a clean set of 'axioms' from which most interesting floating point results can be derived more transparently. The idea of encapsulating floating point arithmetic in a set of axioms has attracted some attention over the years. However, the main point of these exercises was not so much to simplify and unify proofs in a *particular* arithmetic, but rather to produce proofs that would cover various different arithmetic implementations. With the almost exclusive use of IEEE arithmetic these days, that motivation has lost much of its force. Nevertheless it is worth looking at whether the axiom sets that have been proposed would be useful for our purposes.

The cleanest axiom systems are those that don't make reference to the underlying floating point representation [58, 60, 31]. However these are also the least useful for deriving results of the kind we consider, where details of the floating point representation are clearly significant. Moreover, at least one axiom in [60] is actually false for IEEE arithmetic, and according to [46], for almost every commercially significant machine except for the Cray X-MP and Y-MP.

---

[12] See [35] for other generalizations that we do not consider.

[13] We are not sure where this result originated; it appears in some of Kahan's lecture notes at http://www.cs.berkeley.edu~wkahan/ieee754status/ieee754.ps.

Generally speaking, in order to make it possible to prove the kind of subtle exactness results that we sometimes need, axioms that are explicit about the floating point representation are needed [16, 6]. Once this step is taken, there don't seem to be many benefits over our own explicit proofs, given that one is working in a precisely defined arithmetic. On the other hand, it is certainly interesting to see how many results can be proved by weaker hypotheses. For example, using the floating point representation explicitly but only assuming about rounding that it is, in Dekker's terminology, *faithful*, Priest [46] deduces several interesting consequences including Sterbenz's theorem about cancellation in subtraction, part of the theorem on exact sums, and the following:[14]

$$0 \le a \le b \wedge fl(b - a) = b - a \Longrightarrow \forall c.\, a \le c \le b \Longrightarrow fl(c - a) = c - a$$

However, he also makes some interesting remarks on the limitations of this axiomatic approach.

4.2   Division

It is not immediately obvious that without tricky and time-consuming bit-twiddling, it is possible to produce an IEEE-correct quotient and set all the IEEE flags correctly via ordinary software. Remarkably, however, fairly short straight-line sequences of fma operations (or negated variants), suffice to do so. This approach to division was pioneered by Markstein [38] on the IBM RS/6000[15] family. It seems that the ability to perform both a multiply and an add or subtract without an intermediate rounding is essential here.

Refining approximations. First we will describe in general terms how we can use fma operations to refine an initial reciprocal approximation (obtained from frcpa) towards a better reciprocal or quotient approximation. For clarity of exposition, we will ignore rounding errors at this stage, and later show how they are taken account of in the formal proof.

Consider determining the reciprocal of some floating point value b. Starting with a reciprocal approximation y with a relative error ϵ:

$$y = \frac{1}{b}(1 + \epsilon)$$

we can perform just one fnma operation:

$$e = 1 - by$$

and get:

$$e = 1 - by$$
$$= 1 - b\frac{1}{b}(1 + \epsilon)$$
$$= 1 - (1 + \epsilon)$$
$$= -\epsilon$$

---

[14] Think of fl as denoting rounding to nearest.
[15] All other trademarks are the property of their respective owners.

Now observe that:

$$\frac{1}{b} = \frac{y}{(1+\epsilon)}$$
$$= y(1 - \epsilon + \epsilon^2 - \epsilon^3 + \cdots)$$
$$= y(1 + e + e^2 + e^3 + \cdots)$$

This suggests that we might improve our reciprocal approximation by multiplying y by some truncation of the series $1 + e + e^2 + e^3 + \cdots$. The simplest case using a linear polynomial in e can be done with just one more `fma` operation:

$$y' = y + ey$$

Now we have

$$y' = y(1 + e)$$
$$= \frac{1}{b}(1 + \epsilon)(1 + e)$$
$$= \frac{1}{b}(1 + \epsilon)(1 - \epsilon)$$
$$= \frac{1}{b}(1 - \epsilon^2)$$

The magnitude of the relative error has thus been squared, or looked at another way, the number of significant bits has been approximately doubled. This, in fact, is exactly a step of the traditional Newton-Raphson iteration for reciprocals. In order to get a still better approximation, one can either use a longer polynomial in e, or repeat the Newton-Raphson linear correction several times. Mathematically speaking, repeating Newton-Raphson iteration n times is equivalent to using a polynomial $1 + e + \cdots + e^{2^n - 1}$, e.g. since $e' = \epsilon^2 = e^2$, two iterations yield:

$$y'' = y(1 + e)(1 + e^2) = y(1 + e + e^2 + e^3)$$

However, whether repeated Newton iteration or a more direct power series evaluation is better depends on a careful analysis of efficiency and the impact of rounding error. The Intel algorithms use both, as appropriate.

Now consider refining an approximation to the quotient with relative error ϵ; we can get such an approximation in the first case by simply multiplying a reciprocal approximation $y \approx \frac{1}{b}$ by a. One approach is simply to refine y as much as possible and then multiply. However, this kind of approach can never guarantee getting the last bit right; instead we also need to consider how to refine q directly. Suppose

$$q = \frac{a}{b}(1 + \epsilon)$$

We can similarly arrive at a remainder term by an `fnma`:

$$r = a - bq$$

when we have:

$$r = a - bq$$
$$= a - b\frac{a}{b}(1 + \epsilon)$$
$$= a - a(1 + \epsilon)$$
$$= -a\epsilon$$

In order to use this remainder term to improve q, we also need a reciprocal approximation $y = \frac{1}{b}(1 + \eta)$. Now the **fma** operation:

$$q' = q + ry$$

results in, ignoring the rounding:

$$q' = q + ry$$
$$= \frac{a}{b}(1 + \epsilon) - a\epsilon\frac{1}{b}(1 + \eta)$$
$$= \frac{a}{b}(1 + \epsilon - \epsilon(1 + \eta))$$
$$= \frac{a}{b}(1 - \epsilon\eta)$$

Obtaining the final result. While we have neglected rounding errors hitherto, it is fairly straightforward to place a sensible bound on their effect. To be precise, the error from rounding is at most half an ulp in round-to-nearest mode and a full ulp in the other modes.

```
⊢   ¬(precision fmt = 0)
    ⟹ (abs(error fmt Nearest x) <= ulp fmt x / &2) ∧
      (abs(error fmt Down x) < ulp fmt x) ∧
      (abs(error fmt Up x) < ulp fmt x) ∧
      (abs(error fmt Zero x) < ulp fmt x)
```

where

```
⊢   error fmt rc x = round fmt rc x - x
```

It turn, we can easily get fairly tight lower $(|x|/2^p \leq ulp(x))$ and upper $(ulp(x) \leq |x|/2^{p-1})$ bounds on an ulp in x relative to the magnitude of x, the upper bound assuming normalization:

```
⊢   abs(x) / &2 pow (precision fmt) <= ulp fmt x
```

and

```
⊢   normalizes fmt x ∧ ¬(precision fmt = 0) ∧ ¬(x = &0)
    ⟹ ulp fmt x <= abs(x) / &2 pow (precision fmt - 1)
```

Putting these together, we can easily prove simple relative error bounds on all the basic operations, which can be propagated through multiple calculations by simple algebra. It is easy to see that while the relative errors in the approximations are significantly above 2^{-p} (where p is the precision of the floating point format), the effects of rounding error on the overall error are minor. However, once we get close to having a perfectly rounded result, rounding error becomes highly significant. A crucial theorem here is the following due to Markstein [38]:

Theorem 1. *If q is a floating point number within 1 ulp of the true quotient a/b of two floating point numbers, and y is the correctly rounded-to-nearest approximation of the exact reciprocal $\frac{1}{b}$, then the following two floating point operations:*

$$r = a - bq$$
$$q' = q + ry$$

using round-to-nearest in each case, yield the correctly rounded-to-nearest quotient q'.

This is not too difficult to prove in HOL. First we observe that because the initial q is a good approximation, the computation of r cancels so much that no rounding error is committed. (This is intuitively plausible and stated by Markstein without proof, but the formal proof was surprisingly messy).

```
⊢   2 <= precision fmt ∧
    a ∈ iformat fmt ∧ b ∈ iformat fmt ∧ q ∈ iformat fmt ∧
    normalizes fmt q ∧ abs(a / b - q) <= ulp fmt (a / b) ∧
    &2 pow (2 * precision fmt - 1) / &2 pow (ulpscale fmt) <= abs(a)
    ⟹ (a - b * q) ∈ iformat fmt
```

Now the overall proof given by Markstein is quite easily formalized. However, we observed that the property actually used in the proof is in general somewhat weaker than requiring y to be a perfectly rounded reciprocal. The theorem actually proved in HOL is:

Theorem 2. *If q is a floating point number within 1 ulp of the true quotient a/b of two floating point numbers, and y approximates the exact reciprocal $\frac{1}{b}$ to a relative error $< \frac{1}{2^p}$, where p is the precision of the floating point format concerned, then the following two floating point operations:*

$$r = a - bq$$
$$q' = q + ry$$

using round-to-nearest in each case, yield the correctly rounded-to-nearest quotient q'.

The formal HOL statement is as follows:

```
⊢   2 <= precision fmt ∧
    a ∈ iformat fmt ∧ b ∈ iformat fmt ∧
    q ∈ iformat fmt ∧ r ∈ iformat fmt ∧
    ¬(b = &0) ∧
    ¬(a / b ∈ iformat fmt) ∧
    normalizes fmt (a / b) ∧
    abs(a / b - q) <= ulp fmt (a / b) ∧
    abs(inv(b) - y) < abs(inv b) / &2 pow (precision fmt) ∧
    r = a - b * q ∧
    q' = q + r * y
    ⟹ round fmt Nearest q' = round fmt Nearest (a / b)
```

Although in the worst case, the preconditions of the original and modified theorem hardly differ (recall that $|x|/2^p \le ulp(x) \le |x|/2^{p-1}$), it turns out that in many situations the relative error condition is much easier to satisfy. In Markstein's original methodology, one needs first to obtain a perfectly rounded reciprocal, which he proves can be done as follows:

Theorem 3. *If y is a floating point number within 1 ulp of the true reciprocal $\frac{1}{b}$, then one iteration of:*

$$e = 1 - by$$
$$y' = y + ey$$

using round-to-nearest in both cases, yields the correctly rounded reciprocal, except possibly when the mantissa of b consists entirely of 1s.

If we rely on this theorem, we need a very good approximation to $\frac{1}{b}$ before these two further serial operations and one more to get the final quotient using the new y'. However, with the weaker requirement on y', we can get away with a correspondingly weaker y. In fact, we prove:

Theorem 4. *If y is a floating point number that results from rounding a value y_0, and the relative error in y_0 w.r.t. $\frac{1}{b}$ is $\le \frac{d}{2^{2p}}$ for some natural number d (assumed $\le 2^{p-2}$), then y will have relative error $< \frac{1}{2^p}$ w.r.t. $\frac{1}{b}$, except possibly if the mantissa of b is one of the d largest. (That is, when scaled up to an integer $2^{p-1} \le m_b < 2^p$, we have in fact $2^p - d \le m_b < 2^p$.)*

Proof. For simplicity we assume $b > 0$, since the general case can be deduced by symmetry from this. We can therefore write $b = 2^e m_b$ for some integer m_b with $2^{p-1} \le m_b < 2^p$. In fact, it is convenient to assume that $2^{p-1} < m_b$, since when b is an exact power of 2 the main result follows easily from $d \le 2^{p-2}$. Now we have:

$$\frac{1}{b} = 2^{-e}\frac{1}{m_b}$$
$$= 2^{-(e+2p-1)}\left(\frac{2^{2p-1}}{m_b}\right)$$

and $ulp(\frac{1}{b}) = 2^{-(e+2p-1)}$. In order to ensure that $|y - \frac{1}{b}| < |\frac{1}{b}|/2^p$ it suffices, since $|y - y_0| \le ulp(\frac{1}{b})/2$, to have:

$$|y_0 - \frac{1}{b}| < (\frac{1}{b})/2^p - ulp(\frac{1}{b})/2$$
$$= (\frac{1}{b})/2^p - 2^{-(e+2p-1)}/2$$
$$= (\frac{1}{b})/2^p - (\frac{1}{b})m_b/2^{2p}$$

By hypothesis, we have $|y_0 - \frac{1}{b}| \le (\frac{1}{b})\frac{d}{2^{2p}}$. So it is sufficient if:

$$(\frac{1}{b})d/2^{2p} < (\frac{1}{b})/2^p - (\frac{1}{b})m_b/2^{2p}$$

Cancelling $(\frac{1}{b})/2^{2p}$ from both sides, we find that this is equivalent to:

$$d < 2^p - m_b$$

Consequently, the required relative error is guaranteed except possibly when $d \ge 2^p - m_b$, or equivalently $m_b \ge 2^p - d$, as claimed.

The HOL statement is as follows. Note that it uses $e = d/2^{2p}$ as compared with the statement we gave above, but this is inconsequential.

```
⊢   2 <= precision fmt ∧
    b ∈ iformat fmt ∧
    y ∈ iformat fmt ∧
    ¬(b = &0) ∧
    normalizes fmt b ∧
    normalizes fmt (inv(b)) ∧
    y = round fmt Nearest y0 ∧
    abs(y0 - inv(b)) <= e * abs(inv(b)) ∧
    e <= inv(&2 pow (precision fmt + 2)) ∧
    &(decode_fraction fmt b) <
    &2 pow (precision fmt) - &2 pow (2 * precision fmt) * e
    ⟹ abs(inv(b) - y) < abs(inv(b)) / &2 pow (precision fmt)
```

Thanks to this stronger theorem, we were actually able to design more efficient algorithms than those based on Markstein's original theorems, a surprising and gratifying effect of our formal verification project. For a more elaborate number-theoretic analysis of a related algorithm, see [30]; the proof described there has also been formalized in HOL Light.

Flag settings. We must ensure not only correct results in all rounding modes, but that the flags are set correctly. However, this essentially follows in general from the correctness of the result in all rounding modes (strictly, in the case of underflow, we need to verify this for a format with slightly larger exponent range). For the correct setting of the inexact flag, we need only prove the following HOL theorem:

> ⊢ ¬(precision fmt = 0) ∧
>   (∀rc. round fmt rc x = round fmt rc y)
>   ⟹ ∀rc. round fmt rc x = x ⇔ round fmt rc y = y

The proof is simple: if x rounds to itself, then it must be representable. But by hypothesis, y rounds to the same thing, that is x, in *all rounding modes*. In particular the roundings up and down imply x <= y and x >= y, so y = x. The other way round is similar.

4.3   Square Root

Similarly, the Intel® Itanium® architecture defers square roots to software, and we have verified a number of sequences for the operation [29]. The process of formal verification follows a methodology established by Cornea [13]. A general analytical proof covers the majority of cases, but a number of potential exceptions are isolated using number-theoretic techniques and dealt with using an explicit case analysis. Proofs of this nature, large parts of which involve intricate but routine error bounding and the exhaustive solution of diophantine equations, are very tedious and error-prone to do by hand. In practice, one would do better to use *some* kind of machine assistance, such as *ad hoc* programs to solve the diophantine equations and check the special cases so derived. Although this can be helpful, it can also create new dangers of incorrectly implemented helper programs and transcription errors when passing results between 'hand' and 'machine' portions of the proof. By contrast, we perform all steps of the proof in HOL Light, and can be quite confident that no errors have been introduced.

In general terms, square root algorithms follow the same pattern as division algorithms: an initial approximation (now obtained by `frsqrta`) is successively refined, and at the end some more subtle steps are undertaken to ensure correct rounding. The initial refinement is similar in kind to those for reciprocals and quotients, though slightly more complicated, and we will not describe them in detail; interested readers can refer to [37, 12, 29]. Instead we focus on ensuring perfect rounding at the end. Note that whatever the final `fma` operation may be, say

$$S := S_3 + e_3 H_3$$

we can regard it, because of the basic IEEE correctness of the `fma`, as the rounding of the *exact* mathematical result $S_3 + e_3 H_3$, which we abbreviate S^*. Thanks to the special properties of the `fma`, we can design the initial refinement to ensure that the relative error in S^* is only a little more than 2^{-2p} where p is the floating-point precision. How can we infer from such a relative error bound that S will always be correctly rounded? We will focus on the round-to-nearest mode here; the proof for the other rounding modes are similar but need special consideration of earlier steps in the algorithm to ensure correct results when the result is exact ($\sqrt{0.25} = 0.5$ etc.)

Exclusion zones. On general grounds we note that $\sqrt{a}$ cannot be exactly the mid-point between two floating-point numbers. This is not hard to see, since the square root of a number in a given format cannot denormalize in that format, and a non-denormal midpoint has $p+1$ significant digits, so its square must have more than p.[16]

```
|- &0 <= a ∧ a ∈ iformat fmt ∧ b ∈ midpoints fmt
    ⟹ ¬(sqrt a = b)
```

This is a useful observation. We'll never be in the tricky case where there are two equally close floating-point numbers (resolved by the 'round to even' rule.) So in round-to-nearest, S^* and $\sqrt{a}$ could only round in different ways if there were a midpoint between them, for only then could the closest floating-point numbers to them differ. For example in the following diagram where large lines indicate floating-point numbers and smaller ones represent midpoints, $\sqrt{a}$ would round 'down' while S^* would round 'up':[17]

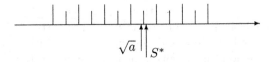

Although analyzing this condition combinatorially would be complicated, there is a much simpler sufficient condition. One can easily see that it would suffice to show that for any midpoint m:

$$|\sqrt{a} - S^*| < |\sqrt{a} - m|$$

In that case $\sqrt{a}$ and S^* couldn't lie on opposite sides of m. Here is the formal theorem in HOL:

```
|- ¬(precision fmt = 0) ∧
   (∀m. m ∈ midpoints fmt ⟹ abs(x - y) < abs(x - m))
   ⟹ round fmt Nearest x = round fmt Nearest y
```

One can arrive at an 'exclusion zone' theorem giving the minimum possible $|\sqrt{a} - m|$. However, this can be quite small, about $2^{-(2p+3)}$ relative to $\sqrt{a}$, where p is the precision. For example, when $p = 64$, consider the square root of the next floating-point number below 1, whose mantissa consists entirely of 1s. Its square root is about 2^{-131} from a midpoint:

$$\sqrt{1 - 2^{-64}} \approx (1 - 2^{65}) - 2^{-131}$$

Therefore, our relative error in S^* of rather more than 2^{-2p} is not adequate to justify perfect rounding based on the simple 'exclusion zone' theorem. However,

---

[16] An analogous result holds for quotients but here the denormal case must be dealt with specially. For example $2^{E min} \times 0.111\cdots111/2$ is exactly a midpoint.

[17] Similarly, in the other rounding modes, misrounding could only occur if $\sqrt{a}$ and S^* are separated by a floating-point number. However we also need to consider the case when $\sqrt{a}$ *is* a floating-point number.

our relative error bounds are far from sharp, and it seems quite plausible that the algorithm does nevertheless work correctly. What can we do?

One solution is to use more refined theorems [37], but this is complicated and may still fail to justify several algorithms that are intuitively believed to work correctly. An ingenious alternative developed by Cornea [13] is to observe that there are relatively few cases like $0.111\cdots1111$ whose square roots come close enough to render the exclusion zone theorem inapplicable, and these can be isolated by fairly straightforward number-theoretic methods. We can therefore:

- Isolate the special cases $a_1,\ldots,a_n$ that have square roots within the critical distance of a midpoint.
- Conclude from the simple exclusion zone theorem that the algorithm will give correct results except possibly for $a_1,\ldots,a_n$.
- Explicitly show that the algorithm is correct for the $a_1,\ldots,a_n$, (effectively by running it on those inputs).

This two-part approach is perhaps a little unusual, but not unknown even in pure mathematics.[18] For example, consider "Bertrand's Conjecture" (first proved by Chebyshev), stating that for any positive integer n there is a prime p with $n \leq p \leq 2n$. The most popular proof, originally due to Erdös [18], involves assuming $n > 4000$ for the main proof and separately checking the assertion for $n \leq 4000$.[19]

By some straightforward mathematics [13] formalized in HOL without difficulty, one can show that the difficult cases for square roots have mantissas m, considered as p-bit integers, such that one of the following diophantine equations has a solution k for some integer $|d| \leq D$, where D is roughly the factor by which the guaranteed relative error is excessive:

$$2^{p+2}m = k^2 + d \qquad 2^{p+1}m = k^2 + d$$

We consider the equations separately for each chosen $|d| \leq D$. For example, we might be interested in whether $2^{p+1}m = k^2 - 7$ has a solution. If so, the possible value(s) of m are added to the set of difficult cases. It's quite easy to program HOL to enumerate all the solutions of such diophantine equations, returning a disjunctive theorem of the form:

$$\vdash 2^{p+1}m = k^2 + d \Longrightarrow m = n_1 \vee \ldots \vee m = n_i$$

The procedure simply uses even-odd reasoning and recursion on the power of two (effectively so-called 'Hensel lifting'). For example, if

$$2^{25}m = k^2 - 7$$

---

[18] A more extreme case is the 4-color theorem, whose proof relies on extensive (computer-assisted) checking of special cases [3].

[19] An 'optimized' way of checking, referred to by [2] as "Landau's trick", is to verify that 3, 5, 7, 13, 23, 43, 83, 163, 317, 631, 1259, 2503 and 4001 are all prime and each is less than twice its predecessor.

then we know k must be odd; we can write $k = 2k' + 1$ and deduce:

$$2^{24}m = 2k'^2 + 2k' - 3$$

By more even/odd reasoning, this has no solutions. In general, we recurse down to an equation that is trivially unsatisfiable, as here, or immediately solvable. One equation can split into two, but never more. For example, we have a formally proved HOL theorem asserting that for any double-extended number a,[20] rounding $\sqrt{a}$ and $\sqrt{a}(1 + \epsilon)$ to double-extended precision using any of the four IEEE rounding modes will give the same results provided $|\epsilon| < 31/2^{131}$, with the possible exceptions of $2^{2e}m$ for:

$$m \in \{\, 10074057467468575321, 10376293541461622781,$$
$$10376293541461622787, 11307741603771905196,$$
$$13812780109330227882, 14928119304823191698,$$
$$16640932189858196938, 18446744073709551611,$$
$$18446744073709551612, 18446744073709551613,$$
$$18446744073709551614, 18446744073709551615\}$$

and $2^{2e+1}m$ for

$$m \in \{\, 9223372036854775809, 9223372036854775811,$$
$$11168682418930654643\}$$

Note that while some of these numbers are obvious special cases like $2^{64} - 1$, the "pattern" in others is only apparent from the kind of mathematical analysis we have undertaken here. They aren't likely to be exercised by random testing, or testing of plausible special cases.[21]

Checking formally that the algorithm works on the special cases can also be automated, by applying theorems on the uniqueness of rounding to the concrete numbers computed. (For a formal proof, it is not sufficient to separately test the implemented algorithm, since such a result has no formal status.) In order to avoid trying all possible even or odd exponents for the various significands, we exploit some results on invariance of the rounding and arithmetic involved in the algorithm under systematic scaling by 2^{2k}, doing a simple form of symbolic simulation by formal proof.

4.4   Transcendental Functions

We have also proven rigorous error bounds for implementations of several common transcendental functions. Note that, according to current standard practice,

---

[20] Note that there is more subtlety required when using such a result in a mixed-precision environment. For example, to obtain a single-precision result for a double-precision input, an algorithm that suffices for single-precision inputs may not be adequate even though the final precision is the same.

[21] On the other hand, we can well consider the mathematical analysis as a *source* of good test cases.

the algorithms do not aim at perfect rounding, but allow a small additional relative error. Although ensuring perfect rounding for transcendental functions is possible, and may become standard in the future, it is highly non-trivial and involves at least some efficiency penalty [42]. We will consider here a floating-point sin and cos function; as will become clear shortly the internal structure is largely identical in the two cases.

As is quite typical for modern transcendental function implementations [56], the algorithm can be considered as three phases:

- Initial range reduction
- Core computation
- Reconstruction

For our trigonometric functions, the initial argument x is reduced modulo $\pi/2$. Mathematically, for any real x we can always write:

$$x = N(\pi/2) + r$$

where N is an integer (the closest to $x \cdot \frac{2}{\pi}$) and $|r| \leq \pi/4$. The core approximation is then a polynomial approximation to $sin(r)$ or $cos(r)$ as appropriate, similar to a truncation of the familiar Taylor series:

$$sin(x) = x - \frac{x^3}{3!} + \frac{x^5}{5!} - \frac{x^7}{7!} + \ldots$$
$$cos(x) = 1 - \frac{x^2}{2!} + \frac{x^4}{4!} - \frac{x^6}{6!} + \ldots$$

but with the pre-stored coefficients computed numerically to minimize the maximum error over r's range, using the so-called *Remez algorithm* [49]. Finally, the reconstruction phase: to obtain either $sin(x)$ and/or $cos(x)$, just return one of $sin(r)$, $cos(r)$, $-sin(r)$ or $-cos(r)$ depending on N modulo 4. For example:

$$sin((4M + 3)(\pi/2) + r) = -cos(r)$$

Verification of range reduction. The principal difficulty of implementing trigonometric range reduction is that the input argument x may be large and yet the reduced argument r very small, because x is unusually close to a multiple of $\pi/2$. In such cases, the computation of r needs to be performed very carefully. Assuming we have calculated N, we need to evaluate:

$$r = x - N\frac{\pi}{2}$$

However, $\frac{\pi}{2}$ is irrational and so cannot be represented exactly by any finite sum of floating point numbers. So however the above is computed, it must in fact calculate

$$r' = x - NP$$

for some approximation $P = \frac{\pi}{2} + \epsilon$. The relative error $\frac{|r'-r|}{|r|}$ is then $\frac{N|\epsilon|}{|r|}$ which is of the order $|\frac{x\epsilon}{r}|$. Therefore, to keep this relative error within acceptable bounds (say 2^{-70}) the accuracy required in the approximation P depends on how small the (true) reduced argument can be relative to the input argument. In order to formally verify the accuracy of the algorithm, we need to answer the purely mathematical question: how close can a double-extended precision floating point number be to an integer multiple of $\frac{\pi}{2}$? Having done that, we can proceed with the verification of the actual computation of the reduced argument in floating point arithmetic. This requires a certain amount of elementary number theory, analyzing *convergents* [4].

The result is that for nonzero inputs the reduced argument has magnitude at least around 2^{-69}. Assuming the input has size $\leq 2^{63}$, this means that an error of ϵ in the approximation of $\pi/2$ can constitute approximately a $2^{132}\epsilon$ relative error in r. Consequently, to keep the relative error down to about 2^{-70} we need $|\epsilon| < 2^{-202}$. Since a floating-point number has only 64 bits of precision, it would seem that we would need to approximate $\pi/2$ by four floating-point numbers $P_1, \ldots, P_4$ and face considerable complications in keeping down the rounding error in computing $x - N(P_1 + P_2 + P_3 + P_4)$. However, using an ingenious technique called *pre-reduction* [55], the difficulties can be reduced.

Verification of the core computation. The core computation is simply a polynomial in the reduced argument; the most general *sin* polynomial used is of the form:[22]

$$p(r) = r + P_1 r^3 + P_2 r^5 + \cdots + P_8 r^{17}$$

where the P_i are all floating point numbers. Note that the P_i are not the same as the coefficients of the familiar Taylor series (which in any case are not exactly representable as floating point numbers), but arrived at using the Remez algorithm to minimize the worst-case error over the possible reduced argument range. The overall error in this phase consists of the approximation error $p(r) - sin(r)$ as well as the rounding errors for the particular evaluation strategy for the polynomial. All of these require some work to verify formally; for example we have implemented an automatic HOL derived rule to provably bound the error in approximating a mathematical function by a polynomial over a given interval. The final general correctness theorems we derive have the following form:

```
|- x ∈ floats Extended ∧ abs(Val x) <= &2 pow 64
    ⟹ prac (Extended,rc,fz) (fcos rc fz x) (cos(Val x))
            (#0.07341 * ulp(rformat Extended) (cos(Val x)))
```

The function prac means 'pre-rounding accuracy'. The theorem states that provided x is a floating point number in the double-extended format, with $|x| \leq 2^{64}$ (a range somewhat wider than needed), the result excluding the final rounding is at most 0.07341 units in the last place from the true answer

---

[22] In fact, the reduced argument needs to be represented as two floating-point numbers, so there is an additional correction term that we ignore in this presentation.

of $cos(x)$. This theorem is generic over all rounding modes `rc` and flush-to-zero settings `fz`. An easy corollary of this is that in round-to-nearest mode without flush-to-zero set the maximum error is 0.57341 ulps, since rounding to nearest can contribute at most 0.5 ulps. In other rounding modes, a more careful analysis is required, paying careful attention to the formal definition of a 'unit in the last place'. The problem is that the true answer and the computed answer before the final rounding may in general lie on opposite sides of a (negative, since $|cos(x)| \leq 1$) power of 2. At this point, the gap between adjacent floating point numbers is different depending on whether one is considering the exact or computed result. In the case of round-to-nearest, however, this does not matter since the result will always round to the straddled power of 2, bringing it even closer to the exact answer.

5   Conclusion and Future Perspectives

Formal verification in this area is a good target for theorem proving. The work outlined here has contributed in several ways: bugs have been found, potential optimizations have been uncovered, and the general level of confidence and intellectual grasp has been raised. In particular, two key strengths of HOL Light are important: (i) available library of formalized real analysis, and (ii) programmability of special-purpose inference rules without compromising soundness. Subsequent improvements might focus on integrating the verification more tightly into the design flow as in [44].

References

1. M. Aagaard and J. Harrison, editors. *Theorem Proving in Higher Order Logics: 13th International Conference, TPHOLs 2000*, volume 1869 of *Lecture Notes in Computer Science*. Springer-Verlag, 2000.
2. M. Aigner and G. M. Ziegler. *Proofs from The Book*. Springer-Verlag, 2nd edition, 2001.
3. K. Appel and W. Haken. Every planar map is four colorable. *Bulletin of the American Mathematical Society*, 82:711–712, 1976.
4. A. Baker. *A Concise Introduction to the Theory of Numbers*. Cambridge University Press, 1985.
5. S. Boldo. *Preuves formelles en arithmétiques à virgule flottante*. PhD thesis, ENS Lyon, 2004. Available on the Web from `http://www.ens-lyon.fr/LIP/Pub/Rapports/PhD/PhD2004/PhD2004-05.pdf`.
6. W. S. Brown. A simple but realistic model of floating-point computation. *ACM Transactions on Mathematical Software*, 7:445–480, 1981.
7. R. E. Bryant. Graph-based algorithms for Boolean function manipulation. *IEEE Transactions on Computers*, C-35:677–691, 1986.
8. J. R. Burch, E. M. Clarke, K. L. McMillan, D. L. Dill, and L. J. Hwang. Symbolic model checking: 10^{20} states and beyond. *Information and Computation*, 98:142–170, 1992.
9. A. Church. A formulation of the Simple Theory of Types. *Journal of Symbolic Logic*, 5:56–68, 1940.

10. E. M. Clarke and E. A. Emerson. Design and synthesis of synchronization skeletons using branching-time temporal logic. In D. Kozen, editor, *Logics of Programs*, volume 131 of *Lecture Notes in Computer Science*, pages 52–71, Yorktown Heights, 1981. Springer-Verlag.

11. C. W. Clenshaw and F. W. J. Olver. Beyond floating point. *Journal of the ACM*, 31:319–328, 1984.

12. M. Cornea, J. Harrison, and P. T. P. Tang. *Scientific Computing for Itanium Based Systems*. Intel Press, 2002.

13. M. Cornea-Hasegan. Proving the IEEE correctness of iterative floating-point square root, divide and remainder algorithms. *Intel Technology Journal*, 1998-Q2:1–11, 1998. Available on the Web as `http://developer.intel.com/technology/itj/q21998/articles/art_3.htm`.

14. G. Cousineau and M. Mauny. *The Functional Approach to Programming*. Cambridge University Press, 1998.

15. M. Davis, G. Logemann, and D. Loveland. A machine program for theorem proving. *Communications of the ACM*, 5:394–397, 1962.

16. T. J. Dekker. A floating-point technique for extending the available precision. *Numerical Mathematics*, 18:224–242, 1971.

17. C. Dulong. The IA-64 architecture at work. *IEEE Computer*, 64(7):24–32, July 1998.

18. P. Erdös. Beweis eines Satzes von Tschebyshev. *Acta Scientiarum Mathematicarum (Szeged)*, 5:194–198, 1930.

19. E. Goldberg and Y. Novikov. BerkMin: a fast and robust Sat-solver. In C. D. Kloos and J. D. Franca, editors, *Design, Automation and Test in Europe Conference and Exhibition (DATE 2002)*, pages 142–149, Paris, France, 2002. IEEE Computer Society Press.

20. M. J. C. Gordon. Representing a logic in the LCF metalanguage. In D. Néel, editor, *Tools and notions for program construction: an advanced course*, pages 163–185. Cambridge University Press, 1982.

21. M. J. C. Gordon and T. F. Melham. *Introduction to HOL: a theorem proving environment for higher order logic*. Cambridge University Press, 1993.

22. M. J. C. Gordon, R. Milner, and C. P. Wadsworth. *Edinburgh LCF: A Mechanised Logic of Computation*, volume 78 of *Lecture Notes in Computer Science*. Springer-Verlag, 1979.

23. J. Harrison. HOL Light: A tutorial introduction. In M. Srivas and A. Camilleri, editors, *Proceedings of the First International Conference on Formal Methods in Computer-Aided Design (FMCAD'96)*, volume 1166 of *Lecture Notes in Computer Science*, pages 265–269. Springer-Verlag, 1996.

24. J. Harrison. Proof style. In E. Giménez and C. Paulin-Mohring, editors, *Types for Proofs and Programs: International Workshop TYPES'96*, volume 1512 of *Lecture Notes in Computer Science*, pages 154–172, Aussois, France, 1996. Springer-Verlag.

25. J. Harrison. *Theorem Proving with the Real Numbers*. Springer-Verlag, 1998. Revised version of author's PhD thesis.

26. J. Harrison. A machine-checked theory of floating point arithmetic. In Y. Bertot, G. Dowek, A. Hirschowitz, C. Paulin, and L. Théry, editors, *Theorem Proving in Higher Order Logics: 12th International Conference, TPHOLs'99*, volume 1690 of *Lecture Notes in Computer Science*, pages 113–130, Nice, France, 1999. Springer-Verlag.

27. J. Harrison. Formal verification of floating point trigonometric functions. In W. A. Hunt and S. D. Johnson, editors, *Formal Methods in Computer-Aided Design: Third International Conference FMCAD 2000*, volume 1954 of *Lecture Notes in Computer Science*, pages 217–233. Springer-Verlag, 2000.

28. J. Harrison. Formal verification of IA-64 division algorithms. In Aagaard and Harrison [1], pages 234–251.

29. J. Harrison. Formal verification of square root algorithms. *Formal Methods in System Design*, 22:143–153, 2003.

30. J. Harrison. Isolating critical cases for reciprocals using integer factorization. In J.-C. Bajard and M. Schulte, editors, *Proceedings, 16th IEEE Symposium on Computer Arithmetic*, pages 148–157, Santiago de Compostela, Spain, 2003. IEEE Computer Society. Currently available from symposium Web site at http://www.dec.usc.es/arith16/papers/paper-150.pdf.

31. J. E. Holm. *Floating-Point Arithmetic and Program Correctness Proofs*. PhD thesis, Cornell University, 1980.

32. IEEE. Standard for binary floating point arithmetic. ANSI/IEEE Standard 754-1985, The Institute of Electrical and Electronic Engineers, Inc., 345 East 47th Street, New York, NY 10017, USA, 1985.

33. C. Jacobi. *Formal Verification of a Fully IEEE Compliant Floating Point Unit*. PhD thesis, University of the Saarland, 2002. Available on the Web as http://engr.smu.edu/ seidel/research/diss-jacobi.ps.gz.

34. R. Kaivola and M. D. Aagaard. Divider circuit verification with model checking and theorem proving. In Aagaard and Harrison [1], pages 338–355.

35. S. Linnainmaa. Analysis of some known methods of improving the accuracy of floating-point sums. *BIT*, 14:167–202, 1974.

36. D. W. Loveland. Mechanical theorem-proving by model elimination. *Journal of the ACM*, 15:236–251, 1968.

37. P. Markstein. *IA-64 and Elementary Functions: Speed and Precision*. Prentice-Hall, 2000.

38. P. W. Markstein. Computation of elementary functions on the IBM RISC System/6000 processor. *IBM Journal of Research and Development*, 34:111–119, 1990.

39. O. Møller. Quasi double-precision in floating-point addition. *BIT*, 5:37–50, 1965.

40. J. S. Moore, T. Lynch, and M. Kaufmann. A mechanically checked proof of the correctness of the kernel of the $AMD5_K86$ floating-point division program. *IEEE Transactions on Computers*, 47:913–926, 1998.

41. M. W. Moskewicz, C. F. Madigan, Y. Zhao, L. Zhang, and S. Malik. Chaff: Engineering an efficient SAT solver. In *Proceedings of the 38th Design Automation Conference (DAC 2001)*, pages 530–535. ACM Press, 2001.

42. J.-M. Muller. *Elementary functions: Algorithms and Implementation*. Birkhäuser, 1997.

43. J.-M. Muller. On the definition of $ulp(x)$. Research Report 2005-09, ENS Lyon, 2005.

44. J. O'Leary, X. Zhao, R. Gerth, and C.-J. H. Seger. Formally verifying IEEE compliance of floating-point hardware. *Intel Technology Journal*, 1999-Q1:1–14, 1999. Available on the Web as http://developer.intel.com/technology/itj/q11999/articles/art_5.htm.

45. V. R. Pratt. Anatomy of the Pentium bug. In P. D. Mosses, M. Nielsen, and M. I. Schwartzbach, editors, *Proceedings of the 5th International Joint Conference on the theory and practice of software development (TAPSOFT'95)*, volume 915 of *Lecture Notes in Computer Science*, pages 97–107, Aarhus, Denmark, 1995. Springer-Verlag.

46. D. M. Priest. *On Properties of Floating Point Arithmetics: Numerical Stability and the Cost of Accurate Computations*. PhD thesis, University of California, Berkeley, 1992. Available on the Web as ftp://ftp.icsi.berkeley.edu/pub/theory/priest-thesis.ps.Z.

47. J. P. Queille and J. Sifakis. Specification and verification of concurrent programs in CESAR. In *Proceedings of the 5th International Symposium on Programming*, volume 137 of *Lecture Notes in Computer Science*, pages 195–220. Springer-Verlag, 1982.

48. K. Quinn. Ever had problems rounding off figures? The stock exchange has. *Wall Street Journal*, November 8, 1983.

49. M. E. Remes. Sur le calcul effectif des polynomes d'approximation de Tchebichef. *Comptes Rendus Hebdomadaires des Séances de l'Académie des Sciences*, 199:337–340, 1934.

50. D. Rusinoff. A mechanically checked proof of IEEE compliance of a register-transfer-level specification of the AMD-K7 floating-point multiplication, division, and square root instructions. *LMS Journal of Computation and Mathematics*, 1:148–200, 1998. Available on the Web via http://www.onr.com/user/russ/david/k7-div-sqrt.html.

51. J. Sawada. Formal verification of divide and square root algorithms using series calculation. In D. Borrione, M. Kaufmann, and J. Moore, editors, *3rd International Workshop on the ACL2 Theorem Prover and its Applications*, pages 31–49. University of Grenoble, 2002.

52. C.-J. H. Seger and R. E. Bryant. Formal verification by symbolic evaluation of partially-ordered trajectories. *Formal Methods in System Design*, 6:147–189, 1995.

53. G. Stålmarck and M. Säflund. Modeling and verifying systems and software in propositional logic. In B. K. Daniels, editor, *Safety of Computer Control Systems, 1990 (SAFECOMP '90)*, pages 31–36, Gatwick, UK, 1990. Pergamon Press.

54. P. H. Sterbenz. *Floating-Point Computation*. Prentice-Hall, 1974.

55. S. Story and P. T. P. Tang. New algorithms for improved transcendental functions on IA-64. In I. Koren and P. Kornerup, editors, *Proceedings, 14th IEEE symposium on on computer arithmetic*, pages 4–11, Adelaide, Australia, 1999. IEEE Computer Society.

56. P. T. P. Tang. Table-lookup algorithms for elementary functions and their error analysis. In P. Kornerup and D. W. Matula, editors, *Proceedings of the 10th Symposium on Computer Arithemtic*, pages 232–236, 1991.

57. P. Weis and X. Leroy. *Le langage Caml*. InterEditions, 1993. See also the CAML Web page: http://pauillac.inria.fr/caml/.

58. A. v. Wijngaarden. Numerical analysis as an independent science. *BIT*, 6:68–81, 1966.

59. J. H. Wilkinson. *Rounding Errors in Algebraic Processes*, volume 32 of *National Physical Laboratory Notes on Applied Science*. Her Majesty's Stationery Office (HMSO), London, 1963.

60. N. Wirth. *Systematic Programming: An Introduction*. Prentice-Hall, 1973.

Author Index

Lecture Notes in Computer Science

For information about Vols. 1–3894

please contact your bookseller or Springer

Vol. 3944: J. Quiñonero-Candela, I. Dagan, B. Magnini, F. d'Alché-Buc (Eds.), Machine Learning Challenges. XIII, 462 pages. 2006. (Sublibrary LNAI).

Vol. 3943: N. Guelfi, A. Savidis (Eds.), Rapid Integration of Software Engineering Techniques. X, 289 pages. 2006.

Vol. 3942: Z. Pan, R. Aylett, H. Diener, X. Jin, S. Göbel, L. Li (Eds.), Technologies for E-Learning and Digital Entertainment. XXV, 1396 pages. 2006.

Vol. 3941: S.W. Gilroy, M.D. Harrison (Eds.), Interactive Systems. XI, 267 pages. 2006.

Vol. 3940: C. Saunders, M. Grobelnik, S. Gunn, J. Shawe-Taylor (Eds.), Subspace, Latent Structure and Feature Selection. X, 209 pages. 2006.

Vol. 3939: C. Priami, L. Cardelli, S. Emmott (Eds.), Transactions on Computational Systems Biology IV. VII, 141 pages. 2006. (Sublibrary LNBI).

Vol. 3936: M. Lalmas, A. MacFarlane, S. Rüger, A. Tombros, T. Tsikrika, A. Yavlinsky (Eds.), Advances in Information Retrieval. XIX, 584 pages. 2006.

Vol. 3935: D. Won, S. Kim (Eds.), Information Security and Cryptology - ICISC 2005. XIV, 458 pages. 2006.

Vol. 3934: J.A. Clark, R.F. Paige, F.A. C. Polack, P.J. Brooke (Eds.), Security in Pervasive Computing. X, 243 pages. 2006.

Vol. 3933: F. Bonchi, J.-F. Boulicaut (Eds.), Knowledge Discovery in Inductive Databases. VIII, 251 pages. 2006.

Vol. 3931: B. Apolloni, M. Marinaro, G. Nicosia, R. Tagliaferri (Eds.), Neural Nets. XIII, 370 pages. 2006.

Vol. 3930: D.S. Yeung, Z.-Q. Liu, X.-Z. Wang, H. Yan (Eds.), Advances in Machine Learning and Cybernetics. XXI, 1110 pages. 2006. (Sublibrary LNAI).

Vol. 3929: W. MacCaull, M. Winter, I. Düntsch (Eds.), Relational Methods in Computer Science. VIII, 263 pages. 2006.

Vol. 3928: J. Domingo-Ferrer, J. Posegga, D. Schreckling (Eds.), Smart Card Research and Advanced Applications. XI, 359 pages. 2006.

Vol. 3927: J. Hespanha, A. Tiwari (Eds.), Hybrid Systems: Computation and Control. XII, 584 pages. 2006.

Vol. 3925: A. Valmari (Ed.), Model Checking Software. X, 307 pages. 2006.

Vol. 3924: P. Sestoft (Ed.), Programming Languages and Systems. XII, 343 pages. 2006.

Vol. 3923: A. Mycroft, A. Zeller (Eds.), Compiler Construction. XIII, 277 pages. 2006.

Vol. 3922: L. Baresi, R. Heckel (Eds.), Fundamental Approaches to Software Engineering. XIII, 427 pages. 2006.

Vol. 3921: L. Aceto, A. Ingólfsdóttir (Eds.), Foundations of Software Science and Computation Structures. XV, 447 pages. 2006.

Vol. 3920: H. Hermanns, J. Palsberg (Eds.), Tools and Algorithms for the Construction and Analysis of Systems. XIV, 506 pages. 2006.

Vol. 3918: W.K. Ng, M. Kitsuregawa, J. Li, K. Chang (Eds.), Advances in Knowledge Discovery and Data Mining. XXIV, 879 pages. 2006. (Sublibrary LNAI).

Vol. 3917: H. Chen, F.Y. Wang, C.C. Yang, D. Zeng, M. Chau, K. Chang (Eds.), Intelligence and Security Informatics. XII, 186 pages. 2006.

Vol. 3916: J. Li, Q. Yang, A.-H. Tan (Eds.), Data Mining for Biomedical Applications. VIII, 155 pages. 2006. (Sublibrary LNBI).

Vol. 3915: R. Nayak, M.J. Zaki (Eds.), Knowledge Discovery from XML Documents. VIII, 105 pages. 2006.

Vol. 3914: A. Garcia, R. Choren, C. Lucena, P. Giorgini, T. Holvoet, A. Romanovsky (Eds.), Software Engineering for Multi-Agent Systems IV. XIV, 255 pages. 2006.

Vol. 3911: R. Wyrzykowski, J. Dongarra, N. Meyer, J. Waśniewski (Eds.), Parallel Processing and Applied Mathematics. XXIII, 1126 pages. 2006.

Vol. 3910: S.A. Brueckner, G.D.M. Serugendo, D. Hales, F. Zambonelli (Eds.), Engineering Self-Organising Systems. XII, 245 pages. 2006. (Sublibrary LNAI).

Vol. 3909: A. Apostolico, C. Guerra, S. Istrail, P. Pevzner, M. Waterman (Eds.), Research in Computational Molecular Biology. XVII, 612 pages. 2006. (Sublibrary LNBI).

Vol. 3908: A. Bui, M. Bui, T. Böhme, H. Unger (Eds.), Innovative Internet Community Systems. VIII, 207 pages. 2006.

Vol. 3907: F. Rothlauf, J. Branke, S. Cagnoni, E. Costa, C. Cotta, R. Drechsler, E. Lutton, P. Machado, J.H. Moore, J. Romero, G.D. Smith, G. Squillero, H. Takagi (Eds.), Applications of Evolutionary Computing. XXIV, 813 pages. 2006.

Vol. 3906: J. Gottlieb, G.R. Raidl (Eds.), Evolutionary Computation in Combinatorial Optimization. XI, 293 pages. 2006.

Vol. 3905: P. Collet, M. Tomassini, M. Ebner, S. Gustafson, A. Ekárt (Eds.), Genetic Programming. XI, 361 pages. 2006.

Vol. 3904: M. Baldoni, U. Endriss, A. Omicini, P. Torroni (Eds.), Declarative Agent Languages and Technologies III. XII, 245 pages. 2006. (Sublibrary LNAI).

Vol. 3903: K. Chen, R. Deng, X. Lai, J. Zhou (Eds.), Information Security Practice and Experience. XIV, 392 pages. 2006.

Vol. 3902: R. Kronland-Martinet, T. Voinier, S. Ystad (Eds.), Computer Music Modeling and Retrieval. XI, 275 pages. 2006.

Vol. 3901: P.M. Hill (Ed.), Logic Based Program Synthesis and Transformation. X, 179 pages. 2006.

Vol. 3900: F. Toni, P. Torroni (Eds.), Computational Logic in Multi-Agent Systems. XVII, 427 pages. 2006. (Sublibrary LNAI).

Vol. 3899: S. Frintrop, VOCUS: A Visual Attention System for Object Detection and Goal-Directed Search. XIV, 216 pages. 2006. (Sublibrary LNAI).

Vol. 3898: K. Tuyls, P.J. 't Hoen, K. Verbeeck, S. Sen (Eds.), Learning and Adaption in Multi-Agent Systems. X, 217 pages. 2006. (Sublibrary LNAI).

Vol. 3897: B. Preneel, S. Tavares (Eds.), Selected Areas in Cryptography. XI, 371 pages. 2006.

Vol. 3896: Y. Ioannidis, M.H. Scholl, J.W. Schmidt, F. Matthes, M. Hatzopoulos, K. Boehm, A. Kemper, T. Grust, C. Boehm (Eds.), Advances in Database Technology - EDBT 2006. XIV, 1208 pages. 2006.

Vol. 3895: O. Goldreich, A.L. Rosenberg, A.L. Selman (Eds.), Theoretical Computer Science. XII, 399 pages. 2006.